Seeing China's Belt and Road

Edited by

EDWARD SCHATZ AND RACHEL SILVEY

T0244394

OXFORD
UNIVERSITY PRESS

OXFORD
UNIVERSITY PRESS

Oxford University Press is a department of the University of Oxford.
It furthers the University's objective of excellence in research, scholarship,
and education by publishing worldwide. Oxford is a registered trade mark of
Oxford University Press in the UK and certain other countries.

Published in the United States of America by Oxford University Press
198 Madison Avenue, New York, NY 10016, United States of America.

Library of Congress Cataloging-in-Publication Data
Names: Schatz, Edward, editor. | Silvey, Rachel, editor.
Title: Seeing China's Belt and Road / edited by Edward Schatz, Rachel Silvey.
Description: New York, NY : Oxford University Press, [2025] |
Includes bibliographical references and index.
Identifiers: LCCN 2024032013 | ISBN 9780197789278 (paperback) |
ISBN 9780197789261 (hardback) | ISBN 9780197789292 (epub) |
ISBN 9780197789285 (pdf) | ISBN 9780197789308 (online)
Subjects: LCSH: Yi dai yi lu (Initiative : China) | Geopolitics—China. |
China—Economic relations. | China—Foreign relations.
Classification: LCC HF1604 .S376 2024 | DDC 337.51—dc23/eng/20240820
LC record available at https://lccn.loc.gov/2024032013

DOI: 10.1093/oso/9780197789261.001.0001

Paperback printed by Marquis Book Printing, Canada
Hardback printed by Bridgeport National Bindery, Inc., United States of America

Seeing China's Belt and Road

We would like to thank our respective partners and families. Rachel thanks her husband for the innumerable large and small ways he enriches and sustains her life, and she appreciates her family, near and far, more than words can say. Ed thanks his wife for the support, grounding, and companionship on this delightful journey, as well as their three boys, who continually fill their parents with pride and joy.

Contents

Acknowledgments

We are grateful to all those who made this book possible.

We received tremendous institutional support from the beginning. The conference that led to the volume was generously funded by the Social Sciences and Humanities Research Council of Canada (SSHRC), which provided a Partnership Development Grant (2020–2024, Grant No. 890-2019-0131). That grant, which supported three conferences, was for the umbrella project entitled "Bolstering Partnerships to Study the Impact of China's Belt and Road." We deeply appreciate that funding. We are also grateful to the Munk School of Global Affairs & Public Policy, which has provided an unusually vibrant space for multidisciplinary area studies research on topics of global significance such as this one.

Within the Munk School, the centers we direct—the Centre for European and Eurasian Studies (Schatz) and the Asian Institute (Silvey)—have afforded exceptionally congenial environments for the development of this work. Our respective home departments—Political Science (Schatz) and Geography & Planning (Silvey)—have also provided excellent support. We are thankful for such enabling conditions.

There are a number of individuals who were key to facilitating this project. The directors of the Munk School, including Randall Hansen, Cheryl Misak, and Peter Loewen, have stood solidly behind our efforts. Particular thanks go to Brenda Yeoh at the National University of Singapore and Neil Collins at Nazarbayev University, Kazakhstan, who were our coapplicants on the Partnership Development Grant from SSHRC that supported our efforts. The superb staff at Munk have brought their professional acumen as well as real joy to the work. We credit Arba Bardhi, Nina Boric, Larysa Iarovenko, Olga Kesarchuk, and Dasha Kuznetsova in particular for their expert management of the international conference we held over Zoom in 2020 and their ongoing support for the broader SSHRC project.

We are especially grateful to all those who offered feedback on early iterations of the work collected here. For their comments on the conference versions of the chapters, we appreciate the paper discussants, including Alima Bissenova, Tyler Harlan, Nargis Kassenova, Katharine Rankin, Hong Shen, James Sidaway, and Jun Zhang. Their participation enlivened and strengthened the conversations. Deep thanks to Joseph McQuade, a postdoctoral research associate on the project, for his keen editorial eye, sustained commitment to the project website, and his grace under pressure when offering closing remarks at the conference.

Our local colleagues at the University of Toronto provided key support as we ushered the project through its many phases. We thank Joshua Barker, Frank Cody, Diana Fu, Seva Gunitsky, Filiz Kahraman, Matthew Light, Katharine Rankin, and Lucan Way. Angela Chnapko, our editor at Oxford University Press, deserves particular mention for her appreciation of the broader intellectual aspirations at stake, as well as her consistent support during the publication process. The external reviewers provided serious, engaged, critical feedback, for which we are enormously grateful; their input has substantially improved the individual chapters and the overall book. Maria Cusano and Richards Paul expertly shepherded the manuscript through proofs to production.

Each author of the nine chapters deserves thanks for sharing their exciting work with us in conference form, for their commitment to the book's vision, and for the patience and trust they showed in the process. It has been immensely rewarding to work with such a knowledgeable and collaborative group of scholars. We have not yet met all of them in person, but we feel as though we know them—and appreciate them—now that we have worked together online with hard deadlines, multiple drafts, and countless email messages. We hope to have the opportunity to meet soon and frequently with all these contributors in real life.

Neekoo Collett, a research assistant and doctoral candidate in political science at the University of Toronto, was central to our efforts all along the way. She masterfully managed logistics for two conferences, diplomatically steered communications among participants, and generously provided editorial feedback on the first draft of the collection prior to submission. We deeply appreciate everything she has done.

Ciara McGarry joined the team as a research assistant in the intense, final phase of preparing the manuscript for submission. She offered a fresh set of editorial eyes, extraordinarily incisive commentary, as well as meticulous attention to detail. We are grateful to have crossed paths with this talented student and to have had the opportunity to work with her during the home stretch.

Contributors

Jasmin Dall'Agnola is a postdoctoral researcher at the Swiss Federal Institute of Technology's Department of Humanities, Social and Political Sciences in Zurich, Switzerland. Her research focuses on the relationship between gender, technology, and surveillance in authoritarian societies. She has published widely in scholarly journals, including *Surveillance & Society*, and is the Associate Editor for Research Notes at *Central Asian Survey*.

Jessica DiCarlo is Assistant Professor in Geography, Environment, and Asian Studies at the University of Utah. She contributes to debates on global China's role in shaping resource politics, development, and geopolitics through long-term ethnographic field-work. She is a 2023–2024 Wilson China Fellow, a 2023–2025 Public Intellectual Program Fellow with the National Committee on US–China Relations, and on the editorial board of the People's Map of Global China and *Global China Pulse*.

Ding Fei is Assistant Professor in the Department of City and Regional Planning, College of Architecture, Art, and Planning at Cornell University. As a development and economic geographer, Fei has areas of expertise in the political economy of international develop-ment, global production networks, infrastructure-led industrialization, capital–labor re-lations, South–South migration, and China–Africa relations.

Bradley Jardine is a Managing Director at the Oxus Society for Central Asian Affairs and Global Fellow at the Wilson Center's Kissinger Institute on China and the United States. Jardine's research focuses on the proliferation of surveillance technology in Central Asia and China's growing security presence in the countries of the former Soviet Union.

Marina Kaneti is Assistant Professor in International Affairs at the Lee Kuan Yew School of Public Policy, National University of Singapore. She draws on visual methods in order to explore questions of global governance and development. Dr. Kaneti's work appears in a number of peer-reviewed journals, including *Journal of Global Ethics, Citizenship Studies, Human Rights Review*, and *Sustainable Development*. She is currently working on two book manuscripts. The first explores the political agency of the stranger, and the second interrogates the nexus of global mobility and hospitality to strangers.

Lena Kaufmann is a Swiss National Science Foundation Ambizione Fellow at the University of Fribourg, where she heads a project on Chinese digital technologies in China and Europe. Trained as an anthropologist and Sinologist in Berlin, Rome, and Shanghai, she earned her PhD from the University of Zurich and authored *Rural-Urban Migration and Agro-Technological Change in Post-Reform China* (Amsterdam University Press, 2021). Serving as the spokesperson for the Regional Group China(s) of the German

Anthropological Association, she has conducted long-term fieldwork on migration and agricultural technologies in China, and Chinese digital infrastructures in Switzerland.

Edward Lemon is Research Assistant Professor at the Bush School of Government and Public Service at Texas A&M University, Washington DC Teaching Site, and President of the Oxus Society for Central Asian Affairs. His research focuses on security issues in Central Asia, as well as the region's relations with external powers.

Galen Murton is Associate Professor of Geography in the School of Integrated Sciences at James Madison University in Harrisonburg, Virginia. A human geographer with broad research and teaching interests in the politics of international development, Galen has published widely on the Belt and Road Initiative (BRI), including in the journals *Political Geography*; *Environment and Planning C: Politics and Space*; and *Territory, Politics, Governance* as well as other edited volumes. He teaches courses on globalization, development, and critical cartography and likes to conduct fieldwork with his students in the mountain ranges of Highland Asia, as well as North America.

Tom Narins is Associate Professor of Geography and Planning with research interests in the critical geopolitics of China's growing engagement with the global economy. As a political and economic geographer with language skills, Tom has published on sovereignty issues relating to China's BRI, as well as on official Chinese lending to BRI-participant countries after COVID-19. His current research interests focus on the geographical contours of China's Digital Silk Road.

Jeremy Paltiel is Professor Emeritus of Political Science at Carleton University in Ottawa. He coedited and contributed a chapter to *Canada and Great Power Competition: Canada among Nations 2021* with David Carment and Laura Macdonald (Palgrave, 2022) and contributed to *The New Asian Disorder: Rivalries Embroiling the Pacific Century*, edited by Lowell Dittmer (Hong Kong University Press, 2022). He also coedited with Huhua Cao, *Facing China as a New Global Superpower: Domestic and International Dynamics from a Multidisciplinary Angle* (Springer, 2015). He has authored numerous other articles on Chinese politics, human rights and the Chinese tradition, civil–military relations in China, East Asian foreign relations and Sino–Canadian relations.

Edward Schatz is Professor of Political Science and the Director of the Centre for European and Eurasian Studies at the Munk School of Global Affairs & Public Policy, University of Toronto. He is the author of *Slow Anti-Americanism: Social Movements and Symbolic Politics in Central Asia* (Stanford University Press, 2021), *Modern Clan Politics* (University of Washington Press, 2004), as well as edited volumes *Paradox of Power: The Logics of State Weakness in Eurasia* (University of Pittsburgh Press, 2017) and *Political Ethnography: What Immersion Contributes to the Study of Power* (University of Chicago, 2009).

Rachel Silvey is Professor of Geography and Planning and Director of the Asian Institute, Munk School of Global Affairs & Public Policy, University of Toronto. Her work has been published in the fields of migration studies, cultural and political geography, gender studies, and critical development studies. Her major funded research projects have fo-cused on migration, gender, social networks, and economic development in Indonesia; immigration and employment among Southeast Asian Americans; migration and mar-ginalization in Bangladesh and Indonesia; and religion, rights, and Indonesian migrant women workers in Saudi Arabia.

Karl Yan is Assistant Professor in the School of Humanities and Social Science at the Chinese University of Hong Kong, Shenzhen. Karl's research sits at the intersection of international and comparative political economy with a particular focus on railway de-velopment and the transformation of China. Karl has published in journals such as the *Review of International Political Economy*, the *British Journal of Politics and International Relations*, and *The Pacific Review*.

Introduction

Seeing the BRI

Edward Schatz and Rachel Silvey

Introduction

China's Belt and Road Initiative (BRI) is a trillion-dollar program of development assistance and infrastructure financing with the potential to transform
states, societies, and economies from Africa and Latin America to Europe and
Asia.[1] Announced in 2013 as the "One Belt, One Road," it would later become
China's signature global policy, potentially playing a central role in the restructuring of the global economy and indeed the world order. There is no doubt as to
the BRI's significance, but there are questions about how best to understand it.

China's rise has been polarizing, and this polarization has spilled into debates
about the BRI. At one end, especially in US policy and media circles, the BRI
is considered a troubling expression of Chinese expansionism. At another end,
particularly in formal announcements emanating from government sources in
China and its state-controlled media, the BRI is promoted as a welcome new
form of win-win international development. For all their differences, both of
these narratives—BRI as either dystopian or utopian, threat or dream, reducible to either geopolitical anxiety or ideological fantasy—are too broad in their
sweep to capture the layers, contestations, and specificities of the development
processes unfolding under the BRI banner. Some aspects of the BRI can indeed
be perceived as threats, while other aspects may provide some positive development outcomes, but it is impossible to paint an accurate picture using broad
brushstrokes.[2]

---

[1] One source suggests that China has allocated $1.5 trillion in funds dedicated to the BRI (Liu,
Zhang, and Xiong, 2020: 139). While money allocated is different from money spent, the trillion-
dollar estimate is a common and reasonable one.

[2] As the chapters in this volume demonstrate, these polar opposite narratives in their most
simplified and ideological forms are most pronounced in coverage of the BRI emerging from the
United States and China. As we argue in this introduction, we aim to shift the lens to understand how
"other" knowledge about the BRI—research produced at the "receiving end" of BRI investment—
diverges from both of these dominant viewpoints (see also Pearson, Rithmire, and Tsai, 2022). This
is especially important if we are to avoid the trap of taking sides in a US–China geopolitical rivalry
(Pearson et al., 2022).

Edward Schatz and Rachel Silvey, *Introduction* In: Seeing China's Belt and Road. Edited by: Edward Schatz
and Rachel Silvey, Oxford University Press. © Oxford University Press 2025.
DOI: 10.1093/oso/9780197789261.003.0001

A framework for studying the BRI should be able to capture the variety of what is an exceptionally varied global project. For this book, we invited top scholars conducting fieldwork in concrete contexts to provide a ground-level view of transformations set in motion by the BRI. Collectively, the book shows how different approaches to the Belt and Road—*different ways of seeing* the BRI—lead us to distinct conclusions about its meanings and effects.[3]

A vibrant, rapidly expanding body of literature seeks to examine the BRI "from the ground" (Klinger and Muldavin, 2019; Oliveira et al., 2020).[4] As with that literature, we ask: How are these projects seen locally, and what are the social and political ramifications of different ways of seeing? We thus build on studies that have examined the cultural and ideological tensions surrounding Belt and Road investments, considering how various claims about the BRI play out empirically and in everyday life. Such dynamics have implications for how we theorize everything from democracy and the state (Rankin et al., 2017, 2018; Narins and Agnew, 2021) and layers of sovereignty (Yeh, 2021) to cartographies of infrastructure (Murton, 2020), international student migration (Sidhu et al., 2019), new racisms (Ang et al., 2022), diasporic citizenship (Ho, 2019), and patterns of development (Klinger and Muldavin, 2019).

Our book extends these lines of research. The chapters are attuned to the particularities of the contexts and processes that are located on the receiving end of BRI ventures. They highlight agency, contingency, resistance, and local dynamics without losing sight of the great power that China increasingly exercises. We do not assume that China's power *determines* outcomes or operates without friction, but we see the power of the BRI developments as nonetheless setting forces in motion that flow in recognizable patterns and identifiable directions. The conclusion takes up the metaphor of *downstream effects*—a commonsense notion that likens the processes of social and political change to what occurs in hydrological basins. As we will discuss, the metaphor highlights how change may be patterned, but it is fundamentally shaped by the unpredictable contingencies of power and direction.

---

[3] The late James Scott's groundbreaking *Seeing Like a State* (1998) provides the inspiration for our volume's title. He famously demonstrated that the efforts of "high-modern states" frequently result in policy failures in part because they oversimplify their objects of intervention. Our aim differs from Scott's, since we ask not how an authoritarian state views its activities but, rather, how different actors implicated in the BRI see their own activities and, in turn, Beijing's efforts.

[4] See the themed issue of the journal *Territory, Politics, Governance*, "New Geographies of Development: Grounding China's Global Integration," edited by Julie Klinger and Joshua Muldavin (2019) with articles by Gustavo Oliveira, Mladen Grgić, Juliet Lu and Oliver Schönweger, Kevin Woods, and Michael Dwyer and Thoumthome Vongvisou. See also the special issue of the journal *Political Geography*, "China's Belt and Road Initiative: Views from the Ground," edited by Gustavo de L. T. Oliveira et al. (2020), with contributions from Galen Murton, Alessandro Rippa, Tyler Harlan, and Yang Yang.

We unify our endeavor by focusing on the politics of sight. Chapters explore how different actors at multiple scales—from Chinese authorities to local businesspeople and political actors, from migrants to ordinary citizens—view the BRI. By implication, we demonstrate that the BRI's power is dynamic and multidimensional. Plans begin with ideas for infrastructure development, which are translated into images and blueprints for building China's vision of future global connectivity. These are then converted into actions and material interventions—enormous ports, new rail connections, expansive digital networks, and complex financing arrangements—but the story neither begins nor ends with this materiality. The bulk of the story is also about rapidly shifting social meanings and lived local encounters and contestations, rather than about straightforward political and economic "effects." It reminds us that the exercise of power and the practice of development are not reducible to their material components, and that the cultural politics of grounded interactions, however closely they may be connected with geopolitical forces, are neither unidirectional nor foreordained. China's BRI is powerfully transformative, but it remains an open question what these transformations look like on the ground.

In this introduction, we first discuss the two polar opposite narratives about the BRI that continue to define the terms of the US–China rivalry. By reviewing these framings at the outset, we set the stage for further analysis. Second, we consider how research on the politics of sight allows us to decenter these discussions by considering them through multiple lenses. This epistemological move allows us to highlight the variety, indeterminacy, and ambiguity that are inherent to the BRI. Third, we underscore how the transformations set in motion necessarily differ from the changes that BRI architects envision. Finally, we conclude with a brief discussion of *downstream effects*, a topic taken up directly in the volume's final chapter; this offers a fresh way of thinking about the consequences of the BRI for the people and places it encounters.

Opposing Narratives

Approaches to the BRI tend to cluster around two poles. In one narrative, China's rise should sound alarm bells. From this perspective, the authoritarian character of the Chinese Communist Party (CCP) and its expanding military and economic role present a growing global threat to international security, liberal democracy, and human rights—some of the cornerstones of the post–Cold War political order (Kliman, 2019; U.S.–China Economic and Security Review Commission, 2022).[5] At this pole, BRI investment around the world in the

---

[5] We recognize that the West's rhetoric about these principles far outpaced the reality on the ground, but the principles nonetheless structured international order for decades after 1989. On the disjuncture between rhetoric and reality, see Schatz (2021).

development of vast networks of roads, ports, high-speed rail lines, and fiber-optic cables is considered inextricable from China's geostrategic aims.[6]

This narrative contains three crucial elements. First, it views the BRI as an essential part of an increasingly assertive Chinese foreign policy. Whereas before Xi Jinping, China was content to "bide time" and "build capabilities" in its international relations (Clarke, 2017: 75–76), Xi has confidently declared that the "China dream" will "benefit the people of the world" (Clarke, 2017: 77). This trajectory and this vocabulary underscore Beijing's intention to compete with the United States and provide the world with its preferred, alternative model of development.

Second, this narrative sees China as a rising power whose economic power is fungible, which is to say it can be converted into geostrategic weight (Reilly, 2021). In this sense, the BRI is an instrument of such influence; it allows China to create new dependencies that cement Beijing's ongoing role, not just in its historical sphere of influence but on every continent across the globe. The logic can be traced to soft realist theorists like Gilpin (1987: 3), who saw a need to integrate analysis of international economics with analysis of international politics. Indeed, before Russia's 2022 war against Ukraine, there was good reason to believe that economic power was the new normal in international affairs, since great powers like the United States, China, or Russia were assumed reluctant to engage militarily in ways that could destabilize the international system. To the extent that China need not exert itself militarily to project its power, the BRI can be viewed as an indispensable instrument of its foreign policy. And, to the extent that China remains intent on distinguishing its approach not just from the United States's but also from Russia's approach to international politics, a China increasingly willing to use military force is different from a China that *leads with* military force.

Third, this narrative—while focusing on economic power instead of military power—nonetheless views China as an expansionist state with its own global agenda. Vibrant debates center on the extent to which this amounts to a threat.[7] Is China a reformist or a revisionist power; that is, does it seek to change international politics around the edges and inscribe a role for itself, or does it want to fundamentally alter how the international system works and unseat the United States? Such debates hinge on how one interprets prior instances of "power transition" (Organski, 1958; Organski and Kugler, 1980). Does the relative

---

[6] While Russia's 2022 war on Ukraine made China's approach to global affairs seem benign by comparison, its longer-term goals may in fact be more ambitious than Russia's, given China's global reach.

[7] As Freymann (2020: 20) puts it, the BRI constitutes a "profound threat to US global leadership . . . because it represents a working model for a future geopolitical bloc led by China, structured along the lines of a modern tributary system." For further perspectives on this broad topic, see Acharya (2017), Hillman (2018), Ikenberry (2018), and Mastro (2019).

decline of the existing hegemon (in this case, the United States) raise the likelihood of conflict—even militarized conflict—between the declining hegemon and the rising challenger? For International Relations theorists concerned with questions of hierarchy, hegemony, and conflict, the BRI—as an instrument of China's rise and foreign influence—is part of a larger story in which a competing power potentially changes the international order.

At the other pole, the BRI is celebrated as delivering infrastructure that enables "win-win" forms of economic development and improved security for all. According to the People's Republic of China's State Council (2015a), at its core the BRI is about economic rationality:

> [The BRI] ... aims to promote orderly and free flow of economic factors, highly efficient allocation of resources and deep integration of markets by enhancing connectivity of Asian, European and African continents and their adjacent seas.

Presenting itself as open to all countries and international and regional organizations for engagement, China's BRI is said to honor mutual respect and market principles in pursuit of common prosperity. By this account, the fruits of economic growth will reach people everywhere as they circulate through trade and investment. As a result,

> The connectivity projects of the Initiative will help align and coordinate the development strategies of the countries along the Belt and Road, tap market potential in this region, promote investment and consumption, create demands and job opportunities, enhance people-to-people and cultural exchanges, and mutual learning among the peoples of the relevant countries, and enable them to understand, trust and respect each other and live in harmony, peace and prosperity (Consulate General, 2013).

Such official language is pitched at a high level of abstraction. For the CCP, the Belt and Road is a broad-gauge statement of intent, a framework for providing development assistance, a plan for increasing connectivity, and a genuinely integrative, positive-sum project that will improve the lot of humanity. Even if its promises of increased employment and investment opportunities with attention to social equity and environmental sustainability prove to be aspirational and excessively optimistic, they motivate policies that are represented as a boon to human and economic development across the globe.

It is not only the CCP that characterizes the BRI in this way; some scholarship is broadly sympathetic to the narrative. Mahmood et al. (2022) argue that BRI projects are indeed a benefit to infrastructure development across Pakistan, and that the China–Pakistan Economic Corridor (CPEC) is roundly supported by Pakistanis in affected regions. Likewise, some authors applaud the salutary intentions of Chinese outward investment, including the BRI, for its promise to reduce economic inequality (Siu, 2019) and to provide greater cultural connectivity (Winter, 2021). From this perspective, the fact that results are mixed does not diminish the essentially beneficial nature of the undertaking. It reflects China's determination to "reshape the world order rather than be shaped by the changing world" (Yu, 2017: 356). The principles undergirding such Chinese state-led approaches to globalization are hardly new, but China has nonetheless scaled them in unprecedented ways and thus presented itself via the BRI as a principled leader of the next chapter of economic globalization.

As we shall see, a ground-level view gives the lie to both narratives, at least in their unqualified forms. However, we do not propose splitting the difference on an assumption that the truth must lie halfway between the two. Some aspects of the BRI are in fact captured by each narrative. Indeed, although they end up in entirely different places analytically, the two narratives share key assumptions.

For example, both narratives tend to assume that BRI plans and projects emanate from an extraordinarily powerful Beijing, and that the CCP is unilaterally driving its expansion. This assumption is evident in Xi Jinping's own speeches about BRI plans, and it seeps to varying degrees into security studies, international relations, and geopolitical accounts wary of China's military expansion.[8] Agreeing about Beijing's extraordinary power, the two narratives differ on the judgment they make about the purpose this power serves, that is, whether China is respectful and visionary or status-seeking and cynical. Either way, it is assigned more power than any state in reality could possibly muster. As Cheng Li (2021: 10) argues, scholars and policymakers must challenge the "dominant assumptions and associated policy measures . . . about the 'all-dimensional China threat,'" myths he views as "simplistic, premature and misguided."

Of course, the CCP has forged its military involvement to pave the way for its expansionist economic agenda, which in turn benefits BRI development projects.[9] In Chapter 1, Lemon and Jardine examine China's military investments along the Belt and Road territories in Central Asia and describe how these large-scale projects enhance China's geopolitical and geoeconomic power through "weaponized interdependence." Thus, the securitization of Chinese overseas development projects leads to an aggressive military buildup, which in turn leads to local pushback and further securitization. Lemon and Jardine demonstrate that civil society actors and foreign states manage to exercise considerable agency in

---

[8] For analysis of the ways that the CCP itself functions, and the ways it drives China's global engagement, see, for example, Freymann (2021); Reilly (2021); Ye (2020), and for a comprehensive discussion of the influence of Xi Jinping's life and leadership, see Chan (2022).

[9] The territorial routes that China's military investments are carving indeed mirror the pathways it has outlined for its economic expansion (Lemon and Jardine, Chapter 1, this volume).

the face of this power, but their evidence makes it hard to miss just how powerful China has become in Central Asia. Whether China's military investments are seen as impressive or concerning, they are clearly intrusive and introduce novel and potentially transformative possibilities into long-standing ways of exercising power in Central Asia.

Likewise, China's investments in digital technologies contain massive potential to generate change; some changes might be applauded, while others might be resisted. In Chapter 8, Dall'Agnola takes perceptions of China as a threat seriously. By examining public opinion surveys among Central Asians, she shows that publics broadly approve of Chinese closed-circuit television (CCTV) cameras widely installed throughout the region. The fact that Central Asians are generally unconcerned about the threat that such cameras pose to privacy rights is itself testimony to the influence that a Chinese model of penetrative, surveillance-led development already has across the region.

Whether the BRI is in fact part of an expansionist Chinese foreign policy with ambitions to control the global economy is open to debate, but the narrative of Chinese power is itself productive in a political sense. Consider the widespread characterization of China as setting "debt traps" for BRI countries. This idea is especially prevalent in discussions of "debt diplomacy," in which China's loans are viewed as part of a predatory suite of investment plans that will subordinate economies that take on the debt (Brautigam, 2020).

However, evidence from a wide range of sources points to the more complex articulations of development agendas with intermediaries, whether these are local elites rechanneling loans for their own purposes, dissatisfied Chinese laborers deployed at stalled projects, or governments focused on leveraging their relationships with China against other powerful countries. As Narins demonstrates in Chapter 2, actual geographies of debt management, as well as the optics of debt for BRI projects, unfolded in diverse patterns during the era of the COVID-19 pandemic. He dives into four national cases (Sri Lanka, Pakistan, Laos, and Zambia) to detail each government's distinct approach to BRI projects and loans, as well as public responses to the BRI in each context. As each of these countries struggled with the economic downturn prompted by the pandemic, BRI projects stalled, expatriate Chinese workers were shortchanged, and it became increasingly difficult for borrower governments to project a positive view of the BRI to local populations.

Thus, there is nothing straightforward about the "rollout" of infrastructure projects required for China's rise to global political-economic hegemony. But the narrative of a powerful China that operates largely without friction across BRI countries itself enhances China's imagined power by underscoring the inevitability of China's model and the futility of seeking alternatives. Moreover, asking about "what China intends"—hegemony or win-win development—ascribes human characteristics to a complex and multilayered state bureaucracy. Strictly speaking, a state cannot "intend" anything; as a result, policymaking may be messy, fickle, and contingent more than it is coherent, rational, and certain.

Particularly useful here is Chapter 3, in which Paltiel and Yan argue that we should view the architects of the BRI as being in a multilayered bureaucracy. No one central office in Beijing controls all BRI projects in the same way. Paltiel and Yan posit two types of diplomatic trajectories attached to BRI projects, one of which is predominately "bottom-up" versus the other, which is largely "top-down." Some bottom-up projects escape direct central oversight, especially if they are not deemed sensitive by Chinese officials. Top-down projects, by contrast, are more centrally coordinated and more tightly aligned with Beijing's explicit state agenda. This heuristic of "top-down" and "bottom-up" allows the chapter to begin to disentangle the range of relationships Beijing has with different BRI project intermediaries. It offers an alternative way of seeing BRI projects that emphasizes both the specificity of interstate negotiations as well as the complexity of the bureaucracy in Beijing. Chapter 3 shows that in fact the BRI's stated ambitions differ dramatically from what is rolled out as its accomplishments. The BRI's big ideas, as grand in scope and ambition as they may be, take empirical form as they interact and intersect with mesoscale political and economic ambitions.

The Politics of Sight and (In)visibility

The BRI carries a clear name, but in practice it is challenging to define. While some prefer to impose crisp analytic categories on messy, lived realities, we take a different tack. Inspired by Mitchell (1991: 77), who contended that "elusiveness should not be overcome by sharper definitions, but explored as a clue" to the nature of the phenomenon, we assume that ambiguity lies at the heart of the BRI. Mitchell was interested in the state, but his logic applies equally to this important, potentially transformative, and yet elusive initiative set in motion by Beijing.

Like Wittgenstein's famous "duck-rabbit" (Pitkin, 1993, in Wedeen, 2010: 266), a drawing that can be seen as a duck or as a rabbit, what people see in the BRI is—to a significant degree—a question of how they approach the topic. Following a constructivist line of argumentation, we contend that the BRI is largely a function of what the actors involved make of it. If it is viewed as a security threat in some quarters, those views will affect how those dynamics unfold. If it is viewed as a visionary development practice, its dynamic will correspondingly shift. Starting from constructivist assumptions attunes us to the great variety of dynamics set in motion by the BRI.

This assumption about variety invites a methodological corollary. The BRI should not be studied in pristine isolation from China's foreign affairs. Rather, it should be considered in light of its relationships with a series of adjacent actions involving Chinese actors.[10] As one of DiCarlo's interlocutors (Chapter 6 of this volume, page 137) underscores, northern Laos was engaged with China long before 2013: "This is China in northern Laos, as usual." Our volume thus considers not just BRI projects that have announced themselves as such, but also BRI-adjacent projects and transformations that would have been unlikely without the BRI. Some of these projects bear other labels, or no labels at all. What you see is in good part a function of how and where you look. Or, in Clifford Geertz's terms, "What you count is what you get."[11]

Of course, any variety has limits. Wittgenstein's "duck-rabbit" may be seen as an image of a duck, as an image of a rabbit, or as an essentially ambiguous image with the possibility of being viewed as either a duck or a rabbit (Pitkin, 1993, in Wedeen, 2010: 266), but it cannot be viewed as a frog, a camel, or a pair of scissors. Likewise, the materiality of the BRI introduces a range of social meanings that can plausibly be ascribed to the BRI, but that range is not infinite.

Our chapters highlight the analytical, substantive, and political significance of shifting our gaze, by attending to scholarship on the politics of sight and (in)visibility. In a sense, all questions about sight are political questions. For Pachirat (2011: 236), seeing is necessarily political, as it involves "organized, concerted attempts to make visible what is hidden and to breach, literally or figuratively, zones of confinement in order to bring about social and political transformation." Since "distance and concealment operate as mechanisms of power in modern society" (Pachirat, 2011: 3), the remedy is clear: reveal to enable change. A normative commitment to shifting perspectives and shedding light on uncomfortable facts drives this approach to thinking about sight.

Our collective goal is indeed to shed light on otherwise hard-to-see facets of the BRI and its varied impact, since much about the initiative in fact lies in shadow. It would be surprising if it were otherwise. After all, transparency has not been a stated priority of the governments or businesses involved in the BRI's rollout. Whether produced by sins of commission or omission, opacity is fairly normal.

Yet "seeing" is not necessarily politically transformative or normatively preferable. English and Zacka (2022: 1026) underscore that uncovering repugnant practices is indeterminate when it comes to instigating change. Indeed, they suggest that the politics of sight may have unintended consequences. Instead

---

[10] Here, we follow Hart (2018: 371), who encourages researchers to develop "relational comparisons," to examine "open, non-teleological conception of dialectics."
[11] As cited in Wolf (1992: 4).

of toppling an unjust status quo, for instance, it may contribute to the normalization and legitimization of harmful practices. This is ultimately because the politics of sight relies on change powered by emotional responses, particularly shock and outrage as a result of discomfort and unfamiliarity (Pachirat, 2011). Yet, repeated exposure may dilute emotions, leading to disengagement and disillusionment. Moreover, as more actors get involved in revealing that which was previously hidden, each revelation competes harder with other revelations for attention and therefore for political potency. The marketplace gets crowded.

Whatever normative preference for visibility and transparency one might have, when it comes to the BRI it is important not to prejudge what drives actors to reveal or conceal. In the end, our endeavor attends to the social meanings that those involved with BRI-related transformations bring to their acts, including their choices to reveal or to conceal. Thus, we seek to see for analytic reasons; without doing so, we argue, too much about the BRI and its transformations remains hard to understand.

We chart our way forward by raising three interrelated questions about the politics of visibility. First, how do various BRI actors—from project planners to engineers to manual laborers, from bankers to project managers to lawyers—see the BRI? What do they want to celebrate, trumpet, and announce, and what do they prefer to leave unsaid, work actively to conceal, or find themselves unwittingly whispering? Second, what choices do observers of the BRI—from pundits to scholars to policymakers—make regarding the BRI as an object of study? How do they construct their observational efforts, and how do they see their own roles in relation to this knowledge production? What do these acts of construction illuminate, and what do they leave in shadow? Third, what do publics affected by the BRI see, how do they locate themselves amid such transformations, and in what ways do these self-understandings invoke the BRI in particular or China more generally?

The Start of Something Potentially Momentous

The current unfolding of global geoeconomic development is an emergent amalgamation of projects with tremendous variety. Historical conjunctures fuel direction and momentum for change without determining how change unfolds, let alone where it ends up. As our chapters elaborate, indeterminacy, ambiguity, and contestation lie at the crux. Recognizing this variety is the first step toward providing a nuanced account of the BRI and its potential effects.

But should we dismiss broad narratives entirely? After all, they provide storylines, usually rooted in some element of truth reflecting and amplifying some interest in particular framings of the BRI. Ordinary people, prominent social or political actors, and even analysts themselves sometimes resort to these analytic shortcuts as they scramble to make sense of the BRI's staggering reach, its rapid development, and the great diversity of projects that bear the BRI label.

The fact that one-size-fits-all accounts are rarely analytically satisfying does not prevent them from traveling widely. In turn, their wide circulation has political and social effects. The chapters collected here ask how they circulate and what political work they accomplish. In so doing, they set the stage for investigating what China's infrastructure projects mean for different people and places around the world.

The book's first part (Chapters 1–3) offers baseline evidence for seeing the BRI as an expansion of China's infrastructural influence. Attentive to Beijing's coercive, economic, and administrative power, respectively, each of these chapters is well attuned to context. Lemon and Jardine show that China's coercive power via "weaponized interdependence" unfolds not in empty space, but amid the rich relationships of Central Asia's existing political dynamics. Narins highlights how Chinese economic power, via its lending capacity, develops not in the abstract but in highly varied and entirely concrete countries across the globe, with their own possibilities and challenges. For their part, Paltiel and Yan show the importance of the administrative context from which the BRI emerges. Together, these chapters ask not only how other state actors influence China's room for maneuver, but also how other features of China's infrastructural expansion may be rendered visible or invisible and what the effects of other ways of seeing the BRI may be.

The second part (Chapters 4–7) elaborates on matters of power and sight, asking a twofold question. First, how are BRI-related phenomena that are designed to guide our gaze (e.g., exhibits and maps) constructed, and what does this construction tell us about China's power? Second, how are BRI projects themselves designed for maximum visibility, and what do people involved in and affected by these projects in fact see?

Kaneti in Chapter 4 traces the challenges that other state actors pose to Beijing in the creation of a highly visible museum exhibition. She shows that although China sought to present a narrative of itself as the original source of the ancient Silk Road, other nations insisted on their own versions of history that positioned their respective countries as key actors. Interestingly, she asks whether symbolic inclusions can also represent and enable China's imperial ambitions. She argues that although the guiding historical narrative of the exhibition was aimed at reaffirming China's primacy in this history, many of the actual exhibits emphasized different storylines that centered other countries' own unique roles in making the Road. She interprets the permission that Beijing granted to these other countries as an indication of China's confidence, as well as evidence that competing historical visions of the *longue durée* are alive and well. By allowing contested details of the Silk Road's history to be featured in the exhibit with thirteen other countries, Beijing could claim that it operated in an inclusive and collaborative manner. The exhibition thus underscored China's interest in presenting a view of itself to counter its reputation as an expansionist, authoritarian regime seeking to create a new hegemony.

The question of limits to China's projection of its power is examined again by Murton in Chapter 5. His research challenges the view of China as an all-seeing actor capable of initiating a straightforward rollout of its vision. He asks what the effects of *not seeing* the BRI may be. His chapter investigates the implications of that which is not represented on BRI maps and focuses on the cartographic absences of road-building projects underway in Tibet and other parts of the Himalayas. His way of seeing the BRI helps illuminate how blanks on the BRI map may support Beijing's pursuit of its geopolitical and geoeconomic imperatives. He points out that by obscuring the specificities of places (e.g., notably Tibet), where human rights abuses or disrupted livelihoods may be conspicuous to local people, the gaps on these maps may support Beijing's exercise of spatial power over vast territorial reaches. Whether and to what extent the absences on these maps are strategic, they provide clues for thinking through the diversity of ways that the BRI is represented, seen, and unseen.

Chapter 6 by DiCarlo explores several hypervisible BRI projects in Laos: the Laos–China Railway (LCR), the Laos–China Economic Corridor (LCEC), and Boten Special Economic Zone (SEZ). She makes visible the labor that is required to produce the infrastructure as spectacle and reveals some ways that people's locations affect their visions. For example, migrant workers in the SEZ work hard to uphold the vision of the place as a good investment destination, performing exaggerated professionalism and industriousness for visits of important guests. Villagers may join the media in celebrating the "China speed" of the railway project's progress, while they blame their own government for the slow pace of land compensation payouts when they are displaced by the construction. Along the corridor, these perceptions vary sharply, and they change over time, depending on people's specific roles and their encounters with the promises and the pitfalls of these megaprojects.

Whereas ports, as well as rail and road networks, are visible, much of the BRI's materiality is largely or partially out of sight. The third part (Chapters 7–9) turns to these key material features, focusing on the infrastructure for digital connectivity and the human labor that—visibly or not—undergird the entire Belt and Road.

Chapter 7 traces the digital path to Switzerland, finding a public that appreciates the benefits that technology investments from China bring. In this chapter, Kaufmann shows that Chinese companies helped to speed up Swiss critical digital infrastructure as part of their effort to improve and extend their companies' reach and the Chinese Digital Silk Road (DSR), more generally. These digital components of the BRI are much less visible than the pipelines, railroads, roads, and harbors whose construction they enable. Their history is largely underground, and it began long before the official announcement of the BRI. Interestingly, both the Swiss and the Chinese governments, along with industry partners from both countries, have planned and installed the digital foundations in Switzerland. The development of "the cloud" and improvements to "the Internet" are sociomaterial infrastructure projects that rest on building fiber-optic networks. As companies headquartered in China have worked with Swiss companies to expand the DSR, they have created the transnational digital underpinnings of smart cities, financial services, and high-speed Internet communication, all of which facilitate the development of other more visible, above-ground BRI projects. These underground roots of the BRI were laid—as transnational corporate connections with interstate cooperation—well before the announcement of any major, visible construction projects.

Like Kaufmann, in Chapter 8, Dall'Agnola decenters discussion of China's DSR. Asking how people on the receiving end of China's technology investments see the new technologies, her chapter examines Central Asian people's responses to the growing use of surveillance cameras produced by Chinese companies such as Huawei, Dahua Technology, and Hikvision. Her research shows that as CCTV systems have been adopted throughout Kazakhstan, Kyrgyzstan, and Tajikistan, they have been met with widespread approval by the public. Indeed, people indicate that, rather than viewing the intensified surveillance as an intrusion into their privacy, they generally see their states' deployments of CCTV as a public good that enhances security. By viewing the DSR from the perspective of public opinion in these three Central Asian states, Dall'Agnola shows that the rollout of BRI projects can be welcomed and that perceptions of the BRI can—as in her case studies—have little or nothing to do with views of China. Indeed, whether or not the technology itself is made in China, Central Asian publics privilege security over privacy protections. In so doing, they create a context that facilitates the DSR's expansion or at least the expanded market share of its affiliated technology companies.

Chapter 9 by Fei turns to the people who remain indispensable for BRI's expansion and development. Exploring the lives of Chinese migrant workers on BRI projects in Ethiopia, she shows the human costs that they pay as downstream workers. Ethiopian leaders have approached BRI investment as a natural outgrowth of the increasing ties between their country and China. Intensified overseas ventures of Chinese companies generate job opportunities for millions of Chinese workers seeking higher salaries or better socioeconomic status by working abroad. However, this dramatic global job expansion produces tremendous social costs in its wake. Overseas BRI jobs usually require that workers undertake repeated sojourns abroad involving long periods of social detachment from China. These jobs rarely translate into the upward socioeconomic mobility that expatriated workers desire, even when migrants are mid-level managers of firms. Workers deployed by China imagine a better future at the expense of building their lives in China, paying the price for years of absence from their social and professional relationships back home.

The disconnect between the shared prosperity narrative of the BRI and the downstream effects on China's expatriated workers is pronounced. As Fei's chapter details, the workers in Ethiopia are disillusioned as they struggle to manage unrealized aspirations. Displacing their hopes onto an imagined future that lies elsewhere, they find it necessary to work abroad on serial contracts; they are resigned to being stuck with low pay and little chance of advancement in these labor circuits. Their lack of socioeconomic mobility over time as they service Belt and Road projects gives them a view of their home country as failing to live up to its promises.

Taken together, these chapters point to the economic and political significance of invisible and partially occluded projects and people. While China is involved in developing the museum exhibits, maps, and digitization efforts everywhere from Switzerland to Central Asia, its role in these projects remains largely unseen by local publics. In the Ethiopian case, it is migrant Chinese workers toiling on BRI-related projects who come to see the nature of their predicaments and in turn to view China itself in a new light. Thus, China's expansion via the BRI has an evident materiality, but the significance of that materiality is a function of the politics of sight.

The BRI, Moving Forward

What is visible or invisible is in part a function of power and how it is conceptualized. As the chapters that follow amply demonstrate, power is not a simple matter of material disparities. If it were, no ground-level analysis would be needed; one could simply infer power relations from the relative size of economies and the relative size of militaries. Instead, there is much room for actors—up and down these overtly visible power hierarchies—to exercise agency and shift the dynamics by which the BRI operates. Paying focused and deliberate attention to this complexity, our collective endeavor foregrounds these long-standing questions of agency and contingency and examines power as residing not in the abstract but in concrete relationships among various parties in specific situations.

At the same time, we recognize the materially important and sometimes truly overwhelming power that China can have. Indeed, the BRI is predicated on

Chinese power; it is impossible without it. To make the point most plainly: if Chinese geoeconomic power hypothetically were to dissipate quickly outside its borders, the BRI would not be the global story that it has become. China's material power is absolutely fundamental for the BRI to be transformative, but how precisely it is transformative is widely variable.

With the BRI, power generally flows in a particular direction, but its effects are highly contingent upon what the flow encounters downstream. Our concluding chapter develops the commonsense notion of *downstream* by showing that shifting sediment, changing tides, a sudden reshaping of the embankment, or a spell of particularly dry (or wet) weather can easily alter the effect that a flow might have. If this is true in hydrological basins, it is doubly true in social systems, where human beings play active roles in making the institutions and relationships consequential to how power operates.

The BRI is not just multifaceted. If it were, studying it might be merely a matter of apprehending its different facets to assemble a holistic picture. Here, we are reminded of the story about four blindfolded people who are tasked to describe an elephant. Using their sense of touch, they each accurately describe a separate part of an elephant but are unable to conjure what the entire beast looks like. Similarly, one cannot expect case studies to "add up" to a complete picture of the BRI as a whole. If the cases aggregated so neatly, the task at hand would be a simple matter of assembling knowledge to produce sight with ever-increasing clarity. Yet the BRI is also dynamic. Ever changing, it creates new facets of interconnection with such rapidity that actors and analysts alike have trouble apprehending such change.

When we initiated this project in 2019, China's BRI was already playing a significant role in shaping globalization. In 2021, as we hosted a virtual conference, chapter authors were in the midst of COVID-19 lockdowns and strove to discuss these issues through our Zoom interfaces. Since then, our discussions—about how to see the BRI and what political work is accomplished by different ways of seeing it—arguably became more significant, and certainly more complicated. The postpandemic economic recovery involved continuing supply chain disruptions, rising debt loads in many BRI-affected countries, alarming increases in anti-Asian racism and violence, as well as crimes directed at BRI workers, Asian citizens, and Chinese construction sites. In addition, climate-related disruptions and seismic shifts in geopolitics caused by Russia's war against Ukraine ensured that the downstream effects of the BRI would continue to shift. When change occurs at breakneck speed, there is no simple way to study it. This book offers a step forward by showing how questions of sight help to reveal new and productive perspectives on an otherwise polarized debate.

PART I

SEEING CHINA'S INFRASTRUCTURAL POWER

1

Securing the Belt and Road and Establishing Hierarchy in Central Asia

Edward Lemon and Bradley Jardine

Introduction

In 2016, in a remote corner of the Pamir mountains in Tajikistan, the Chinese military quietly built Sitod, a base that can accommodate over 300 personnel. The base is located near the border with Afghanistan and China. Two years earlier, in a speech in China's Xinjiang Uyghur Autonomous Region (XUAR), Xi Jinping had stated that "after the United States pulls out of Afghanistan, terrorist organizations positioned on the frontiers of Afghanistan and Pakistan may quickly infiltrate Central Asia" (Ramzy and Buckley, 2019). Sitod forms a nodal point in China's increasingly extensive security networks in Central Asia.

Chinese security activities in Central Asia are motivated by an interest in pacifying the XUAR. Beijing views Central Asia's 2,387-km border with Afghanistan and its ethnic Uyghur diaspora, numbering an estimated 300,000 people, as security threats (Yau, 2022a: 6–12). The instability in Afghanistan following the 2021 withdrawal of US and NATO troops further intensified Beijing's securitization of the region.

Sinophobic violence has also constituted security challenges for China as it seeks to expand its economic footprint around the world through its Belt and Road Initiative (BRI). The allure of the BRI for developing states is not difficult to understand. On the one hand, the world economy suffers from an infrastructure investment gap estimated to stand at some $15 trillion by 2040 (Mohseni-Cheraghlou and Aladekoba, 2022). But in regions like Central Asia, locals contend that Beijing exhibits too much control over their governments, erodes their environment, undermines justice, and leaves their economies saddled with debt (Peyrouse, 2016; Burkhanov and Chen, 2016).

In response to these developments and heightened concerns over the security threats emanating from the region, China has increased its role as a security provider in Central Asia, building a complex web of ties with the region's regimes. The density of these ties has grown dramatically since the BRI was launched in 2013. China established its first overseas military facility in the region in

Edward Lemon and Bradley Jardine, *Securing the Belt and Road and Establishing Hierarchy in Central Asia*
In: Seeing China's Belt and Road. Edited by: Edward Schatz and Rachel Silvey, Oxford University Press.
© Oxford University Press 2025. DOI: 10.1093/oso/9780197789261.003.0002

Tajikistan in 2016. China's share of arms imports to Central Asia increased from 1.5 percent to 16 percent from 2010 to 2020 (Lemon and Jardine, 2020b). The Chinese military and security apparatus has developed its defense diplomacy, increasing the number of training activities and joint exercises.

At the same time, Central Asia has also proven to be a testing ground for China to develop its own parallel order building and expansionist experiments with forms of security cooperation, increasingly without the region's former external hegemon, Russia, which has seen its role as a security guarantor undermined since its February 2022 full-scale invasion of Ukraine. Chinese efforts to work outside the Shanghai Cooperation Organisation (SCO) and create new regional initiatives without Russia, such as the Quadrilateral Cooperation and Coordination Mechanism (QCCM) or the China + Central Asia platform, as well as bilateral strategic initiatives such as Chinese-run reconnaissance facilities in Tajikistan's Pamir mountains, indicate that China is strengthening efforts to extend its sphere of influence in the region.

This chapter examines how China's BRI is received locally in Central Asia. The increasing downstream friction as a result of China's presence in the region is shaping Beijing's practices and making it see the BRI through an increasingly securitized lens as something that needs protecting. Our focus is not on the BRI itself, but on developments in China's security governance that have evolved since the launch of the BRI in 2013. We argue that China's rising security role along the BRI in Central Asia is in part driven by perceived threats to China's security and the safety of Chinese investors. But it is also part of a longer-term strategy by which China strategically builds networks to lock Central Asian states into hierarchical relations of (inter)dependence according to a hub-and-spoke model. Our way of seeing China's role in the region therefore aligns with the China threat narrative outlined in the book's introduction, in which BRI is considered inextricable from China's geostrategic aims. China enhances its security networks with the view to exploiting its network positions to extend its influence in the region. Material resources (arms, military aid) and nonmaterial products (knowledge, norms) flow through these networks. Arms transfers, joint exercises, and training enhance interoperability, socialize militaries into the Chinese way of thinking about security, and intensify reliance on Chinese technology. Military bases offer the Chinese military an opportunity to project force within Central Asia. Safe city projects and intelligence cooperation allow China to gather data on Uyghurs and other groups they deem threatening.

In the long term, we see Beijing as laying the foundations for "weaponized interdependence." This refers to the ways in which actors can use their position within networks to leverage informational and financial exchange for strategic advantage (Newman and Farrell, 2019). Actors use weaponized interdependence in two ways. First, they use the "panopticon effect" to gather strategically valuable information. Second, they employ the "chokepoint effect" to deny network access to adversaries. We argue that China is laying the groundwork through the BRI to use the panopticon and chokepoint effects in the future. Thus, while it is true that "the exercise of power and the practice of development are not reducible to their material components" (Schatz and Silvey, introduction to this volume: 3), a clear view of how power is exercised and how new hierarchies are created must attend to these material developments and their likely (if not inevitable) consequences.

To make these arguments, we use three main data sources. To quantify the density of China's security networks with Central Asian republics, we rely on the Central Asia Exercises Database, a comprehensive data set of 256 joint exercises involving the militaries from the region since 1991, and the Central Asia Arms Tracker, a data set of arms flows into the region based on figures from the Stockholm International Peace Research Initiative (SIPRI), supplemented by figures from the EU, Military Balance, and local media.[1] To track rising protests against China in the region, including attacks on Chinese BRI investments, we utilize the Oxus Society for Central Asian Affairs' Central Asia Protest Tracker, a protest event data set with detailed data on China-related protests from 2011 to 2022.[2]

The BRI and the Question of "Weaponized Interdependence"

We contend that through the BRI, China creates networks of (inter)dependence that it can use to coerce actors into helping it achieve its goals. In doing so, we turn to the concept of "weaponized interdependence" (Newman and Farrell, 2019: 308), which refers to "how some states have used their privileged position in the networks that underpin global interdependence to achieve coercive outcomes." For many, the era of complex interdependence meant an end to traditional power politics. As economies became entangled through flows of capital and goods, states were more likely to cooperate for mutual gain (Keohane and Nye, 1973). But such global networks also created opportunities for powerful actors to leverage network structures as a coercive tool. Key nodes accumulate power, gain a "first mover" advantage, and produce something more akin to a "hub-and-spoke" system.

---

[1] The arms data are available at https://oxussociety.org/viz/arms-flows/. The data on exercises can be downloaded at https://oxussociety.org/wp-content/uploads/2021/09/Central-Asia-Military-Exercises-Database.xlsx.

[2] This database can be accessed at https://oxussociety.org/viz/protest-tracker/.

When a country establishes itself atop a hierarchy of coercion, it builds power and information asymmetries that work in tandem to shape domestic institutions and norms of independent countries. For example, the United States cut Iran off from the SWIFT system, the primary system that facilitates international payments, and used its power over the Internet to establish a global surveillance system under the National Security Agency. As noted earlier, Newman and Farrell (2019) theorize two types of coercion enabled by networks: *panopticon effects*, or the ability to glean information from networks, and *chokepoint effects*, or the ability to deny access to networks for certain actors. In short, "if [a state has] appropriate domestic institutions, [it] can weaponize networks to gather information or choke off economic and information flows, discover and exploit vulnerabilities, compel policy change, and deter unwanted actions" (Newman and Farrell, 2019: 45).

While most scholarship on this relatively new concept has focused on the United States (Newman and Farrell 2019, Drezner, Newman, and Farrell 2021), Cavanna's (2021) research analyzes the BRI as an attempt to form alternative networks to mitigate the United States's future use of weaponized interdependence. Goddard's (2018) notion of "embedded revisionism" is a fruitful way to think through how China may use BRI for its own weaponization of interdependence in the long term. Goddard (2018: 764) argues that "Revisionists build [. . .] networks strategically, seeking power and influence through their ties with other states." In this view, revisionists' ability to influence global politics is built on two components. The first component is *access*, which is "the extent to which a revisionist is integrated into the dominant network, measured by the density and frequency of its institutionalized relations" (Goddard, 2018: 769). Such states have strong ties with great powers in the system, allowing them to leverage material and ideational ties to give them influence. The second component is *brokerage*, that is, the ability to create and mobilize ties across different networks, and often to act as an exclusive conduit between subgroups in the international system such as isolated states like Iran and North Korea (Goddard, 2018: 771).

While networks are asymmetrical, existing in a hub-and-spoke arrangement, the different nodes do derive some power from their network positions (Izumikawa, 2020). Horizontally weaker states can build alternative networks among themselves, and vertically they can strengthen networks with alternative patrons to break free of their dependence on single patrons via hub-and-spoke networks. Within global politics, scholars have pointed to the way that weaker states can maximize their autonomy and actively resist great powers.

A number of studies have developed these arguments with reference to Central Asia. Cooley (2012) points to the way Central Asian states are not merely pawns on the "grand chessboard" (Brzezinski, 1998), but agents who have developed strategies to play great powers against one another to maximize their sovereign authority under conditions of inequality. Costa Buranelli (2017) argues that Central Asia's interactions with great powers are part of a pattern of "negotiated hegemony," whereby weaker states use their sovereignty to shape the influence and legitimacy of external powers. One way of achieving this is "balancing regionalism," where weaker states build horizontal ties among themselves and diversify external partnerships to reduce reliance on single patrons (Tskhay and Costa Buranelli, 2020). In doing so, they build on a substantial literature on "multivectorism," the attempts to maintain ties with multiple external powers, in Central Asia (Contessi, 2015; Cooley, 2012; Dadabaev, 2019; Fumagalli, 2007; Nourzhanov, 2012; Teles Fazendeiro, 2018; Vanderhill, Joireman, and Tulepbayeva, 2020).

Securitizing the BRI

Following the Soviet collapse and the emergence of independent states in Central Asia, China began to develop ties with its new neighbors. Early priorities included delimiting the 4,380-km border with the former Soviet republics, preventing the Central Asian states from becoming havens for accused separatists from Xinjiang, and developing economic ties. The latter grew substantially, with trade volumes between China and Central Asia rising from $4 billion in 2003 to $70 billion in 2022 (Panamarov, 2005; Xinhua News Agency, 2023). Ties increasingly became asymmetrical; China owns an estimated 40 percent of the external debt of Tajikistan and Kyrgyzstan (Imamova, 2023) and accounts for 90 percent of Turkmenistan's exports in the form of gas supplies (European Bank for Reconstruction and Development, 2021). As relations developed, China's interests expanded. Three overarching interests now stand out. First, China views the region, in particular Tajikistan, as a buffer zone between its restive province of Xinjiang and Afghanistan and fears that Afghan-based Uyghur militants will use it as a staging ground for attacks. Second, China capitalizes on Central Asia's energy reserves for its growing domestic needs. Third, China sees the region as a key transit hub for the Eurasian continent and a central point for its BRI.

The BRI codified China's strategy toward Central Asia and repackaged investments under its auspices. Wang Jisi, the dean of the School of International Studies at Peking University, wrote a widely circulated op-ed entitled *"Xijin"* [Marching West] (Jisi, 2014). Facing pressure from the United States in the east and with the central regions of the country lagging behind the coastal provinces, he argued, the government should turn its attention toward Eurasia. One year later, on a visit to Kazakhstan, Xi Jinping launched the Silk Road Economic Belt to link China to Eurasia. The initiative, which would later become the BRI, was driven economically by a need to find new outlets for Chinese capital and exports in order to sustain domestic growth. Politically, China sought to demonstrate its ability to construct a viable alternative to the current international order dominated by the United States (Clarke, 2017).

As China has expanded its role in Central Asia through the BRI, local populations have pushed back. In turn, this generates insecurities for Chinese investors, which drives Beijing to take a greater role in Central Asian security. Sinophobia remains relatively widespread in Central Asia, particularly in Kazakhstan and Kyrgyzstan (Peyrouse, 2016; Burkhanov and Chen, 2016). According to survey data from the Central Asia Barometer shared with the authors, 39 percent of Kazakhs and 34 percent of Kyrgyz had negative views toward China in 2022, compared with lower percentages in 2017 (16 percent and 32 percent, respectively).

Protests against China's rising role in the region, perceived by some as taking jobs from locals, polluting the environment, and being part of a broader strategy to "colonize" Central Asia, have been on the rise. The Kazakhstani government's proposal to reform the Land Code in 2016 to allow foreigners to buy land sparked protests on a scale not before seen in the country's independent history, with protesters claiming China would buy swathes of land and threaten Kazakhstan's sovereignty (BBC, 2016). Protests would become more common in Kazakhstan as the transition of power from Nursultan Nazarbayev, who resigned in March 2019, to his successor Kassym-Jomart Tokayev opened greater opportunities for citizens to express grievances. According to the Oxus Society's Central Asia Protest Tracker, 195 separate protests related to China took place in Central Asia from 2011 and 2022, 129 of which occurred in Kazakhstan. China's detention of thousands of ethnic Kazakhs and Kyrgyz in Xinjiang also generated protests in Central Asia. Families of those affected protested in front of the Chinese consulate in Almaty on a daily basis from February 2021.

In Kyrgyzstan, anti-China protests are also common, with 65 entries in the Central Asia Protest Tracker. The mining sector, which makes up around one-third of the economy and where China is a significant investor, has been a particular target. While relations with elites are most important in China's efforts to strengthen networks with Central Asia's authoritarian regimes, Central Asia's governments cannot totally ignore popular sentiments. In February 2020, a series of protests in Naryn led to the abandonment of plans for a $280 million Chinese-funded logistics center in Kyrgyzstan (RFE/RL, 2020). In the same village three months prior, hundreds of locals had clashed with workers from a Chinese mining company, accusing it of poisoning the water supply.

China also perceives terrorism as a threat to BRI projects. This stems from two sources: Uyghur nationalists historically based in the region and possible spillovers from Afghanistan. According to census data, Central Asia had a large Uyghur diaspora of some 300,000, mostly located in Kazakhstan and Kyrgyzstan. Immediately after independence, several organizations dedicated to promoting Uyghur culture, human rights, or, in some cases, statehood were established in Central Asia. But the region was also a base for more violent groups such as the East Turkestan Liberation Organization (ETLO)[3] and the Uyghur Liberation Organization.[4] Chinese authorities viewed their activities with suspicion, blaming them for various attacks. In 2000, four Uyghurs were convicted in Kyrgyzstan for an attack on a Chinese delegation that left one dead. Two years later, the first secretary at the Chinese embassy in Bishkek and his assistant were murdered (CNN, 2002). In 2016, a car exploded outside of the embassy in Bishkek. A year later, a court sentenced three for the attack, blaming it on the Turkestan Islamic Party, a Uyghur militant group based in Pakistan and Syria.[5] Each of these cases was muddled by murky investigations and contradictory case details that have led scholars such as Sean Roberts (2020: 204–5) to question their validity.

The launch of the BRI in 2013 also coincided with a shift in Chinese strategic thinking from one of economic development as the root of stability to one more focused on political control. Since the 2014 launch of the People's War on Terror in Xinjiang, Beijing has come to view Central Asia as a bulwark preventing instability in Afghanistan from pouring across its western borders. The 2019 "Xinjiang Papers," which included a series of speeches given by Xi Jinping in 2014, revealed that he had been concerned about Central Asia's stability for five years (Ramzy and Buckley, 2019). In this context, China has begun to view Tajikistan as a particularly important barrier against spillover from Afghanistan.

China's Expanding Security Cooperation in Central Asia

While Xi Jinping has framed BRI as "a community of common destiny" to promote "peace, development, cooperation and mutual benefit" (China Internet Information Center, 2014) through the provision of mutually beneficial economic exchanges and the renewal of the ancient Silk Road's traditions of dialogue between civilizations, in reality, we see that China's strategy is to build hierarchical relations with its partners. Through the BRI, China is creating a complex series of networks (financial flows, data, roads, railways, pipelines) linked to

---

[3] ETLO was a Uyghur separatist group founded in the early 1990s in Turkey. It was labeled a terrorist organization by China, Kyrgyzstan, and Kazakhstan. As of 2024, it appeared to be inactive.

[4] Uyghur Liberation Organization, also known as Xinjiang Liberation Organization, was a group based in Kyrgyzstan and Uzbekistan in the late 1990s and early 2000s.

[5] Founded in 1989 by Zeydin Yusup as the East Turkestan Islamic Party and referred to as the East Turkestan Independence Movement by the Chinese government, the organization rebranded itself as the Turkestan Islamic Party in 2008.

hundreds of nodes (ports, free economic zones, transit hubs), which are often asymmetrical in China's favor and create relations of (inter)dependence.

China also builds hierarchical networks of (inter)dependence with the security apparatuses of the Central Asian republics and positions itself as superior to the region's regimes. First, China has established a military facility in Tajikistan from which it can project force and protect Xinjiang from potential spillovers from Afghanistan. Second, through joint exercises, training activities, and arms transfers, Central Asian militaries are increasingly dependent on China for technology and training (Lemon and Jardine, 2020b).

Military bases are nodes in networks of great power influence that give their operators the ability to project force but also generate rents for host states and opportunities to play patrons off against each other (Cooley, 2008). As China has expanded its global economic footprint, it faces a growing need to protect its investments and citizens, as well as provide more global public goods (Guifang and Jie, 2019). To facilitate these out-of-area operations, China has started to build overseas military installations. China established the first such facility, the People's Liberation Army Support Base in Djibouti, in 2016 to protect shipping through the Bab-el-Mandeb Strait and facilitate antipiracy operations in the Horn of Africa. Exaggerated fears of Uyghur militancy from Afghanistan into Central Asia, which shares a short, remote border with China and a longer, more populated border with Tajikistan, have led Beijing to establish an installation code-named Sitod, on the Tajik–Afghan border (Eurasianet, 2020). Satellite imagery suggests that the site could house around 300 troops and has a helicopter landing pad (Standish, 2021). According to a 2021 International Criminal Court case (Reuters, 2021b), the base has likely facilitated cooperation between China's security services and their Tajik equivalent, resulting in raids against Uyghur businesses in the country. In addition to the base, China has also renovated barracks in the capital Dushanbe and built 11 border posts in the country as part of a 2016 deal (Putz, 2016; Van Der Kley, 2019).

Building on these nodes, joint training, and military technology transfers are also growing means by which China can expand its hierarchical linkages in the region. The SCO, founded by China, Russia, Uzbekistan, Tajikistan, Kyrgyzstan, and Kazakhstan in 2001 to facilitate security cooperation, has been the traditional vehicle for Chinese defense diplomacy in the region. In 2002, China took part in its first known bilateral exercise, with Kyrgyzstan. The drill, organized by the SCO, involved under 100 soldiers armed with light weapons, antitank missiles, and armored personnel vehicles. The following year, China held its first multilateral exercises in the region in Kazakhstan and Xinjiang, with every SCO member state but Uzbekistan participating. Chinese drills have increased substantially in the decades that followed. The SCO organized 26 exercises

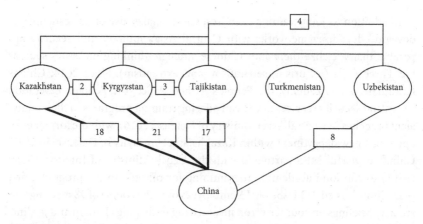

Figure 1.1 Network chart: military exercises in Central Asia.

involving Central Asian militaries between 2002 and 2021.[6] China was involved in 22 of these (compared with Russia at 17). Uzbekistan was the most reluctant Central Asian state, participating in just 8 exercises, with Tajikistan involved in 18, Kazakhstan participating in 20, and Kyrgyzstan involved in 23. As Figure 1.1 shows, China has built the strongest vertical security ties via exercises with Kyrgyzstan; Turkmenistan, which is permanently neutral, remains isolated from these new networks.

Some 59 percent of Chinese-led exercises in the region involve security services, followed by special operations forces and police units, which reflects China's extramilitary methods for expanding its reach. This security mix differs markedly from exercises led by other states in the region, which have prioritized collaboration with the military. In 2014, Xi made a number of speeches in XUAR, in which he expressed concern that "Uyghur fighters" could infiltrate Tajikistan and destabilize China's westernmost province (Ramzy and Buckley, 2019). This fixation on stabilizing these contested frontiers led to China launching "Cooperation-2019," a series of drills designed to enhance interoperability between its own People's Armed Police (PAP) and local national guard formations. Kyrgyzstan, Uzbekistan, and Tajikistan all took part in 2019, which marks the first instance in which their national guard units had cooperated with China on issues relating to counterterrorism. In addition to the PAP, the Chinese Ministry of Public Security (MPS) conducted its first exercises abroad in 2015, when MPS forces trained with their Tajik counterparts near Dushanbe.

---

[6] For a list, see https://oxussociety.org/wp-content/uploads/2021/09/Central-Asia-Military-Exercises-Database.xlsx.

In addition to joint-training exercises, China makes use of its academies to develop educational networks with Central Asia's military and security apparatus that socialize them into Chinese strategic thinking on issues such as the Three Evils (terrorism, separatism, and extremism). Since 2014, China's Criminal Police Academy, the People's Armed Police, the People's Liberation Army, and security services have been offering training programs to their equivalent branches in Central Asia (Ministry of Defense, 2016), with the former even opening a new department within Kazakhstan's University of Defense. In 2017, China's powerful MPS partnered with the Uzbek Ministry of Interior Affairs (MIA) to run joint academic programming for officers. In the program's first year, China hosted 213 Uzbek MIA employees over the course of 38 meetings for security briefings on counterterrorism and drug trafficking (Lemon and Jardine, 2020b). China also uses the SCO as a framework for training exercises. In 2014, the MPS founded the China National Institute for SCO International Exchange and Judicial Cooperation in Shanghai with the express purpose of training senior SCO officials on counteracting terrorism and organized crime. By 2018, the Institute had trained some 300 officials from SCO member states, an average of 75 per year (Van Der Key, 2019: 83).

This network of Chinese-funded facilities, joint exercises, and training programs deepens the reliance of the Central Asian security apparatuses on China. They bolster interoperability and socialization into Chinese strategic thinking while enhancing China's ability to project military power in the region. This is not purely a process of Chinese-led coercion; in their efforts to maintain their power, the authoritarian regimes of the region have demanded an increased Chinese role in security. For example, in response to violent protests in Kazakhstan in January 2022, China reportedly offered assistance. Kazakhstan's Foreign Minister told journalists "[China] was ready to provide necessary assistance [...] but we do not have a legal basis to accept foreign forces from countries outside the CSTO" (Tengri News, 2022). In October 2021, the government of Tajikistan announced that China would fund and construct new facilities for a Tajik special rapid response unit in the Gorno-Badakhshan Autonomous Region on the border with Afghanistan (Standish, 2021).

Arming Central Asia

China has also ramped up its arms transfers to the region. According to the SIPRI Arms Database, China exported $446 million worth of arms to Central Asia from 2000 to 2020, with 97 percent of those occurring after 2014—at the time of Xi Jinping's Xinjiang speeches arguing for heightened security. Additional data gathered by the authors suggest that the SIPRI data set is limited, missing

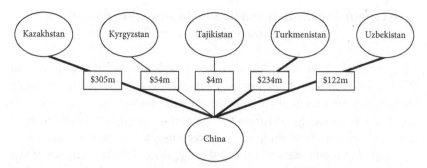

Figure 1.2 Network chart: Chinese arms transfers to Central Asia.

several key large-scale transfers that push China's total exports to the region over $719 million.[7]

With the 2014 shift in Chinese strategic thinking, arms transfers to Central Asia skyrocketed. As Figure 1.2 shows, Kazakhstan has received the largest value in arms transfers, followed closely by Turkmenistan, with Tajikistan receiving the fewest arms.

Crucially, China is shifting the regional balance of power by advancing arms sales in technological areas previously unavailable in Central Asia. Kazakhstan, Turkmenistan, and Uzbekistan have each purchased drones from China, including the CH-3, CH-4, CH-5, and Wing Loong (Security Assistance Monitor, 2014). Such technology has already increased China's leverage in the region, offering Beijing a number of "chokepoints" to advance its interests. In 2019, for example, China placed Turkmenistan on a military blacklist, which ceased all military exports to the country after Ashgabat struggled to pay back a loan issued by Beijing after its gas production plummeted (Sina Military, 2019).[8] These power asymmetries have much larger implications for the broader region.

China has become a major arms supplier in Central Asia—a role set to grow with Russia's declining presence in the aftermath of its full-scale invasion of Ukraine. Russia has already seen its share of the arms market decline from 65 percent between 2010 and 2015 to 52 percent between 2016 and 2021 (Lemon and Jardine, 2020a). The reliance on Chinese technologies, many of which can be utilized to protect their regimes, will lead to continued dependence on spare parts, training and maintenance, overhaul, and repair. This will grant the Chinese government crucial leverage over the Central Asian governments in the coming decades.

---

[7] For example, SIPRI does not include the $296 million sale of eight Chinese-made Y-8F-200W to Kazakhstan in 2018.

[8] On debt diplomacy see also Narins, Chapter 2, this volume.

Weaponizing the Belt and Road: "Information Panopticons" and Strategic Asymmetries

Cavanna (2021: 225) notes, "there are undeniable affinities between Belt and Road and the concept of weaponized interdependence." The BRI is generating the potential for structural coercion. As Newman and Farrell (2019: 55) have noted, the BRI's energy and transit infrastructure could help China to exert major panopticon effects using "physical access to or jurisdiction over hub nodes [. . .] to obtain information" passing through them. For the purposes of this chapter, these "hubs" refer to intermediaries operating within decentralized communication structures.

As technology has grown more sophisticated and centralized, state capacity to surveil the activities of adversaries has only grown. Under the framework of an "information panopticon," states like China can supercharge their information-gathering and information-generating activities by utilizing wide networks of semiprivate actors. For Farrell and Newman (2019: 55), "such information offers privileged states a key window into the activity of adversaries, partly compensating for the weak information environment that is otherwise charac-teristic of global politics." The state with the most control over hubs maintains a strategic advantage, using its privileged information sources to counter rivals and negotiate from a position of strength.

The Chinese state has been achieving these goals in Central Asia in a number of ways. It has established a new "Belt and Road National Security Intelligence System," which aims to utilize private actors, particularly Chinese private se-curity contractors, to aid Chinese embassies in information gathering, which will be located in a central database accessible across various government ministries. In addition, growing trade networks with Central Asia have also pro-vided power asymmetries that allow for growing data gathering from individual traders. In July 2019, *The Guardian* reported that Chinese border guards at the Irkeshtam crossing were forcing travelers from Central Asia to download spy-ware granting them access to emails, texts, and contact information (Osborne and Cutler, 2019).

China rewired global information flows within its "Digital Silk Road" frame-work, aiming to turn China into the world's primary data hub by 2025—a goal that would grant the CCP oversight over much of the world's digital supply chain. To achieve its targets, Beijing created information nodes in Central Asia known as "smart cities," a catch-all term for cities with advanced data-processing capabilities. These projects also featured a security dimension.[9] For example, Kyrgyzstan opened a new police command center in its capital

---

[9] See also Dall'Agnola, Chapter 8, this volume.

Bishkek, which makes use of facial recognition software supplied by the China National Electronics Import and Export Corporation (Bowdler, 2019). In neighboring Uzbekistan, Chinese telecommunications giant Huawei closed a $1 billion deal to build a traffic monitoring system involving some 883 cameras (Sputnik, 2019). Meanwhile, Hikvision, a Chinese company that advertises its ability to spot members of China's Uyghur minority in crowds, supplies major urban centers across Kazakhstan, including Almaty and Shymkent (Jardine, 2019). Chinese companies also increase their information asymmetry vis-à-vis Central Asia through expansion into the region's digital infrastructure. In 2019, Uzbekistan's telecommunications operators began using soft loans from Chinese partners to introduce Huawei's 5G technology to the country. Huawei also connects 8 in every 10 Kyrgyz residents to the outside world and owns nearly 90 percent of neighboring Tajikistan's telecommunications infrastructure (Jardine, 2019). Huawei also works closely with Kazakhstan's top telecommunications companies Kazakhtelecom, Kcell, Beeline, and Tele2.

In addition, China has covert data gathering methods at its disposal, including hacks and the use of malware in the region. In Central Asia, Chinese telecommunications giant Huawei owns more standard-essential patents in 5G than any other company. Combined with its Chinese rival ZTE, it accounts for some 40 percent of global 5G infrastructure—a situation that Western officials have been left scrambling to challenge. Former Secretary of State Mike Pompeo, for example, told Maria Bartiromo, "If it's the case that the CCP wanted to get information from technology that was in possession of Huawei, it is almost certainly the case that Huawei would provide that to them" (Congressional Research Service, 2021: 1). Similarly, in response to a question from a journalist about the European use of Huawei technology, Deputy Assistant Secretary of State Rob Strayer said,

> We think that as the technology used in [smart] cities is integrated into broader wireless networks, that would be a cause for concern because that data could end up back in places such as Beijing where it would not be used for the purposes that we want to see all of our data subject to which is protected uses, limited uses, and not to be exploited for authoritarian purposes (Segal, 2021).

Dependence on Chinese technology may create heightened regional vulnerability to Chinese government-affiliated hacks. In September 2019, Reuters reported that Chinese hackers had exploited weaknesses in telecommunications companies in Kazakhstan, Turkey, India, Thailand, and Malaysia (Stubbs, 2019). The hacks allegedly used call record details to search for "high-value individuals," including Uyghurs living abroad and the people they are in contact with back in Xinjiang (Stubbs, 2019). In 2021, Chinese hackers were revealed by Facebook to have targeted Uyghurs living abroad through its platform by disseminating links to download malware. These hackers, from a group called Evil Eye, also created proxy websites and fake Android apps targeting some 500 Uyghurs, including in Kazakhstan.

Finally, China utilizes its own international structures to obtain sensitive information on policing and counterterrorism from allies. The SCO operates mainly through two administrative bodies: a Secretariat based in Beijing and the Regional Anti-Terrorism Structure (RATS) based in Tashkent. Established in January 2006, RATS is a consolidated list of extremist, terrorist, and separatist individuals and groups that would balloon to include 2,500 individuals and 69 groups by September 2016. According to Thomas Ambrosio (2016), "the RATS serves as the central locus of the process of 'sharing worst practices' amongst the SCO member states." The European Court of Human Rights has described these norms as "an absolute negation of the rule of law" (Amnesty International, 2013). Several counterterror drills under a series of "Peace Missions" have been staged under the RATS framework in Pakistan since 2018 and strengthened Islamabad's security cooperation with China.

While these asymmetries have primarily been utilized to pursue Uyghurs as a form of transnational repression, there are a number of scenarios in which Chinese strategic asymmetries may have wider implications for the region's sovereignty as a whole. For example, Chinese companies may gain sensitive information on the activities of competitors, including internal documents shared only within their servers. In another scenario, government officials may access sensitive information on Central Asian political figures, thereby leveraging economic or political concessions.

Parallel Order Building

China has traditionally been aware that Russia views Central Asia as part of its near abroad, or principal sphere of influence. With bases in three of the countries (Kazakhstan, Kyrgyzstan, Tajikistan), bilateral security ties, and multilateral organizations (Commonwealth of Independent States [CIS], Collective Security Treaty Organization [CSTO]) led by Moscow, Russia has the densest security networks with Central Asia of any great power, and this remained the case after its February 2022 invasion of Ukraine. China has shown deference to Russia on such matters in the past and tends to inform Moscow well in advance of its policies. In 2017, the Development Research Center, a powerful think tank under China's cabinet, invited Russian researchers to a private seminar to ascertain Russia's red lines regarding Chinese regional policy (Shih, 2019). The limited emphasis of the Chinese-led drills on border security and counter-terrorism, as described earlier, may serve the additional purpose of placating Russia, which sees itself as the prime security guarantor of the region. But the situation is slowly changing as China strengthens its own security networks.

China has increasingly developed networks in the region without Russia. Bilaterally, as described previously, it has organized its own joint exercises, created training programs, provided military aid, established a military facility in Tajikistan, and provided arms to the region. Multilaterally, it has established its own platforms for security and political cooperation, such as the SCO and China + Central Asia.

Outside the SCO, China established a new security mechanism in 2016 called the QCCM made up of itself, Tajikistan, Afghanistan, and Pakistan. The organization is tasked with jointly combating terrorism and further advancing security cooperation among these states (Kucera, 2016). The chiefs of staff of the four military forces met in Ürümchi in 2016 to announce the creation of the QCCM and stated it would coordinate efforts on the "study and judgment of the counter-terrorism situation, confirmation of clues, intelligence sharing, anti-terrorist capability building, joint anti-terrorist training, and personnel training" (Kucera, 2016). China combines its security coordination with these countries with pledges of large development projects as part of the BRI, and vice versa. In a 2020 report to Congress, the Pentagon highlighted how China's security and development interests are complementary and described how China was seeking new ways to increase its power projection in Central and South Asia. The report detailed how the Chinese military was planning to build "military logistics facilities" in several countries including Tajikistan, Afghanistan, and Pakistan in order to better protect China's economic and security interests (Department of Defense, 2020).

Leaked internal CCP documents obtained by the *New York Times* in 2019 provide further evidence regarding China's focus on securitizing Xinjiang. Set against a backdrop of the 2009 unrest in Ürümchi and the looming specter of a US withdrawal from Afghanistan, the leaked documents reveal how Xi pushed for a new strategy of expanding China's security apparatus in the XUAR and Central and South Asia. In closed-door speeches found in these documents, Xi states that economic development "does not automatically bring lasting order and security" and that China would have to wage a "People's War" in the region by emulating the US-led Global War on Terror (Ramzy and Buckley, 2019). These speeches signaled that, moving forward, the Chinese strategy in Central and South Asia would have to integrate traditional economic development projects with new military and security systems. These policies have resulted in an unprecedented crackdown in Xinjiang, including internment camps, forced sterilization, and large-scale use of coerced labor, indicating a shift toward viewing Uyghur society as a security threat, whereas past campaigns had largely targeted political activists. In addition, China's security activities and use of transnational repression around the globe grew significantly from 2014 to 2021 and indicated not only a nascent internationalization of the "Uyghur problem" in the eyes of the Chinese government (Jardine, Lemon, and Hall, 2023), but also an increasingly aggressive stance on the part of China in all international affairs.

In July 2020, China launched a new initiative "China + Central Asia (C+C5)," which brings together foreign ministers from the five republics and China. The platform focuses on coordinating cooperation on BRI transit projects, boosting cultural exchanges, and discussing joint security concerns. The initiative was elevated to the heads of state level in May 2023 when Xi Jinping hosted all five Central Asia presidents for an inaugural summit. In his welcoming remarks, Xi hailed the summit as signaling "a new era of China-Central Asia relations." Xi said that "China is ready to help Central Asian countries strengthen capacity building on law enforcement, security and defence in an effort to safeguard peace in the region" (State Council of the People's Republic of China, 2023).

Central Asia's Response: Balancing Regionalism

Although China's security networks are asymmetrical, Central Asia's governments do have agency and the power derived from their network positions to negotiate China's hegemonic ambitions (Cooley, 2012; Costa Buranelli, 2017). On the one hand, ruling regimes welcome China's growing role in Central Asian security. First, China's overtures allow the region's governments to reduce reliance on Russia and pursue multivector foreign policies, and to develop ties with a number of external partners as a means of avoiding overdependence on any single patron. Second, it fills a vacuum, coming at a time when the United States has largely exited the region, with military assistance falling 98 percent between 2012 and 2020 (Lemon and Jardine, 2020a). Third, Chinese assistance, which comes with no human rights conditionalities, provides opportunities to strengthen the repressive capacity of authoritarian regimes.

At the same time, the region's governments have to placate citizens who are wary of China's role as well as to avoid becoming too dependent on Beijing. Central Asian states utilize their network positions to maintain their sovereignty in two ways. First, *vertically*, they pursue multivector foreign policies by building network ties with multiple different external powers. Although Russia accounted for 52 percent of the arms imports to the region between 2016 and 2020 and China 16 percent, Central Asia managed to diversify weapon suppliers to Italy (11 percent), France (7 percent), and Turkey (6 percent), according to our data set. In terms of military exercises, Russia, either bilaterally or through the Commonwealth of Independent States or Collective Security Treaty Organization, organized 110 drills with Central Asian militaries by the end of 2021, while NATO and the United States organized 85 and India organized 12. Ultimately, Russia continues to be the node with the strongest security networks in the region, both in terms of the density and frequency of its institutionalized relations.

Second, *horizontally* they develop network ties among themselves. In recent years, the states of the region have pursued a strategy of "balancing regionalism" (Tshkay and Costa Buranelli, 2020). This involves both bolstering regional cooperation within Central Asia and developing ties with multiple actors as part of multivector foreign policies to protect themselves from the establishment of an exclusively Russian or Chinese sphere of influence in Central Asia.

For many years following independence, Central Asia was one of the least integrated parts of the world with low levels of trade, undelimited borders, and tensions between neighboring states. Regionalism was often exogenously enforced by external powers pursuing their own agendas. But after the death of Islam Karimov in Uzbekistan in 2016 and the rise of his successor Shavkat Mirziyoyev, this started to change. Mirziyoyev made improving ties with his neighbors the centerpiece of his foreign policy. As a result, security cooperation has developed with eight joint exercises between Central Asian militaries between 2011 and 2021. The first joint exercises between Kyrgyzstan and Tajikistan were a small, largely symbolic affair involving around 30 troops. This was followed by the second exercise in 2015. A first exercise, Sapper's Friendship, took place between Kazakhstan and Kyrgyzstan in 2017. In a move that would have been unthinkable a decade earlier, when tensions between Uzbekistan and Tajikistan were at their peak, the two countries held their first bilateral exercise, in the south of Tajikistan in 2018. The next year Tajikistan and Uzbekistan signed an agreement on military-technical cooperation and envisaged bilateral exercises and joint production of military equipment (Kerimkhanov, 2019). Under the new agreement, the two countries had held three further exercises by 2021, all involving special operations forces.

Rising regionalism also allows the governments to address regional issues, such as border delimitation, collective security, and trade, without external mediation. When Tajikistan and Kyrgyzstan engaged in the bloodiest conflict on their border since independence in April 2021, regional organizations and external powers were apathetic in their response, while the governments of Kazakhstan and Uzbekistan took the lead in mediation.

Conclusion: Security and Hierarchy along the BRI

As China continues to expand its footprint in Central Asia through the BRI, a number of events indicate that we can expect China's investments to come under threat. First, ongoing political transitions in Kyrgyzstan, Kazakhstan, and Uzbekistan have created greater opportunities for citizens to express their grievances, with opposition actors capitalizing on existing Sinophobia to channel protests against the BRI. Second, as the United States and NATO have withdrawn from Afghanistan, the situation in the country has worsened, heightening the spillover of militancy north of the Amu Darya River. These developments have led the Chinese government to increasingly see the BRI through the lens of security, as investments that need protecting.

Concerns over security have also drawn China into complex, overlapping security networks in Central Asia. These networks have developed rapidly, with China becoming a major arms supplier, setting up its first military facility, organizing exercises, and enhancing the surveillance capacity of regimes. In the long term, these networks could be exploited by China to "weaponize interdependence" by exercising a "panopticon effect" to collect data on actors within Central Asia.

That said, China is not omnipotent in the region and has to consider the positions of other nodes in the regional network. First, at present, China is less and less deferential to Russia, the historically dominant external security provider in Central Asia, despite pledges in March 2023 to "strengthen mutual coordination to support the countries of Central Asia in ensuring their sovereignty and national development" and to "not accept attempts to import 'color revolutions' and external interference in the affairs of the region" (Kremlin, 2022). The war in Ukraine has weakened Russia materially and symbolically, offering increased opportunities for China to expand its role as a security provider. There is growing evidence that China has developed its own bilateral security networks, through exercises, training activities, arms supplies and surveillance, and multilateral ties through forums that exclude Russia, such as the QCCM and China + Central Asia. As these ties develop, they could start to undermine and weaken Russia's security networks. It remains to be seen whether Russia would be able to resist this by mobilizing its own resources to lessen Beijing's influence. Second, the Central Asian governments, and especially their populations, remain wary of becoming too dependent on China or Russia. As a result, they have developed ties with other external powers such as the United States, Turkey, India, and EU countries to diversify their portfolio of security networks as part of multivector foreign policies.

While China's BRI infrastructure in Central Asia has remained economically oriented over the past decade, developments in South and East Asia suggest that militarization of infrastructure may be on the horizon. Since 2015, China has operated a number of military roads in the South Asian country of Bhutan with the aim of creating strategic depth for a potential conflict against great power rival India (Barnett, 2021). In addition, Cambodia has growing debts to China—equal to those of Kyrgyzstan and Tajikistan—which have resulted in a number of strategic concessions, including a rumored naval facility run by China's armed forces. Such developments show an increasingly militaristic orientation for sensitive border regions along the BRI.

All these military developments along the Belt and Road territories lead us to see the BRI as characterized by a security–development nexus aimed at enhancing China's geopolitical and geoeconomic power and reach. While this volume correctly attends to the diverse ways of seeing the BRI, our contention is that these material developments remain crucial to appreciating the BRI's broad contours. Seeing the Belt and Road in this way offers insight into the "sinews of war and trade" (Khalili, 2020) that underpin the expansion of not only China's control over the infrastructure projects that increase its role in market expansion but also China's active involvement in the aggressive military buildup that emerges in tandem with infrastructure developments. Attention to these elements of the BRI sheds light on the ways that China securitizes its overseas development projects, and it reveals the BRI projects as both enabling and providing the rationale for China's increasing military role beyond its borders. However, this chapter has also demonstrated some ways that Central Asian states push back against the BRI's intertwined development and security investments. Attention to the agency of people and regions at the frontiers of China's expansionary push has allowed this chapter to demonstrate that even when Beijing presents a unified strategy backed by increasing military investments as part of the BRI's progress, the path that the BRI ultimately takes will be shaped by a wide range of actors with a tremendous diversity of interests.

2

Official Lending, Optics, and Outliers

Chinese Debt and the Belt and Road Initiative after COVID-19

Tom Narins

Introduction

During the four decades leading up to 2020, the Chinese state became increasingly visible in developing economies for a variety of reasons (Zhang, 2019), including as an official lender to governments in need of financing for infrastructural projects. In so doing, the Chinese state garnered both positive and negative attention as an international lender (Afrobarometer, 2016; Zhang, 2019). In particular, Chinese lending practices became increasingly important, and increasingly controversial, within the context of South–South Cooperation (SSC). This chapter examines four Belt and Road Initiative (BRI)-debtor countries (Pakistan, Laos, Sri Lanka, and Zambia) to highlight what implications their economic struggles have for the BRI as an initiative and China as a lender. Where appropriate, this examination involves a survey-level discussion within each country of three comparative angles: academic/policy observers, government spokespeople, and citizens, as a way of providing a more complete picture of the economic impact of Chinese debt and associated economic activities in light of the COVID-19-triggered economic downturn.

SSC broadly refers to "the transfer and exchange of resources, technology and knowledge, set within claims to . . . shared colonial . . . experiences . . . and anchored within a wider framework of promoting the collective strength and development of the global South" (Mawdsley, 2019: 1). In the SSC's most recent incarnation, dubbed "South–South Cooperation 3.0," China expanded onto the geopolitical stage with greater exposure than ever before (Mawdsley, 2019).

Increased exposure of Chinese official lending to developing countries stems from the economic uncertainties brought on by the COVID-19 pandemic, which caused many emerging countries' debt levels to rise precipitously (Narins and Agnew, 2021). This pronounced rise in Chinese debt among select BRI countries symbolized a type of national financial distress among recipients of Chinese lending and increased the scrutiny of Chinese-funded infrastructure

Tom Narins, *Official Lending, Optics, and Outliers* In: Seeing China's Belt and Road. Edited by: Edward Schatz and Rachel Silvey, Oxford University Press. © Oxford University Press 2025.
DOI: 10.1093/oso/9780197789261.003.0003

projects worldwide. Such Chinese lending came at a time of increased public demand for national accountability focused on spending on healthcare and economic recovery in light of the deleterious effects of COVID-19 (Dehghan, 2021). Although China's lending to BRI-participant countries began before the onset of COVID-19, such exposure became more pronounced in international public forums given the immediacy of containing the political and economic setbacks associated with the onset of the COVID-19-triggered "pandemic depression"— a term coined to describe the global economic fallout caused by the pandemic (Reinhart and Reinhart, 2020).

This shift in perception of China as an international lender is noteworthy. Conventional accounts of China as an international lender posit that the country was a major "lender of *last* resort" (Stallings, 2021: 42, emphasis in original) to developing economies, some of which are viewed as pariah states (Gallagher, Irwin, and Koleski, 2012) and many of which were unable to borrow from established, multilateral lending organizations. A more recent study suggests that China became a "lender of *first* resort" because for many developing countries, including several BRI participants, China's government became the easiest, quickest option for financing development projects over the last few decades, oftentimes providing financing when traditional lenders, such as Western lenders / financial institutions, were unwilling to do so (Dreher et al., 2022). This shift in terminology, though subtle, underscores how the spotlight of international financial attention focuses more than ever on Chinese economic actors.

A series of important Chinese state policy announcements helped to gradually position China as a high-visibility, official lender on a global scale. This process started in 1978 with the "Reform and Opening Up" (*gǎi gé kāi fàng*) of China's economy and its subsequent increasing connection with the broader world economy. This action set the stage for the state-sanctioned internationalization of the Chinese economy. In 1999, Beijing officially adopted the "Going Out" strategy (*zǒu chū qù zhàn lüè*) and "Develop the West" (*xī bù dà kāi fā*) policies, both of which encouraged Chinese state and private investment beyond China's borders. In 2001, China's accession into the World Trade Organization marked another defining moment of China's interconnection with the global economy.

Of special significance for this chapter, in 2013, Chinese leadership publicly formalized its interest in international infrastructure construction and financing expertise when Chinese President Xi Jinping announced the "One Belt, One Road" (*yī dài yī lù*) Initiative (OBOR). During visits to Kazakhstan and Indonesia in 2013, Chinese President Xi Jinping called for the development of a "Silk Road Economic Belt" (*sī chóu zhī lù jīng jì dài*) and a "21st Century Maritime Silk Road" (*21 shì jì hǎi shàng sī chóu zhī lù*), respectively, which together comprised OBOR (ASEAN–China Center, 2013; Ministry of Foreign

Affairs, 2013). OBOR officially changed its English-language name change to Belt and Road Initiative in 2016. Chinese foreign policymakers selected a more inclusive sounding name (Belt and Road Initiative) and moved away from the original English translation (One Belt, One Road), to avoid the uncertainties associated with the plan's routes and avoid perceptions that this initiative centered on and around Chinese institutions building (Bērziņa-Čerenkova, 2016).

In spite of Beijing's preoccupation with adapting the English translation of the initiative's name to appeal to a broader international audience, the impetus for the BRI's launch stemmed from a desire among the Chinese leadership to address *domestic* priorities "to deflect the US–China rivalry, search for alternative diplomatic space, and find new opportunities for industry" (Ye, 2021: 93). However, as understood and interpreted by countries partnering with China, the BRI was popularized in the press (both inside and outside of China) and was given tangible meaning by being portrayed as an attempt by the largest country in East Asia to use infrastructure to *internationalize* China's economy. In particular, the press portrayed the BRI as symbolizing an opportunity to connect China with the economies of 145 countries (Belt and Road Portal, 2021) by using China's expertise and experience in financing and constructing "new roads, railways, and other infrastructure beyond its borders" (Hillman, 2020: 4). Both the "Belt" and the "Road" are visual representations linking Beijing's efforts to leverage Chinese companies' expertise in infrastructural construction and logistics with cultural and historical nostalgia for the ancient Silk Roads "in which people, cultures and continents were woven together" through international trade (Frankopan, 2018: x). Importantly, these efforts occurred in a Eurasian geopolitical environment where reception to connectivity efforts symbolized by the BRI was at an all-time high (Frankopan, 2018; Narins and Agnew, 2020).

As a major official (sovereign) lender to developing countries, contemporary China's international financing is more widespread than ever before (Zhang, 2020), even while the pace of official lending to BRI-participant countries decreased from 2020 to 2021 (White, 2021). At the same time, Chinese official lending is conducted largely without publicizing the conditions and terms of its loans. This reality has led to ongoing concern among international financial regulatory observers and among BRI-participant countries (Chilkoti and Steinhauser, 2020; Horn, Reinhart, and Trebesch, 2020) and translated into increased scrutiny over China's four-decade-long push to "go global."[1] This is the case in part because recipients of Chinese loans have recently shifted from central banks to special-purpose corporations, resulting in Chinese debt failing to appear on developing countries' balance sheets (Areddy, 2021; White, 2021).

---

[1] See, for example, Shambaugh (2013), for background on the Chinese leadership's thinking on global engagement prior to the BRI's launch.

The global economic shock triggered by the COVID-19 pandemic catapulted Chinese-issued debt in the developing world into a cause célèbre of concerned world leaders (Ramaphosa, 2020), critics of the BRI (Hillman, 2020), and development and human rights organizations (World Bank, 2020; Breuer and Cohen, 2020). As a result, in Western media depictions, Chinese lending became more *visible* than ever—even if the details of the loan amounts were not revealed and the terms often lacked transparency.

This veiled nature of the amounts and details relating to Chinese lending was at the heart of concerns relating to sovereignty among BRI debtor countries (Narins and Agnew, 2021) and occurred at a time when China's official lending agencies "extended many more loans to developing countries than previously known" (Horn et al., 2020). With the onset of the COVID-19 pandemic, BRI debtor countries faced a difficult geopolitical and geoeconomic paradox. The governments of these countries were, on the one hand, politically motivated to emphasize cooperative and mutually productive bilateral relations with Chinese official lenders, yet, on the other hand, these same governments struggled with the uncertainties of how such official Chinese lending influenced their ability to guide and protect their own national development and territorial sovereignty (Narins and Agnew, 2021).

One 2021 study indicates that BRI participant countries owed $385 billion in "hidden debts" to China (Malik et al., 2021). After the BRI's announcement in 2013, and even more so after the onset of the pandemic in January 2020, official Chinese lending garnered increased visibility in part because many of China's loans to BRI participant countries posed major repayment challenges for receiving governments (Narins and Agnew, 2021). Therefore, by examining the multiple ways in which Chinese financing and debt within the BRI are *seen* from various vantage points along with exploring the likely economic trajectories of four outlier BRI debtor countries (Pakistan, Laos, Sri Lanka, and Zambia) moving forward (see Figure 2.1), this chapter considers the implications that these countries' economic struggles have for the BRI as this initiative enters its second decade.

Each of the countries selected here is an outlier with regard to its relationship toward official Chinese debt within the broader BRI framework. Pakistan is an outlier, for its flagship political economic relationship within China's BRI; Laos, for its government's acquiescence allowing heavy Chinese debt to be linked to several infrastructure projects of dubious national importance; Sri Lanka, for its flawed symbolism as a target of China's debt-trap diplomacy; and Zambia, for: (1) its unusually high level of Chinese indebtedness (being one of three African countries where Chinese loans are considered "major or dominant" (Eom, Bräutigam, and Benebdallah, 2018; Ofstad and Tjønneland, 2019: 3), and for (2) being a country that went from having almost no external debt in 2005

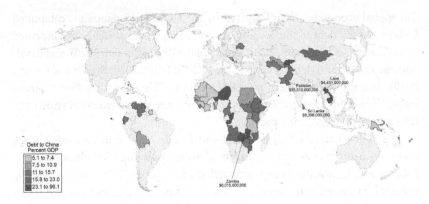

Figure 2.1 Four selected countries: Pakistan, Laos, Sri Lanka, and Zambia (labeled) with high Chinese debt-to-GDP ratios and their outstanding Chinese debt. Note: Countries that are shaded (but not labeled) rank among the top 50 countries holding Chinese debt. Source: Horn et al. (2019).

to becoming the first African country to default on its loans (due to its heavy borrowing starting in 2012) (Ofstad and Tjønneland, 2019: 4) after the onset of COVID-19.

Analyzing Chinese official lending to these countries offers practical and theoretical insights into the evolution of the BRI as a power-imbalanced and finance-dependent development effort. Furthermore, because "the identification of an outlier case may immediately suggest a new theoretical specification with potentially broader application" (Lieberman, 2005: 440), studying these four BRI debtor countries in relation to Chinese debt promotes understanding of the varied contours of the BRI, where, up until recently, so much of the official government, media, and scholarly focus was on China as the dominant actor in an effort that involves over 140 countries. Consistent with the volume's efforts to decenter the study of the BRI (Schatz and Silvey, introduction to this volume), this chapter critically questions this China-centric vantage point. By providing empirically grounded information about these BRI debtor countries, the chapter aims to consider potential future pathways toward economic recovery.

Pakistan

BRI Observers

Among popular and scholarly observers of the BRI, Pakistan was arguably the most important BRI partner country. In part this has to do with the geopolitics of South Asia, where Pakistan was seen as a potential Chinese counterweight to US-aligned India. In terms of geoeconomics, the proposed China–Pakistan Economic Corridor (CPEC), which launched in 2015, was touted as a way for China to ensure its future energy security by representing an alternative land-based route connecting Western China to the oil-rich countries of the Middle East. In so doing, Chinese economic actors could avoid the sea-based route to the Middle East via the Strait of Malacca, which is widely viewed as a potential bottleneck for world economic trade flows, especially in times of crisis. From the Chinese perspective, CPEC initially appeared to be a pathway for China to address multiple objectives simultaneously, "stabilizing its western periphery, outsourcing overcapacity, bolstering its strategic partner, and setting the stage for a more expansive form of cooperation between the two countries that others would see and wish to imitate" (Small, 2020: 18).

From the Pakistani perspective, early on, there was broad support for CPEC because it was believed that it would "alleviate Pakistan's severe energy crisis" with "most of the power projects" slated to be built in the economically less developed regions of Balochistan and Sindh (Boni and Adeney, 2020: 457). However, as construction projects associated with CPEC commenced, it became clear that information about the details and financing of such projects was not easily obtainable. In general, the details of the CPEC agreements between China and Pakistan were notable for their lack of transparency (Boni and Adeney, 2020).

In addition, CPEC observers often portrayed the BRI as representing "a uni-directional Chinese endeavor" (Adeney and Boni, 2021: 1) where all roads lead to China. This aligns with a popular perception that "Beijing is merely imposing the CPEC on its all-weather partners in Islamabad" (Adeney and Boni, 2021: 1). This depiction stood at odds with the reality that China's construction of the Port of Gwadar—one of the key infrastructural sights in the CPEC—was carried out specifically at the request of Pakistan's then-president and head of the army, Pervez Musharraf (Markey, 2020: vii). In reality, on-the-ground experiences in Pakistan highlighted the fact that Pakistani and Chinese priorities were mediated and resulted in "*negotiated* outcomes as opposed to having terms unilaterally set by Beijing (Adeney and Boni, 2021: 10, original emphasis)."

Another widely discussed perception about Pakistan's involvement with the BRI was that CPEC functioned as a transportation "corridor" between Western China and the Pakistani Port of Gwadar on Balochistan's Arabian Sea coast.[2] While leaders in Beijing aimed to extend China's reach to the Arabian Sea and to promote stability on its western border, with the ultimate goal of "consolidating China's strategic influence along its western horizon"

---

[2] For analysis of another BRI "corridor" linking China to Laos, see DiCarlo, Chapter 6, this volume.

(Markey, 2020: 78–79), the notion of a functioning corridor from China to Pakistan did not reflect the realities on the ground. CPEC represented a set of site-based infrastructural projects driven by partisan politics, each of which portrayed a conservative agenda in terms of bringing change to Pakistan's political economy (Adeney and Boni, 2021; Boni and Adeney, 2020). In fact, as a September 2020 report clearly stated in referring to CPEC: "despite the use of the term 'corridor,' it was never intended as a serious cross-border artery, and there are no plans for railways, pipelines, or even large-scale road traffic between Pakistan and China" (Small, 2020: 5). This suggested that the motivations for China's long-term presence in Pakistan may be more "geopolitical rather than geo-economic" (Garlick, 201: 519). CPEC, however, resulted in improvement and upgrades to Pakistan's domestic infrastructure as well as "some cross-border fiber-optic cabling" (Small, 2020: 5). This important reality was perhaps the most impactful and significant development included in the BRI—the expansion of China's digital infrastructure and computer networks beyond its borders (Hillman, 2021).[3]

Another reason why BRI observers view Pakistan as an outlier is that it is the *only* country whose land territory represents the full extent of one of the six widely discussed BRI economic corridors that emanated from China. These six economic corridors represented broad international pathways of logistics and transportation investments originating in China, around which the BRI was framed (State Council Information Office, 2020), even though discussions of these corridors suggest "that more is known about the initiative as a whole and what it has so far achieved than is in fact the case" (Narins and Agnew, 2019: 2). Each of the other five BRI economic corridors is comprised of China plus *multiple* BRI participant countries (State Council Information Office, 2020).

There is also a perception that Pakistan received as much as $62 billion in Chinese financing for infrastructural projects associated with CPEC after its inception in 2015 and that such a large amount of investment would significantly improve Pakistan's economic prospects moving forward. Recent scholarship, however, has clarified that such investment levels are "no longer accurate, [and] investments of that magnitude are not under consideration either" (Small, 2020: 3). Other estimates of Chinese investments in Pakistan ranged from approximately $19 billion (Small, 2020: 40) to $35.3 billion (Horn, Reinhart, and Trebesch, 2019). In addition, the perception that CPEC was designed to

---

[3] For further discussion of how China's technology transfers and the "Digital Silk Road" have been received, see Kaufmann, Chapter 7, and Dall'Agnola, Chapter 8, this volume.

"foster development in otherwise marginalized regions or countries" (Guluzian, 2017: 137) with the implication that *all* of Pakistan would benefit from CPEC's investments did not take into account how partisan politics made such investments unevenly distributed across Pakistan's four main provinces, with the more economically developed and more populous Punjab province receiving a disproportionate share of China's investment capital.

Like other BRI debtor countries, Pakistan was poised to renegotiate its Chinese debt, but such negotiations, despite Pakistan's flagship role in the BRI, most likely meant a revision of the original CPEC contracts as opposed to an outright forgiveness of debt owed (Small, 2020: 7). At the same time, however, because of the actual completion and success of multiple Chinese investments in Pakistan, "more electricity [was added] to its faltering grid and is now better connecting its own cities with new roads and public transit systems" (Saeed, 2021). Despite these successes, experts raised concerns regarding the possibility that CPEC might compromise Pakistan's fiscal and political sovereignty, especially considering "the size and terms of China's investment . . . at a time when [Pakistan's] economy is squeezed by the coronavirus pandemic" (Saeed, 2021). This domestic, fiscally based critique of Pakistan's political economy and relationship to the global financial system stood in counterpoint to a principal tenet of China's domestic impetus for the BRI's expansion: "to create a more energetic growth environment in South and Central Asia that would synergise with economic development and stability in western China" (Gordon, Tong, and Anderson, 2020: 6).

The Pakistani Government's Depiction of Chinese Debt

After the inception of CPEC in 2015, the Pakistani government under the Pakistan Muslim League (Nawaz) party, which was closely aligned with the Pakistani army, viewed Chinese debt as a means to generate much needed economic development. However, beginning in 2018, populist Prime Minister Imran Khan voiced concerned over Pakistan's rising debt levels and expressed the importance of not depending on foreign loans. Such unease was similar to that expressed by new administrations assuming office in Sri Lanka, Malaysia, and the Maldives (Jorgic, 2018). Over time, however, the new Pakistan Tehreek-e-Insaf administration continued to promote the public narrative that CPEC's development would lead to progress and economic success for Pakistan. Importantly, with regard to Pakistan's China debt load, "CPEC's reputation has become as important as the substance of any of the projects and [Pakistan and China] will take the steps required to maintain that" (Small, 2020: 4). Because of China's strategic interests in CPEC—more as a large flagship project with

an "all-weather friend" than as an actual, functioning economic corridor—
Pakistani officials with knowledge about the country's negotiations with China
stated that in the event of future Chinese debt problems, Pakistan could negotiate better terms at a later stage. Tellingly, one Chinese expert commented about
Chinese debt financing in Pakistan: "Pakistan is not a place where our main priority is to make money—if we have to revisit loans and contracts at a later point,
we can do that."[4]

Where Chinese Debt Cannot Help: Pakistani Citizenry's Lack of a Social Safety Net and Fiscal Mismanagement since COVID-19

The negative health ramifications of COVID-19 did not impact Pakistan as severely as other countries due to the country's demographic makeup: Pakistan
has a young population and a low urbanization rate. These two factors were in-
strumental in preventing the spread of the virus in Pakistan (Zakaria, 2020). At
the same time, however, the Pakistani state did not have social welfare programs
to protect its citizens during the prolonged period of economic hardship that
followed the COVID-19 outbreak (Zakaria, 2020). This lack of a social safety
net placed a greater burden on family ties as a means of survival. This intensified
the economic and social burdens of the pandemic because, according to one
Pakistani social critic, "these familial networks will not be a successful source of
support, given the widespread nature of the economic pain caused by the pandemic" (Zakaria, 2020).

While the Pakistani government, in consultation with United Nations
agencies, developed a "Covid-19 Socio-economic Impact Assessment and
Response Plan" as a way of responding to and coping with the most ur-
gent impacts and risks brought on by the then-unfolding economic depression, the imbalance between Pakistan's long history of lacking social planning
mechanisms coupled with the country's fiscal mismanagement made Pakistan's
economic recovery trajectory highly uncertain. This reality highlighted the se-
verity of the near-term challenges faced by those especially vulnerable, large
segments of Pakistan's population including the "nearly half of all households in
the country [that] rely on agriculture and livestock as their primary and/or secondary source of livelihood" (UNDP, 2020: 5).

---

[4] Anonymous interview quoted in Small (2020: 30).

Laos

BRI Observers

Numerous scholarly studies have focused on the relationship between the Lao government and the increasing role of Chinese foreign capital and investment in the country. These studies highlighted the irresponsible nature and lack of capacity of the Lao People's Revolutionary Party (LPRP) in planning and managing the country's debt (Barney and Souksakoun, 2021: 105). In 2015, Laos joined a list of Global South states that "entered into formalized agreements to borrow from Chinese policy banks for BRI infrastructure" (Chen, 2020: 296; see also Fernholz, 2018). While scholarship had been very critical of claims of a China-led "debt-trap" (e.g., Bräutigam, 2021; Bräutigam and Rithmire, 2021; Dreher et al., 2022; Jones and Hameiri, 2020) affecting countries across the developing world, experts have accurately described Laos as a BRI debtor country that had a "ballooning external debt profile" (Sims, 2020) and in this sense fit into the dominant Western media narrative (and concern) that such fiscal weakness "could affect the rebalancing of geopolitical power in the future" (Chen, 2020: 297; see also Lai, Lin, and Sidaway, 2020).

Research points to the likely increase of Laos's dependence on China due to large-scale Chinese-financed infrastructure investments (Kuik and Rosli, 2023). While some observers quickly criticized Chinese lenders' role in Laos, one scholar noted that "far from eroding the power of the Lao communist regime, the new Chinese transnational networks . . . play a key role in the production of a neoliberal governmentality, that allowed the Lao state to consolidate its grip over its territorial margins" (Tan, 2017: 141). This pattern of Chinese official lending strengthening the sovereignty of a recipient government occurred in the relationship between Chinese government-backed investment and the government of another small, poor, landlocked Asian country—Nepal (Murton, Lord, and Beazley, 2016). Elites in other small Asian countries, such as Sri Lanka, also tried to enhance their legitimacy and authority by connecting their time in office with BRI-associated Chinese debt (e.g., Freymann, 2020: 95–129).

With regard to the Laos–China Railway (LCR), which was touted as the infrastructure project that would help to transform Laos from a "pass-through country" (Sun, 2017) to a "land-linked" country (Rowedder, 2020; World Bank, 2020a), critical scholarship noted that "Laos' function of merely being a passageway of larger external visions of regional economic integration, now increasingly expedited by China, becomes clear once again" (Rowedder, 2020: 156). Nevertheless, the completion of LCR in December 2021 was viewed with an increase in positive, state-run media emanating from the Chinese state and local Lao media outlets (Thanabouasy, 2021; Global Times, 2021).

The Lao Government's Depiction of Chinese Debt

While Laos "always looked to China more as a protector against powerful neighbors (Thailand and Vietnam) than as a threatening great power" (Stuart-Fox, 2004: 134), the rapid expansion of China's economic footprint in the early 2000s led to widely divergent outcomes for various actors depending on their position in Lao society. From the perspective of the country's government and business elites, China's growing investment inflows, infrastructure-linked debt, and general increased involvement in the Lao economy were welcomed and encouraged (Kuik, 2021: 741). The Lao government's view of Chinese debt stemmed from the connection between Chinese-backed infrastructural investment (e.g., rail and hydropower projects) and enhancing the authority and legitimacy of the ruling LPRP (Kuik, 2021: 736).

On the domestic front, LPRP leaders have leveraged their country's power asymmetry with China and encouraged and courted Chinese investment and expertise, "with the ultimate goal of enhancing the LPRP's authority and legitimacy" (Kuik, 2021: 736; see also Rathie, 2017: 41–43). Similar to other developmentalist states in Asia, such as China, Laos's party-state viewed consistent economic growth connected with development as the way to maintain power. For the LPRP, the LCR was a key part "of the party's vision of transforming Laos into a 'land-linked' nation" (Kuik, 2021: 736). In addition, Laos's government and business elites considered the railway to be a "river of iron" (Lampton, Ho, and Kuik, 2020) around and from which Laos's economic future will emanate.

The Lao Citizenry's Views of BRI Investments

Recent work by geographers noted that there are "quite particular and contingent ways in which Chinese capital enters Laos" (Suhardiman et al., 2021: 80). Most of this work was critical of such investment and questioned the extent to which "flagship projects" such as the LCR, also referred to as the Vientiane–Boten Railway, and numerous hydropower projects contributed to Laos's debt vulnerability (Barney and Souksakoun, 2021: 95) without necessarily improving the economic opportunities or standard of living of Lao citizens.

At the same time, grassroots movements became increasingly critical of China's increasing involvement in Laos over this same period (Zhu, 2015; Fujimura, 2010). In 2008, for example, "strong grievances were voiced against a planned real estate project in the capital's That Luang marshlands because it was rumored the project would be a gated community to house thousands of Chinese migrants" (Kuik, 2021: 741). Discontent also arose because of this proposed project's location near the golden That Luang stupa, which was a symbol of Lao religion, sovereignty, and identity (Strangio, 2020).

In addition, evidence from scholarship in economic geography revealed that Laos appears to be an outlier in terms of which group of laborers (expatriate Chinese or local citizens) may be most exploited by BRI infrastructural projects. Whereas in most cases it appears that expatriate workers fared better than local labor, according to one study, it was Chinese workers (*not* Lao workers) who bore the heaviest brunt of the financial losses associated with the LCR project (Chen, 2020: 296). This appeared to be of little concern to the government of the Lao People's Democratic Republic, which relied mainly on Chinese debt to the exclusion of two other pandemic-related financial assistance frameworks: the G20's Debt Service Suspension Initiative and the International Monetary Fund's (IMF) Rapid Credit Facility (Chen, 2020).

Of direct concern to the Lao public was the fact that the completion of the LCR was not connected with any sustainable, long-term benefits directed at the economic development of the country (Rowedder, 2020: 155). In the case of Laos in particular, the people most impacted by the country's high debt, credit downgrades, and increased borrowing costs were Laos's rural and urban poor, as the Lao government increasingly "face[d] reduced capacity to extend social protection programs" (Barney and Souksakoun, 2021: 105).

Sri Lanka

BRI Observers

For many years, Western media portrayed Sri Lanka as the "poster child" victim of what some observers call China's "debt-trap" diplomacy, a narrative "which emphasizes deliberate Chinese entrapment with the goal of seeking assets or strategic leverage" (Bräutigam, 2021: 8). After a pundit's misreading of a Chinese contract with the debt-burdened port of Hambantota (Bräutigam, 2021; Bräutigam and Rithmire, 2021), critics viewed Sri Lanka as symbolic of the dangers of engaging in Chinese-financed infrastructure projects, particularly with regard to the maintenance and protection of a BRI-borrowing state's national territorial sovereignty. Such a widely repeated narrative also stoked geopolitical concerns in the West that the Hambantota port may have represented another "pearl" in the string of pearls (SoP) theory—a theory suggesting that the buildup of Chinese naval bases in maritime South and Southeast Asia translates to Chinese political and military expansion in the Indo-Pacific region. This narrative was widely circulated despite the lack of empirical support (e.g., Barton, 2020).

As was the case with the construction of the Gwadar port in Pakistan, it was the Sri Lankan government's idea to build the Hambantota port (Freymann, 2020: 107) and not the idea of China's government. Bräutigam and Rithmire (2021), however, highlighted the conditions that led Sri Lanka's prime minister to choose Chinese lenders (after lenders from India, Japan, and the West refused to offer credit) to move forward with his own politically fueled desire for building a port in the extreme southern city of Hambantota (see Hillman, 2020: 151–70).

The Sri Lankan Government's Depiction of Chinese Debt

Before recent contributions clarified how the financing of the Hambantota port came to be closely associated with Chinese official lending (Bräutigam and Rithmire, 2021; Freymann, 2020), most Western scholars treated the Hambantota port case as evidence of China's nefarious intentions to use debt-trap diplomacy to push forward the BRI across the developing world (Robertson, 2018). However, Hambantota's debt financing was more complex than this narrative suggests. Sri Lankan Prime Minister Mahinda Rajapaksa and his patronage network courted funding to build the port, and they were supported by a practical, domestic political faction that stood to profit from its construction.

In 2002, two Canadian firms negotiated with the Sri Lankan government to build the Hambantota port with no success (Ladduwahetty, 2002). Then, around 2006, Japan, as well as other large donor countries, was encouraged to bid on the port construction project but declined to do so. Around this same time India had been "offered" the port, but Delhi passed on the deal due to budgetary limitations and because of concerns that "the project was not credit worthy" (Freymann, 2020: 109). Only after these numerous initial attempts at securing funding did China submit a proposal to develop the port (Freymann, 2020). This evidence supports the view that China's role in the Hambantota port project was as the lender of *last* resort. The fact that China's proposal for Phase I of the project "went through a secret approval process" (Freymann, 2020: 109) did not facilitate China's desired image of itself as having purely economic interests in this project. This fact-based account of the story of the Hambantota port reveals that the optics of Chinese debt from a Sri Lankan public and Western public perspective did not reflect the process that the Sri Lankan government itself went through.

Recent scholarship highlighted an important lesson for those wishing to understand the nature of the BRI: the domestic predilections and policy decisions of national-level politicians participating in BRI projects could be the main driving factors contributing to the apparent financial stranglehold that observers argue Chinese debt assumed. The reality—as the real case of the port at Hambantota made clear—was much more complex and domestically driven than the coverage in international media shaping views of the fast-evolving BRI suggested (Carrai, 2021).

The Sri Lankan Citizenry's Views on the Pandemic-Inspired Economic Downturn

As with all countries, the full extent and duration of the negative economic impacts of the pandemic remain unknown. A 2020 UNICEF report, however, stated that the crisis continued to take a significant human toll on the citizens of Sri Lanka. According to UNICEF simulations, "average household incomes could fall by up to 27 percent during the crisis" (UNICEF, 2020: 7). This occurred against the backdrop of the Sri Lankan government's high levels of indebtedness to Chinese as well as other international lenders. The government's debt loads made it nearly impossible to organize and carry out much-needed cash transfers to the country's most economically vulnerable citizens (UNICEF, 2020: 12).

To most Sri Lankan citizens, however, perceptions of illegal immigration felt like more of a threat than did Chinese debt held by the government in Colombo. While Chinese infrastructural engineering companies were responsible for big development projects including Colombo Port City, only 22.4 percent of the workers on this project were Chinese migrants (Wignaraja et al., 2020). In addition, Colombo International Container Terminals Ltd., a joint venture company between China Merchants Port Holdings Company Limited and the Sri Lanka Ports Authority, which operated a terminal at the port of Colombo, had a staff comprised of only two percent Chinese workers as of 2019 (Wignaraja et al., 2020). Finally, the southeastern Sri Lankan port of Hambantota which employed about 900 workers in 2020, had a Chinese labor force of only 3.3 percent (Wignaraja et al., 2020).

Zambia

BRI Observers

During the early years of the COVID-19 pandemic, Zambia was unique among African countries, "for its high level of Chinese loan commitments relative to its economy and its outstanding debt" (Bräutigam, 2021: 3). In November 2020 Zambia became the first African country to default on its foreign debt after the onset of COVID-19 (Bariyo, 2021), leading to fears of a "debt tsunami" on the continent (Steinhauser and Wallace, 2020; Williams, 2020). The Zambian state was at greater risk of debt distress than other African countries in part because it has 18 distinct Chinese creditors, more than any other African country (Bräutigam, 2021). In addition, Zambia was one of only four African countries to have a Chinese debt-to-GNI percentage above 40 percent (Bräutigam, 2021: 4). Zambia was a quintessential example of a developing country whose government was highly leveraged with respect to Chinese lenders (27 percent of Zambia's external debt stock was held by Chinese creditors in 2020) (Ministry of Finance and National Planning, 2020), in a global economic landscape where "the coronavirus pandemic . . . caused debt levels to soar, subsequently raising many questions about the ability of emerging countries to pay back their debts in the future" (Economist Intelligence Unit, 2021).

The Zambian Government's Depiction of Chinese Debt

Zambia's debt to China was difficult to ascertain in part because of the 18 Chinese lenders involved, as well as the fact that the Zambian government had "been hiding the identity of some significant Chinese creditors" (Bräutigam and Wang, 2021). Chinese loan amounts were apparently underreported by the previous Lungu administration by a factor of 2 (Bräutigam and Wang, 2021). The Lungu administration stated its highest Chinese debt figure as $3.4 billion, whereas researchers at the China Africa Research Initiative estimated Zambia's external loans to all Chinese lenders totaled approximately $6.6 billion (Bräutigam and Wang, 2021: 1). This discrepancy between government and independent reporting of Chinese loans was possibly due to the terms of the nondisclosure agreements stipulated in China's loans with the Zambian government.

The Zambian Citizenry's Views of the BRI

Since 2010, Zambia has been one of the poorest countries in Africa with 54 percent of its citizens suffering from high and chronic poverty (International Household Survey Network, 2010). Beginning in 2015, following four consecutive years of drought and a slump in the price of copper, the country faced a growing debt crisis. The crisis was fueled in part by the secrecy of the loans that enabled Chinese lenders to impose terms that slowed economic growth in Zambia during the four years prior to the COVID-19 pandemic. The onset of the COVID-19 pandemic exacerbated "these negative developments by pushing vulnerable households into poverty and increasing the poverty gap further for chronically poor households" (Paul et al., 2021: 3). The country's Social Cash Transfer (SCT) program, which began in 2003, had the potential to provide major economic relief to a substantial portion of the population (Paul et al., 2021: 3–4). However, the Zambian government faced difficulty providing the SCT unless it improved its fiscal position. In order to do this, the government needed to openly publicize more information about China's "hidden loans," thereby allowing other international creditors, such as the IMF, World Bank, and the African Development Bank, to assist with debt relief in a more transparent and sustained manner (Bräutigam and Wang, 2021).

Following the IMF's approval in June 2023, the Zambian government reached a deal with China, its largest creditor, and other creditors to restructure its $6.3 billion in loans (Corbet, 2023). This deal may act as "a roadmap for how China will handle restructuring deals with other nations in debt distress" (Corbet, 2023).

Conclusion: Implications for the BRI Moving Forward

This chapter adopts a political economic approach toward understanding the geographies of Chinese debt management and the optics of addressing such debt during the COVID-19 pandemic era. By examining four national cases—Pakistan, Laos, Sri Lanka, and Zambia—this work employs the responses from the distinct viewpoints of academic/policy observers, government spokespeople, and citizens, as a way of providing a more complete picture of the economic impact of Chinese debt and associated economic activities in light of the COVID-19-triggered economic downturn.

If policymakers in Beijing had continued to guide the BRI in ways consistent with their actions before the pandemic, their efforts to "stay the course" may have helped their reputation in a world that grew increasingly wary of China's political intentions after the beginning of the COVID-19 pandemic. However, ongoing post-COVID-19 global economic challenges posed major challenges for China—a country that sought to enhance and expand its geopolitical stature and goodwill while it simultaneously aimed to translate its economic power into political influence around the world. These lofty goals could only be achieved if China could act as a collaborator in helping its BRI partner countries with one of the most ambitious global economic recoveries attempted in modern times. But what sort of recovery could this be?

During the initial stages of the pandemic, little information was available about the economic impacts of this global public health crisis (Demirgüç-Kunt, Lokshin, and Torre, 2020). This was especially remarkable considering that evidence confirmed that the pandemic triggered one of the most pronounced declines in global economic output ever recorded (Hannon and Chaudhuri, 2020). One factor, however, that was known *prior* to the onset of COVID-19 was that by the end of 2019, emerging market and developing economies (EMDEs) took on "the largest, fastest, and most broad-based increase in debt . . . in the past 50 years" (Kose et al., 2020). By 2020, the indebtedness of these countries was already unsustainably high and "further complicated by other weaknesses, such as growing fiscal and current account deficits and a shift toward riskier debt" (Kose et al., 2020). EMDEs' debt was projected to increase as a result of the COVID-19 pandemic (Kose et al., 2020).

All four of the BRI debtor countries examined in this study have significant amounts of Chinese debt (Horn et al., 2020), much of which is nontransparent in nature. Taken together, these factors contribute to the likelihood of a slow economic recovery for all four countries. In light of the devastating financial repercussions brought on by the COVID-19 pandemic, which intensified debt distress in many developing countries and intensified negative public perceptions of Chinese investments overseas, it is possible that the geopolitical importance of the BRI could be waning.[5]

Each of the four target countries considered here poses unique challenges to the successful "optics" of the BRI, challenging the claim that the BRI is a cooperative, mutually beneficial globe-spanning endeavor. In the case of Laos, judging by the experiences of Chinese workers who were brought in to work on sections of the LCR that were contracted out to Chinese state-owned enterprises, one possible—though unintended—implication of Chinese debt-financed projects in the BRI may be a backlash driven by expatriate Chinese workers directed at their Chinese supervisors abroad. This is important because Chinese workers are often viewed as being among the primary beneficiaries of Chinese-backed construction and infrastructure projects in other countries. The recurring and ongoing LCR debt shortfalls not only reveal the "cascading impacts" of making sovereign debt under the BRI (Chen, 2020) but also show that expatriate Chinese workers can bear the brunt of the financial loss in such arrangements.

Pakistan and Sri Lanka, in different ways, highlight the ongoing role and importance of government-to-government relationships in maintaining "good optics" for the BRI. Many of the efforts to frame the BRI as bringing benefits to borrower countries are domestic-political in nature, having little or nothing to do with the Chinese leadership's approach to or implementation of BRI projects. In the case of Zambia, domestic political motivations have played a role in keeping Chinese loans hidden from the public gaze. The experiences of these three countries also highlight the disruptions in development that arise when loan repayment to official lenders in Beijing is delayed. When the debts are not being serviced, the BRI projects stall, and with delays, public perception grows increasingly negative.

---

[5] Personal communication with John Agnew, December 19, 2021.

3

Conceptualizing the BRI

Complex Bilateralism in Theory and Practice

Jeremy Paltiel and Karl Yan

Introduction

In a book about "seeing" the Belt and Road Initiative (BRI), this chapter views it by looking at the bowels of its engine room and focusing on the institutions that implement and coordinate it inside the Chinese state. There are many interpretations of China's strategic purpose, economic objectives, and even President Xi Jinping's personal political calculations in launching the BRI. Numerous overlapping calculations were involved with new ones added as the initiative moved forward. It is neither necessary nor especially pertinent to prioritize one motivation over another, and without detailed information about internal communications between Xi Jinping and his aides and advisors in the period leading up to the announcement of the initiative in Jakarta and Astana, respectively, we cannot know which motivations took priority. If, however, we examine the institutional development of the BRI, that is, the "black box" within which BRI projects are developed and implemented, we can gain a better idea of how the BRI is constructed and the path-dependent constraints that frame its scope and possibilities.

The chapter asks: How did the Chinese state organize resources and institutions to implement the BRI? How did state institutions evolve, in terms of their mandate and scope of activities, in light of the BRI? What are the actors that most decisively shape the negotiation, implementation, and supervision of China's BRI projects? Finally, are bilateral negotiations of BRI projects and the behavior of Chinese state actors implementing agencies amenable to multilateral rules-based scrutiny? How could the BRI become more multilateral?

Considering these analytical questions, this chapter argues that the National Development and Reform Commission (NDRC) is a pilot agency for the "going global" of Chinese firms and the internationalization of Chinese capacities, as long as those global activities fall under the strategic considerations of the Chinese state. The Commission also serves as an interface between the top leadership and the state-owned enterprises (SOEs) to promote the globalization of

Jeremy Paltiel and Karl Yan, *Conceptualizing the BRI* In: Seeing China's Belt and Road. Edited by: Edward Schatz and Rachel Silvey, Oxford University Press. © Oxford University Press 2025. DOI: 10.1093/oso/9780197789261.003.0004

China's industrial strategy. This new role grew out of the domestic industrial policy of the "Develop the West" program. Like the BRI itself, this domestic development program concentrated on infrastructure by relying on Chinese SOEs. We make these analyses based on our fieldwork in China between 2017 and 2021. The authors conducted archival research and semistructured interviews. Interviewees include cadres inside Chinese ministries, including the NDRC, managers from SOEs and their international offices, and officials in Malaysia and Jakarta. They were recruited through the snowball method.

However, the interface described works best bilaterally and is not well adapted to answer to multiple stakeholders in a multilateral environment. We have termed this type of structure "complex bilateralism"—complex because there is an overriding strategic framework with an institutional steering mechanism at its center, but bilateral because each project is undertaken through bilateral initiatives that are not accountable to other stakeholders except through the central Chinese "hub."[1] The typical basis of BRI projects was the announcement of a bilateral agreement subsequent to a state visit by the Chinese president or premier.

Our chapter addresses the main themes of the book concerning the characterizations and visibility of the BRI by looking at the machinery of its implementation within the state apparatus. At the 2018 Annual Meetings of the International Monetary Fund and the World Bank, which took place in Bali Nusa Dua, Indonesia, on October 12–14, 2018, China's vice minister of finance, Zou Jiayi, gave a speech in which she asserted that the BRI's development initiatives are driven mostly by commercial interests, rather than by a central platform with an overarching coordination mechanism emanating from Beijing. Our research confirms this assertion in terms of the ways BRI projects play out at intergovernmental and multilateral levels. Yet we challenge her characterization of China's role in global market expansion as depoliticized. We propose an alternative way of seeing the projects that fall under the label of the BRI, distinguishing those that are "bottom-up" from those that are "top-down." Bottom-up projects are those initiated by China's state-owned or private firms and subnational-level projects that all fall under the regulatory purview of the NDRC. They are bottom-up because the initiators are not China's top decision makers, contrasting with top-down projects initiated by central government agencies. Therefore, the key distinction is the different sources of projects that the NDRC manages—whether they come from the top leadership or from other actors. As a result, some bottom-up projects escape direct central oversight, especially if they are not deemed sensitive by the Chinese state. "Top-down"

---

[1] In this sense, it is similar to the hub-and-spoke networks that Lemon and Jardine describe in Chapter 1 of this volume.

projects, by contrast, are more centrally coordinated and more tightly aligned with Beijing's explicit state agendas. To manage these two distinct types of BRI initiatives, the NDRC both undertakes the direct implementation of centrally initiated projects and coordinates the implementation of BRI projects initiated at lower levels, particularly once these lower-profile projects become mired in bilateral controversy. In effect, the Chinese state at the central level "sees" the BRI through the NDRC to bring the BRI into its strategic scope even when such projects are not the strategic initiatives of top leaders.

This heuristic of "top-down" and "bottom-up" allows us to begin to parse the range of relationships Beijing has with different BRI projects. In addition, it lays the groundwork for examining subnational BRI interests and their regional downstream effects. Indeed, Chinese provinces have tended to develop their own plans for the BRI despite state mobilization and coordination (Ye, 2020). They also gained much autonomy in terms of lobbying for central-level support or bargaining and shirking international responsibilities (Wong, 2018).

To illustrate the particular impact of "bottom-up" projects on bilateral relations, Guangxi region and Jiangsu province are actively involved in promoting their own businesses in Southeast Asia, but the rollout of plans has been turbulent in practice. In Sulawesi, Indonesia, locals responded to Jiangsu Delong Nickel Industry Ltd.'s smelting operation with protests. This smelting operation was endorsed by the Jiangsu Province as one of its "'Belt and Road' International Industrial Capacity Cooperation Key Projects." This provincial-level project courted opposition from Indonesian parliamentarians concerning further BRI projects, highlighting the "bottom-up" effects on the subnational BRI interests, and the challenges faced by governments who may court Chinese investment.

Moreover, BRI projects offer opportunities for local actors to bargain for more resources. When one of the authors was in Guangdong conducting fieldwork, he was surprised by the provincial and Guangzhou municipal court, public security, and procuratorate systems' efforts to integrate their prison education with the broader agenda of the BRI. These efforts showed that they are also responsive to the national strategy and, at the same time, can compete for grants supporting their prison education system and relevant hardware upgrades. Private entrepreneurs also did not hesitate to jump on the BRI bandwagon when they saw opportunities that could serve their business interests. Businesspeople in the Baltic states advertised tourism and business travel as "BRI-related." The aims of such tactics were to align themselves with China's national narrative of progress, win the trust of local officials and business communities, and eventually access the Chinese market.

In all these cases, it is evident that BRI activities on the ground are shaped by local dynamics and connections. More importantly, these events show that while the Chinese state has undeniable geopolitical and geoeconomic ambitions tied to this grand project, strategies on this scale ultimately draw in opportunistic participants who do not subscribe to the vision and instead choose to be a part of it for potential economic and financial gain. Thus, the BRI has many faces and is engaged from a tremendous range of perspectives from within and beyond state agencies. Indeed, the BRI gradually became a catchphrase for Chinese actors (central and local) to refer to any development project that involved foreign parties. For this reason, it is wrong to assume that every project that claims the BRI label or brand is a strategic initiative of the Chinese state. And yet, as we shall see, the Chinese state has put in place an agency to troubleshoot and coordinate (sometimes after the fact) the BRI projects. Indeed, provincial-level projects often do not fall under the purview of the NDRC—they instead fall under provincial jurisdictions. Therefore, when speaking of "top-down" or "bottom up," this chapter mainly focuses on projects that are centrally managed or approved (hé zhǔn) or kept on central-level governments' files (bèi àn).

The chapter is organized as follows. The first part discusses the institutional organization of the BRI within the Chinese state as revealed by published documents. Next, we analyze two cases of BRI projects and the decision-making processes involving them within the Chinese bureaucracy and between the Chinese state and their BRI partners. The two cases are the East Coast Railway in Malaysia and the Jakarta–Bandung High-Speed Rail project in Java, Indonesia. Finally, we analyze what the project selection and implementation process tell us about key institutions in China and what this means for how we see the BRI. We go beyond looking at structures alone to examine institutional norms and how these fit into bilateral and multilateral diplomacy to arrive at how the BRI exemplifies the diplomatic and strategic culture of the Chinese state. Specifically, we reference a bilateralist bias, a holistic view of relationships as opposed to legal-rational issue compartmentalization and the role of beneficence and deference in managing concrete outcomes.

Putting the BRI in Place: From a Regional Agenda to a Geopolitical One

The timing of the BRI is instructive: it emerged in the first year of Xi Jinping's assumption of full office, and in the context of China's full domestic recovery from the effects of the 2008 global recession, when global trade still had not attained its pre-2008 momentum. China was looking for ways to stoke the engine of its economic development in the face of slower growth in the global economy. It was doing so in the context of a more competitive geopolitical climate that was indexed by Obama's Asian Pivot. Xi Jinping adopted a series of measures to cement China's regional position at the same time as he was searching for a new platform to project China's ambitions on the world stage. The BRI from the outset had both geopolitical and economic objectives yet was an extension of China's domestic economic strategy.[2] Domestic infrastructure construction was the key driver of China's recovery from the 2008 recession, but by 2013 the country was facing a crisis of overaccumulation. The BRI was a strategy for China to deleverage its domestic growth.

Seeing China's BRI strategy as an extension of its domestic growth strategy helps to explain both the institutional pattern of the implementation of the BRI and how it came to form a keystone of what Xi Jinping would allude to as the "China solution" (*zhōng guó fāng àn*), a development strategy premised on key drivers of China's domestic governance.

The Two Silk Roads

On September 7, 2013, in a speech at Nazarbayev University in Astana, the capital of Kazakhstan, Xi Jinping announced his vision of a "21st Century Silk Road" and called for a "Silk Road Economic Belt" (Du, Ding, and Huang, 2013). A month later, on October 2, in a speech before the Indonesian parliament in Jakarta, Xi called for building a "maritime silk road" and summoned up the spirit of the Ming Dynasty admiral Zheng He, in linking together China, Southeast Asia, East Africa and the Middle East. He called for a broad belt of connectivity linked through physical infrastructure going all the way to Europe (ASEAN-China Center, 2013). The same speech pledged to create a new multilateral bank dedicated to building Asian infrastructure. This was to become the Asian Infrastructure Investment Bank (AIIB), which was announced during the lead-up to the Asia Pacific Economic Cooperation (APEC) Summit in Beijing in November 2014 China. By September 2015, Xi was ready to package these initiatives as part of a comprehensive global initiative by China to provide global public goods. He announced increased funding for the United Nations Development Fund alongside new funding for security in the form of an African Union peacekeeping fund (Perlez, 2015). Xi called for an open, innovative, and inclusive approach to economic development that would bring benefits to all.

"It is important for us to use both the invisible hand and visible hand," Xi contended, "to form synergy between market forces and government function and strive to achieve both efficiency and fairness" (China Internet Information Center, 2015). This dual emphasis on the visible and invisible hand neatly

---

[2] Shortly after announcing the twin "silk road initiatives" that became the BRI, Xi Jinping convened a major conference of China's top diplomats in the region in October 2013. For more on this meeting and its significance see Smith (2021).

corresponds to China's own development model, one that a leading Chinese economist, Justin Yifu Lin, has urged together with his fellow former Chief Economist at the World Bank Joseph Stiglitz (Esteban, Lin, and Stiglitz, 2013).

Taken as an ensemble, without expressly marketing its own model of development to the rest of the world, China provides global public goods in a form that tends to replicate its own domestic state-driven model of market economics. China's development practice emphasizes state-to-state loans, prioritizing infrastructure development where the state is the primary client and contractor. China's Export-Import Bank and the China Development Bank play a key role in these loans, while Chinese construction companies are key beneficiaries of lending. Repayment models are linked to commodity exports channeled into imports by Chinese state-owned enterprises. This pattern shows a clear preference for a state-centric model of development congenial with China's own. As we shall see, the structural characteristics of the BRI suggest that China's industrial policy has globalized in line with its domestic ordering.

The Formation of the Belt and Road Office

In the effort to institutionalize the BRI within the Chinese state and party structure, the BRI became the subject of a Central Work Conference in February 2015.[3] This meeting established a leadership small group[4] under Politburo Standing Committee member and Executive Vice Premier Zhang Gaoli, and including Politburo members Wang Huning, vice-premier (in charge of foreign economic policy) Wang Yang, member of the Chinese Communist Party (CCP) Secretariat and State Councilor Yang Xin, and State Councilor (and Executive Secretary of the leading group on Foreign Affairs) Yang Jiechi. Following this work conference, the State Council issued a framework document under the joint authority of the State Council Development and Reform Commission, the Foreign Ministry, and the Ministry of Commerce. The initial amount of funding pledged to the new "Silk Road Fund" was $40 billion (People's Daily, 2014). The lead agencies under the state council were the National Development and Reform Commission, Ministry of Foreign Affairs, and Ministry of Commerce of the People's Republic of China.

The State Council Belt and Road Office was established on the basis of the old domestic Develop the West Office and Party Small Group.[5] The makeup of

---

[3] Central Work Conferences are high-level state forums that demonstrate the importance of a project, establishing the administrative structure through which it is to be implemented.

[4] A leadership small group is a special organ directly subordinated to the CCP's Politburo.

[5] Interview at Peking University, Wang Yong, June 23, 2016. Other subsequent interviews with other sources confirm this information regarding the relationship of the BRI to the Develop the West Office.

the Develop the West Office set up in 2000 was largely cognate (State Council Gazette, 2000). This type of dual-purpose organ is known in Chinese as "one administrative unit, two signboards." This body under the Chinese State Council was largely involved in the construction of infrastructure in China's western provinces. A prominent role was allocated to China's State Planning Commission (the organization responsible for the Five-Year Plans), whose successor organization is the NDRC. Because the Western Development program anticipated funds from multilateral donors, Western development aid agencies, and foreign investment, it also contained an international interface through what became the Chinese Ministry of Commerce (State Council, 2001). Effectively, the BRI "reverse engineered" the international aspects of the Western Development office and maintained NDRC's close relations with state-owned enterprises (SOEs) involved in infrastructure construction. According to several interviewees, the reincarnation of the Develop the West Office, the Opening to the Outside Office, remains one of the most important offices within the commission and is responsible for strategizing BRI development and implementation. Its previous work in coordinating balanced development between eastern and western parts of China was internationalized so that the newly created office could continue to play a salient role in coordinating China's opening to the outside via the BRI (see Chart 3.1).[6]

Party Committee and Secretariat	Administrative Offices/Bureaus	Policy Research Room
		Planning Office
		National Economy Office
		Using Foreign Capital and Overseas Investment Office
		Commerce Office
		Regional Opening Office (BRI Leadership Group)
		International Cooperation Office
		Regional Economy Office
		Regional Revitalization Office
		Economic and National Defense Coordination Office
		Regional Development Center
		Institute of Comprehensive Transportation
	Direct Affiliations	International Cooperation Center
		BRI Construction Promotion Center
		International Economic Exchange Center
		State Geospatial Information Center
		State Information Center

Chart 3.1 An organization chart of the National Development and Reform Commission (with relevance to the BRI)

---

[6] These bureaus and departments within the NDRC have dual roles, and their international roles have domestic origins. For example, the Regional Economy Office strategizes the integration of China's Greater Bay Area with BRI projects.

The Belt and Road Action Plan

In the Action Plan of the BRI issued by the State Council of the PRC on March 30, 2015, the "Cooperation Mechanisms" are described as follows (State Council, 2015a):

> We should strengthen bilateral cooperation, and promote comprehensive development of bilateral relations through multilevel and multichannel communication and consultation. We should encourage the signing of cooperation [Memorandums of Understanding or MoUs] or plans, and develop a number of bilateral cooperation pilot projects. We should establish and improve bilateral joint working mechanisms, and draw up implementation plans and road maps for advancing the Belt and Road Initiative. In addition, we should give full play to the existing bilateral mechanisms such as joint committees, mixed committees, coordinating committees, steering committees, and management committees to coordinate and promote the implementation of cooperation projects.

Also in the Action Plan, the relationship with multilateral organizations was clearly outlined as "hub and spoke" with the Chinese State Council in bilateral arrangements with existing multilateral organizations (State Council, 2015a). The following quotation gives a flavor of the "catch-all" aspiration of coordination with diverse multilateral bodies without deference to any particular multilateral process:

> We should enhance the role of multilateral cooperation mechanisms, make full use of existing mechanisms such as the Shanghai Cooperation Organization (SCO), ASEAN Plus China (10+1), Asia-Pacific Economic Cooperation (APEC), Asia-Europe Meeting (ASEM), Asia Cooperation Dialogue (ACD), Conference on Interaction and Confidence-Building Measures in Asia (CICA), China-Arab States Cooperation Forum (CASCF), China-Gulf Cooperation Council Strategic Dialogue, Greater Mekong Subregion (GMS) Economic Cooperation, and Central Asia Regional Economic Cooperation (CAREC) to strengthen communication with relevant countries, and attract more countries and regions to participate in the Belt and Road Initiative.
>
> We should continue to encourage the constructive role of the international forums and exhibitions at regional and subregional levels hosted by countries along the Belt and Road, as well as such platforms as Boao Forum for Asia, China-ASEAN Expo, China-Eurasia Expo, Euro-Asia Economic Forum, China International Fair for Investment and Trade, China-South Asia Expo, China-Arab States Expo, Western China International Fair, China-Russia Expo, and

Qianhai Cooperation Forum. We should support the local authorities and general public of countries along the Belt and Road to explore the historical and cultural heritage of the Belt and Road, jointly hold investment, trade and cultural exchange activities, and ensure the success of the Silk Road (Dunhuang) International Culture Expo, Silk Road International Film Festival and Silk Road International Book Fair. We propose to set up an international summit forum on the Belt and Road Initiative.

Following the announcement of the "Action Plan" the State Council mobilized China's SOEs to implement the Initiative. On June 18–19, 2015, the State Assets Supervision Administration Commission, the body under the state Council that is the shareholder of central SOEs, convened a work conference on the promotion of SOE participation in the construction of the BRI and international cooperation in productive capacity and equipment manufacturing. This meeting was addressed by the former Chinese Premier, Li Keqiang (State Council, 2015c). This conference made it clear that SOEs were expected to take the lead in the BRI and fully utilize the opportunities provided by the BRI to promote their "Going Out" strategy (internationalization and outward investment strategy). Subsequent commentaries from the State Council made it clear that SOEs were lead players in this initiative (Wang, 2015).

The 13th Five-Year Plan and the BRI

The BRI was written into the 13th Five-Year Plan (FYP), which ran from 2016 to 2020. It was considered one of the major platforms for China's "Going Out" strategy (Wang et al., 2015). Indeed, prior to the announcement of the 13th FYP, the Chinese state already incorporated the BRI as one of its "Three Big Strategies." The other two included the development of the Beijing–Tianjin–Hebei (Jing–Jin–Ji) Economic Circle and the Yangtze River Economic Belt. In response to this task, the NDRC mandated that its administrative departments, bureaus, and subsidiary work units cooperate on the implementation of these strategies. The inclusion of the BRI as an official platform for "going global" was confirmed in Premier Li Keqiang's speech introducing the 13th FYP to the NPC in March 2016. The lead agency for formulating and implementing the Five-Year Plan is of, course, the NDRC. The BRI received separate treatment in the NDRC's "Outline of the 13th Five Year Plan" (NDRC, 2016). The commission was tasked to promote mutual gain in neighboring countries and create a platform on which eastern and western parts of China could connect with foreign countries via land and sea (Yan, 2021). The third initiative redesigned the "going global" of Chinese SOEs.

The AIIB and Its Relationship to the BRI

Because the AIIB came into being as a result of Xi's initiative in proclaiming the Belt and Road, some observers assume it is aligned with the strategic purpose of the BRI (Haga, 2021; Macikenaite, 2020; Stuart-Haentjens, 2017; Zhao and Lee, 2021). From a structural public policy perspective, this is a mistake. The AIIB is a multilateral lending institution that answers to a board made up of its shareholding countries; it sets its own lending policies independently of the Chinese government. According to Zhu (2019), the Chinese state has provided the bank with space for the latter to build its credibility as a multilateral bank. While the bank's target lending opportunities do overlap with the BRI, its procedures and guiding principles are separate. For example, a plurality of the early loan projects provided by the AIIB has been to India, a country that refused to sign onto the BRI. India was one of the AIIB's founding members in June 2015. It is the second largest shareholder with approximately 8 percent and has a single member constituency on the Board (Marandi, 2018).[7] Moreover, whereas the AIIB has not authorized a single thermal coal project in the energy sector, the BRI's China–Pakistan Economic Corridor includes several large-scale coal mining and energy producing projects. The AIIB is able to establish its own multilateral lending criteria, and it often lends in tandem with other multilateral lending institutions, such as the Asian Development Bank and the European Development Bank.

The Belt and Road Forums

The First Belt and Road Forum for International Cooperation was convened in May 2017; it reinforced the "hub and spoke" arrangement of governance that had been put forward in the "Action Plan." The Forum produced a joint communiqué announcing a number of principles for cooperation as well as a number of aspirations in the form of nonbinding "Cooperation Principles" (Belt and Road Forum for International Cooperation, 2017). The tenor of the communiqué was triumphant:

> We uphold the spirit of peace, cooperation, openness, transparency, inclusiveness, equality, mutual learning, mutual benefit and mutual respect by strengthening cooperation on the basis of extensive consultation and the rule of law, joint efforts, shared benefits and equal opportunities for all. In this context we highlight the following principles guiding our cooperation, in accordance with our respective national laws and policies.

---

[7] The AIIB also keeps a list of approved projects.

The emphasis on "respective national laws and policies" underscored the bilateral nature of BRI governance. None of the cooperation principles were vested in a permanent secretariat accountable to forum members. Neither this forum nor its follow-up meeting in 2019 established a permanent secretariat or any permanent body or institution accountable to stakeholders. Following a number of setbacks and criticisms, such as the paring down of the China–Pakistan Economic Corridor (CPEC) and the Malaysian railway project, the tone of the second forum was more circumspect (Financial Tribune, 2018). For instance, Xi Jinping's keynote speech to the second forum was more sober than at the first forum (Xi, 2019). The key focus of the Second BRI Forum was "high quality projects" (The Second Belt and Road Forum for International Cooperation, 2019).

The NDRC and the BRI's "Black Box"

During the authors' fieldwork in Beijing, many interviews, both inside and outside the NDRC, confirmed that the commission remains a major player in coordinating BRI projects. During the height of the COVID-19 pandemic, the Chinese state revised the original development strategy of "coordinating the domestic and international situations." Instead, this strategy was replaced with an emphasis on "accelerating the construction of a new development outlook focused on the domestic big cycle and the mutual promotion of the domestic and international economic cycles" (Liu, 2020). This has become known as the "dual circulation" model. Though the domestic "big cycle" (dà xún huán) had been considered as the mainstay of the Chinese economic opening in Liu He's speech on a draft version of the 14th Five-Year Plan, China's opening to the outside remains the leitmotif of its economic development. Therefore, the NDRC remains as the most important ministry, or the mini–State Council, in terms of implementing national strategies.

While Yan (2021) discovered that the NDRC is responsible for approving Chinese firms' overseas investment activities, this chapter sees that there is a path-dependent nature in the role of the commission. Indeed, many BRI projects, either initiated through a top-down or bottom-up fashion, remain under the purview of the NDRC, especially the Regional Opening Bureau. Interestingly, there are two institutional legacies that helped shape the commission's path-dependent nature. First, created to become the mini–State Council, the NDRC took on the role of the gatekeeper of the Chinese national economy. One specific role that the commission has played is being the manager of "new things." Though becoming such a manager might be accidental, the commission's internal organization certainly allows it to serve in that position. The NDRC is organized in a way so that its functional departments line up perfectly with the State Council's line ministries. For example, the commission's Resource Saving and Environmental Protection Bureau, National Defense Bureau, and International Bureau mirror the responsibilities of the State Council's Ministry of Ecology and Environment, Ministry of National Defense, and Ministry of Foreign Affairs, respectively. This type of alignment allows the NDRC to better coordinate both sectoral and cross-sectoral action in terms of making and implementing strategic industrial policies.

An important implication of this arrangement has been the offloading of important executive and often strategic initiatives of the state to the NDRC. Beyond the implementation of the BRI, after elevating the joint development of Beijing, Tianjin, and Hebei as a national strategy, the Leading Group for the Joint Development of Jing–Jin–Ji was nested under the NDRC's Regions Bureau. There seems to be a tradition within China that the commission is tasked with coordinating the strategy and implementation of "new things" yet to be fully understood for which responsibilities have yet to be demarcated.[8] Additional examples of "new things" that initially fell under the purview of the NDRC then later moved to other line ministries include the establishment of a national credit system, antimonopoly laws, and bankruptcy regulations. As a whole, when the BRI was promoted as a national strategy, the NDRC was the body responsible for BRI project implementation.

Second, the internationalization of the NDRC can be argued to represent the internationalization of the Develop the West Office. One of the major tasks of the original Develop the West Office was to link capital and investment from eastern China and direct it to improve economic development in western regions. Therefore, the decision to internationalize the Develop the West Office was rationalized with reference to the office's familiarity with economic cooperation between eastern and western parts of China. As the reincarnation of the NDRC into its global from, the office would be able use its domestic experience to coordinate China's opening to the outside via the BRI.

The new office was no longer responsible for providing detailed administrative approvals. Instead, an adjustment in operation occurred with the Regional Opening Office taking on macro and political coordination. Precisely, this bureau now hosts the central government's BRI Leading Group, responsible for strategy and coordination of BRI implementation.[9] Further below this office, the

---

[8] Interviews with cadres from the State Council and the NDRC confirm this line of analysis. Interviewees concur that when the state wants to do something about which no one has any prior knowledge, the task is often assigned to the NDRC to study and coordinate action, thus rendering the commission the "manager of new things." Against this backdrop, only after a set of norms of practices have been established by the NDRC can the task then be transferred to appropriate line ministries, either through a reshuffling of responsibilities or the creation of new agencies.

[9] Interviews with cadres in the State Council, the NDRC, and the Ministry of Commerce confirm this understanding concerning the role of the NDRC.

NDRC also established specific bureaus such as the Maritime Silk Road Bureau and the Silk Road Economic Belt Bureau responsible for strategizing BRI implementation in ASEAN and Central Asia, respectively.

The more detailed implementation, however, was divided among other offices within the NDRC. For example, the Using Foreign Capital and Overseas Investment Office is responsible for approving capital inflow and outflow that fall under the broad umbrella of BRI projects. After an overseas investment has been approved, especially if it is deemed of national importance, the decision is then forwarded to the State Administration of Foreign Exchange and China's Policy Banks for financing and implementation. Under the broad umbrella of the NDRC is the International Cooperation Office, which hosts the Mitigation Team of the BRI Leadership Group and tracks the progress of projects that fall under the CPEC and the Bangladesh–China–India–Myanmar Forum for Regional Cooperation.

However, the division of labor with the NDRC is not always clear. Rather, project assignment takes place on a path-dependent basis. The most important decision-making mechanism within the commission is the Leadership Group Work Meetings. At these meetings, top leaders of the NDRC discuss and decide which office/department gets to work on which project. Though there is no specific policy justification concerning project assignment despite an ostensible demarcation of responsibilities, the commission's top leadership prefers to see specific offices working consistently on similar-scale projects. For example, the Bangladesh–China–India–Myanmar Forum for Regional Cooperation was assigned to the International Cooperation Office (ICO) mainly because of the ICO's experience in handling the CPEC.[10]

There are two sources for incoming projects that the NDRC must handle: top-down and bottom-up. There are also two types of top-down projects. The first type is bilateral strategic cooperation, which is often initiated by China. The second type of project is usually initiated by overseas countries. Importantly, however, both types of top-down projects undergo a similar process: bilateral framework agreements→ NDRC evaluation→ Ministry of Finance of Budgeting and Financing→ NDRC implementation. Implementation here refers to the selection of SOEs responsible for detailed execution. The Jakarta–Bandung High-Speed Rail project is an example of the second type of top-down project, initiated not by China but by a foreign country. Nonetheless, during this process, the central government and higher authorities are initiators, so they collect and propose projects to the NDRC based on MoUs that have been signed at high-level

---

[10] The authors learned the internal workings of the NDRC through field interviews in Beijing with academics and cadres within the system. However, and admittedly, some of the more specific details, for example, who and which state ministries or offices within the commission are involved, remain unclear.

meetings and overseas visits. Within this setting, state planning plays an important role.

By way of contrast, SOEs and private enterprises initiate bottom-up projects, which can therefore be considered purely commercial endeavors. As part of this process, SOEs report to the State Council, local development and reform commissions, and the NDRC for potential overseas projects. The NDRC is then responsible for conducting preliminary research. As a gatekeeper of the State Council and the Central Government, the NDRC decides whether the proposed projects fall under national/central or local/provincial authorities. They also gauge the salience of each project based on economic returns, bilateral relations, regional influence, and strategic and political considerations. Based on these criteria, the NDRC decides whether a project can be considered of national importance. If the NDRC finds a project to be strategically important to the state, it can suggest a specific way of managing the project (either business-to-business or government-to-government) and consider the potential profit margin vis-à-vis other concerns such as access to other resources, influence, and improvement in bilateral relations.

During the implementation of both top-down and bottom-up projects, the NDRC can intervene as needed. Indeed, when a project goes awry, the State Council, foreign governments, and SOEs can invite the NDRC to intervene. However, interventions are also carefully calibrated as the commission considers whether the project can continue and, once finished, will still benefit and improve bilateral relations. It must also consider SOEs' willingness to continue a project. If the commission finds a project to be helpful for bilateral relations and mutual gain between China and the host country, it can guide SOEs to renegotiate and reach an agreement with foreign governments. The Malaysian East Coast Rail Link is an example of a bottom-up project in which the NDRC intervened to finalize negotiations.

Through this process, it seems that other state ministries have a limited role in influencing the NDRC's decision-making. Although the specific bargaining processes across these vertically organized bureaucratic units remain to be seen, this analysis of the internal workings of the NDRC suggests that line ministries have been integrated into the NDRC decision-making process. According to a scholar at the Chinese Academy of Social Science, the BRI Leading Group consists of members from various ministries such as the Ministry of Foreign Affair (MOFA) and the Ministry of Commerce (MOCOMM). Moreover, both the MOFA and the MOCOMM have representatives stationed in the NDRC to improve communication and coordination among these line ministries. However, we should also understand that the NDRC has more leverage vis-à-vis these line ministries because of its position in the domestic economy. In domestic national planning and economic operations, the NDRC coordinates line ministries to make cross-sectoral and medium-long-term industrial policies. And the composition of the NDRC highly corresponds to the tasks of line ministries. Concerning the "going global" of China, which has been couched in the BRI, the NDRC remains the only pilot organization that has the authority and power to coordinate action among central SOEs within and outside of China. Other line ministries lack such leverage.

Institutionalizing "Complex Bilateralism"

China has an impressive capacity to deliver turnkey projects on time.[11] However, the implementing companies see this mainly as an engineering challenge and a commercial opportunity with financing of the project essentially guaranteed by the Chinese executing agency through contracts with the host countries. The construction companies hedge for economic viability through the oversight of the NDRC and see the projects essentially like a domestic transaction in which a Chinese company is contracted to deliver a Chinese project paid in Chinese funds. There is nothing inherently wrong with this except that it leaves the host government with a substantial debt risk, and as we have already seen in Malaysia and Pakistan, governments change, and a new government may see the risk in a very different light. The new emphasis on "quality" projects reflects a growing Chinese understanding that China faces substantial political risk by naively assuming that "lack of conditionality" guarantees smoother intergovernmental relations.[12] Under these circumstances, increasing consideration will have to be paid by the Chinese granting authority to capacity building in the host country to ensure that projects are chosen with a view to their economic sustainability.

In keeping with the general strategic orientation of the initiative, the BRI can be characterized as a form of complex bilateralism with China as its hub rather than an exercise of multilateral institutionalism. Complex bilateralism can be defined as a structure where the initiator country forges multiple bilateral relationships centered on itself with an overarching aim of enhancing regional and transregional integration without a common coordinating institution commonly accountable to all stakeholders. In the rest of this chapter, we outline what

---

[11] The pandemic had a palpable effect on the implementation of overseas Chinese projects; however, the impacts were due to a combination of factors. China's domestic pandemic prevention measures forced many production facilities to discontinue their operations, therefore affecting China's export volume. At the same time, host countries' pandemic prevention measures and economic contractions during the pandemic also rendered them unable to continue the pace at which infrastructure development proceeded before the pandemic.

[12] An interview with Professor Ren Xiao of the Department of International Politics at Fudan University in July 2019 indicated that the advent of the BRI saw a new wave of hiring of political science graduates of his department by China's commercial banks for newly established political risk analysis departments.

this means for Chinese foreign policy and Chinese views of regional and global order, as well as some preliminary thoughts regarding the likely impact of this initiative on the regional and global order.

The Belt and Road Initiative can be construed as China's effort to support its role in global trade by providing public goods that will enhance China's role as a global provider of engineering and infrastructure development and boost immediate demand for Chinese construction services as well as the physical goods involved in infrastructure. At the same time infrastructure development should boost local economic activity, creating local employment as well as demand for other Chinese exports. With the focus on connectivity, however, rising demand is meant to extend to major centers of economic activity in Europe, thus accelerating general economic growth along the BRI corridor. While there is little doubt that BRI projects are designed to link economies along the Belt and Road corridors more closely with the Chinese economy, we argue that there is nothing inherently suspicious or nefarious about this. In concept, and in its self-presentation, the BRI is win-win. The criticism of Belt and Road projects as "debt traps" does not arise from the design of the BRI itself, but from the way in which it is financed and the fact that the primary onus of project selection rests with host governments, which may not have the capacity to select and evaluate projects wisely.[13]

To examine the structural components of the BRI and the way these have grown out of China's industrial strategy, we examine two key BRI projects: the Indonesian Jakarta–Bandung High-Speed Rail and the Malaysian East Coast Railway.

The "Top-Down" High-Speed Rail in Indonesia

The Jakarta–Bandung High-Speed Rail (HSR) project was initially proposed by the Japanese International Cooperation Agency based on a 2012 study. China's BRI project set off an intense bidding war between China and Japan, which was won in September 2015 by China on the basis of the Indonesian government providing no cash contribution to the project (Clark, 2021; Yan, 2023). This project was the first major overseas construction project by the China Railway Corporation (CRC). The contract was signed on October 16, 2015, between the CRC and four Indonesian corporations, with the Chinese side holding 40 percent of the shares and the Indonesian side, 60 percent. Groundbreaking on the project was announced on January 21, 2016. There were many delays and cost overruns in the construction process, but the project appears now to

---

[13] See also the discussion of indebtedness in Narins, Chapter 2, this volume.

be assuming its final shape (People's Daily, 2020; Reuters, 2021a; Xinhua News Agency, 2021).

The Jakarta–Bandung Project is a clear example of a project that was initiated and maintained through high-level contacts. The process began when Indonesian President Joko Widodo met with Xi Jinping during the APEC summit in November 2014, when Widodo first invited Chinese investment. He met again with Xi in March 2015. On that occasion the NDRC and the Indonesian Ministry of SOEs signed an MoU. Prior to the signing of the MoU, the NDRC's Wang Xiaoming visited Jakarta many times to probe the possibility of Chinese investment in Indonesia. The NDRC allocated $5 million for a feasibility study to be completed in July. When President Xi visited Jakarta in April, and the NDRC also visited Jakarta, another framework agreement was signed. China then allocated a $6 billion package through China Development Bank. The NDRC asked the CRC to prepare a feasibility study and then commissioned China Railway Design Corporation (CRDC) for the actual work. Staff from the CRDC spent 90 days in Jakarta for the project. The NDRC's Planning Department, International Cooperation Department, and Foreign Capital and Overseas Department collaborated with the CRC for the bidding process, preparation of the feasibility study, and project implementation. In addition, the China Railway Rollingstock Co. was asked to consider establishing a rolling stock plant in Indonesia. The Indonesian public was lukewarm with many in local governments opposed to the Chinese bid. Finally, the NDRC Chair Xu Shaoshi and representatives from the CRC lobbied Jakarta to improve their bid. The Chinese were determined to use this bid to showcase China's railway technology and the reduced financial guarantees expected of Indonesia. Nonetheless, the winning bid did not come without some last-minute dramatics with Widodo first vetoing the bid in early September 2015 and then reversing himself less than a month later.

In October 2015, the Kereta Cepat Indonesia China (KCIC) was established as a joint venture between four Indonesian SOEs and the CRC. On the Chinese side, the KCIC was directly answerable to the NDRC and the CRC. The engineering, procurement, and construction (EPC) contract was awarded to another Sino-Indonesian consortium—the High-Speed Railway Contractor Consortium (HSRCC). Project implementation was supervised directly from within China's NDRC under a process that demanded monthly reports and supervision. Reports were sent to the NDRC's party committee and leadership team, with copies going to the international cooperation department and the CRC's head office. The NDRC evaluated the reports, and four teams were dispatched to supervise and accelerate project implementation. Notable high-level inspections include Li Xuedong in 2017, associate director of NDRC's International Cooperation Office and the director of the

BRI Steering Group's External Affairs Team, and Li Bin in 2019, associate director of the NDRC's International Cooperation Bureau. Li Bin visited Jakarta (virtually) again in 2021. The NDRC also supervised the organization of study groups to China, from Indonesia. Three sessions were held in total between 2015 and 2018 for technology transfer purposes (see Chart 3.2. for the overall flow of the project).

The "Bottom-Up" Malaysian East Coast Rail Link

China Communications Construction Company (CCCC) had been active in Malaysia for several years working on infrastructure projects. In response to domestic and international efforts to solve the "Malacca bottleneck" constraining shipping between the Indian Ocean and the South China Sea, the CCCC proposed to take on the East Coast Rail Link (ECRL) in direct negotiations between the CCCC and the Malaysian state actors (Malaysia Rail Link [MRL]). This is a typical "bottom-up" project, as its initiator was a state-owned firm—meaning the project itself did not emerge through direct bilateral negotiations between the top leadership of the two countries. Despite its "bottom-up" nature, as we will see in the ensuing discussion, the NDRC intervened to ensure this "bottom-up" project would improve China's international image and at the same time not damage Sino-Malaysian relations.

To secure the contract, the CCCC argued that awarding the contract to the CCCC would help secure soft loans from China through the Exim Bank. As the project was presented to the Chinese government, it evaluated the proposal in light of its importance for bilateral relations. For the government of

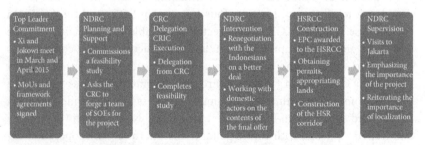

Chart 3.2 Indonesian Jakarta–Bandung High-Speed Rail Project (Top-Down)[a]

[a] This chart shows the processes and the actors involved concerning a top-down infrastructure project. The decision-making process begins with top leadership exchange, framework agreements signed between the two governments, and then execution by China's state-owned firms. The NDRC plays a salient role in ensuring successful implementation of overseas projects.

Malaysian Prime Minister Najib Razak, it was an opportunity to boost domestic legitimacy through a major investment project. Solving the "Malacca dilemma" for China became a linchpin in the BRI concept of "connectivity" and a flagship project for the BRI in Malaysia. A total of 14 business-to-business MoUs were signed in 2016 during Najib's visit to China including one on the ECRL. A formal financing agreement was reached with Exim Bank and a MoU signed between MRL and CCCC (the CCCC is the EPC contractor for the project). The project started in August 2017, but only limited work had been done before the official suspension of the project after the 2018 Malaysian general election.

During the 2018 Malaysian election, the ECRL became a target for Malay nationalist sentiments, together with other issues such as debt-trap, China threat, and poor contract terms. As a result of the election in which former Prime Minister Mahathir Mohamad returned from retirement to lead a coalition to oust his former political party, the United Malays National Organisation, the project was officially suspended on July 3, 2018. The CCCC was shocked by this turn of events. To deal with the diplomatic fallout, Mahathir named Daim Zainuddin, Chairman of the Commission of Eminent Experts, to serve as a special envoy to China. The Chinese wanted the negotiations to be done through a business-to-business model whereas the Malaysians insisted that the negotiations take place on a government-to-government basis. The CCCC was the principal Chinese actor behind the renegotiations. It did not want to build a cheaper version of the ECRL, thus rejecting Malaysia's requests for a reconsideration of the project. In the wake of this disagreement about negotiation strategy, negative perceptions about the BRI's infrastructure projects rose in Malaysia (Weng et al., 2021).

The Chinese state was forced to reconsider its stance. It ended up sending a signal to assuage negative views "in order to respond to local conditions and truly pursue win-win cooperation" and as a result soften their approach concerning the project. At this point the NDRC intervened to guide the CCCC toward a peaceful resolution to salvage the project. It stepped in during the second renegotiation phase to bring SOEs in line with the state's international objectives/ambitions. The Chinese leadership calculated that conceding to Malaysia's request would improve China's international image. This outcome bowed to China's strategic considerations, in addition to beating back accusations about the BRI and debt-trap diplomacy. This was done in light of historical relations with Malaysia (Sinophobia among the Bhumi political base) and calculations about future strategic cooperation with this key ASEAN neighbor. The outcome emphasized future bilateral and multilateral cooperation. The project resumed in April 2019 after having been reduced by four stations in return for a two billion Ringgit reduction in cost (see Chart 3.3. for the overall flow of this project).

Chart 3.3 Malaysian East Coast Rail Link (Bottom-Up)[b]

[b] This chart shows the processes and actors involved concerning a bottom-up infrastructure project. Though projects are initially proposed by China's state-owned firms, the NDRC nonetheless intervened to ensure that the project would not hamper China's bilateral relations with the host country and international image as a responsible donor.

The NDRC as the Key Bureaucratic Player from "Develop the West" to the BRI

The key role played by the NDRC in the implementation of the Jakarta–Bandung High-Speed Rail Project as well as the rescuing of the East Coast Rail Link highlights the relationship between the BRI and China's industrial policy, in which the NDRC is the key agency. The hands-on role played by the NDRC and its close relationship to the Chinese SOEs that were the contracting parties in project implementation illustrate the way the BRI replicated and extended the infrastructure development program that began with China's Develop the West campaign, and that was a key driver in promoting the role of central SOEs in 21st-century China. In this case, the BRI drove forward the internationalization of these SOEs "going out," but the role of the NDRC suggests not just the internationalization of the SOEs through maturation and scale, but more directly an administrative push and the guiding role of the state seeking to extend and capitalize on its earlier domestic experience. In important respects, the BRI can be termed as the "internationalization of China's NDRC," driving SOEs to extend excess capacity outside, facilitating the role of Chinese banks in financing international projects by linking China's policy banks and commercial banks. It is worth noting that many commentators view the 2018 reorganization of the Chinese State Council as significantly reducing the role of the NDRC in the domestic economy. Despite these changes, the NDRC's core functions as a macroeconomic and medium- and long-term planner were unscathed (Wei, 2018; Xinhua News Agency, 2018). The offloading of microeconomic responsibilities could be viewed as a way to concentrate the commission's efforts in coordinating the domestic and international situations and pay greater attention to overall planning (Yan, 2021). The Vice-Premier in charge of the NDRC not only remains concurrently the Chair of the BRI Construction Small Group Office but has also become one of the four central officials who regularly accompany Xi Jinping on his overseas travels.

As we saw in the case of the Malaysia East Coast Rail, Chinese contractors tend to minimize their financial risk by building that risk into the cost of project construction, which is then transferred to the host country as debt. There is a further risk of overreach through bilateral contracts: while the overall goal is one of "connectivity," the idea of a high-speed rail running smoothly between China's Yunnan province through Laos, Thailand, and Malaysia to Singapore and Indonesia may never be realized even though contracts exist for railway construction between China and each of the countries. That is because bilateral relations govern the construction projects, and the key oversight body, the NDRC, is mainly answerable for the viability of the SOE construction project, not to some overarching international design uniting all stakeholders. In domestic infrastructure construction, the NDRC facilitates overall network rationality in a centralized plan that realizes network synergies, which can become a weakness in international projects where it is beholden to other states' agendas and bilateral relations.

The Bilateral Bias Baked into Chinese Foreign Policy

Chinese foreign policy is not naturally multilateral (Johnston, 2003; Paltiel, 2009). This is not simply or even principally because of a hierarchic bias in the Sinocentric world order. The key to the hub-and-spoke relationship is that it depends on particularized relationships between China (and sometimes Chinese leaders) and select countries and their leaders. The point about these particularized relations is that they valorize the continued relationship over the contractual details of any one particular issue or project. The key value is the maintenance of the relationship itself rather than the details of any deliverable. In the railway case, projects, either top-down or bottom-up, are the tangible result of a relationship, not the other way around. That is why the Chinese state renegotiated the details of the East Coast Railway project to satisfy the incoming government of Mahathir, and why it continued to acquiesce to changes with the following coalition. Certainly, fostering a mutually beneficial relationship and continuing the friendship narrative with Malaysia remains salient to the Chinese, especially because the ECRL could serve as an example of how China and a BRI country have settled their disagreements. It is also worth highlighting that the Jakarta–Bandung project was one fruit in a basket of projects and pledges that Xi Jinping and Li Keqiang had promised Widodo during their meetings in Beijing in March 2015. In turn, this high-speed rail project is emblematic of the friend-ship between China and Indonesia, not the start or cause of a deepening in bilat-eral relations, according to an interview with a senior cadre in China's Economic and Commercial Office in Jakarta.

Therefore, reciprocity is arrived at through a wide-angle lens of multiple exchanges, not through the particular lens of a single project and its details. It answers to the rationality of relationality not to some other contractual principle (Qin, 2018; Qin and Nordin, 2019). According to Yang Jiechi, the BRI Forum was a success because it showcased China's ability to host high-level, multi-lateral diplomatic events. More importantly, 29 heads of states and over 1,500 delegates from over 130 countries and 70 international organizations had agreed to participate in the event. Being present and expressing hopeful wishes con-cerning the development of the BRI are also important to the Chinese, in ad-dition to contract signing at the forum (Belt and Road Forum for International Cooperation, 2017).

Of course, the contractual details matter greatly to the parties directly in-volved in the contract. However, if a partnership is to be sustained, there are many details of the relationship that are not captured in the language of the con-tract. The distribution of the costs may be haggled over in private, rather than disclosed to outsiders. The role of a central agency like the NDRC is to connect the concerns of the state leadership to the implementing construction parties; it provides an interface through which the Chinese state aims to negotiate its de-velopment projects with both SOEs and external parties.

CPEC and the Perils of Bilateralism

Time and space preclude a detailed case study for this chapter, but the excru-ciating saga of the CPEC provides a useful contrast and foil to the relatively successful management of complex bilateralism in the cases mentioned earlier (Sohail, 2022). The CPEC illustrates both the incremental and the strategic elements of the BRI. There is an incremental element because it is linked to the strategic push to develop Xinjiang (especially Uyghur South Xinjiang) through the Develop the West campaign and to link it to the sea and overseas trade through Pakistan, China's "all-weather friend." This strategic purpose has collided with the harsh realities of Pakistan's governance. Security problems and unprofitable projects have contributed to Pakistan's ballooning debt. In April 2015 Chinese President Xi Jinping made a state visit to Pakistan. Nawaz Sharif, the Prime Minister of Pakistan, had already agreed to a series of Chinese infra-structure investments in 2013 and was eager to become the first to publicly ac-cept a role in the development of the BRI. Despite some caution from Foreign

Ministry officials, who warned that signing with Pakistan could jeopardize potential plans with India, Xi was determined to move ahead with the first signature on his great initiative. He proceeded to announce the CPEC, which passes through contested areas of Jammu and Kashmir. Predictably, India rejected the initiative (Nataraj and Sekhani, 2015). From the perspective of Chinese officials, this was the first missed opportunity to generalize the benefits of the BRI beyond bilateral advantage (Schneider, 2021). Wishful thinking on both sides premised on close bilateral relations severely tests the limits of complex bilateralism in this case.

Conclusion

The role of the NDRC in the BRI provided a set of training wheels for Chinese SOEs in their "Going Out" strategy. However, it operates differently depending on the destination. Its dual role in domestic and international industrial policy initially helped to hedge the risks to the SOEs as they ventured abroad, and it amplified the political direction of the CCP's leadership as communicated through high-level visits and bilateral agreements. However, the NDRC, despite its objective of strengthening and expanding China's organizational role in global connectivity, may in practice risk overreach. It keeps projects politically viable and economically sustainable for the Chinese SOEs but may weaken the overall strategic success of the connectivity plan by skewing the strategy to complex bilateral calculations. The NDRC undeniably is geared toward promoting the internationalization of Chinese SOEs and Chinese technology, but because it ultimately rests on bilateral negotiations, in practice it does not uniformly serve Beijing's geopolitical strategic interests.

The two case studies examined in this chapter addressed the BRI through the empirical lens of path-dependent political economy. We have asked how the ideas communicated by state leaders—in this case the ideas about the BRI put forward by President Xi Jinping and CCP officials in the NDRC—take shape only as they pass through filters of existing bureaucratic structures and procedures. We have argued that these path dependencies inform the scope and limits of the implementation of BRI projects. As Beijing aims to build high-speed rails in both Malaysia and Indonesia, the negotiation and implementation of these infrastructure projects take distinct forms in the two countries. The reasons for these differences are not least because of the distinct origins of the projects (i.e., "top-down" in the case of Indonesia and "bottom-up" in the case of Malaysia), but also because expansion in practice is always messier than the centralized dreams of authoritarian planners. In these cases, complex bilateralism has been key to the successful development of Malaysia's new high-speed rail, while in Indonesia's case it has meant long delays in seeing their railway open. The differences between these cases offer a challenge to the simplistic supposition that Beijing can, via offices such as the NDRC, roll out the BRI in the same way everywhere.

PART II
SEEING EXHIBITS, MAPS, AND CORRIDORS

4

China and the Visual Politics of World Order

Marina Kaneti

Introduction

In 2019,[1] alongside the grandiose spectacle of the Second Belt Road Forum (BRF),[2] Beijing also hosted a unique collaborative exhibit, "Sharing a Common Future" (SCF).[3] Staged at the Beijing National Museum, the SCF exhibit subtly, yet unmistakably, alluded to the overarching vision of the Forum, and the Belt and Road Initiative (BRI) more broadly: a millennia-old transboundary connection on the historical Silk Road that is bound to inspire a new era of a shared common future. Granted, the exhibit made no explicit references to the forum or the BRI; however, the title "Sharing a Common Future" was a direct reference to a key phrase in the BRI political lexicon: "community of shared future for mankind."[4] Other aspects of the exhibit also alluded to the BRI mantra. Unique and unprecedented in the museum world, the Beijing National Museum cocurated the SCF alongside 12 national museums from across the world.[5] This was precisely the type of international cooperation, peaceful exchange, and

[1] Fieldwork for this chapter was funded by NUS LKYSPP grant # R-603-000-295-133 and India China Institute/Ford Foundation Emerging Scholars Grant. I am immensely grateful to Rachel Silvey and Edward Schatz, as well as the many museum curators, for their comments on earlier versions of this chapter. My deepest gratitude also goes to Gao Peng, Akanksha Narode, Jenny Jenish Kyzy, Arief Rizky Bakhtiar, Israruddin, Christy Tsang, and David Ng for their outstanding research support.
[2] Hosted in Beijing, the BRFs are meant to provide a platform for BRI partners to take stock of collaborative engagements and kick-start the next phase of BRI engagement. There have been three such forums thus far: 2017, 2019, and 2023. See http://www.beltandroadforum.org/english/index.html.
[3] Details on the exhibit are available at the official Beijing National Museum website: http://www.chnmuseum.cn/portals/0/web/zt/20190411sfgx/. All images discussed in this chapter are available at the Visual Archives of the Silk and Spice Route: https://visual-archives.com/image-repository/.
[4] This refers only to the English language title of the exhibit. The Chinese title of the exhibit "shū fāng gòng xiǎng" was a reference to a Han Dynasty classic and suggestive of a shared glorious past. See https://www.chinesethought.cn/EN/detail.aspx?nid = 92&pid = 97&id = 8409. On the variants of English language translations of "community of shared future" (rén lèi mìng yùn gòng tóng tǐ) see, for example, Zeng, 2020.
[5] For background on the exhibit, see, for example, Art China (2019) and Chen (2019).

Marina Kaneti, *China and the Visual Politics of World Order* In: Seeing China's Belt and Road. Edited by: Edward Schatz and Rachel Silvey, Oxford University Press. © Oxford University Press 2025.
DOI: 10.1093/oso/9780197789261.003.0005

people-to-people connections that the Chinese leadership envisioned under the BRI (Ministry of Foreign Affairs, 2019). And, most importantly, there was the reference to the Silk Road: from the time of the BRI launch in 2013, the Silk Road was singularly positioned as both the model and mode for the BRI vision, with the BRI itself touted as "emulating the Silk Road spirit of peace, cooperation, openness and mutual learning" (Xi, 2017). By weaving in an integral link between the past and present, the Chinese government used the Silk Road to ascribe the broader BRI vision: in addition to the initial formulations of the 21st Century Maritime and Land Silk Road, there are, for example, the Digital Silk Road, the Health Silk Road, the Polar Silk Road, the Space Silk Road, and the Green Silk Road. Not coincidentally, the two events—the BRF and SCF—also shared a similar timeline so that delegates could attend both the forum plenaries and the exhibit.[6]

With all these factors at play, it was easy to see the significance of the SCF at the time of its launch. Centered on the formative role of the ancient Silk Road, the exhibit was meant as a spectacular display of a world of common past and shared future stretching from Japan to Slovenia, and Mongolia to Oman. At the same time, it reaffirmed Beijing's unique ability to be the platform for such a multinational undertaking.[7] The SCF was designed as evidence of the collaborative opportunities enabled by the BRI.

Yet, for all the grandeur, the SCF displays did not match the aforementioned vision. Even if the thirteen museums' collaboration had one collective source of inspiration in the ancient Silk Road and had gone through a process of prescreening and selection,[8] the visual effects did not invoke a sense of a shared past and common history. To the contrary, the artifacts and narratives on display suggested vastly different stories, claims, and visions of the Silk Road.[9] In the exhibit space, even the imaginary of the Silk Road itself was often invisible. And, instead of convergence and mutual cooperation on a shared vision, the visitors

[6] The exhibit opened on April 11, 2019, and the BRF on April 25, 2019. The exhibit lasted three months, through July 2019. Although an official number of visitations for the SFC exhibit does not exist, at least 1.5 million people saw the exhibit, based on the 30,000 daily visitation records of the museum. See https://www.chnmuseum.cn/zx/gbxw/202001/t20200123_191603.shtml. In addition to the BRF, the exhibit coincided with the Conference on Dialogue of Asian Civilizations held in May 2019, also dedicated to the Belt and Road.

[7] The rest of the national museums included those in Russia, South Korea, Poland, Latvia, Tajikistan, Kazakhstan, Cambodia, and Romania.

[8] The initial call for participation was sent to 68 museums across the world. Submissions were judged on how they reflected "i) land and sea routes; ii) people and objects on the Silk Road; or iii) cultural transmissions and mutual encounters." Of the return submissions, 12 made the final cut. See Chen (2019).

[9] One researcher describes this as a "bold move" on the part of the Beijing curatorial team: the invited cocurators were given the freedom to write an introduction to their portion of the exhibit without this having to be aligned or prescreened by their Chinese counterparts (Chen, 2019).

could ponder a different sight: acts of resistance to Beijing's efforts to develop a recognizable and acceptable value system based on a shared past.

This chapter explores the disjunction between grand aspirations and actual displays. It asks how such effects were produced and how we might think of their significance. Certainly, it would be tempting to conclude that the exhibit was no different than the BRI itself: a collection of aspirational grand narratives that run into myriad complications on the ground (Hillman, 2020); or to classify the divergence as another example of the many pushbacks and opposition to the Chinese-led vision for world order (Patey, 2020); or to simply accept the statement of the Chinese curatorial team that multiplicity and diversity were central to the display (Chen, 2019). Indeed, just as the BRI itself, the SCF exhibit could be interpreted in multiple ways, for—as the editors of this volume remind us— "What you see is in good part a function of how and where you look" (Schatz and Silvey, introduction, this volume: 9).

Taking this latter insight as a starting point, this chapter uses the SCF exhibit to explore questions of where, what, and how we look at the BRI and China's global ambitions. Here, the question of *where* is a reminder that, in terms of staging and location, the SCF exhibit occupied a unique place in the context of both the BRI and Xi Jinping's own historical legacy.[10] If these were to be understood as acts of resistance, it is important to note they did not take place in remote villages, the edges of rainforests, or the streets of distant capital cities—where most opposition to BRI is said to take place. Instead, such acts of resistance were on full display at the heart of Chinese political power (Beijing) and took place at a moment of a great international scrutiny of the government's global vision (the Second Belt Road Forum). Similarly, the question of *what you are looking at* prompts consideration not only of the subtle acts of resistance to a singular Silk Road narrative, but also the *permission* for such acts to be conjured in the first place. Attending to where, what, and how of resistance, this chapter suggests, allows for exploration of the multiscalar nature of Belt Road–Silk Road interactions. And, following the premise of this book that there are different ways of seeing the BRI, this chapter draws on the literature on visual politics to examine the multiscalar nature of interactions at SCF.

In taking a visual approach, the chapter investigates not simply the possibilities for resistance to Beijing's vision, but also what Beijing makes of such resistance. In addition to power and political agency, the latter point is important, as it illuminates the Chinese government's capacity to recognize and acknowledge difference—and to do so at a moment of heightened visibility by both domestic

[10] As is well known, Xi's first public appearance after donning the Chinese government leadership mantle in 2012 was at the Beijing National Museum where he pledged to carry out the "Great Renewal of the Chinese nation" (Wu and Yan, 2012). On the significance of the National Museum in the context of the BRI, see Chen (2019).

and international audiences. Rhetorically, recognition and acceptance of difference are critical components in Beijing's strategy to gain legitimacy for both the BRI and its overarching vision for world order. This is also how the government counters criticisms of its alleged hegemonic ambition and fear of unilateral imposition of Beijing's views.[11]

My visual analysis is facilitated by the "visual turn" in international relations,[12] particularly the proposition that images have the power to sculpt our collective "common sense" perception of social reality. Images, therefore, delineate how politics and global relations are framed, articulated, carried out, and legitimized (Bleiker, 2018). At stake in deploying visuality, I suggest, is the affective validation not only of a particular "common sense" imaginary of a shared past and common future, but also of questions pertaining to state ideology, political censorship, and the space for contestation of narratives and ideas. Attention to visuality therefore complements analyses of China's hegemonic ambitions by offering insights into how Beijing's vision and actions find global resonance, legitimacy, and acceptance. If the battle for global dominance is a battle over global imaginaries (Bottici, 2011), this chapter examines how China uses visuality to ensure the viability of its preferred global imaginary.

This is not to suggest that the SCF exhibit, or a "visual turn," is representative of the BRI or the full spectrum of China's global ambitions and evolving engagement in global politics. Rather, a critical interrogation of the politics of sight and the visual construction of China's ambitions is meant to supplement investigations concerning Beijing's use of material and discursive power (Foot, 2020; Ho, 2020; Khong, 2013). It also speaks to the divergence between Beijing's policy pronouncements and alleged aspiration to create a universal, inclusive, egalitarian world order on the one hand, and the "wolf-warrior"-type diplomatic engagements that seek to defend national interest, realpolitik, and hierarchy on the other (Acharya, 2019; Foot, 2020). Attending to the politics of sight, I suggest, provides tangible means for understanding the multiscalar nature of interactions emerging across the BRI, as discussed in this volume's introduction. It also provides insights into how Beijing seeks to validate its vision for global order and gain international legitimacy and trust.

To explore how a shared sense of the past is crafted through visuality, I draw primarily on Jacques Rancière (2013a, 2013b) on the politics of images and aesthetics. His approach to the politics of sight allows for interrogating the multiple layers of "what is seen and what is said" about the past, as well as assessing the very allowance for divergent interpretations to be made visible (2013b: 35).

---

[11] This is a recurrent trope in the Chinese government political lexicon (e.g., Xinhua News Agency, 2019).
[12] See, for example, Berents and Duncombe (2020); Bleiker (2009); Bleiker (2018); and Callahan (2020).

I use the case of the SCF exhibit to explore this dynamic duality and show how the politics of sight is key to structuring an overarching sense of credibility and legitimacy of China's global ambitions. The *permission* to make different narratives visible and sayable, this chapter suggests, allows Beijing's proposition for a shared past and common future to gain traction and resonate with others. Here, the perceived opportunity to express different views acts as a reassurance that Beijing is willing to recognize and accept a certain degree of diversity in the rendering of a different world order. Beijing's use of the politics of sight therefore produces a distinctive and acceptable pattern of order that resonates broadly within international society (Clark, 2011, 2014).

Attending to the politics of visuality provides a means to understand the messy, complex processes through which Beijing seeks to validate a vision for global order and gain international legitimacy and trust. In the following section, I explicate these points further before turning to the SCF exhibit and the politics of sight.

The "Visual Turn" in IR ... and China

The proposition that images play a major role in international relations and inform every aspect of social interactions, emotions, and thinking is not new. Over the past two decades, a growing engagement with visuality and the politics of sight has enriched and complicated the study of international relations.[13] Yet, despite the growing recognition that we live in a visual age, the role of visual politics in the context of China's rise and global ambitions remains largely unexamined.[14] To date, questions concerning China's multilateral engagements and visions for world order are typically analyzed through the prism of finance and infrastructure investments, policy proposals and discursive rhetoric, or strategic adherence to established multilateral norms. Partially, here as elsewhere, the lacunae of visual analysis can be attributed to a methodological challenge: a critical consideration on the incompatibility between visuals and the logic of causality (Schlag, 2019). As Rancière (2013a: 142–43) states, "there is no straight path from the viewing of a spectacle to an understanding of the state of the world, and none from intellectual awareness to political action." And, as the editors to this volume remind us, neither visuals nor "seeing" are in and of themselves politically transformative or normatively preferable (Schatz and Silvey, introduction, this volume).

---

[13] Again, see, for example, Berents and Duncombe (2020); Bleiker (2009); Bleiker (2018); and Callahan (2020).

[14] Some notable exceptions include Callahan (2020); Karavas (2020); and Morisson (2021).

As many scholars have argued, however, approaching visuals or the politics of sight through the angle of causality misses the point entirely (Bleiker, 2019). A critical analysis of the visual realm eschews the logic of positivism (Williams, 2018). Instead, such analysis must begin with an interrogation of the visual ordering of the social reality, our collective understanding of "common sense," and affective validation of a course of action. At stake in such interrogation is an analysis of what Rancière (2013a: 143) describes as a shift, a process of dis-association: "a move from one given world to another in which capacities and incapacities, forms of tolerance and intolerance, are differently identified." As such, visual artifacts can be understood as structuring the "conditions of possibility" for a particular "distribution of the sensible,"[15] and therefore sculpting collective perceptions of what is proper, acceptable, or legitimate (Rancière, 2013a; Bleiker, 2018).

Certainly, this approach poses a different challenge. The exceptionally dark history of the use of visuals during the interwar period of the 20th century and corresponding "aestheticization of politics" led to a belief that images are dangerous, linked closely with fascism, war, and totalitarianism. The affective validation of fascist ideology, ideals and principles was mediated through visuality—particularly through the spectacle of military parades and film (Williams, 2018). In the aftermath of the wars, the turn to "scientific" explanations and the rise of positivism and rationalism was, in part, a reaction against images, affect, aesthetics, "nonsense," and the power of myth (Williams, 2018). Consequently, the near erasure of visual politics from international relations scholarship for many decades was associated with the inability to construct a causal, logical, or scientific explanation of the mythical, affective power of visuality to mobilize and activate people in extreme ways. Instead, the politics of sight and the use of visuals was equated with the type of propaganda and cultural governance imposed by authoritarian and totalitarian regimes. Today, the relative lack of critical engagement with the role of visuals in the formulation of China's global ambitions could very well be the product of this complex and uneasy history of the discipline itself. This is not to say the Chinese government does not use visuality and political optics for propaganda purposes,[16] nor to claim there are no ethical consequences to such use. Rather, given the profound impact of visual politics in ordering "common sense" perceptions of reality today, a study

---

[15] Rancière describes the distribution of the sensible as "the system of self-evident facts of sense perception that simultaneously discloses the existence of something in common and the delimitations that define the respective parts and positions within it" (2013b: 12), and the "ways of framing a sensory space, of seeing or not seeing common objects in it, of hearing or not hearing in it subjects that designate them or reason in their relation" (2013a: 92).

[16] On the use of visuality for propaganda purposes in China see, for example, Denton (2014), Morrison (2021), and Varutti (2014).

of both the politics of sight and the power of images in any context becomes all the more critical.

It is also important to position visual politics in relation to dominant readings of China's international engagements. As mentioned, a prevailing approach among international relations scholars is to analyze Beijing's hegemonic ambitions through the lens of economics and material capabilities.[17] Accordingly, both China's global visions and the appeal of a "China model" are seen as a function of the country's spectacular economic prowess and rising material power. As Hugh White suggested nearly a decade ago, the only source of national power is "sheer economic scale," and economic growth directly increases political and diplomatic influence (cited in Khong, 2013: 162). Yet, many have challenged the primacy of analysis that hinges exclusively on economic development and material power, arguing that China's material capabilities alone do not necessarily translate into influence (Foot, 2019; Ho, 2020). Furthermore, if hegemony is understood not as an exercise in dominance, but as the "creation of a distinctive, and acceptable, pattern of order" (Clark, 2017), China's global ambitions need to find a source of resonance and legitimacy beyond the materiality of bridges, ports, bilateral financial agreements, or its own economic achievements and spectacular growth. Scholars have therefore highlighted Beijing's use of discursive power (*huà yǔ quán*). New terminology such as "building a community of shared future for mankind" (*rén lèi mìng yùn gòng tóng tǐ*), which is in turn sculpted in the "spirit of the ancient Silk Road," is understood as an attempt to describe China's peaceful ambitions for global cooperation, indicate its benign intent, and demonstrate the "mutual interest and win-win" potential of BRI projects (Foot, 2020). As some analysts have argued, material capabilities and discursive tactics can be seen as complementary: aimed at promoting a vision of order and focused on stability and development. Nevertheless, others contend that China's charm offensive remains too abstract (Hillman, 2020); reassurances for benign intent are not matched by policies (Foot, 2020; Acharya, 2019); and Beijing still fails to elaborate on a vision of global order that is beneficial to anyone else but China (Mastro, 2019).

An alternative way to interject in such conversations is to point to the critical need to understand both the BRI and the Chinese government in a global context. A study of Beijing's power and hegemonic ambitions is not just a matter of assessing economic capabilities or discursive power; rather, it necessitates critical ground-level analyses. This is because, as Schatz and Silvey (introduction, this volume: 14) remind us, "power is not a simple matter of material disparities." Instead, power is multifaceted, dynamic, and subject to the downstream effects

---

[17] Such work can contribute much, as Chapter 1 by Lemon and Jardine, Chapter 2 by Narins, and Chapter 3 by Paltiel and Yan, this volume, all demonstrate.

that it encounters. To this end, questions of resonance and legitimacy demand investigation of how others see, and potentially (re)shape, Beijing's narratives and visions, as well as how Beijing reacts to such multifaceted, transformative dynamics. This chapter's critical analysis of the visual construction of China's global ambitions is meant to supplement such investigations. For example, starting from the premise that China does not have exclusive claim to the history and interactions along the Silk Road, a turn to the politics of sight enables an interrogation of how others understand and subscribe to the imaginary of a shared past and common future. At issue here is not only Beijing's use of shared historical imaginaries but also *how* or *why* others might find these convincing. This, especially given the fact that the homogenous rendering of a Silk Road past, has a long history of contestation and has been the subject of vociferous opposition, especially in Asia (Chin, 2013; Winter, 2019).[18]

To explore the downstream effects of China's imaginary and the use of visuals to both accept and reject a vision of collective past and common future, the next sections turn to the SCF exhibit. I begin with a description of some overarching notions concerning Beijing's use of history, and the narrative of the ancient Silk Road in particular. Then, I use visual analysis to explore how an acceptable pattern of order (Clark, 2011) resonates with others. I suggest that such resonance becomes possible not because of the nature of any one concrete representation of the links between the past and the future, but because of the visibility given to the messiness, incompatibility, and diversity of views, memories, and affective associations with the past. To this end, the creation of a "common sense" understanding of a shared Silk Road past and common future is a matter of visual politics; a turn to the politics of sight highlights the presence of a space where divergence and disharmony become visible, sayable, and acceptable as part of an overarching narrative.

Remembering the Past, Sculpting the Future

> This will be my first trip to Iran, yet like many other Chinese, I do not feel like a stranger in your ancient and beautiful country, thanks to the Silk Road that linked our two great nations for centuries and to the many legendary stories recorded in history books of our friendly exchanges.
>
> (Xi, 2016)

---

[18] This information has been gleaned from fieldwork and interviews across multiple parts of Asia from 2016 to 2019.

As mentioned in this chapter's introduction, since the launch of the BRI in 2013, the Chinese government has sought to anchor a vision for alternative world order on the notion of an alleged common Silk Road past (Mayer, 2017, 2018a; Winter, 2019). Just as in the passage from Xi's remarks quoted at the beginning of this section, the Silk Road history of peaceful interactions and prolific exchanges enables a sense of shared commonality and security ("I do not feel like a stranger"). In addition, this sense of affective cohesion serves as a model upon which to (re)establish connectivity and deepen future interactions. Prior to the COVID-19 pandemic, this shared past-future imaginary sought to give concrete substance to the phrase "community of shared future." Within China, this is also how "community of shared future" came to occupy a prominent place in the Chinese government's political lexicon. Indeed, since the pandemic, the phrase has taken on a life of its own: it is central to Beijing's vision for global order and is meant to reaffirm Beijing's commitment to globalization and multilateralism.[19]

The invocation of the ancient Silk Road alongside the language of a "community of shared future" suggests that future collaboration is possible because of a history of past interactions and exchanges. In turn, the combination of the two translates into an overarching vision of global order emulating the "spirit of the ancient Silk Road" (Sidaway and Woon, 2017). Unlike notions of legitimacy derived from the country's economic prowess, the alleged Silk Road legitimacy traces back to deeper and longer-lasting historical connections. This, in turn, suggests that the Silk Road–Belt Road vision is located within a teleological process of historical inevitability (Mayer, 2018a; Winter, 2019). Accordingly, the forces of convergence on a path to common future and shared prosperity emanate from a joint history of interactions and exchanges along the ancient Silk Road. An added aspect of this shared history is the organization of relationships under the principle of *tiān xià*, or as is commonly translated, "all under Heaven." As one of the leading Chinese International relations scholars, Zhao Tingyang, characterizes it, *tiān xià* is "a common choice made by all peoples in the world or a universal agreement in the "hearts of all people"; it is "a political system for the world with a global institution to ensure universal order" (Zhao Tingyang, quoted in Acharya, 2019: 475). In this view, the ancient Silk Road itself represents the factual historical precedence of an overarching *tiān xià* order.

But what does a "community of shared future" look like? Organizing a "common sense" imaginary around such claims demands spectacular visual renderings. Along with the initial announcement of the BRI in 2013, this meant a significant push across China and BRI countries to establish a concrete, factual basis for the claims of shared past of Silk Road interactions. The mobilization of

---

[19] The phrase appears in many high-level speeches to international audiences, often in conjunction with affirmations on China's commitment to globalization and multilateralism.

historical/cultural narratives was so pronounced that even the COVID-19 pandemic managed only to disrupt, but not entirely shut down, the complex circuit of dazzling Silk Road-themed displays, including elaborate musicals performed both in China and abroad, TV shows, and dedicated domestic and international museum exhibits and exchanges. For example, the International Alliance of Museums on the Silk Road (IAMS) sponsored a steady flow of Silk Road-themed international events throughout the pandemic. The intent was not simply to counter the growing push toward deglobalization (Arase, 2020); it also was to allow Beijing to maintain an imaginary of a "natural" state of interconnectedness and provide a platform for interaction and exchange at a time when traditional in-person engagements were severely limited. By partaking in various museums and cultural displays, the virtual spectators could still acquire some of the direct, intimate connection with the flows of history and experience the links between the past, present, and future on their own terms (Tidy and Turner, 2020).

Staged prior to the pandemic, the SCF exhibit was part of this newly created genre of spectacular, spectator-immersive, Silk Road-themed displays. Yet, in many ways, it was also different from prior museum exhibits or cultural events. In addition to the auspicious timing, discussed at the opening of this chapter, the SCF exhibit was the first multilateral event to ever feature a large-scale global museum collaboration: an unprecedented joint curation from thirteen national institutions across the world.[20] The narrative of interconnected past and common future was based on individual museums' curatorial decisions and told through exquisite antique objects and official statements by each respective national museum. Thematically, the exhibit was divided into a Land Silk Road, represented by China, Russia, Mongolia, Kazakhstan, Tajikistan, Slovenia, Latvia, Poland, and Romania, and a Maritime Silk Road, represented by Japan, Korea, Oman, Cambodia, and China. Each museum was assigned a separate gallery to display objects and official museum statements. In total, 246 objects were displayed.

Coinciding with the high-level Second Belt and Road Forum, the exhibit aligned with the Chinese government's vision to "extend the splendid history of the Silk Road and to create a brighter future" (Wang, 2019). As alluded by the title, the exhibit sought to represent a wide-ranging convergence around the memories of ancient transboundary interactions and seamlessly align these into a vision for a common future. From the point of view of the organizers, the exhibit had two simultaneous goals. On the one hand, the displays were meant to reaffirm the teleological vision of a "community of shared future" by showcasing

---

[20] Statement by Yan Zhi, curator of the exhibition and deputy director of the International Liaison Department of the National Museum: http://www.chnmuseum.cn/portals/0/web/zt/20190411sfgx/.

a tiān xià–type interactions across the ancient Silk Road, spanning two millennia. On the other, the joint participation was also meant to highlight the scope of global collaboration across multiple museums (IAMS, 2019). The claim to inclusiveness was bolstered by the prominent list of international participants known for their divergent views regarding the Silk Road past, most prominently Japan, Russia, and the countries of Central Asia (Mayer, 2018b; Ito, 2019; Xu, 2019). Both explicitly (in terms of timing with the BRF) and implicitly (in terms of messaging), the exhibit was planned as an effort to cement an international-style alignment with Beijing's vision for a future of "peace and cooperation, openness and inclusiveness, mutual learning and mutual benefit" (Wang, 2019).

Notably, the rhetorical maneuvering and attempts at alignment of historical narratives were not lost on the prospective museum invitees. The museum curators from invited countries were aware of the contested terrain at stake in the exhibit. During field interviews, a number of museum curators from countries with significant historical connections to the ancient Silk Road spoke of their general unease with the exhibit. Many voiced concerns with participating in the spectacle of a shared past and common future that could be interpreted as an outright endorsement of a Chinese-style rendering of history. Moreover, as will be discussed further, it would have been easy to see the grandiose display as proof of the sophistication and civilizational advancement of Chinese artisans, artists, and architects. Indeed, such reasoning led some prospective invitees to decide against participation at the SCF, or to altogether ignore the generous invitation by the Chinese organizers.[21] Beyond the exhibition itself, uncertainty as to the intended messages of the exhibit was also a reflection of overarching suspicions of Beijing's global ambitions (Ho, 2020).

Granted, declining the invitation to participate meant different things to different curators. Depending on their own positionality, some of my interlocutors were quite adamant on the incompatibility of historical imaginaries and insistent about the need of other representations, and names, associated with the past. Yet others were eager to point out that their own renderings of the past were not meant to counter the BRI or the Silk Road. Nevertheless, both national governments and local communities have been keen to (re)assert and revive a different sense of history and heritage. In India, for example, there are attempts to promote initiatives such as Project Mausam and Project Museris, focusing on religious exchanges and the history of the spice trade (Ray, 2019, 2020). In Indonesia, the Ministry of Education and Culture leads a nationwide effort to collect and revive memories and traditions associated with ancient maritime interactions, similarly focused on the history of the spice trade (Kumoratih

---

[21] Author's field work and interviews with museum curators and government officials from 2018 to 2022.

et al., 2021). Within China itself, provincial governments, especially in prominent maritime ports such as Guangzhou (ancient Canton) and Quanzhou (also known as Zayton in ancient times), organize a "common sense" narrative of the past not so much in relation to the Silk Road, but around memories and traditions linked to the cosmopolitan multi-religious history of the ports, the trade in ceramics and spices, and decentralized decision-making.[22]

In the face of such multifaceted divergences, Beijing's prospects for legitimizing a vision of a shared future on the premise of a common past appear to be limited if not far-fetched. How, then, might Beijing use the politics of sight to cultivate a "common sense" understanding and gain acceptance and legitimacy for its global vision?

I explore this question by turning to the displays at the SCF exhibit and offering three different interpretations of the exhibit's space and artifacts. I highlight how, even in the singular space of a museum exhibit, there are multiple ways of seeing and understanding how visual artifacts can organize and structure a "common sense" impression of the past. These interpretations show how acceptance and legitimacy were contingent on a complex process that involved the politics of sight, the rendering of space, and the allowance for diverse, incompatible narratives to coexist. By making distinct interpretations of the Silk Road seeable and sayable, the SCF exhibit did not provide a uniform, singular vision. Instead, it became a platform where complex, messy, and sometimes incompatible representations could coexist. Indeed, this "messiness"—or what the Beijing hosts envisioned as "multicenter" (duō zhōng xīn)—was part of the original design (Chen, 2019). This is because, for the Chinese curators, the complexity and ambiguity were themselves integral to the plurality and diversity of the Silk Road. To start, the Chinese curators were cognizant of their adoption of a Western terminology and imaginary, in other words, the Silk Road, to represent something far more complex than what a name and neat lines on a map could capture. Resorting to a "multicenter" meant allowing multiple, divergent narratives and representations to coexist. This is also how the SCF signaled the "conditions of possibility" for transformative impressions and viewpoints to emerge, or, in the language of Rancière, a "re-distribution of the sensible" to take place (2013a). Here, divergences were also indicative of a freedom of expression, challenging concerns that the exhibit necessarily imposed the views of the Chinese hosts, and by extension the Chinese government. Indeed, given that differences and

---

[22] Author's fieldwork and interviews across Asia from 2016 to 2022. This included visits to museums, heritage sites, and public displays related to the BRI and the Silk/Spice Road in China, India, Indonesia, Vietnam, Cambodia, Singapore, and Malaysia. In addition to field visits, I conducted interviews with curators, museum experts, and grassroots community organizers engaged in heritage preservation. Much of the fieldwork, including blogs, images, and maps, is documented at Visual Archives of the Silk and Spice Routes: https://visual-archives.com/.

dissonance in historical narratives were themselves made a central part of the SCF display, the exhibit illuminated broader contestations about who gets to lay claim to the historical roots of the Silk Road and, therefore, also project a claim for a future world order.

Distributing the Sensible: Visualizing a Community of Shared Past

The ancient Silk Road stretched for tens of thousands of miles and lasted for thousands of years. The Silk Road embodies the spirit that transcends time and space, transcends national borders, embodies eternal charm, and exhibits values that can also be applied in contemporary time including peace and cooperation, openness inclusiveness mutual learning and mutual benefit.

(Wang, 2019)

What did the vision of a shared past and common future look like?[23] Was there an overarching sense of commonality cutting across all 13 museums' displays? How did visual artifacts translate abstract political discourse into an imaginary of connectivity, peace, and cooperation?

At first sight, the exhibit seemed to reaffirm the aforementioned apprehensions about Beijing's assertion of a singular, hegemonic view of the past. The organization of the space, as well as the choice of select objects and textual references, often seemed to suggest China's central role in the Silk Road past. Most strikingly, irrespective of how a visitor was to enter the SCF exhibit space, she would have to start and end the journey of a "shared past and common future" with China.[24] This was because the first display, immediately at the exhibit entry, featured China's Land Silk Road, and the last display, immediately next to the exit, featured China's Maritime Silk Road. Yet, apart from these curatorial devices, China's centrality was hardly the theme across most of the exhibit. As I will show further, even the mentions of the Silk Road were few and far between. Thus, the notion that the exhibit would only channel a singular China-driven narrative was not substantiated by the material displays or the textual references. Rather, the exhibit created a space for multiple representations and divergent voices. As such, there appeared to be hardly any convergence across the 13 museums. The

---

[23] All images described in the following sections are available at https://visual-archives.com/image-repository/.

[24] I am grateful to Ben Nienass for urging me to develop this point.

Figure 4.1 Chinese ceramics on display from Oman, Romania, and Poland.
Source: Author.

use of visuality for propaganda narratives of a shared past was instead drowned in the creative multiplicity of objects, associations, and themes.

Act 1: China at the Center?

As previously suggested, at first glance, the SCF exhibit could easily be seen as a grandiose display and reaffirmation of a Sinocentric world, with the history and origin of the Silk Road directly linked to China (Chin, 2013). Three examples explicate the point. First, in terms of staging, China was the only country featured within both "maritime" and "land" sections, and therefore allotted two galleries; all other national museums had their displays exhibited in one section. Exhibit viewers were thus socialized in a space that effortlessly depicted an "all roads lead to China" perspective. Moreover, as mentioned earlier, it was impossible to miss China in the exhibit because of the positionality of artifacts from the Beijing National Museum at the entry and exit. Second, the notion of fluid connectivity across space, time, and physical boundaries was reaffirmed with the help of material and visual representations evocative of Chinese civilization and culture: for example, the conspicuous display of Ming-style porcelain in multiple gallery spaces, including Oman, Romania, Poland, and Latvia (see Figure 4.1). The Polish, Russian, and Cambodian displays also featured various objects crafted with Chinese motifs, therefore suggestive of the ubiquity and

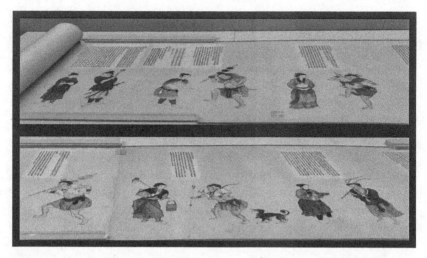

Figure 4.2 Scrolls from the *Atlas of the Western Regions*, 18th century and 6th century. Source: Author.

universal reach of the Chinese cultural and civilizational influence. At the same time, the widespread influence of Chinese styles and crafts channeled a sense of millennia-old recognition and attempts at emulation of the "superior" Chinese styles. This point was made unabashedly clear in news media reports of the exhibit, such as commentaries suggesting the prominent acceptance and emulation of the Chinese architectural imaginary (*zhōng guó jiàn zhù de xiǎng xiàng*) even in faraway lands such as Poland (Art.China, 2019).

Possibly the most overt reference to a China-centered world was the prominent showcase of two sizable scrolls in the China Land Silk Road section. One was the Atlas of the Western Regions (*xī chéng tú cè*), originally commissioned by the Qianlong Emperor after the conquest of the Xinjiang region in the 18th century (Zhang, 2019), and the other—a copy of a similar atlas, *Zhí gòng tú*—from the sixth century (see Figure 4.2). Both scrolls, displayed at the very first gallery of the exhibit, featured drawings of foreign envoys to China, and the peoples of the world paying tribute to the Chinese emperor. A full explication of the multiple symbolic and political meanings of both scrolls goes beyond the scope of this chapter.[25] Suffice it to say that the not-so-subtle reference to the conquest of Xinjiang, and the evocation of tributes to the Chinese emperors, could hardly be suggestive of messages of peaceful interaction or freedom of cooperation and

---

[25] The Qing dynasty's Atlas of the Western Regions (xicheng tuce) is considered to be one of the very few remaining copies of the original book commissioned by the Qianlong Emperor. Part of a long-standing genre, Qianlong's nine volumes on tributary offerings also allegedly provided more realistic representation of foreigners than volumes from previous dynasties (Ge, 2017).

exchange (Callahan, 2020; Smith, 2013). Within the context of an exhibit, the very act of displaying the two scrolls further underscored the notion of Beijing's ambition to (re)construct a China-centered universe with a tributary system and hierarchy of relationships. Beyond the SCF exhibit, the scrolls also appeared to validate one prevailing assessment of Beijing's foreign policy: that China's global ambition amounts to an attempt to reimpose a *tiān xià* world and recreate a hierarchical tributary system modeled on its imperial past (Rolland, 2017, 2020).

Yet such visual narratives, and especially the imaginary of tributary relations, found no resonance with the rest of the displays in the SCF exhibit. Even if they featured Chinese artifacts as part of their displays, the remaining 12 national museums chose not to adopt a China-centered narrative of interactions along the ancient Silk Road. Instead, and as elaborated in the next section, they rendered visible an entirely different spectrum of interactions and significations of the past.

Act 2: A Community of Shared Past?

The notion of the exhibit as the common source of shared Silk Road memories dissipated as soon as the visitor would turn to the official statements and objects displayed by the participating museums. A simple textual analysis (see Table 4.1), conducted using natural language processing, of official messages (National Museum of China, 2019) (see Figure 4.3) shows that there was hardly any cohesion in the respective depictions of the past. For example, in the two official statements of the Beijing National Museum, the phrase "Silk Road" appeared 11 times—more than any other combination of words. In contrast, the phrase was not even mentioned in the official messages of the Japanese, Romanian, and Slovenian national museums and was referenced only once or twice by Tajikistan, Oman, Russia, Poland, and Cambodia. In other words, in terms of official messaging, the majority of participating museums deviated significantly from the Chinese hosts' narrative of a shared Silk Road past.

In fact, the majority of participating museums seemed to downplay the historical significance of both the Silk Road and China. Certainly, in a gesture to the Chinese hosts, some museums referenced the Chinese influence on their culture and civilization, especially Poland (see Table 4.1). However, even such references did not create an impression of an overarching commonality, close interactions, and constancy of exchanges. At the same time, the only official statements that made explicit connections with the Silk Road, by Mongolia and South Korea, barely referenced China. Furthermore, none of the statements positioned China as the original source for ancient interactions and assigned no particular relevance to relationships with China. As such the official statements

Table 4.1 Textual analysis of 13 museum statements in the "Sharing a Common Future" exhibit, Beijing 2019.

National Museum	Total word count	Silk Road	China	Chinese	Reference to the word "Chinese"
China	491	11	15	0	—
Cambodia	268	1	4	6	culture, books, Buddhist stone pillar, dragon
Japan	183	0	0	0	—
Kazakhstan	272	3	1	1	merchants
Latvia	200	3	1	2	culture, cup
Mongolia	263	7	2	2	civilization, dynasty
Oman	330	2	3	5	relics, name, fleet
Poland	322	2	1	9	art, history, metal, paintings, artworks, architecture, pavilions
Romania	327	0	1	1	items
Russia	189	1	1	0	—
Slovenia	360	0	1	0.	—
South Korea	198	7	2	0	—
Tajikistan	202	1	2	2	traveler, coexisted

created an overwhelming sense of ignoring, rather than endorsing, a shared Silk Road past. Especially puzzling was the Japanese museum's silence on the subject of the Silk Road, given the long-standing history of Japanese governments' use of Silk Road language to promote internationalism and boost their own diplomatic credentials (Winter, 2020, 2022).

The textual dissonance and the limited nods to China's role were further mirrored in the visual and material displays across the different galleries. Except for the aforementioned artifacts referencing the influence of Chinese art or culture (and some occasional portraits of 19th-century Chinese merchants), there appeared to be no connecting themes across the 13 countries. A visitor would have a hard time seeing any common threads across the individual galleries. Objects of different makes, time periods, and varied use often seemed to reaffirm the significance of particular territories and peoples rather than speak to a sense of shared community and interaction. For example, a 19th-century inkstand in

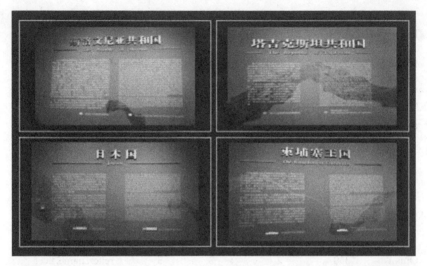

Figure 4.3 Museum statements on display at the *Sharing a Common Future* exhibit. Source: Author.

the form of a Chinese sailing ship from the Moscow National Museum sat across from a replica of the Golden Man of Kazakhstan, dated to the fourth–third century BCE. Then, in an adjacent gallery connected with a long, darkened corridor, the exhibit showcased two 18th-century longcase clocks made in England and a wood cabinet made in Germany. Coming from the National Museum in Warsaw, Poland, these clocks and cabinets had no obvious link to an ancient Silk Road or any of the other objects on display (Figure 4.4).

In the Maritime Silk Road section of the exhibit, a stronger sense of commonality was made visible through objects associated with various religious traditions, including the mysterious *Dongson* drums,[26] known to exist across numerous locations throughout Southeast Asia (Miksic, 2013; Ray, 2003), and multiple Buddhist statues. Still, beyond religion, it was hard to imagine overarching patterns of connectivity and a shared past, especially for visitors unfamiliar with the long-standing history of connectivity stretching from the Indian Ocean to the Pacific. For example, for all their historical value and significance, it was unclear how objects on display from Oman might be linked to the Japanese

---

[26] The drums are mysterious precisely because of their unprecedented spread across Southeast Asia. While the region is well known for its long-standing traditions of mobility and transience, the massive drums required far more complex transport infrastructure. That the drums have been found in multiple locations suggests there was indeed a highly sophisticated transport infrastructure that went beyond the movement patterns of fishermen, sailors, and small traders (Miksic, 2013; Ray, 2003).

Figure 4.4 Images of dissonance: Golden Man, inkstand, and clocks.
Source: Author.

or Korean sections, let alone formulate an impression of a network of maritime connectivity. From the Major Moon book on maritime navigation from the 18th century, featured as part of the Oman display, to the Japanese *Dotaku* bell from the first century, and the corner post stone of the Korean Silla period, the exhibited objects showcased distinct historical and cultural achievements rather than the precedence of a shared past, peaceful interactions, and maritime exchange (Figure 4.5).

Across the exhibit space, three curatorial devices served as the only reminder that the objects and narratives were to be understood as part of an interconnected past and meant to be viewed as objects of a singular exhibit. These devices were, first, a depiction of a thread of flowing silk connecting the different sections; second, the visitors' ability to move freely across the space and displays; and, third, the brightly lit panel with the words "Sharing a common future" at the end of the exhibit. Yet, neither the concept of a Silk Road nor the sense of a common past seemed to resonate with the individual displays and how they sought to organize and link into a constitutive whole.[27] Just as with the official statements, the material displays seem to produce a similar impression: disjointed, singular narratives that could not sustain an imaginary of a shared past, let alone an aspiration to a common future. If anything, given the interpretations discussed, the exhibit instead appeared as a showcase of dissonance and divergence across time, space, and memories associated with the past.

---

[27] The lack of synergy could partially be due to the limited time to plan the exhibit. I am grateful to a museum curator for pointing this out. However, the limited planning time does not discount the argument that ultimately there was no one singular (propaganda-style) reading of a shared Silk Road past.

Figure 4.5 Corner post stone (Korea), Major Moon book (Oman), *Dotaku* bell (Japan). Source: Author.

How then to think of this extensive emphasis on difference and seeming rejection of an imaginary of a shared past? What does it signify in terms of the limited attempts at collaboration? Were they a clear sign of the rejection of Beijing's vision of world order? Before exploring such questions further, I turn to one more interpretation of the exhibit space. Here, I take into account the interactions on the Silk Road that preceded the formation of modern nation-states. I highlight the visibility of connectivities and linkages that appeared in spite of the heavy emphasis on national histories and state-led crafting of history. These linkages transcended state boundaries and clear-cut identifications with singular nationalities or cultures.

Act 3: Visualizing Transnational Communities of a Shared Past

In this last interpretation, I draw on the insight that viewers (or spectators) are not merely passive observers of the exhibit but have the capacity to co-construct the meanings and significance of the performative space (Rancière, 2011). To this end, I suggest an interpretation that gives primacy to the visual objects themselves. Allowing the visual artifacts, instead of the museum curators, to tell the story of the past might draw a visitor's attention to seemingly inconspicuous objects that invoke a different kind of premodern time, space, and connectivity.[28] One such example is the bronze *kazan*. In the exhibit, the *kazan* was

[28] Granted, there was some curatorial intent to "read" the exhibit through objects—this is how, for example, the Chinese curatorial team included drums in one of the Chinese sections in an effort to match the Cambodian *Dongson* drums (Chen, 2019).

Figure 4.6 Visualizing transnational connections: the *kazan* and the camel bell. Source: Author.

featured as part of the Kazakhstan museum display (see Figure 4.6). Allegedly, there was nothing special about a *kazan*: it was a commonly used cooking pot. For all its understated appearance, however, the *kazan* could have been part of nearly every display, stretching from the lands of Mongolia and Kazakhstan all the way to the western territories of the Ottoman Empire and modern Turkey. An everyday cooking utensil, commonly used by nomads and later appropriated and utilized by both nomadic and settled households across Eurasia, the *kazan* is precisely the type of object that symbolizes unity and interconnectivity across space and time that a Silk Road narrative also strives to achieve. In the SCF exhibit space, however, the *kazan* would have to be "discovered" and put in a relational context by the museum visitors themselves, thereby enabling them to become active interpreters and cocreators of an imaginary of an interconnected past.

A similar story could have also been told about the camel bell from the Mongolian section of the exhibit. Just as with the bronze *kazan*, camel bells were widespread throughout Africa and Eurasia and once again associated with the type of nomadic lifestyle and interactions constitutive of the Silk Road exchanges. Camel caravans and their bells also hold a special place in the new discourse on the Silk Road–Belt Road connectivity. For Chinese domestic audiences, the object could have found further resonance because of Xi's famous reference to camel bells in his unveiling of the BRI in 2013 in Kazakhstan, as well as the "legend of the camel bell" (*zhí gòng tú*) musical staged in Xi'an shortly thereafter.

Finally, occasional displays of weapons and armor across the exhibit hallways could have served as a reminder that, rather than aspirations for peace, historical interactions across Eurasia entailed violent confrontations and war. For an exhibit and vision that aspired to promote peace, such objects could trigger multiple conversations, including reflections on the formative role of war in structuring identities, or the price of peace and the types of means necessary for its achievement.

The Politics of Sight: Seeing Difference and the "Re-distribution of the Sensible"

Based on the previous discussions, it would be easy to dismiss the exhibit's attempt at singular narrative and collective understanding of a shared past and common future. Yet, it could also be argued that the pronounced display of divergence and multiple points of view served a different purpose. Namely, by allowing visitors to bear witness to the diversity of visualizations, the exhibit sculpted a perception of wide-ranging possibilities for both expression and freedom for interpretation. By permitting a range of different narratives and visualizations, Beijing may have in practice enhanced its legitimacy and quelled apprehensions regarding hegemonic impositions.

Such an interpretation aligns with one philosophical tradition that informs the Chinese government's approach to international relations: the principle of *zhōng yōng* and its three formative elements—inclusivity, complementarity, and harmony. According to this approach, "opposites constitute life for each other and tend to co-evolve into a new, harmonious synthesis." As a central tenet of governance, harmony depends on the coevolution, complementarity, and process of continuously "maintaining, adjusting, and managing complex and fluid human relations" (Qin, 2016). Applied to international relations, *zhōng yōng* signals a refusal of the view that relations are dictated solely by the interests of rational, unitary actors (Qin, 2016). Starting from a *zhōng yōng* perspective, the divergence and expression of different perspectives within the SCF exhibit could therefore be understood as complementing the larger process of interaction and an opportunity for co-creation of a vision for a shared past and common future.

A different philosophical perspective could also inform the analysis. Although not posited in the context of international relations, the value of divergence and disagreement is central to Rancière's (2013a) conceptualizations of the politics of aesthetics and of *dissensus*. He describes *dissensus* as moments of "re-framing the given by inventing new ways of making sense of the sensible, new configurations between the visible and invisible, and between the audible and the inaudible, new distributions of space and time" (2013a: 143). Accordingly, at the SCF exhibit, the permission granted to divergent narratives could be an offering to challenge the China-centric understandings of the past. As demonstrated in the previous section, the fact of visual and narrative divergence stimulated different notions of a shared past, and of China's significance on the ancient Silk Road.

Yet, beyond *zhongyong* and *dissensus*, the conclusion that the visual representations undermined Beijing's vision for a shared past and common future might be premature. Indeed, Rancière (2013a) warns of the possibilities for misreading the politics of sight, the alleged spaces for disagreement, or what counts as *dissensus*. As he points out, the expression of different views or the sight of divergent visions do not—in and of themselves—amount to an alternative configuration of what is seen and understood. Instead, they can very well be or become embedded *within* existing structures and understandings of the world. These different interests, values, and aspirations thus bring forth a sense of "one unique reality to which everything must be related, a reality that . . . has only one possible signification" (Rancière, 2013a: 144). Consequently, when channeled within the framework of one reality, differences do not trigger a transformative rupture that changes the collective sense of social order or overarching perceptions of reality.

At the SCF exhibit, neither the Silk Road nor a tiān xià hierarchical order appeared as dominant messages. Nevertheless, the exhibit's overarching message still highlighted China's prominence in leading historical connectivity across time, space, and communities. The "multiple centers" (duō zhōng xīn) and divergent expressions were situated in a larger encirclement that started and ended with China. Even if not in a narrative form, the essence of tiān xià was produced by the circular space: an aesthetic reminder that no matter which way a visitor might go, all the roads would lead China.[29] As such, the politics of sight was not limited to the visuals but permeated through the spatial arrangement and architectural design of the exhibit (English and Zacka, 2022). The fluidity and openness of the space allowed for different expressions to coexist but also reinforced a sense that all these differences amount to one singular point of departure and conclusion. Furthermore, the allowance of differences did not enable a radical rupture or a dominant alternative reading of the past (for example, one involving struggles for power, the predominance of Islam across the Silk Road, or the role of autonomous merchant networks). There was also no interrogation of the underlying premise that the past and future should be understood as part of one smoothly flowing continuum (Winter, 2019). While there was an opportunity for divergence within the space of the exhibit, all the interactions and interpretations appeared within the already prescribed space of a Silk Road narrative. Or, as the editors to this volume point out, Wittgenstein's "duck-rabbit" could be seen as a duck, rabbit, or an ambiguous image, but it cannot be

---

[29] Starting and ending the exhibit with China was an explicit curatorial decision made by the Beijing team (Chen, 2019).

seen as a frog or a camel (see Schatz and Silvey, introduction to this volume: 9). Similarly, with the SCF exhibit, there were multiple possibilities for divergent visualizations and narratives, but the permission for display and interpretation was still within a bounded circle of interactions: the world of a "shared past and common future" envisioned by China.

Conclusion

Critical analyses of China's vision for a new world order have become a top priority for Washington and many of its allies (Rolland, 2020). While China's ambition to establish its own international authority is no longer subject to debate, many observers still argue that Beijing lacks the credibility and legitimacy to assert its global visions (Mastro, 2019). Partially, this lack is associated with the ambiguity of official statements, convoluted investment deals, and instances of pushback from various partners, especially as part of BRI projects (Patey, 2020).

Given the profound impact of visuality in structuring our collective "common sense," this chapter argued that a critical analysis of the visual construction of China's global ambitions can bring further understanding to questions concerning authoritarian imposition, legitimacy, and acceptance of visions for world order. The chapter showed how a critical engagement with the politics of sight allows for an exploration of Beijing's attempts to assign a "common sense" understanding of a new world order with itself at the center. In problematizing the different levels at which the politics of sight operates, the chapter also offered an interrogation of the concrete (i.e., visible) sources of legitimacy and acceptance for such an order.

Using the case of the collaborative SCF exhibit, the chapter highlighted how visual artifacts both promoted and disrupted a sense of China's historical prominence in Silk Road interactions. Instead of a singular narrative, the chapter showed how the space of the exhibit created an opportunity for multiple representations and interpretations to gain affective hold. At stake in showcasing divergence was a shift of "common sense" perceptions away from authoritarian censorship and toward a mode of collective expression that aligned with Beijing's vision of convergence across time and space toward a shared future. The exhibit showcased the Chinese hosts' capacity to accommodate different and sometimes incongruent narratives. Yet, this was not to argue that China is moving toward a Western-style plurality and freedom of expression, nor to suggest that China might be allowing for the type of collaborative engagements that might lead to a "re-distribution of the sensible." Even in the context of the exhibit, the notable acts of divergence did not amount to a construction of a non–Silk Road narrative.

Nevertheless, the politics of sight revealed that, where perceptions of the past were concerned, Beijing was willing to forgo a singular, dominant narrative. Further, in an effort to build credibility and legitimacy, it sought to provide a space for multiple expressions and opinions, however incompatible they might be with the Chinese representations. Certainly, this could be understood as China's quest for presenting a vision for an alternative world order that has universal validity. For, as Lisa Wedeen (1999) reminds us, when state propaganda wages an universal claim, it has to appear flexible and accommodating of the conditions of all "the people."

Thus, in the interest of its geocultural hegemony, Beijing appears open to a plurivocal "common sense" notion of the past. The openness may amount to relatively small gestures, such as shifting the focus away from China, stripping the imaginary of "barbarian" others, and privileging the role of multiple communities with shared interactions. Ultimately, such acts enhance Beijing's global legitimacy and credibility. As BRI projects enable Beijing to steer growing segments of the visual and digital space, many observers will do well to ask how the Chinese government constructs "common sense" imaginaries on a global scale and what they might mean to others. And even more importantly, it is worth pondering how China's quest for global legitimacy creates opportunities to both disrupt and co-construct such imaginaries.

5

The Power of Blank Spaces

A Critical Cartography of China's Belt and Road Initiative in the Himalayan Region

Galen Murton

Cartographers manufacture power. They create a spatial panopticon. It is a power embedded in the map text. We can talk about the power of the map just as we already talk about the power of the word or about the book as a force for change. In this sense maps have politics. It is a power that intersects and is embedded in knowledge. It is universal.

—J. B. Harley (2001: 21–22)

Introduction

A variety of maps depict a usefully approximate but inexact network of roads, rails, sea lanes, and other transport infrastructures to represent something called China's Belt and Road Initiative (BRI). And yet, for a global infrastructural program that reflects and advances Beijing's ambition to become the global leader of international development, BRI maps are surprisingly imprecise and unofficial. Taking this "useful fuzziness" (Narins and Agnew, 2020) of cartographic ambiguity as a starting point and drawing on methods of historical and critical cartography, this chapter reads BRI maps as texts of "cartographic silence" (Harley, 2001) to show how they "do work" (Wood, 2010) in the negative register of empty space. A critical reading of BRI maps thus provides yet another and "different way of seeing the BRI" and helps illuminate how Chinese power moves with discursive agency, as "the exercise of power and the practice of development are not reducible to their material components" (Schatz and Silvey, introduction, this volume: 3).

Inspired by Krishna's work on "cartographic anxiety" in South Asia (1994), I focus on Tibet, Nepal, and the broader Himalayan region to highlight an important paradox that reflects China's own cartographic anxieties related to BRI development. On the one hand, a brief look at any number of popular BRI maps

Galen Murton, *The Power of Blank Spaces* In: Seeing China's Belt and Road. Edited by: Edward Schatz and Rachel Silvey, Oxford University Press. © Oxford University Press 2025.
DOI: 10.1093/oso/9780197789261.003.0006

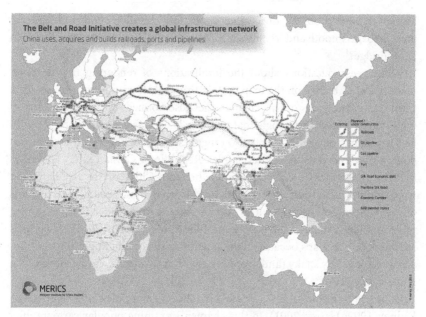

Figure 5.1 Map: The Belt and Road Initiative Creates a Global Infrastructure *Network*. Source: MERICS (2018)

(see Figure 5.1) reveals that Tibet and the Himalayan region remain conspicuously absent from most large-scale cartographic representations of the BRI. On the other hand, these "blanks on the map" exist despite the presence of numerous BRI projects that pass through this "sensitive space" (Cons, 2019). For example, new road, rail, hydropower, and telecommunication networks linked to international BRI agendas are today being built across the Tibetan Plateau and through multiple Himalayan valleys en route to new Chinese development zones in Nepal and elsewhere in South Asia (Chettri and Eilenberg, 2021; Murton, 2021; Plachta, 2021).

A concurrence of major infrastructure development and increasingly authoritarian policy in Tibet and Xinjiang also shows that blanks on the BRI map can simultaneously support Beijing's pursuit of geopolitical and geoeconomic power by obscuring the specificities of place where human rights abuses are otherwise conspicuous. That is, the fact that BRI maps consistently fail to depict BRI projects in Tibetan and Himalayan regions raises important questions concerning China's own territorializing activities related to restive minority populations (Szadziewski, Mostafanezhad, and Murton, 2022). Why, for example, are roads and rails that run through the Tibetan Autonomous Region all but absent from most BRI maps, even if such infrastructures are ultimately meant to connect with the China–Pakistan Economic Corridor (CPEC)?

Moreover, what problems do Uyghur education-detention centers in Xinjiang present to the smooth and free-flowing infrastructural imaginary of the Eurasian Land Bridge?[1]

While these questions about the implications of rendering BRI development spaces as blanks on the map pertain primarily to minority regions within China, as in the focus of this chapter, they also connect more generally to an important extraterritorial logic that transcends China's geographic borders. To be sure, blanks on the BRI map also range across spaces occupied by Tibetans both within and outside of the People's Republic of China (PRC) as well as numerous locations of territorial dispute between China on the one hand and Nepal, Bhutan, and India on the other. In addition to these geopolitical concerns of cartographic obfuscation, it is also important to consider if development projects undertaken in such "geographic blindspots" (Harris, 2013) are perhaps left blank on the maps because of the inherent risks in building infrastructures across geologically shaky (and geopolitically shifty) landscapes of Tibet and the Himalayas.

Informed by historical processes and practices of mapping empire across Asia (Edney, 1999; Harley, 2001), in this chapter, I examine popular cartographies of the BRI to illustrate and amplify Schatz and Silvey's assertion (introduction, this volume: 14) that "[w]hat is visible or invisible is in part a function of power and how it is conceptualized" as "power is not a simple matter of material disparities." Toward this objective, I argue that cartographic ambiguity is not only at the heart of BRI maps but is itself a discursive practice and performance of strategically eliding what might actually be present and otherwise apparent. In conversation with other chapters comprising this volume and considering that "[w]hether produced by sins of commission or omission, opacity is fairly normal" (Schatz and Silvey, introduction, this volume: 9), I demonstrate that contradictory instances of cartographic ambiguity work to advance China's global ambitions, even if such ambitions are not always accomplished. However, rather than looking squarely at the political or military operations of the PRC or the immediate effects of Xi's authoritarian power on the bodies of subject populations, I instead take an oblique view to the ways in which maps "do [the] work" (Wood, 2010) of advancing and communicating particular territorial interests in contemporary China.

After reviewing some fundamental, historical connections between cartography and empire, this chapter argues that cartographic invisibility—or what goes "missing from the map" in the case of China's current BRI program—paradoxically illustrates a spatial operation of Chinese power in discursive form. In concert with other chapters, I add another critical framework to advance

---

[1] On China's security-first approach to Xinjiang, see Lemon and Jardine, Chapter 1, this volume.

the book's greater goal to disrupt and challenge persistent misconceptions about the BRI. Correcting erroneous notions that a monolithic China follows a coherent policy to advance its neoimperial power and accomplish outsized ambitions, I instead show that BRI maps are also complex and incomplete—just like the BRI itself. In subtle ways, maps help to accomplish goals and reconcile paradoxes: they highlight some BRI imaginaries and hide other ambiguities, from infrastructures that symbolize economic productivity and environmental sustainability to shortcomings related to the (ir)rational (il)logics of China's so-called project of the century itself.

Contexts of the Missing Map and Questions of Visibility

A pioneer in the discursive reading of maps as texts, the eminent critical cartographer J. B. Harley asserted that "it is better to begin from the premise that cartography is *seldom* (but *not always*) what cartographers say it is."[2] Bringing poststructuralist critique to bear on cartography, Harley argued that it is imperative to recognize and amplify particular "cartographic silences" in order to fully understand the power of maps. Emphasizing that maps must be situated and read according to multiple contexts, Harley's analytical framework for cartographic deconstruction includes reading maps as texts according to the context of the cartographer, the context of other maps, and the context of society (Harley, 2001). Applying Harley's framework to three interrelated questions posed by Schatz and Silvey about visibility helps to further contextualize and illuminate the importance of blanks on BRI maps. That is, in relation to the context of the cartographer, we must also consider "how do various BRI actors ... see the BRI?" (Schatz and Silvey, introduction, this volume: 10). Secondly, with respect to the contexts of other maps, one must further ask "what choices do observers of the BRI ... make regarding the BRI as an object of study?" (Schatz and Silvey, introduction, this volume: 10). And third, in the face of many forces working across a range of actors that constitute the context of society, it is imperative to also ask "what do publics affected by the BRI see, how do they locate themselves amid such transformations, and in what ways do these self-understandings invoke the BRI in particular or China more generally?" (Schatz and Silvey, introduction, this volume: 10). When reading BRI maps through these analytical lenses, if "that which is absent from maps is as much a proper field of enquiry as that which is present" (Harley, 2001: 58), what then are we to make of the geographic blind spots located in such centrally important spaces of China's foremost international project of the twenty-first century?

[2] Harley (1989: 2), as cited, with emphasis added, by Andrews (2001: 6).

To be sure, there is no official map of the BRI. The BRI is an idea, not a thing: it is a discursive vision rather than a coherent project. It is a policy agenda comprising major transportation infrastructures like roads and railways as well as education and humanitarian enterprises in the shape of schools and hospitals; even more, it also includes the development of broader mobile connections via telecommunication networks and diplomatic relationships. That is, the BRI is material and social, physical and political (Oliveira et al., 2020; Sidaway et al., 2020). As a dynamic and ever-evolving project of global ambition motivated by Chinese ideologies of "going out" (Yeh and Wharton, 2016), the BRI cannot be mapped as a two-dimensional cartographic still life. And yet, despite this expansive ambiguity, the BRI has been reified by advocates and critics alike. This includes think tank pundits and policy experts who identify and enunciate the Belt and Road as a development project that will connect and modernize (or threaten and destabilize) the world like never before (Schatz and Silvey, introduction, this volume) to constituents of Chinese development projects in BRI recipient countries, including in places like Nepal where such BRI projects have barely taken any shape in material form (Murton, 2024; Paudel, 2021). Accordingly, Harley's cartographers can be seen as the very "BRI actors" for whom it is imperative to celebrate, trumpet, and announce the grandeur of the BRI even while centrally important aspects of the initiative are left unsaid or actively concealed in cartographic form. From Chinese Communist Party (CCP) cadres to activists in rural Nepal, the BRI often gets work done by its name alone (Murton and Lord, 2020). But who then truly is "the cartographer," and why is there no definitive or official map?

While a singular map of the BRI may well be impossible to produce, it is surely no accident that no official map exists. A trove of reports, agreements, plans, and documents has filled the website of the PRC's official Belt and Road Portal (Belt and Road Portal, 2019, 2021), and yet this state-led mouthpiece nevertheless neglects to map its eponymous self. Moreover, it is critical to see that this is in no way accidental. As Narins and Agnew argue (2019), a "missing map" has allowed the BRI to exist and operate as both concrete and ethereal, a "useful fuzziness" that makes the BRI appear inevitable but at the same time flexible (if not also wholly uncertain). Having already committed over $1 trillion toward a myriad number of infrastructure projects comprising the BRI (Lai, Lin, and Sidaway, 2020), the CCP could surely have built a sophisticated GIS platform to document, track, and project the latest and greatest aspects of the Initiative. But this is not underway, and it is unlikely to happen. As Oakes (2021, original emphasis) states in *The BRI as an Exercise in Infrastructural Thinking*,

The hole in the middle of the Belt and Road—a hole where there should have been plans and policies [and a map]—was *intentional*. Where actual content

might be expected to be clarified and laid-out, there was instead a sort-of "fill
in the blank" space. The Belt and Road was only ever meant to be a vague idea,
a notion, a gesture, the beginning of a sentence waiting to be completed by
someone else.... We all love filling in the blank.

Although no *official* BRI map exists, a great number of unofficial BRI maps circulate around the world; that is, in Harley's formulation, there are indeed many
"other maps." As such, it becomes productive to further inquire not only, "what
choices do observers of the BRI make regarding their object of study?," but also,
"how do they construct their observational efforts, and how do they see their
own roles in relation to this knowledge production? What do these acts of construction illuminate and what do they leave in shadow?" (Schatz and Silvey, introduction, this volume: 10). To be sure, countless "other" BRI maps emphasize
the six major "Economic Corridors" comprising the Silk Road Economic Belt;
still others prioritize the "Maritime Silk Road" as a host of sea lanes running from
the South China Sea to the Atlantic and Arctic Oceans and all places in between.
A close look at a representative sample of these maps reveals general and consistent patterns of what is normally depicted where, including the CPEC and the
Bangladesh–China–India–Myanmar Economic Corridor (BCIM-EC). And yet
a great number of other projects that frequently fit into various BRI cartographic
landscapes are nevertheless illustrated more sparingly or inconsistently. These
include, for example, the new and dubious Hambantota seaport in Sri Lanka[3]
as well as the historical megaport of Rotterdam at the western terminus of the
BRI's ambitious Eurasian Land Bridge. For example, a quick look at two widely
circulated and oft-cited maps produced by MERICS (Figure 5.1) and the Leiden
Asia Centre (Figure 5.2) illustrate the geographical contexts and most common
particulars of some of these "other maps."

When it comes to cartographic invisibility, these popular maps are consistent in two key ways. First, they emphasize the primary corridors and
major development priorities of the BRI such as CPEC, BCIM-EC, and other
megainfrastructures as discussed earlier. Second, the maps largely neglect other
important development programs in regions where BRI projects are formalized
and highly public undertakings. Even a quick glance shows this to be evidently
true with respect to Tibet, Nepal, and much of the wider South Asian region.
This omission betrays yet another paradox, as BRI developments in such "invisible regions" are in fact located within close proximity to the primary BRI development corridors themselves.

In the case of this analysis, a close look at Tibet and the Himalayas suggests
that nothing much is going on there in terms of BRI development and that it·

---

[3] See Narins, Chapter 2, this volume.

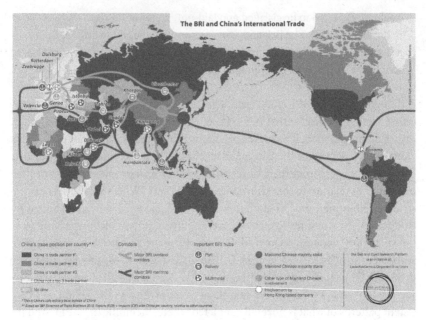

Figure 5.2 Map: *The BRI and China's International Trade.* Source: The Belt and Road Research Platform, Leiden Asia Centre (2021)

is best rendered as a mere blank on the map—an empty space in between the greater commitments to corridors being made in Pakistan and Burma. But it is precisely the interests in and commitments to the BRI for "society" in these blank spaces that must be considered in Harley's third context as well. Following this line of thinking with respect to Harley's tripartite framework in turn requires a more localized analysis of what is empirically evident on the ground with the BRI. This is, of course, true not just on the map, but in everyday life as well.

A view to Nepal, Tibet, and the Himalayas effectively grounds this cartographic study in a "sensitive space" (Cons, 2019) that is a significant target for BRI investment and development. To be clear, attention to this trans-Himalayan region productively illuminates how "cartographic anxieties" themselves (Krishna, 1994)—or place-based societal concerns that motivate distinct territorial action by the state—are frequently rendered blanks on most BRI maps, even while the presence of the BRI is far from invisible or nonexistent in everyday life for innumerable peoples across these very same areas. For example, the so-called Sky Train extension of the Qinghai–Tibet railroad from the Tibetan Plateau down into Nepal is hardly an unknown or irrelevant project. Indeed, it is a central piece of the nine Belt and Road projects that the Government of Nepal signed with the CCP in 2019 (Murton and Plachta, 2021).

Anticipation of an international railroad running into and through Nepal ran especially high in the months immediately following the 2nd Belt and Road Forum in Beijing in April–May 2019 (Paudel, 2021), when the project was discussed officially between Nepali and Chinese leaders. A highly publicized diplomatic achievement, energy and hopefulness around the "Sky Train" grew exponentially with Xi Jinping's official state visit to Nepal in October 2019, when the project was again a key topic of conversation. And yet nearly five years after such earnest discussions on the railroad, no concretely significant work on the project has been completed to date, and progress has not moved beyond stalled discussions over initial Environmental Impact Assessments and financial modalities for undertaking the project (Murton, 2023).

However, beyond the conspicuous and yet nonexistent "Sky Train" and eight other largely unrealized BRI projects in Nepal, numerous other BRI initiatives exist in proximate areas of South Asia and beyond. Some of these have been materially successful and others remain merely fanciful, as will be discussed in more detail. More importantly, from Nepal and Tibet to Bangladesh and the Maldives, a vast array of BRI programs remains missing from the map. And that is, I argue, not only highly problematic but also a strategically effective form of spatial and territorial logic employed by China's leaders.

Histories of Cartography as a Territorial Tool

In *Rethinking the Power of Maps*, Denis Wood provides an introduction to the philosophy and practice of critical cartography. At the very outset of the book, Wood proposes that maps do all kinds of political things: "maps do work"; "maps operate effectively"; "maps leverage words"; "maps apply social forces"; and "maps convert energy to work by linking things in space" (Wood, 2010: 1). Arguing that maps are fundamentally (if not nothing more than) a "discourse function" that advances the power and interests of the central state, Wood's poststructuralist critique of cartography reveals the many ways in which maps reinforce authority with textual force. Motivated by Wood's provocations, an examination of BRI maps—and the lack thereof of an official BRI map—shows some of the ways by which the CCP has communicated cartographically and leveraged sociopolitical power through the broader discursive currency of the BRI. In the geohistorical context of territorial practice and imperial anxiety expressed cartographically, the lack of geospatial accuracy in BRI maps even reiterates previous global powers' intentional "mis-mapping" of their territorial dominions, such as the Spanish Crown's selective mapping of the Americas in the 15th–16th centuries, as explained next.

It is well established that cartography was central to European imperial expansion, such that mapping was both a strategic "state of the art" and an imperial "art of the state" (Mundy, 1996: 11). As a fundamental tool of empire, maps allowed the authoritative power of the metropole to not just imagine but actually see and approximately know its peripheral domains. However, this cartographic knowledge was itself a precious resource, and thus protection and manipulation of the map were also a form of imperial artistry. In the context of the Spanish Empire in Mexico, "the space of the nation was not pictured as autonomous and competitive cities, but as a continuous and politically undifferentiated geographic expanse" (Mundy, 1996: 6). As such, from Isabella and Ferdinand to Phillip II, the cartographic project to know, show, and control the Spanish Empire with maps became a task of supreme importance.

Moving from the 17th to 19th centuries, in *Cartographic Mexico*, Raymond Craib (2004) shows that national maps of postcolonial Mexico served as a strategic "stage" for the production and consolidation of more forceful state power. Conceptualizing the "stage" metaphorically for the ways in which space is coordinated, captured, displayed, and performed, Craib's critical cartographic analysis works to reconcile tensions between historical and geographic approaches to time and space, respectively. In the case of Mexico, that is, the map as stage functioned to control space (a stage for actors) and to observe time (in stages of history). And yet, as a way to "see through the space of history" (Carter, 2010: xiv, quoted in Craib, 2004: 3), Craib's stage thus serves as another analytical platform to reveal how maps work to cartographically transform space into territory. It is then by projecting that representation to wider populations that the state asserts its territorial authority.

In the context of China today, the BRI is surely a stage from which Beijing announces, performs, and communicates its global ambitions.[4] The illustration of economic corridors throughout Central Asia emphasizes China's outsized role in connecting East Asia with Europe just as railways and pipelines to the Arctic Ocean and Arabian Sea index the imagined advent of a greater Chinese presence along historical and future sea lanes of world trade. And yet, what is seen on the stage is of course only partial at best, as blanks left on the map allow for the pursuit of development projects in places where politics remain highly sensitive and territorial anxieties abound. This, then, is just one of the many ways that BRI

[4] Whether or not the PRC constitutes a modern empire, or "neoimperial" power, is of course a topic of great (and far from resolved) debate. Scholarship taking up this issue runs through numerous disciplines, from humanistic methodologies in history and Asian studies to more quantitative and positivist approaches of political science and economics to recent critical and grounded analyses in geography, development sociology, and other social sciences.

maps' "fuzziness" can be so useful (Narins and Agnew, 2020), and this despite the CCP's truly advanced digital technologies and cartographic capacities.[5]

In other historical contexts, the British East India Company's scientific development of advanced trigonometric practices enabled an unprecedented expansion of colonial power across Asia and the wider world in the 18th and 19th centuries (Fleetwood, 2022; Gardner, 2021). For British interests in the Indian subcontinent, Mughal India was reimagined and became a "real" colony of the crown as a function of cartography (Edney, 1999; Ramaswamy, 2017). A truly epistemological transformation, cartographic knowledge and representation in India—or the way that maps and globes made people see the world in particularly new and European (or Cartesian) ways—facilitated a further diffusion of the imperial gaze. As a consequence of the Great Trigonometric Survey of India and the normalization of its cartographic assumptions, India was transformed from a collection of princely states partially consolidated under the Mughal Empire into a singular entity framed and controlled by the British Empire (Edney, 1999). Having organized the subcontinent's multiple places and vast territories into a legible space to be ruled, Britain created yet another new way to see and know its empire, a spatial practice of territorial visibility that was subsequently rationalized and expanded—via maps—to more distant corners of the earth as well.

How then has BRI planning also consolidated distant places into what is promoted and imagined by the Chinese state as a coordinated if not altogether coherent space? Although the territorial scope of the BRI is surely not one of direct rule akin to the British Raj in India, the BRI nevertheless appears as intended to extend China's political economic reach and territorial power into countless distant landscapes across the continents. Might we critically ask, then, if this effort is not so unlike a modernist and digitized rendition of the red-colored dominions mapped as the British Empire, where the sun was said to never set? Moreover, while many of the most widely circulated BRI maps illustrate only a small selection of priority megaprojects, China's potential infrastructural reach to Europe, Africa, the South Pacific, and even the Arctic is increasingly normalized and depicted definitively. Beyond these territorial targets of development, however, a key blind spot that remains missing from BRI maps betrays some of the very same blanks on the British maps of previous imperial eras (Shipton, 2010)—once again, it is Tibet and the broader Himalayan region.

While brief, the historical examples underscore the enduring importance of cartographic science (and silence) for imperial, territorial, political, and economic power. As Harley states, "the power of the map, an act of control over

---

[5] For a timely and critical analysis of China's Digital Silk Road, for example, see Kaufmann, Chapter 7, this volume.

the image of the world, is like the power of print in general. Since the age of Columbus, maps have helped to create some of the most pervasive stereotypes of our world" (2001: 49). As social constructions, maps thus generate and convey a special kind of spatial power. In order to advance a state's political projects, the map thus becomes not merely art or science, a stage or image, but an ideology. That is, much like the census and the museum in Benedict Anderson's historical study of the making of nationalism in Southeast Asia and Latin America (2006), the map likewise enables a state to become itself.

As the cartographic form allows state making to happen, historical and iconological analysis—to "explore the discourse of maps in the context of political power" (Harley, 2001: 53)—can in turn illuminate the critical relationship between a state and its map. As Harley states, "Cartographers manufacture power. They create a spatial panopticon. It is a power embedded in the map text . . . [m]aps have politics. It is a power that intersects and is embedded in knowledge. It is universal" (Harley, 2001: 21–22). To be sure, not only do maps have politics, and their own kind of power, but there can also be a contradictory relationship between the cartographic picture and its power. That is, the political power manufactured via the cartographic text is deployed not just by what is mapped therein but also, paradoxically, by what is left out and missing from the map itself.

China's Downstream Extraterritorial Concerns, or, What to Do about Tibetans in Nepal

No shortage of ink has been spilled in mapping the BRI, but little of that ink has belonged to Beijing, nor has much been spent filling in infrastructure development projects across the Himalayan region. From think tanks and leading media outlets to academic journals, corporate consultants, and the World Bank, maps of the BRI abound. While the details of planned BRI roads, rails, sea lanes, and other transport infrastructures appear to have increased in cartographic granularity and real-time accuracy (Center for Strategic and International Studies, 2021), BRI infrastructure crossing the Tibetan Plateau and descending the Himalayan range into South Asia remains all but absent from the vast majority of cartographic renderings. For example, recent World Bank publications on the potential global economic impacts of the BRI are but one testament to this persistent invisibility.

Both the stylized BRI "subway" map (Figure 5.3) depicted on the cover of World Bank's *Belt and Road Economics: Opportunities and Risks of Transport Corridors* (2019) and the more statistically analytical cartography (Figure 5.4) created for "Assessing the Value of Market Access from Belt and Road Projects"

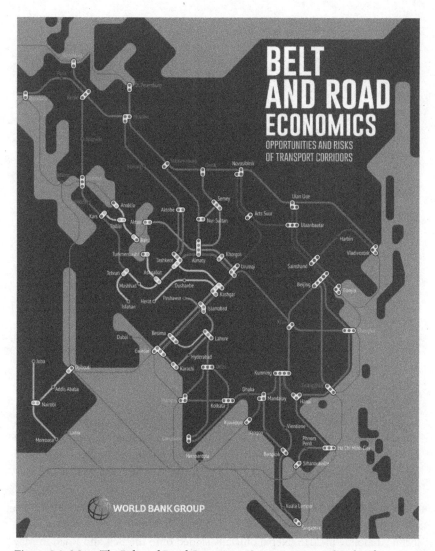

Figure 5.3 Map: *The Belt and Road Economics: Opportunities and Risks of Transport Corridors.* Source: World Bank (2019)

(Reed and Trubetskoy, 2020) continue to reproduce many of the same recurring blanks on the BRI map. On the one hand, China is time and again shown to be a leading force for development between Pakistan and the Caspian region, as well as along the eastern seaboard of the African continent and throughout peninsular Southeast Asia, among many other spaces. Corridors into Mongolia, Russia, and Central Europe continue to recycle the great Silk Road tropes, as

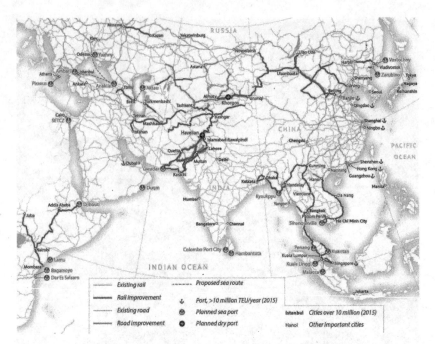

Figure 5.4 Map: *BRI Improvements in Eurasia.* Source: adapted from Reed and Trubetskoy (2020)

Beijing would have it (Sidaway and Woon, 2017).[6] And yet, on the other hand, some of the largest and most ambitious development initiatives ever promoted in Nepal, which are themselves BRI projects extending from other BRI-related infrastructural programs in China's Tibet Autonomous Region, are consistently missing.

Nepal has been part of the BRI movement since it was first articulated from and promoted by Beijing as the One Belt One Road program. Beginning with formal dialogue in 2015, Nepal officially signed onto the Belt and Road in May 2017 with a proposal of 35 BRI development projects for the country. Primarily focused on construction in the energy and transport sectors as well as the creation of new economic corridors and special economic zones, Nepal's original BRI vision was estimated to require significant investments upward of $10 billion (Murton and Plachta, 2021). However, after Beijing balked at such levels of BRI investment for Nepal, protracted negotiations brought Kathmandu's BRI development target down to a select nine key projects. This comprised four road projects connecting central Nepal with roads and trading centers along

---

[6] See also Kaneti, Chapter 4, this volume.

China's Tibetan border, including Rasuwagadhi–Kathmandu, Tokha–Bidu, Kimathanka–Hile, and Dipayal; two hydroelectric power projects, including the 762 MW Tamor Hydropower and the 426 MW Phukot Karnali Hydroelectric projects; the Galchhi–Rasuwagadhi–Kyirong 400 kv transmission line; construction of the Kyirong–Kathmandu railroad (otherwise known as the "Sky Train"); and the Madan Bhandari Technical Institute, named after a previous communist leader of Nepal (Murton and Plachta, 2021).

Complementing this BRI framework for Nepal, Kathmandu and Beijing also reached agreements at the Second Belt and Road Forum in April 2019 to coordinate new policy procedures for greater trade and transport connectivity as well as bilateral commitments to surveillance and security of human populations across the countries' Himalayan borderlands. This comes forth most conspicuously in Nepal's rearticulation of its observance of the "One China Policy"[7] and many of the conditions embedded within the Nepal–China Trans-Himalayan Multi-dimensional Connectivity Network (THMDCN). Most importantly, such infrastructure-meets-security mechanisms—or what I have elsewhere conceptualized as a form of Sino-Nepali "infrastructural relations" (Murton, 2020)—entails a truly bilateral agenda, as the THMDCN project prioritizes the operationalization of six economic corridors between Nepal and China with enhanced border facilities for trade and security as well as advanced transport infrastructure.[8] And still, very few international BRI maps depict any of the components of this *Connectivity Network*, let alone any other BRI projects in Nepal.

It has become evident that BRI development programs between Nepal and China are increasingly connected to transborder, bilateral security regimes. Yet another mechanism to assuage Beijing's anxieties over restive Tibetan populations both inside and outside of the PRC, the *List of Instruments Signed and Exchanged between Nepal and China* in October 2019 during Xi Jinping's state visit to Nepal following the 2nd Belt and Road Forum outlines several new surveillance systems inextricably linked to BRI projects. Most conspicuous of these mechanisms are the *Agreement between the Governments of Nepal and the PRC on the Boundary Management System*, the *Treaty between Nepal and the PRC on Mutual Legal Assistance in Criminal Matters*, and the *Exchange of*

---

[7] Concerning the relationship between the PRC's "One China" policy and its comanagement of both domestic space and international relations, Szadziewksi et al. (2022: 138) write, "The One-China narrative has evolved from the One China policy, a condition of diplomatic relations with the PRC designating the administration in Beijing as sole sovereign over the territories of 'China,' to a totalizing state practice of spatial and social fusion incorporating China's border and heartlands. This practice is totalizing in the sense that technological surveillance has compressed the management of space; as a result, the state is able to identify and modify through disciplinary measures behaviors that deviate from Party and Han norms."

[8] In Chapter 8 of this volume, Dall'Agnola also explores this relationship between economic corridors, international trade, and state security in Central Asia.

Letter for Border Security Equipment and Office Equipment (Ministry of Foreign Affairs, 2019).

It is worth noting that such "infrastructural security cooperation is especially prominent in border areas, which are themselves traditionally home to a large number of culturally Tibetan communities. Control over these minority groups has long been a central concern of the Chinese Communist Party" (Murton and Plachta, 2021: 337). As such, foreign investment and BRI development in Nepal indicates just some of the ways that Chinese actors implement new surveillance operations and leverage extraterritorial influence over what Beijing considers Tibetan-related threats beyond the PRC. And yet, the Belt and Road linkage between infrastructure development and control over Tibetan populations does not appear to be something mapped from Beijing—at least not in any publicly available channels. Nor do the human rights politics of BRI development seem to have been mapped by other infrastructure analysts or cartographers working in the relevant fields of human security studies or policy-oriented think tank outlets, for that matter.

From the beginning, Tibet itself has been central to BRI development for both geographical and political reasons. According to the Tibetan historian and policy analyst Tsering Shakya (2018),

> [T]here are some imperatives that place Tibet within the core objective of the Belt and Road strategy. There is a growing disparity in development between the coastal regions, and Tibet and the Western provinces; they remain the poorest in all economic and social indices. Tibet's economy has mostly depended on state subsidies. Under the Western Development project.... China has focused on developing infrastructure, roads, railway and power supply to facilitate the industrialisation of the area. China sees this as a way of addressing inequalities between the regions. This unequal development—and the geographical, cultural and ethnic divide between the rest of China and Tibet (and other areas with minority groups)—is seen as accentuating local nationalisms, manifesting in incidents like protests.

From the urban enclaves of Tibet to the riverside villages of Nepal, the BRI is not only present across the Himalayas but has become a truly conspicuous and discursive force even if the region is routinely elided as a blank on many BRI maps. Going well beyond the promises of given BRI projects in Nepal, I have elsewhere conceived of this form of political power related to Chinese development capacity as a particular kind of "presence" (Murton, 2024). This presence has been felt, perceived, and experienced by a range of constituents subject to China's investment and development agenda across the Himalayan region (Murton, 2023: 13):

> [T]he discursive power of China's presence throughout Nepal is evident in two fundamental but paradoxical ways. First, innumerable Chinese development projects are identified and called BRI even when they have nothing to do with the BRI. In public conversation as well as popular perception across the country, decidedly non-BRI projects—such as rural hydropower and road development programs or post-earthquake urban reconstruction efforts that are not included in Nepal's nine-project BRI framework—are called "BRI" because the Belt and Road has brand recognition and instils confidence in Nepali constituents; in other words, the BRI gets work done in name alone. Second and conversely, actual BRI projects are relatively invisible, sometimes because very little work has yet been accomplished and, at other times, because such projects are routinely absent from cartographic representations.

To be sure, even when BRI projects are not illustrated in cartographic form, the discursive power of the Belt and Road nevertheless continues to "do [the] work" that Wood (2010) conceptualizes as the fundamental "power of maps." As a multitude of studies have shown, elite political actors and rural communities alike routinely embrace and enunciate particular visions of the BRI as potential futures of imagined modernity (Oliveira et al., 2020).

As argued elsewhere with respect to Nepal, analysis of the BRI—blanks and all—shows how "politics are articulated through infrastructural developments and, vice versa, how infrastructures also articulate political relations" (Murton and Lord, 2020: 2). In conversation with these other cases both in and beyond Nepal, I hope to join an expanding chorus about the uneven intersections of BRI development. In doing so, this can help to amplify what Schatz and Silvey identify as the critical importance of seeing the BRI in new and different ways, contributing to further analyses that attend "to the social meanings that those involved with BRI-related transformations bring to their acts, including their choices to reveal or to conceal" (introduction, this volume: 10).

Conclusion: China's Cartographic Anxieties

In *Mapping: A Critical Introduction*, Jeremy Crampton (2010) begins by identifying two important "silences" that exist in relation to power in the cartographic tradition. First is the silence of cultural and political geographers in terms of not critically engaging with mapping and cartography. Second is the obverse tradition of GIS practitioners and contemporary cartographers not engaging with critical theory in the geographic tradition and fully addressing the sociopolitical power of maps. In response to Crampton's call, my own task in this chapter has been to bridge these two divides and in so doing employ methods of critical cartography to illuminate how Chinese power moves with and through maps. As I have argued, this kind of analysis is especially important insofar as what is, and is *not*, depicted on the maps themselves. And so rather than taking a positivist approach to cartography—which itself is routinely (mis)construed as a predominantly positivist science—I have instead followed Harley's "non-positivist" framework to read maps not as the world they purport to depict but rather "inwards and backwards to its maker[s] and outwards or forwards to its readers" (2001: 6).

Taking the mapping of BRI development as a place and process of inquiry, this chapter also puts critical cartography to work with the "infrastructural inversion" (Bowker and Star, 1999; Rippa, Murton, and Rest, 2020) to illustrate and highlight what ordinarily appears invisible. This allows one to see how the BRI operates to extend and communicate China's spatial power through the infrastructure of maps themselves. But because my analysis is merely preliminary and the BRI continues to expand as both material projects on the ground and discursive formations that circulate between Beijing and the rest of the world, ongoing analyses must also examine the multiple ways by which BRI programs are imagined, implemented, and mapped across global and local scales. Without a doubt,

> China's BRI is not a monolithic program designed in Beijing and imposed upon others. Rather, it is better understood as a bundle of intertwined discourses, policies, and projects that sometimes align and are sometimes contradictory. Focusing on these entanglements inverts analysis of the BRI from a top-down coherent strategy to a relational, contested process that occurs in specific places. (Oliveira et al., 2020: 1)

Keeping these relational and contested processes in mind, it remains true that unmapped BRI development projects—particularly in the form of roads and railways crisscrossing the Himalayas between Tibet and Nepal—indeed do work to accomplish many of China's ambitious objectives of territorialization in the 21st century. Moreover, the very "cartographic anxieties" that these projects often obfuscate also index the stubborn and sensitive ways in which states imagine and project themselves via maps. According to Crampton (2010: 9), on the one hand maps are incredibly powerful devices for creating knowledge and trapping people within their cool gleaming grid lines, on the other hand they seem to be nothing at all, just mere bits of fluff in the air. Maps are sovereign; maps are dead.

Following these critiques, it remains important to ask once again what BRI maps are worth and what they do for China today. As fuzzy blanks on the map belie Beijing's commitments to infrastructural development, they also advance China's geoeconomic and geopolitical priorities, all the while obscuring place-based experiences where extraterritorial power is sometimes extreme but not always conspicuous. As such, it is essential to critically consider the political and social implications of such maps, and to bear in mind that what is seen cartographically is sometimes hardly half the story of what is really being done on the ground. To end with Crampton's formulation, while vague and intentionally ambiguous, BRI maps are surely not dead, and the work they do, even in spaces that remain absent of cartographic detail, is nevertheless central to Beijing's exercise of spatial power against vast territorial concerns.

6

Behind the Spectacle of the Belt and Road Initiative

Corridor Perspectives, In/visibility, and

a Politics of Sight

Jessica DiCarlo

Introduction

China's Belt and Road Initiative (BRI) is frequently characterized as elusive and difficult to define. More than a decade into the initiative, commentators, policymakers, and the media continue to grapple to understand its intentions, its effects, and what projects "count" as the BRI. The BRI's dynamic nature only adds to its complexity. Indeed, "ambiguity lies at [its] heart" (Schatz and Silvey, introduction, this volume: 8). However, this inherent elusiveness, rather than being a puzzle to solve, points to important areas for inquiry. Some argue that the BRI is deliberately vague, only meant to be "a notion, a gesture, the beginning of a sentence waiting to be completed by someone else" (Oakes, 2021). From this perspective, ambiguity allows the BRI to adapt to different contexts and remain flexible for the purposes of both the state and capital (Braga and Sangar, 2020). In this way, the BRI is not a rigid policy, but an aspirational statement that invites imaginative interpretations of its lines and corridors (Oakes, 2021).

While the initiative may be difficult to define, its visibility and deployment of spectacle are undeniable. Ambitious endeavors, from regional train systems and new cities to colossal dams and ports, are markers of the BRI. As a result, BRI corridors across the globe have been inundated with concrete, commodities, people, and massive projects that symbolize state power and progress. Such infrastructural ambitions are hypervisible, constructed as objects of great fanfare, and embody not only progress but also immense potential. The spectacle of the BRI, I suggest, lies in the interplay between its ambiguous omnipresence and the massive, hypervisible projects.

However, the spectacle animating the BRI can obscure more than it reveals. Political and public attention often focuses on the scale of projects or speculates

Jessica DiCarlo, *Behind the Spectacle of the Belt and Road Initiative* In: Seeing China's Belt and Road. Edited by: Edward Schatz and Rachel Silvey, Oxford University Press. © Oxford University Press 2025. DOI: 10.1093/oso/9780197789261.003.0007 on Chinese intentions behind them, occluding the less visible practices and effects that underpin and sustain its production and the BRI's concrete, localized, and context-dependent manifestations. As this volume demonstrates, the BRI's story is one of rapidly shifting and highly differentiated social meanings, yet views of the BRI are often homogenized. For example, I am often confronted with the question "What do people in X country (here, Laos) think about the BRI?" This chapter seeks to reorient this line of questioning. It offers a partial answer while reminding us not to view countries and their populations as homogenous in intention or perspective. Human experiences, uneven effects, differentiated views, and complex social relations and politics lie behind the hypervisible spectacle of the BRI. With this in mind, I develop insights on the BRI's differentiated downstream effects.[1]

Drawing on the viewpoints of residents, Chinese workers, and officials across northern Laos, I ask how people see the BRI. For whom is the BRI hypervisible or invisible, and what might either obscure? What do these perspectives reveal about the BRI and China's global integration? Lastly, I probe what seeing or *not* seeing the BRI means for global China. To address these questions, I attend to the everyday experiences of BRI infrastructure through a politics of sight. In doing so, I amplify Schatz and Silvey's claim, as laid out in this volume's introduction, that the political, cultural, and social effects of the BRI are a function of what is rendered visible and what is kept concealed. Through a politics of sight, I hold the promise of development and infrastructure in tension with less visible forms of infrastructural ambiguity and violence. This approach also addresses a critical challenge of studying Chinese infrastructure-led development: to balance China's rising power with local dynamics, contingency, and agency. Both are central to the production of the BRI.

This chapter extends conceptual and theoretical engagements with infrastructure by examining how projects are seen locally, as well as the social and political ramifications of different ways of seeing. My approach illuminates the downstream effects and experiences for Chinese and Lao people alike. While hope and aspiration feature prominently, projects often result in a significant disparity between the intentions motivating the initiative and the lived experiences of those involved. I thus address two important aspects in global China scholarship: dynamics within host countries and more grounded and granular understandings of how China operates globally (Klinger and Muldavin, 2019; Lee, 2017; Lu, 2021; Yeh, 2016), recognizing that BRI extends beyond planners and policymakers to differently affect people in its processes of becoming.

Through a *follow-the-corridor* approach, this chapter offers a mobile and patchwork ethnography of an economic corridor across northern Laos (see

---

[1] See also Fei, Chapter 9, this volume.

DiCarlo, 2021). In contrast to ethnography rooted in one location, my research relied on movement within the corridor and returning to the same places over multiple visits. The fieldwork for this chapter encompassed a variety of locations, including construction sites, homes, and offices throughout the Laos–China Corridor between 2017 and 2023. In my conceptualization, the corridor offers an opportunity to examine global China's infrastructural engagements from diverse vantage points. This approach illustrates the BRI's simultaneous ambiguity and spectacle by moving beyond elusive corridor maps and highly visible projects to the ground. I build on the river analogy discussed in this book's conclusion, extending the gaze "downstream" to develop a politics of sight associated with the BRI.

In the next section, I suggest reading the BRI through the politics of sight to theorize the infrastructure's visibility on a spectrum, probing how BRI projects are seen and the ramifications of different ways of seeing. I then outline three key BRI projects in Laos that have informed public and political visions of development and shape how people see or do not see the BRI. The following section brings readers to the corridor to analyze the visions and blind spots of people engaged in and affected by infrastructural becoming. The chapter concludes by reflecting on how corridor perspectives in northern Laos challenge and provide nuance to our understandings of the BRI and its effects.

Infrastructure, In/visibility, and the Politics of Sight

This chapter builds on Oakes's (2021) provocation to use an infrastructural analysis to understand BRI development impacts as they unfold. Infrastructure's dual nature makes it conceptually intriguing: it is both a thing and a relation among things (Anand, Gupta, and Appel, 2018; Larkin, 2013). It is thus not only an object of study but a powerful analytical framework that illuminates the intricate interdependencies within a system. Infrastructure encompasses the tangible elements that enable the flow and functioning of other entities (e.g., roads, pipes, and wires). Such objects, intricate interconnected systems themselves, serve as the foundation on which other systems operate (Larkin, 2013: 329). Infrastructure often presents as a vast, expansive, and all-encompassing network that resists traditional social frameworks and methodologies (Harvey, Jensen, and Morita, 2016). It extends beyond the visible and concrete to the less visible: from digital technologies to practices like the construction process, and calculative technology, statecraft, or spectacle.

The infrastructural turn in the social sciences produced compelling analytical lenses through concepts of visibility and invisibility. Scholars contend that infrastructure often becomes visible upon breakdown (Star, 1999). However, even without disruption or breakdown, infrastructure is inherently visible and present, a spectacle that showcases state power while seamlessly integrating into daily life (Larkin, 2013; Schwenkel, 2015). In some cases, visibility is the whole point. When presented as a spectacle, infrastructure can evoke both awe and fear.[2] Infrastructure embodies the promise of state power, advancement, and societal development; however, infrastructure's ubiquity makes it less visible. This dual nature as both a spectacle and an everyday backdrop illustrates the complex interplay between visibility and invisibility. Infrastructure simultaneously captivates attention through its grandeur and fades into the background through its pervasive presence.

Infrastructure then is productively understood on a spectrum of visibility, ranging from opacity to spectacle. At one end of the spectrum, infrastructure may remain relatively concealed or opaque, functionally blending into the background. Underground systems, communication networks, and logistical frameworks often go unnoticed until a malfunction. The other end of the spectrum includes infrastructure designed to be highly visible and spectacular, symbols of power, progress, or national identity. These projects are often monumental in scale, visually striking, and capable of attracting local and global attention and of contributing to narratives of modernity, development, or legitimacy (as we shall see with the Laos–China Railway [LCR]). Importantly, this is not a binary; infrastructure can simultaneously exhibit varying degrees of visibility. Recognizing this spectrum helps us appreciate how infrastructure shapes societies, as it can potentially be both subtle and unnoticed and grand and captivating. The visibility of infrastructure can influence perceptions, generate social and political meanings, and shape collective experiences.

The spectrum of visibility raises important questions about how infrastructure is perceived and experienced. I suggest approaching the BRI through what Pachirat (2011) termed a "politics of sight." Pachirat's research on slaughterhouses suggests that the politics of sight involves revealing what has been hidden to bring about political or social change. Other scholars have expanded on Pachirat's work by exploring the dynamics of social violence in contexts of slums and slum tourism (Davis, 2006; Henry, 2020). These studies demonstrate how violence is often outsourced or concealed to make it less visible. Infrastructure development projects, too, are sites where violence is hidden or obscured (DiCarlo, 2024), particularly by the commonsense logic of projects as progress, or what Gurung (2021) called "infrastructural orthodoxies." Infrastructure promises to benefit certain segments of the population while disregarding or concealing the violence endured by others. This hidden violence is often accepted as an inherent feature of infrastructure development. Applying

---

[2] For example, consider Larkin's (2020) concept of the colonial sublime.

a politics of sight to infrastructure makes visible the uneven development, dis-possession, unequal labor practices, and performances of different bodies across the corridor. This approach illuminates tensions between spectacular state-led infrastructure development, which I turn to in the next section, and everyday encounters that condition people's lives and sustain the BRI.

Laos and BRI Megaprojects

Laos is situated within the China–Indochina Peninsula Economic Corridor, one of six BRI economic corridors. The country joined the BRI in 2016 after signing a memorandum of understanding to collaboratively develop a BRI plan with the Chinese government. The first master plan was drafted in May 2017, and Laos is also included in provincial BRI plans with Guangxi, Sichuan, and Yunnan provinces. Flagship projects include connective infrastructures such as roads, railways, and ports. Additionally, investors have proposed smaller-scale investments within the corridor, encompassing tourism, agriculture, new cities, logistics, small and medium enterprises, and special economic zones.

This chapter is centered around three interrelated megaprojects that are em-blematic of the BRI: the LCR, the Laos–China Economic Corridor (LCEC), and Boten Special Economic Zone (SEZ) (Figure 6.1). First, the LCR, a sec-tion of the Kunming–Singapore Railway, is significant for China's vision for the Pan-Asia Railway network and serves as the backbone of the regional corridor. Construction on the 414-km standard-gauge railway commenced in 2016 and was completed in late 2021. Widespread debates have emerged about the po-tential benefits for Laos and the impacts on local communities, while boosting tourism to Laos.

Second, in a visit to Vientiane in November 2017, Chinese President Xi Jinping introduced the LCEC to enhance integration with China, foster devel-opment in Laos, and attract investment along the railway. This vision echoed on a front-page headline in the *Vientiane Times* (Vaenkeo, 2018) proclaiming that the railway would encourage the establishment of SEZs and offer opportunities to attract foreign investment, diversify the economy, and reduce dependence on natural resources. Across Southeast Asia, corridors and zones have re-emerged as tools of development and accumulation. Despite their past failures, the trans-formative potential of railway connectivity elevated the LCEC and several SEZs to the status of flagship BRI projects.

Together, the railway, corridor, and BRI have helped revive Boten SEZ. Boten has witnessed dramatic transformations over the past two decades, evolving from a remote border crossing in the pre-2000s to a booming casino town be-tween 2007 and 2011. It declined from 2011 to 2015, only to be revived under

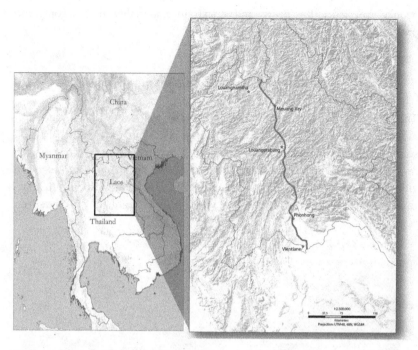

Figure 6.1 Route of the Laos–China Railway and Laos–China Economic Corridor in northern Laos. Source: Author.

a new city plan; it has been an active construction site and city in the making since 2016 (DiCarlo, 2022). Under a new Chinese developer, the SEZ is being refashioned into an urban and tourism center, as well as a trade and logistics hub. While these developments are largely driven by private sector investment, the developer has leaned on the BRI to legitimize its projects in Laos. Boten has emerged as a high-priority project for the Chinese and the Lao governments, garnering special attention due to its strategic position and potential to connect Southeast Asia and the southern Chinese province of Yunnan.

These three projects have garnered attention with their scale, spectacle, and promise, symbolizing the essence of the BRI in Laos and Southeast Asia broadly. As recently as 2023, Lao Deputy Prime Minister and Minister of Foreign Affairs Saleumxay Kommasith declared that the BRI "has achieved fruitful results... It is fair to say that the China–Laos Railway is the most successful cooperation under the BRI" (China Global Television Network, 2023). However, such statements and images seldom translate to the people who see, build, and relate to these projects on a daily basis. On the ground, infrastructure shapes the ambient conditions of everyday life throughout the corridor, as both Lao and Chinese people experience the dusty and uncertain materiality that accompanies projects.

Corridor Perspectives in Northern Laos

The following sections use the LCEC as a transect to investigate varied development experiences and imaginaries, providing insight into the broader BRI landscape in northern Laos. This section begins in the corridor's northernmost point on China's border; it then moves southward (downstream) through a series of villages and construction sites, concluding in the final destination of Vientiane capital (Figure 6.2). In what follows, I present ethnographic perspectives from

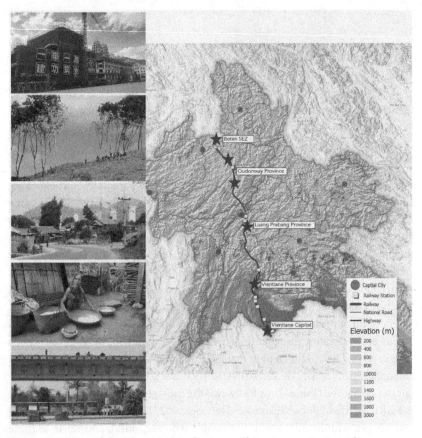

Figure 6.2 Research locations within the Laos–China Economic Corridor. Source: Author.

multiple vantage points to challenge prevailing top-down views of the corridor and the BRI, underscoring the differentiated views of residents, laborers, and officials to consider what is made visible, what is concealed, and with what effect.

Chinese Labor in a Border SEZ: From Building to Performing the BRI

Infrastructure and large-scale development projects like Boten SEZ involve an array of stakeholders. In the case of Boten, Chinese and Lao individuals ranging from company employees to casual laborers, shopkeepers, restaurant owners, hotel staff, and workers in entertainment establishments such as karaoke bars and massage parlors are all integral in its construction and becoming. This pattern is prevalent across the BRI, as Chinese firms frequently deploy workers overseas to implement projects. The contrast between the expectations and actual experiences of Chinese workers in Boten underscores the interplay between the imaginative allure of the BRI and the pragmatic challenges faced by those involved in its implementation.[3] Chinese laborers recruited to work in Boten were motivated by various factors. Most were hired by Haicheng, a Yunnan-based developer, to develop "the next Shenzhen." Thus, one motivation was rooted in the concept of development. Workers often expressed that Laos lagged behind Yunnan Province by 30 years. Many saw their role as contributing to Laos's development and helping the country catch up to China. This perception of development as a linear progression played a significant role in their decision to participate.

Workers were also attracted to Boten by the grandiose vision of what the city could become, enticed by the prospect of employment and economic opportunities associated with the BRI. For them, the BRI represented a pathway to secure livelihoods and futures through stable positions. However, the reality often diverged from the grand vision that they were initially presented with, as their tasks in Boten were more about performing a spectacle than participating in glamorous development projects. Upon moving to the SEZ, the daily lives of these workers oscillated between monotonous tasks and the production of small-scale events designed to create an illusion of luxury for visiting elites and VIPs. Despite the exhausting nature of their work, the laborers played a pivotal role in crafting the visibility of Boten during high-profile conferences and events. Much investment in Boten relies on such performance of possibility and prosperity.

This performance—a sort of development theater enacted by the laborers—rendered the BRI visible and thus "successful" to some visiting observers. In

---

[3] See Fei, Chapter 9, this volume, for similar dynamics among Chinese expatriates in Ethiopia.

other words, the cycles of development theater played a crucial role in shaping perceptions of Boten as an attractive investment opportunity. The BRI, seen in this context, is a performance for some, relying on the imaginative labor of workers who embody and enact the zone's development. However, the vibrant facade of a thriving city dissipates as guests depart, leaving a stark contrast between the heightened activity and vacancy. After one such conference, I asked employees about a coffee stand in the hotel lobby that had been packed away. They looked at me as if it had never existed. Many workers live in this rhythm of hype and lulls as they produce and sustain the spectacle of Boten, which in turn shapes how they see the legitimacy of the BRI.

At the same time, due to the backing of the BRI, potential developers and investors saw projects as too significant to fail. Various groups, including migrant workers, investors, and small business owners, were willing to invest their time, labor, and capital in the zone. Chinese individuals and companies increasingly viewed the zone as a "good investment" due to the workers' performance of zone futures and the BRI's facade of state backing. Growing confidence in the area's potential was evidenced by families who contemplated buying second homes in Boten instead of across the border in Xishuangbanna, Yunnan, and those considering establishing medical clinics specifically for the zone. These promises unfold in offices, streets, shops, and even in the minds and bodies of the workers and residents who contribute to the realization of the BRI. The BRI provides Boten with a sense of legitimacy, transforming perceptions and fueling the belief that the zone holds significant potential. This collective perception influences the decisions and investments made by individuals and businesses, shaping the trajectory of Boten's development.

The BRI's visibility in Boten extended beyond physical infrastructure projects; it was intimately tied to the performative labor of workers and legitimacy engendered by the BRI banner. The everyday lives of laborers became a stage for enacting the BRI, presenting a facade of development. The cycles of performance shape the perception of Boten as a space worthy of investment, rendering the BRI visible for some while concealing the very experiences and dynamics that make the spectacle possible.

On the "Chineseness" of Projects: Lao Residents along the Railway

Moving south from Boten, I followed the railway corridor into Oudomxay Province, where tracks cut through mountains, farmland, and villages (Figure 6.3). The railway has garnered significant media and public attention, with a focus on its rapid progress—sometimes referred to as "China speed." However,

Figure 6.3 Elevated railway tracks built above village homes in Oudomxay Province. Source: Carl Zoch (2019).

I found that views about the railway were rarely connected to the BRI. Between 2017 and 2023, it became evident that locals' complaints did not always align with the narratives surrounding Chinese-backed projects in international and regional media. Local Lao villagers framed the influx of infrastructure not solely through their "Chineseness" but by invoking a larger constellation of Lao government-led development. Contrary to the idea that Chinese companies and projects dominate smaller countries through BRI infrastructure, many people along the railway corridor understand the projects through their encounters with the Lao state. The focus on the BRI's "Chineseness" is thus in stark contrast with locals' perception of it as a project of the Lao state.

The immediate and visible impacts of large Chinese projects received attention, while the less visible effects often went unnoticed. The railway was not necessarily synonymous with the BRI for those affected by the construction. Local complaints often focused on the Lao government and land appropriation, not on China or the project itself. Some villagers who lost their land even speculated that Chinese workers or companies might have handled the situation better. In some cases, Lao villagers noted that Chinese workers supported local businesses or allowed them to complete agricultural cycles.

A resident I spoke with expressed concern about the railway's impact on his village, particularly about the large amount of land appropriated by the Lao government. He believed that the Chinese were willing to pay compensation, but the Lao government acted as an intermediary and reduced the compensation received. One Lao resident explained,

> You know it is all money. What the Chinese say is true, they *would* pay for the land, but our government did not allow them to pay compensation directly. Compensation must be paid through the [Lao] government, and the government organizes compensation. So, they take some of the money and say land is cheap.

His mother-in-law agreed that the Chinese company should be responsible for land compensation because they have more money. Both shared the common complaint that railway compensation was slow because it was determined and paid by the Lao government. They cited contrasting private projects like the Vang Vieng expressway, which they believed was quicker to compensate people because the developer (not the government) was charged with compensation and capital was available before construction. The slow compensation from the Lao government was a common complaint among locals.

Such views persisted in other provinces. For example, many other changes over the past 30 years were visible further south in Vientiane Province and around the tourist town of Vang Vieng. A longtime resident summarized the town's transformation: "There are big hotels and shops coming; it's not small anymore, and people do not come for village life." He recalled a once free-flowing river shaded by trees with small family-run shops along its shores. Many trees were felled for multistory hotels, new roads, bars, and restaurants. There was now a stark contrast between the hot, dusty, bustling town and its outskirts, where the riverbank remained shaded by tall trees. Like many locals, he watched the level of the *Nam Song* (Song River) drop and worried that it could dry up within five years due to deforestation, construction projects, and chemical dumping. He attributed the situation to numerous projects and no proper oversight:

> It is very low because the government allows too many projects and doesn't [monitor them]. They chopped down too many trees, not just here but also north on the river. It's getting low these days, so I worry that one day in the near future, maybe just five years, the river will be cut off [dry] from March or April to June or July [the hot, dry season].

He explained that "there has been a lot of chemical dumping [at Pathang Tunnel]. We know because we live here, see it daily, and understand the changes." This perspective was shared across the corridor. Local officials were seen to enable local issues by facilitating large investment projects and disregarding the known harmful consequences.

For many villagers I encountered across provinces, local Lao officials are the main (perhaps only) point of contact with a project. Most Lao people I spoke with had little to no contact with construction companies and Chinese workers, if only because of the vast linguistic divide. Several people also reminded me that Chinese construction companies seek direct approval from the central Lao government to proceed swiftly with construction. It was the Lao government that facilitated the movement and removal of people, homes, and agricultural land. Here, a politics of sight challenges the common "China threat" narrative associated with the global boom of large Chinese infrastructures and instead sheds light on challenges related to the Lao government, local politics, and a lack of trust in officials. It also shows how people focused on a project's immediate effects and how they are treated throughout development.

(Not) Seeing the BRI

Much of the discussion thus far has centered on how Lao and Chinese people in northern Laos see and are seen in light of BRI infrastructure development. However, infrastructure projects are not necessarily a proxy for the BRI. Even in the villages most profoundly impacted by construction, the BRI did not register as meaningful for all people. Many individuals were unfamiliar with or totally unaware of the BRI. Instead, they regarded BRI projects as a continuation of existing trends in the broader landscape of development and investment. A cohesive understanding and interpretation of the BRI was not always readily discernible, even when explicitly labeled as such.

"What is the BRI?" asked a local woman as we shared noodle soup at a small roadside shop in Oudomxay Province. I had not expected such a question, especially since we sat only a few kilometers from the new railway tracks. My two Lao research colleagues seemed equally surprised. We offered the standard definitions: the BRI is a global initiative for infrastructure-led development; the Lao government says it will help Laos modernize, develop, and reduce poverty. We gave examples: the railway, special economic zones, the corridor, and natural resource investments. Her family had gathered to listen, and an older woman interjected to explain that Chinese people and projects have long existed in Laos and that these infrastructures were like many past development projects. The woman shared that her sister had married a Chinese man who came to work in Laos years ago: "This is China in northern Laos, as usual." As if to drive the point home, Chinese pop music was quietly playing on the radio in the background.

Our conversation flagged several tensions in how people see the BRI within a longer history and larger context of development and regional relations.

This point was reinforced after the railway was operational. In January 2023, I returned to a village near Vang Vieng station to meet with an interlocutor who traveled between the capital for work and this cluster of villages where most of his family lives. I asked what people thought about the BRI now that the railway was operational. "People in my village do not know the BRI. We have no idea what that means. And it does not matter what we think about it." I pressed him on that last point, insisting that their thoughts on the railway matter. He agreed that community members frequently discussed projects, questioned their purpose, and asked who would benefit and why they were not included in planning processes. However, he reminded me, "people outside the capital do not talk about the BRI." Instead, they focus on the rapidly evolving day-to-day project construction, migrant labor, and what they hope to gain from the changes.

Others corroborated this position that the BRI as an object itself primarily has meaning in the capital. I raised this point with a young activist there. She reflected on her family and friends: "The villagers just don't get it. They ask what is that [the BRI]? Maybe some people who live closer to the main roads have started to see more. But people living far away do not know how [the BRI] works." District authorities were the main point of contact for villagers with questions or grievances and offer no explanation of the BRI itself. "The BRI is too far away," my friend concluded, "for villagers and local officials."

Multiple Views from the Capital

The BRI does come into sharper focus in Vientiane, where interlocutors tended to be government officials and professionals working in development, business, and education. This southernmost part of the corridor is where most policy and project decisions were made. Political offices, multilateral development institutions, nongovernmental organizations, and private firms are scattered throughout the city. Therefore, it is unsurprising that people in the capital see the BRI as more geopolitical and strategic than other corridor locations.

However, that does not mean that views are homogenous; instead, a diverse range of perspectives rather than a unanimous consensus emerges. Various ministry and National Assembly officials frequently aimed to generate state legitimacy through large-scale projects. In contrast, bureaucrats and technocrats, particularly those engaged in the energy sector, focused on the financial benefits of infrastructure development and the overall efficiency of energy systems, irrespective of their origins. An expert suggested that officials who may initially harbor reservations about sizable infrastructure ventures can be swayed by their sheer magnitude and grandeur. A planning expert from Vientiane explained how individuals change their perspectives upon witnessing the colossal presence of a dam or railway for the first time: "The gigantic, concrete structure is like nothing most Lao people have ever seen . . . everything about the structure and its purpose points to the future." When confronted with the expansive scope and scale of substantial energy projects, many officials are compelled to re-evaluate their stance.

Officials' ways of seeing the BRI and large infrastructure carry significant and tangible consequences. The Lao government has established and redirected bureaucracies to effectively negotiate and oversee projects, particularly those that collaborate with Chinese counterparts. Many Lao ministries seek to capitalize on the influx of projects and investments. Dedicated research units have been established to guide Lao engagement with the BRI and the related LCEC. Often, they conduct macroeconomic analyses to identify how to reap benefits from the railway through sectors such as agriculture, processing, services, tourism, finance, and customs. Such departments seek to gain "a better understanding of the Chinese way" and apply it to state development plans. Similarly, the Prime Minister's Office established a BRI committee to make decisions about costs, benefits, and strategic directions and identify sectors to prioritize for development. According to a Ministry of Planning and Investment (MPI) official, this is where all the "real work" on the BRI happens. Notably, the BRI serves as a cornerstone for the recently initiated five-year plan (2021–2025 National Socio-Economic Development Plan [NSEDP]). They also often frame the BRI by the Sustainable Development Goals, highlighting its significance in the pursuit of sustainable development objectives.

In addition to official ways of seeing the BRI, some Lao citizens residing in the capital spoke favorably of BRI projects, similarly citing them as opportunities for economic development, job creation, improved transportation, and increased tourism. However, uncertainties remained about the long-term sustainability of projects. One resident explained, "We do not know how long the benefits of transportation will last in terms of people taking the train." There were also concerns about the time it would take for the promised poverty alleviation benefits to materialize. Still, she expressed a sense of optimism, "There are so many opportunities that will come eventually." As with the workers in Boten, hope was anchored in the notion of future possibilities. However, families in the capital who lost their land to railway construction did not share this stance (as in the corridor villages). The most skeptical characterized the BRI as "China taking over Laos."

Finally, people associated with Chinese business organizations in Vientiane viewed the BRI as a lucrative opportunity. Private capital and smaller-scale investments are significant to the BRI and deserve further study. One Chinese business organization saw the BRI as a gateway to expand business operations, access markets, and establish strategic partnerships in the region and with other Chinese firms. For such businesses, the BRI goes beyond large-scale infrastructure projects and encompasses a wide range of sectors and industries, including trade, manufacturing, logistics, finance, and tourism. Businesses have become not only implementors but ambassadors of the initiative, and their investments are legitimated by the BRI. The Chinese state recognizes the significance of these businesses in realizing the BRI and supports them through various means (e.g., financial incentives, policy support, and diplomatic assistance). They play an important role within the BRI and potentially drive economic growth and influence in the regions where they operate.

Proximity and a Politics of Sight

Throughout my time traversing the corridor, it became evident that proximity to Vientiane as well as border regions played a role in shaping how the BRI is seen and how people interact with its projects. In Vientiane, it was more common to encounter discussions about political sensitivities and apprehensions around "China in Laos." The concentration of political institutions and decision-making centers in the capital likely contributed to a heightened geopolitical awareness. Conversely, perspectives in border regions were shaped by proximity to neighboring countries and the intricate dynamics of cross-border trade and cultural interactions. For some in these areas, the BRI is seen as a catalyst for economic opportunities and connectivity, while others experience the BRI as a hindrance to traditional routes for trade and movement as borders were tightened and movement funneled through official crossings. A politics of sight thus underscores the shifting perceptions of the BRI. Proximity to projects and people from China, as well as the politics of the project itself, influences how individuals and communities see the BRI, if they see it at all.

However, proximity is more than a fact of geographical distance. Rather, it encompasses a complex interplay of factors—shared historical ties, cultural affinities, and economic interdependencies between Laos and China—that play meaningful roles in shaping a politics of sight regarding the BRI. The notion of proximity and its influence on perceptions of the BRI was also dynamic. Narratives surrounding the BRI varied and evolved as people traversed the corridor and encountered the BRI in individually specific ways, interacted with different stakeholders, and gained firsthand experiences with projects. Understanding the politics of sight goes beyond examining how people see the BRI; it also considers how they are seen, adding a layer to the downstream dynamics surrounding the initiative.

Critically, then, a politics of sight considers what is seen and hidden in individual experiences of the BRI. At the local level, changes resulting from BRI projects often manifest themselves gradually and subtly. These gradual shifts became normalized as commonsense thinking about infrastructure development. Project impacts were observed through incremental improvements in local transportation, connectivity, and economic activities. Over time, changes such as lost land, improved connectivity, increased labor presence, or traffic congestion became part of the local landscape and were perceived as a natural progression that aligned with expectations of progress and development. Understanding infrastructure on a spectrum of visibility underscores how local experiences of the subtle and gradual changes become normalized within the logic of infrastructure development, while large-scale projects create a spectacle that blinds observers to subtler shifts. Distant offices in the United States and Europe or even Vientiane that view the BRI as primarily a geopolitical initiative may overlook the social and material aspects of the projects. Instead, as megaprojects captured the attention and imagination of external observers, these monumental endeavors created a captivating spectacle that overshadowed the more nuanced and incremental local changes.

Conclusion

Examining infrastructure development through a politics of sight reveals that the BRI is a function of what is rendered visible and what is concealed. It helps to reconcile the simultaneous ambiguity and spectacle of the BRI with its concrete manifestations, while holding in tension the promise and violence of infrastructure. Through this approach, I suggest the visibility of infrastructure is best conceived as being on a spectrum and often shifting. Exploring the diverse ways of seeing the BRI and its downstream effects also allows for a deeper understanding of power and the multifaceted nature of China's global engagements and how they take shape on the ground. As Schatz and Silvey suggest in this book's introduction, power moves downstream, but its effects are contingent upon what it encounters. Power not only flows from country to country but also ebbs and flows in less visible ways within downstream contexts. Chinese workers continue to construct and perform projects, showcasing the contingent nature of the BRI. Local officials implement the BRI according to local models of development. While individuals and communities who navigate the BRI's sociopolitical landscape also demonstrate potential forms of agency and transformative capacity. In this way, power is not a unidirectional force imposed from above; it is also derived by ways of seeing or not seeing the BRI and the ways it shapes how people are seen. Just as a flowing river continuously shifts due to changing sediment, tides, and weather conditions, the places and spaces influenced by the BRI are shaped by local agency and ways of seeing.

Understanding global China more broadly therefore requires grounded and project-based approaches. As this chapter attests, there is no single way of seeing the BRI. Indeed, dualistic narratives of China as a threat or savior are absent in the varied ways the BRI is perceived in Laos. This mirrors the lack of cohesion in the plans, projects, and outcomes of the BRI itself. It is essential not to conflate individual projects and the whole BRI. People experiencing project effects commonly do *not* perceive the constellation of Chinese-backed projects to be part of the BRI. As such, this chapter yields broader insights for understanding the global China by questioning prevailing narratives, unpacking complex host country dynamics, and emphasizing the localized experiences and responses to China's global engagements. As projects are implemented in diverse contexts and encounter friction, it is crucial to attend to the BRI's emergent nature in place, how localities shape projects, and the diversity of meanings and effects associated with global infrastructure development.

PART III

SEEING CONNECTIVITY, PRIVACY, AND LABOR

7

Prefiguring China's Digital Silk Road to Europe

Connecting Switzerland

Lena Kaufmann

Introduction

"You don't feel it, even though it carries the whole Swiss economy!" Ms. Wang,[1] a leading Huawei network engineer in Switzerland, proudly told me in an interview in August 2019. Ms. Wang was referring to the information and telecommunication backbone structure supported by her company. Her exclamation was sparked by a company video she had watched, showing a remote village in Switzerland, which had until recently relied on satellites and the old copper network for telecommunication. The Internet connection there had been so slow that villagers had time to drink a coffee while waiting for their computers to connect. Ms. Wang explained that, thanks to a Huawei device called "micro CAN (Copper Access Node)," which connects the older copper lines to the newer fiber-optic lines (see Figure 7.1), the village now had access to high-speed Internet without long connection times. In addition, residents could access high-quality television via the Internet, as well as various streaming services. "To see this progress," Ms. Wang said, "was such a touching moment, it moved me to tears." In fact, just a few years earlier it would have been unthinkable that technology from China, a country long associated with backwardness, copycat attitudes, and a lack of innovativeness (Lindtner, 2020), would offer "progress" to other countries, especially Switzerland, which not only is one of the richest countries in the world but also prides itself on its innovative capacity.

In truth, Huawei's devices clearly do not carry the whole Swiss economy; Huawei's competitors, such as Finland's Nokia, Sweden's Ericsson, and the United

---

[1] For privacy reasons, some of the personal names in this chapter have been omitted or changed. All translations of Chinese and (Swiss) German sources and interviews are by the author. I would like to thank my interlocutors for sharing their time, insights, and experiences. This research was funded in whole or in part by the Swiss National Science Foundation, Grant number 192205.

Lena Kaufmann, *Prefiguring China's Digital Silk Road to Europe* In: Seeing China's Belt and Road. Edited by: Edward Schatz and Rachel Silvey, Oxford University Press. © Oxford University Press 2025. DOI: 10.1093/oso/9780197789261.003.0008

Figure 7.1 A micro CAN (Copper Access Node) inside a manhole. Source: Author.

States's Cisco Systems, also play a tremendous role in Switzerland. Nevertheless, her statement highlights the transnationality of critical digital infrastructures, alluding to the key role of transnational—particularly Chinese—corporations in making Swiss and other economies tick in the information age. Moreover, it points to the fact that, despite its relevance, transnational engagement in digital infrastructures remains largely invisible. In this context, broad narratives that depict global Chinese infrastructures as either a form of neocolonial power or win-win development projects do not necessarily enhance our understanding of these digital infrastructures and their "downstream effects" (Schatz and Silvey, conclusion to the volume). Instead, it is valuable to examine these infrastructures through the perspectives of the multiple actors involved—both Chinese and Swiss—as well as the "politics of sight" (Schatz and Silvey, introduction to this volume). This approach reveals that it is the Chinese companies in this field that are largely driving the Chinese engagement in Swiss digital infrastructures, rather than it being solely a top-down government strategy. Moreover, Swiss politicians and company representatives also play an active role, not only in collaborating with Chinese actors, but also in keeping infrastructures and related Chinese collaborations mostly concealed from the general public.

In the case of Huawei, recent media reporting about the company in the United States, Europe, and Australia has raised public awareness.[2] It has also increased fears about the company's relationship to the Chinese government and issues of cybersecurity. Nevertheless, in everyday life the general public remains largely unaware of the materiality of transnational digital infrastructures: most people imagine that their emails, text messages, online orders, financial transactions, photos, and posts on social media are stored somewhere in "the cloud" (Hu, 2015; Schubert and Marinica, 2020; Vonderau, 2019). This is not surprising, as most digital infrastructures are buried underground, in the ocean, or hidden from the public in remote and inaccessible data centers.

Through a case study of fiber-optic cables and networks in Switzerland, I shed light on the sociotechnical materiality and, relatedly, the politics of sight of these infrastructures. I provide insights into a commonly overlooked—though crucial—component of the Chinese Belt and Road Initiative (BRI): the Chinese Digital Silk Road (DSR).[3] The digital components of the BRI are usually much less visible than the pipelines, railroads, roads, and harbors that they accompany. Exploring how the DSR has unfolded in Switzerland, I argue that the effects of digitalization in Switzerland (as well as in many other countries) cannot be fully understood without taking into consideration Chinese engagement in the field of digital infrastructures. Although discursive references that link Switzerland to the DSR are rather recent, I show that what is now framed as part of the DSR in fact began long before the official announcement of the BRI. Moreover, I demonstrate that the Chinese–Swiss entanglements in digital infrastructures are not as unidirectional and coherently top-down as one may assume.

This chapter builds on an emerging body of studies on digital infrastructures in the social sciences. Infrastructure studies tend to focus on visible infrastructures, such as railways, roads, and pipelines (see, e.g., Anand, Gupta, and Appel, 2018; Harvey, Jensen, and Atsuro, 2017; Harvey and Knox, 2015; Heslop and Murton, 2021; Larkin, 2013). Digital infrastructures have only recently become objects of study. Studies in this field highlight the materiality of "the cloud" and "the Internet," showing that digital infrastructures are deeply rooted in sociomaterial practices, with specific imaginaries attached to them (Boellstorff, 2010; Easterling, 2016; Fish, 2011; Furlong, 2021; Graham and Marvin, 2004; Knox, 2021). Moreover, they demonstrate that these seemingly new infrastructures are often built upon layers of existing infrastructures such as railroads, military bases, or telegraph lines (Dommann, Rickli, and Stadler, 2020; Hu, 2015; Johnson, 2019; Starosielski, 2015; Thorat, 2019). While

---

[2] For example, see NL Times (2021).
[3] See also Dall'Agnola, Chapter 8, this volume.

transnational entanglements do play a role in some of these studies, the DSR is largely absent from the analysis.

Instead, the DSR, as an important part of the BRI, has so far mainly attracted the attention of political scientists, security and international relations scholars, economists, journalists, and think tanks, in contrast to social scientists who study digital infrastructures using qualitative-ethnographic methods. While these analysts have provided important overviews of the political framework and scope of Chinese investments (e.g., Gordon and Nouwens, 2022; Hillman, 2021; Shen, 2018), there are few in-depth case studies on the DSR, especially regarding Western Europe. To date, most of the texts about the DSR are brief overviews, blog posts, or policy analyses, and there is very little empirical literature on the topic,[4] especially tracing the actual materiality of the DSR.

This chapter is a first step toward filling this gap, contributing a social science and historical perspective on China's Digital Silk Road to Europe, especially in Switzerland. This chapter also raises awareness of the digital infrastructures— fiber-optic networks in particular—that enable digitalization and DSR projects such as smart cities, financial services, and communication networks, which are fundamental to other infrastructure projects in the context of the BRI.

Conceptualizing the Digital Silk Road

Since around 2015, the DSR has become an important component of the BRI, making its way into major Chinese policy documents such as "Made in China 2025" and the 13th and 14th Five-Year Plans (FYPs). In practice, however, the DSR, just like the overarching BRI, is not easy to define. On the one hand, it has a tangible material base that mostly remains invisible, including the massive, though commonly overlooked, investments in fiber-optic cables, data centers, and smart cities built together with BRI energy and transportation projects. On the other hand, the DSR is also a broader and vaguer branding effort and narrative, enabling the Chinese government "to promote its global vision across a range of technology areas and projects" (Eurasia Group, 2020: 1). Often it is private or state-owned companies, rather than the Chinese government, driving this endeavor, "using the DSR label to gain policy support to pursue overseas commercial expansion" (Eurasia Group, 2020: 1). The DSR has thus come to embrace "virtually any telecommunications or data-related business operations or product sales by China-based tech firms" along the BRI (Greene and Triolo, 2020). While only a few countries have signed specific DSR agreements, these

---

[4] Exceptions include Fei (2021a), Kassenova and Duprey (2021), and van der Lugt (2021). See also the comprehensive literature review provided by Heeks et al. (2023).

numbers are much higher if we include Chinese state and corporate information and communications technology (ICT) activities abroad. In fact, Huawei alone lists employees in more than 170 countries, many of which are also BRI countries (Huawei, 2021).

Hence, the DSR comprises both a discursive construct and tangible sociomaterial practices of ICT firms. Here, Switzerland is an interesting Western European example. The Swiss BRI agreement builds on long-standing diplomatic and economic relationships (see Coduri, Keller, and Baumberger, 2009). In 1950, Switzerland was one of the first countries to recognize the People's Republic of China (PRC). Furthermore, it was a Swiss company—the elevator producer Schindler—that established the first-ever joint venture with China in 1980 (Schindler, 2019). In 2014, a Free Trade Agreement (FTA) was ratified, and by 2022 the PRC was Switzerland's third-biggest trading partner after Germany and the United States (Rosenberger, 2022). In 2019, Switzerland was among the first Western European countries to sign a BRI Memorandum of Understanding (MoU) (The Federal Council, 2019), although no official BRI infrastructure projects had been established in the country as of 2024. Nevertheless, as this chapter will explain, the DSR had already begun to manifest itself in Switzerland before Xi Jinping officially launched the BRI in 2013.

Observing the Digital Silk Road

Accessing the physical infrastructure of the DSR is not easy. This is arguably one of the reasons why most observers have directed their attention to other aspects of the BRI. On the one hand, the digital infrastructures in question are considered critical by governments and, for that reason, remain largely invisible for national security reasons. Moreover, they usually appear as infrastructures devoid of human beings. The human work behind them often becomes visible only when construction workers build cable networks and data centers. Meanwhile, much of the maintenance, repair, and installation work takes place out of sight in cellars, manholes, or on cable ships. On the other hand, due to the ongoing cybersecurity debates on Chinese companies such as Huawei (e.g., Häberli, 2022), the employees of Swiss companies in this sector typically prefer not to publish many details about collaborations between their companies and Chinese business partners. Similarly, Chinese companies in the ICT field are cautious about disclosing information. This is because the highly competitive high-tech sector generally demands a certain degree of secrecy to protect intellectual property among other reasons, but also due to the delicate situation of contested Chinese companies. One employee at the Huawei Research Center in Zurich began our informal interview in March 2022 by stating, "I cannot tell you very much," implying that he was limited in what he could say about the Center's collaborations with Swiss partners. It is thus necessary to go beyond mere policy analyses to draw on a mix of methods to gain insights into the DSR.

This chapter builds on archival and ethnographic field research between March 2019 and March 2022, with a focus on fiber-optic networks. Data were gleaned through in-person and virtual semistructured interviews and informal conversations with employees of Swiss and Chinese ICT companies based in Switzerland; the use of digital platforms and media such as LinkedIn, WeChat, and email; a media content analysis; and written sources such as policy documents, industry reports, cable maps, trade registers, company websites, and marketing material. Moreover, data were collected through participant observation during industry fairs, conferences, and business events of the Swiss–Chinese Chamber of Commerce and Chinese companies in Switzerland, as well as seven days of technical fiber-optic training. During site visits I observed how fiber-optic cables were produced on factory floors and how cables were laid across the Swiss countryside. I watched how they became connected to large data storage systems in often highly secured data centers, which I could enter only after completing a strict security check. Neither photos nor phone calls were allowed. Often, site visits meant going underground: removing manhole covers and climbing down steep ladders into dark humid manholes to see how fiber-optic equipment was installed and maintained; descending into cellars or narrow ducts under the streets of Bern to follow cables along part of their path; visiting the impressive Milchbuck Tunnel, which traverses Zurich, carrying not only car traffic, but, in the seventh underground floor, also the city's major telecommunication and energy infrastructures (see Figure 7.2).

The outcome of this research, which I will present, can be regarded as analogous to accessing the key points of a network: I start from the cables that make up this network, before touching upon "Points of Presence" (access points connecting different countries' networks), data centers, and other network components.

Optical Fibers and Cables: Producing the Basis for the DSR

Chinese cables play a crucial role in the expanding global information infrastructure. A closer historical look reveals, however, that much of the Chinese fiber and cable-making know-how vital for building the DSR originated in the United States, Japan, and Europe decades earlier. Moreover, while Chinese cables are crucial for connecting other countries along the DSR, foreign cables, including those from Swiss cable makers, also provide connectivity to major infrastructure sites within China. From this perspective, the DSR appears less a

Figure 7.2   Fiber-optic and energy cables in the Milchbuck Tunnel. Source: Author.

simple move from China abroad and more a historical and multidirectional entanglement of people, knowledge, ideas, and technologies. This way of seeing the BRI challenges and adds nuance to sweeping, broad-stroke narratives about the BRI—whether as a threat or a development project—by highlighting the local and translocal complexities at play, as well as the roles of multiple human and nonhuman actors.

Spurred by advances in laser technology in the 1960s, fiber-optic production took off in the 1980s and 1990s. Fiber optics are made from thin strands of silica glass that resemble fishing lines. By transmitting light signals instead of electrical signals, fiber optics can transmit more data at a higher speed and over longer distances than copper cables (Hecht, 1999). They are thus the basis of digitalization. The global centers of production were the United States and Japan. Western Europe, especially the United Kingdom, France, and West Germany, also played a role (IGI Consulting, 2001: 201). Several enterprises based in Switzerland with decades of cable-making experience, such as Dätwyler, Brugg Telecom (now partially Solifos), Huber + Suhner, and the French Nexans also produced fiber-optic cables for use abroad, including in China. As the production of raw fibers, which is more challenging, was not successful in Switzerland, these companies now focus on making cables with fibers imported mainly from the United States.

Today, Dätwyler cables outfit not only iconic places such as Shanghai's Oriental Pearl Tower, Beijing's CITIC Tower, and a Communist Party school, but also major infrastructure sites such as international airports and the Shanghai Sea Port. Moreover, Dätwyler has equipped data centers in China, including one owned by Huawei, and the headquarters of Ant Financial, in other words, two companies that are active in the framework of the BRI (Dätwyler IT Infra, 2021).[5]

In comparison with their international competitors, Chinese companies did not have much experience in glasswork or cable-manufacturing when they first began to engage in fiber-optic production in the 1970s. As a result, their initial efforts largely failed. Today, the situation is radically different. Supported by related policies, Chinese companies have learned from importing optical-fiber manufacturing equipment from Finland, the United Kingdom, France, Germany, and the United States, as well as from joint ventures with Japanese, American, and European companies. As a result, by the mid-2000s the Chinese fiber optics and cable industry had already become one of the global centers of fiber optics, along with the United States and Japan (Fu, 2015: 242–43; IGI Consulting, 2001: 101–7; Research and Markets, 2019). Nowadays, the PRC has the full supply chain, from preform making and glass drawing to cable making. The Chinese city Wuhan became one of the global centers of fiber-optic production by the beginning of the fourteenth FYP (2021–2025). The government of Hubei Province dubbed the area "Optics Valley" (*guāng gǔ*) over a decade ago (Hubei Government, 2023) as a way to claim worldwide recognition and visibility for optical fibers made in China, and to challenge the supremacy of Silicon Valley in global digitalization.

Fibers from the top Chinese producers—YOFC, FiberHome, ZTT, Futong, and Hengtong—increasingly spark concerns in other parts of the world. While Hengtong is an important submarine cable maker, especially since it acquired Huawei Marine (now HMN Tech) in 2019–2020, its alleged links to the Chinese military (Hillman, 2021) are a source of controversy. Similarly, FiberHome was recently added to the US Bureau of Industry and Security's restricted Entity List due to allegedly supporting Uyghur surveillance in Xinjiang (Hardy, 2020; US Bureau of Industry and Security, 2021). Meanwhile, the oversupply, low prices, and growing quality that make Chinese cables more competitive are also increasing concerns among fiber producers from other countries. For instance, a Danish–Japanese fiber producer employee said in frustration, "We helped China [to launch fiber-optic production] from zero [. . .] but they have a 77 percent tariff [on foreign fiber imports and] you can't sell [foreign fiber] to China!"[6] This has resulted in an ongoing investigation into dumping in relation

---

[5] This information is supported by interviews with Dätwyler managers and employees.
[6] Based on personal communication with a fiber producer employee, October 26, 2020.

to Chinese fibers—though not cables—in the European Union. Nevertheless, Chinese fibers continue to be sold in Europe and are often the basis for connecting China with Europe within the BRI framework.

Chinese Fiber-Optic Connections: Establishing the Networks of the DSR

An increasing number of both terrestrial and submarine fiber-optic cables connect the PRC to the rest of the world. The global spread of Chinese fiber-optic cables and connections began in the 1990s. The basic infrastructures and current routes of the DSR were therefore laid out about two decades before the BRI's official launch, and much earlier, if we take into consideration prior infrastructures such as railway or telegraph lines, which often served as a basis for constructing fiber-optic networks.

Previously, Western countries, especially the United Kingdom and the United States, had long controlled global telegraph and, subsequently, coaxial and fiber-optic cables (Starosielski, 2015). Since the mid-2000s, however, global fiber-optic connections, including from China, have been growing rapidly. Generally, submarine optical cables are more important than terrestrial cables in terms of overall global connectivity, carrying almost all data traffic.[7] This is, as Nicole Starosielski (2015) points out, related to security reasons: when cables are buried deep in the sea, they are least likely to be affected by human and other disturbances. Nevertheless, according to Mr. Zhang, a management-level employee from China Unicom in Switzerland, terrestrial cables play a greater role and have several advantages in connecting China and Europe. Despite more complex routing and more regional restrictions, they require lower investment, have lower latency (due to the shorter distances), are more stable, and are easier to install and maintain. Moreover, they usually have an enormous capacity compared with submarine cables.[8]

The first undersea cables used for regular traffic were introduced in the mid-1980s. They followed the routes of earlier telegraph and coaxial networks, continuing to materially reflect "the imagined sources of friction and security of those periods—from the debates over territorial security in the colonial era to the spatial decentralization and institutional interconnections of the Cold War era" (Starosielski, 2015: 45). American, British, French, and Japanese operators

---

[7] That submarine cables carry about 95 percent of data traffic is commonly repeated in white papers and media and industry reports; however, the number is difficult to verify as these publications do not list sources.

[8] Mr. Zhang, written conversation, April 19, 2021.

were at the forefront of fiber-optic development (see Starosielski, 2015: 45; Hecht, 1999: 209–10; 213).

Chinese transnational optical cables appeared almost a decade after the first Western and Japanese cables. The first was a Chinese submarine optical cable connecting China and Japan in 1993 (China Academy of Information and Communications Technology, 2018: 11). The first submarine fiber-optic cable between China and Europe, the FLAG Europe-Asia cable, was built and ready for service in November 1997. It was owned by the India-based company Reliance Globalcom (Submarine Telecoms Forum, 2012: 51).[9] The earliest terrestrial fiber-optic cable between China and Europe was the Transit Europe-Asia cable (TEA, in Chinese TAE), with endings in Shanghai and Frankfurt, respectively. The construction of that cable was an initiative of the Chinese Ministry of Posts and Telecommunications. At a meeting in Geneva in December 1992, organized by the International Telecommunication Union, the Chinese Ministry of Posts and Telecommunications along with heads of foreign telecommunication enterprises had concretized the idea to construct the TEA. The Ministry also sent delegations to Russia, Ukraine, Belarus, Poland, Hungary, Austria, and other countries to garner support for the project and organized two international planning conferences, one of them in collaboration with Germany (Liu, 1993). The official opening ceremony took place in 1998 (Pan, 1999: 213). In the mid-2000s, Chinese officials and company representatives officially intensified cooperation with Russia on the cable system and China Telecom and Rostelecom signed a memorandum to upgrade and expand the existing system (Lu, 2004). Subsequently, the TEA became the shortest route between Asia and Europe, with higher speed and quality than alternative routes across the Pacific and Atlantic Oceans or Southeast Asia and the Middle East.

In terms of connections to Europe, Russia continues to play a central role as a terrestrial-cable transit country. Today's fiber-optic routes through Russia roughly follow the telegraph lines laid in the mid-19th century, which connected Europe to Imperial China and established Moscow, as well as St Petersburg, as key telegraph communication hubs (Colton, J.H. & Co., 2020 [1871]). While Chinese–Russian relations have not always been amicable, following the end of the Cold War in the 1990s and the collapse of the Soviet Union, the Chinese government renewed its interest in a close relationship with Russia to counter the dominance of the United States. As a result of strategic diplomatic relations, in the late 1990s Russia not only became the first foreign market for Huawei (Wen, 2020: 67) but also attracted Chinese attention with regard to transnational fiber-optic connections. Today, various cable systems are run

---

[9] Mr. Zhang, the China Unicom representative, also wrote about this in a conversation, April 19, 2021.

by the three major Chinese operators, either unilaterally or in collaboration. These operators are China Telecom, China Unicom, and China Mobile. Their networks to Europe pass through Russia as well as in part through Mongolia and Kazakhstan (CAICT, 2018: 10). The Russian segment of the Chinese operators' cables makes use of the Russian Rostelecom's DWDM network.[10] As Chinese and Russian operators continue to collaborate, the Russian war in Ukraine has further highlighted the geopolitical fragility of these transnational cable networks. Following the destruction of the Russian Nord Stream gas pipelines in September 2022, in June 2023 former Russian president and Putin ally Dmitry Medvedev reportedly responded by declaring that Russia has a "moral" right to destroy subsea Internet cables (Bennetts, 2023).

Regarding ownership, there was a significant increase in both single-owner and multiowner submarine cables between 2012 and 2022. While single-owner systems are on the rise, amounting to 57 percent of all cable systems installed in this period, multiowner systems remain important, particularly for securing access to funding and in the context of transnational arrangements (Submarine Telecoms Forum, 2022: 33). The submarine South East Asia Middle East Western Europe 3 cable (SEA-ME-WE 3), for instance, is owned by France's Orange, Italy's Telecom Italia Sparkle, Germany's Deutsche Telekom, and China's China Telecom, along with a range of other European, African, and Asian partners (TeleGeography, 2021). The SEA-ME-WE 5, which follows a similar route, is owned by a 19-member consortium, including Orange, China Mobile International, China Telecom Global, and China Unicom (SEA-ME-WE 5, 2015). As Mr. Zhang explained,

> You cannot build a cable in other countries with your name, you must have an agreement with a local operator to buy or rent fiber-optic capacity. Most utility companies will install "dark" [i.e., unused surplus] fiber along a highway or railway or pipeline, the operator or wholesales player will build an optical transmission network in one region or multiple regions, based on the installed dark fiber.

Hence, "normally each cable includes at least one operator in a different country."[11]

Nowadays, China has direct connections to North America, Central Asia, Europe, and Africa, in addition to transit connections to South America, Africa, and Oceania. There are direct network connections to countries perceived as

---

[10] Mr. Zhang, written conversation, April 19, 2021. DWDM (Dense Wavelength Division Multiplexing) is a transmission technology that increases the amount of data that can be sent over a single fiber.

[11] Mr. Zhang, written conversation, April 19, 2021.

especially important, such as the United States, Japan, Singapore, and the United Kingdom. The four major international submarine cable-landing stations in mainland China are located in Qingdao, Nanhui and Chongming in Shanghai, and Shantou, while Fuzhou and Xiamen connect Taiwan. Finally, Hong Kong is another major hub for cable-landing stations, established by mainland Chinese companies. By the end of 2017, the PRC already had 17 international terrestrial cable border stations and cross-border terrestrial optical-cable systems connecting it to 12 of its 14 neighboring countries (except for Bhutan and Afghanistan) (CAICT, 2018: 10). Apart from Moscow and St Petersburg, the major arrival points of Chinese terrestrial cables in Europe are Helsinki, Stockholm, London, and Frankfurt. Moreover, there are important submarine cable landing points on the coasts of Southern France, Portugal, and Southern Italy (China Mobile International, 2020; China Telecom Americas, 2023; China Unicom, 2021).

The number of transnational Chinese optical cables has been growing fast.[12] In 2017 there were 12 Chinese terrestrial and 10 submarine cables (CAICT, 2018: 10–11). By 2023, China Telecom alone listed 20 terrestrial and 51 submarine cables (China Telecom Americas, 2023), of which 12 terrestrial cables and five submarine cables with varying latencies connected Asia to Europe in 2020 (China Telecom Europe, 2020). Two cable connections, tellingly named "Silk Road North Line" and "Silk Road South Line," have come into use around 2023, both starting in Ürümqi in Xinjiang. The northern cable ends in Frankfurt, Germany. The southern cable runs to Karachi, Pakistan; from there, it connects to the AFRICA-1 submarine cable, which has landing stations in Italy, France, and South Africa (China Telecom Americas, 2023; PEACE Cable, 2023).

Alongside Chinese cables, those of other global operators are also increasing, resulting in what the *Wall Street Journal* called "America's undersea battle with China for control of the global Internet grid" (Page, O'Keeffe, and Taylor, 2019). Major American tech companies, such as Google, Amazon, Facebook, and Microsoft, are investing in their own cables. Although it is difficult to know exactly how many transnational fiber-optic cables there are across the globe due to the dynamic industry, as of early 2024 there were more than 500 active and planned under the world's oceans (Submarine Telecoms Forum, 2023; TeleGeography, 2024). According to some observers, Chinese companies were part of one-fifth of all cable projects worldwide between 2016 and 2019 (Perragin, 2021). However, the Chinese government aims to seize 60 percent of

---

[12] "Chinese cables" refer to cables that have landing points in mainland China or Hong Kong and are operated by China Telecom, China Unicom, or China Mobile. This does not mean, however, that they are fully owned by Chinese companies.

the global fiber-optic communications market by 2025,[13] to gain both commercial and strategic advantages (Hillman, 2021).

One important new cable system is the PEACE cable. According to its website, the cable was ready for service in December 2022, spanning Pakistan, East Africa, and France (PEACE Cable, 2023). It provides an important high-speed link between China (via Pakistan) and Europe, and a connection to Singapore is currently under construction and is expected to be completed in mid-2024 (PEACE Cable, 2023). PEACE Cable International Network Co., Ltd., privately owns, invests, operates, and maintains the cable system. Founded in 2018, PEACE Cable is a subsidiary of Hengtong, the company that acquired Huawei Marine and "aims to be [the] leading international submarine cable system operator" (PEACE Cable, 2023). The United States and allied governments watch such developments with caution, fearing espionage or cyberattacks (Drew and Purnell, 2021).

In the case of Switzerland, the country is now connected to China via undersea cables through Italy and France and via terrestrial networks through Germany. There seem to be fewer cybersecurity fears among the government officials and technical experts in Switzerland compared with other European countries like Germany or the United Kingdom. One Swiss fiber network expert explained that it is generally possible to spy through cables because, when you bend them, the light might leak, and the signals may be read by outsiders. He recalled that this had happened, for example, to cables originating in West Berlin passing through the territory of the former German Democratic Republic. For this very reason, however, Swiss banks transmitting sensitive data via fiber optics constantly monitor the attenuation of their cables in order to immediately identify any potential leaks.[14] Generally, however, the security risk seems less related to passive network components such as cables, which simply transmit data, and more to the active network components to be discussed.

Data Centers and PoPs: DSR Nodes

Along the cable networks, there are data centers and so-called Points of Presence (PoPs). These access points are located inside data centers and connect two or more different countries' networks with each other. In general, because they store valuable information, data centers are deliberately kept out of sight.

---

[13] This is stated in a roadmap for "Made in China 2025" (Strategic Advisory Committee for Building a Manufacturing Superpower, 2015: 8).

[14] Based on an interview with a Swiss network expert, April 14, 2021.

Although not easily visible, the three big, mostly state-owned Chinese tel-ecom operators—China Telecom, China Unicom, and China Mobile—all have a growing number of data centers and PoPs in Europe. London and Frankfurt are especially popular locations, for historical reasons that relate to existing tele-graph and banking infrastructures. China Telecom, for example, which used to belong to the Chinese Ministry of Posts and Telecommunications and is there-fore the country's largest telecom company, has about 23 PoPs in Europe, with the highest density in London and Frankfurt. There is also one near Zurich, the Interxion Zurich Campus at Glattbrugg (China Telecom Americas, 2021). In 2019, a second PoP was planned near Geneva[15] but had not yet officially opened by mid-2024.

In Switzerland, China Telecom, China Unicom, and China Mobile, which are competitors, have all recently registered local branch offices, followed by lavish opening ceremonies several months later. While this is relatively recent, their history precedes the BRI. China Telecom established its first European subsid-iary in 2006 in London (China Telecom Europe, 2021). As a management-level employee of China Telecom Europe (CTE) explained in excellent German, the company started doing business in Switzerland around 2011. At that time, CTE branches in Constance, Munich, and Frankfurt already generated 20 percent of their revenue in Switzerland and had around five customers there).[16] After registering an office in Zurich in May 2018 (Commercial Register Office of the Canton of Zurich, 2018), CTE celebrated the opening of its Swiss subsidiary in November 2019. During the ceremony, CTE representatives announced plans to expand further in Europe. The event was organized by the Swiss–Chinese Chamber of Commerce. The Greater Zurich Area, an institution whose task is to attract foreign investment to the broader Zurich area, was a special guest and facilitator. Further guests included high-ranking Chinese diplomats, repre-sentatives of Swiss companies that also operate in China, and members of the Chamber of Commerce. The whole ceremony was held under the English slogan "Your Digital Silk Road to China" (see Figure 7.3).

China Unicom, China's second-biggest telecom operator, officially registered a Zurich branch in October 2016 with the aim of "providing international private lines, the Internet of Things (IoT) and cloud computing services to multinational enterprises between China and Switzerland" (quoted in Shao, 2017). Benefiting from the FTA between the two countries, it was the first Chinese telecom oper-ator to establish a business in Switzerland (Commercial Register Office of the Canton of Zurich, 2016; Shao, 2017). As in the case of China Telecom, China

---

[15] Based on a presentation by Moti Khan from China Telecom Europe in Zurich, November 21, 2019.

[16] Based on a presentation by a China Telecom Europe manager in Zurich, November 21, 2019.

Figure 7.3 "Your Digital Silk Road to China." Source: Author.

Unicom's Zurich office is also a subsidiary of the company's London branch. The then-ambassador Geng Wenbing, among others, attended the official opening ceremony in September 2017, pointing out that "the promotion of Sino-Swiss 'Belt and Road' cooperation requires a higher level of interconnection" and that,

Figure 7.4 Green Data Center in Lupfig, Switzerland. Source: Author.

in this regard, China Unicom "will also make positive contributions to the 'Belt and Road' cooperation between the two countries" (Wang, 2017).

In June 2019, the company celebrated the opening of its PoP at the Green Data Center in Lupfig, near Zurich (see Figure 7.4). Prior to hosting China Unicom's PoP, Green had maintained "links with China for more than 15 years" and had "expertise in networking Swiss and Chinese companies," according to one of the data center's heads. He added that he was "very proud" to become part of the Digital Silk Road, enthusiastically exclaiming that the new high-speed fiber-optic connection to China "is a Ferrari!"[17] Similarly, Mr. Zhang, a high-ranking China Unicom Switzerland employee, had previous links to Switzerland. According to two former colleagues at Huawei Technologies Switzerland who also attended the ceremony, Mr. Zhang had formerly worked for Huawei,[18] a company that I return to in the next section.

[17] One of the Green Data Center's heads said this during the opening speech in Lupfig, June 24, 2019.
[18] Personal communication with two Huawei employees, June 24, 2019.

Active Network Components: Equipping the DSR

PoPs and data centers are equipped with active or optoelectronic components. These are powered components, such as routers, switches, multiplexers, and servers, that can transmit, direct, convert, or amplify data, which serves a variety of purposes, such as to ensure that the data reach their intended destination or are properly stored in data centers. The two major well-known competing Chinese component providers in this industry are the state-owned ZTE and the privately owned Huawei Technologies. Although ZTE had opened an office in Switzerland, it was liquidated soon afterward (Swiss Official Gazette of Commerce, 2021). According to a Huawei employee, this failure was because ZTE "did a lousy job in Switzerland."[19]

Huawei, on the other hand, has been highly successful in Switzerland (Huawei, 2024), despite lower global revenues and decreased success in Europe following US sanctions imposed in 2023 (Cerulus and Wheaton, 2022). In the company's history, however, with the exception of Russia, Europe was low on Huawei founder Ren Zhengfei's agenda, who prioritized emerging markets in African and Latin American countries. In fact, Switzerland was the last country in Europe where Huawei opened an office, in the late 2000s. The Swiss branch was officially founded in 2008 and initially reported to the Italian office. The opening was spurred by a major tender from Switzerland's largest telecom operator, Swisscom, which required Huawei to have a local office (Kaufmann, 2020). While Huawei Switzerland did encounter some pressures, including from the US government (Burg and Aebi, 2020), the company has nevertheless grown steadily in Switzerland. As of 2024, there were around 400 employees of various nationalities in offices near Bern, Zurich, and Lausanne (Huawei, 2024), equipping Swiss networks with switches, routers, antenna components, wireless local area networks, Internet of Things (IoT) gateways, and security products. By 2018, the company already had more than 40 business partners in Switzerland, collaborating not only with the cable manufacturer Dätwyler, but also with all the big telecom operators. According to one Huawei employee, Huawei provides "weapons" to the latter in their "war for more bandwidth."[20]

For a long time, Switzerland did not play a strategic role in the company's expansion to Europe, but this is beginning to change. With the opening of Huawei research centers in proximity to the Swiss Federal Institutes of Technology in Zurich and Lausanne between 2019 and 2020, Switzerland gained new significance for the company. Although Huawei managers intended to hire more than 1,000 staff and invest several hundred million Swiss francs, they have

---

[19] Personal communication, Huawei employee, August 21, 2019.
[20] Personal communication, Huawei employee, June 24, 2019.

kept these plans rather quiet so far (Greater Zurich Area, 2019; Marti, 2019). While the company's public communication stresses that Swiss innovation and education systems were reasons why they chose Switzerland, one Huawei employee confided that the company had originally planned to locate their centers in the United States. Because of the increasing US–China friction, however, Switzerland emerged as a more neutral but still research-intensive alternative.[21] Here a focus on the politics of sight points to the geopolitical sensitivities at stake and therefore the interest that a particular company like Huawei or government like that of Switzerland may have in being discreet about their plans.

The Effects of the BRI's Digital Side in Switzerland

As of 2024, the overarching effects of the BRI in Switzerland remained modest. The MoU between China and Switzerland focuses mainly on Swiss cooperation on BRI projects located in third countries and in the financial sector. As a result, the MoU has raised relatively little criticism in Switzerland. As of 2020 only a few large Swiss companies like ABB or the banks Credit Suisse and Vontobel, which already had close relationships with China, had reportedly participated in such projects—doing so both prior to and following the BRI's 2013 launch (Büchenbacher, 2020).

Notably, the BRI policy as a whole has shifted its focus from large, expensive infrastructure projects toward health, ecology, and digitalization. Chinese transnational dataflows have increased greatly in recent years and now head the global flow of cross-border data, accounting for almost one-quarter (Tsunashima, 2020). Moreover, by October 2020, the COVID-19 pandemic had already resulted in a 30–50 percent growth of overall network traffic.[22]

In view of these developments, the effects of the DSR seem to be stronger in Switzerland than the effects of other BRI projects. Nevertheless, these effects remain difficult to pinpoint because of the general invisibility of digital projects. The multiple players that constitute a fiber-optic network are not individually identifiable by digital services' end users. As long as the Internet works, people do not know whether it is due to Scandinavian, American, or Chinese involvement in the Swiss network, or a combination of the actions of all these countries. Moreover, the public usually only hears about Chinese digital infrastructures, if at all, through media reports. For these two reasons, there is generally unawareness of the DSR.

[21] Personal communication, Huawei employee, June 24, 2019.
[22] Wing Kin Leung, a Huawei Chief Technology Officer, online presentation during the Huawei Eco-Connect Europe event, October 21, 2020.

The effects of the DSR in Switzerland are thus not specifically related to the BRI or China in particular but, rather, to digitalization in general—in which Chinese companies play a crucial role. It is difficult to relate the effects of particular transnational cable networks just to Chinese companies, despite the fact that the comparatively small Swiss telecommunication companies do not run their own cross-border networks. Nevertheless, Chinese companies are not alone, as some of the bigger European telecommunication providers such as Deutsche Telekom also have cross-border networks spanning Europe and China (Deutsche Telekom, 2021).

In any case, the effects of the fiber-optic connections between China and Europe remain tangible. While individual end users may not be aware of this, Chinese enterprises in Switzerland, and Swiss multinational enterprises with a presence in China, feel especially strongly the difference that improved fiber-optic connections make. These enterprises, such as the multinational Swiss Bühler Group or the China Construction Bank's Zurich branch, are currently also the main target group for Chinese telecommunication companies in Switzerland. For example, the computers the multinational Swiss Bühler Group uses for its Chinese factories' operations are based in Switzerland. As Bühler's Chief Information Officer pointed out, "We need reliable data lines, especially to China. If the line is down, the factory is also down."[23]

Finally, the geopolitical question of who contributes components and builds, controls, or has potential access to data arguably always lingers in the background. While the question of what counts as risk and what counts as security is a social one, the more physical aspect of the technical possibilities of network abuse and espionage is beyond the scope of this chapter. In my interviews and visits to sites and events, Swiss telecommunication providers displayed a rather pragmatic attitude toward integrating Chinese technologies into their networks. This does not mean, however, that the Swiss government and companies in this sector are unaware of the cybersecurity risks related to the Chinese involvement in 5G or the challenges posed by the IoT (see, e.g., Federal Department of Foreign Affairs, 2021; Swisscom, 2021). Vulnerability to cybersecurity threats, whether perceived or real, is certainly one effect of the DSR that the Swiss public, companies, and politicians need to address.

Conclusion

This chapter has made clear that we need to consider the BRI in general and the DSR in particular over a time frame that predates their official launch in

---

[23] Bühler's Chief Information Officer, company presentation, November 21, 2019.

the 2010s. Digital technologies and the DSR may at first appear to be recent developments, as they have gained increasing public visibility alongside growing geopolitical tensions. Yet, rather invisibly, Chinese companies have engaged in the large-scale production of fiber-optic cables, the transnational laying of cables, and the sale of their active components to Europe since the 1990s. Although Chinese ICT companies began accelerating development in the 1990s with support from government policies, they have been preparing to catch up with North America, Western Europe, and Japan in this field since at least the 1950s (Cortada, 2012).

These developments have, however, occurred mostly out of sight. The fact that observers are only now beginning to "see" Chinese fiber-optic networks should be viewed in the wider context of the PRC's economic growth, increased international technological competition, and the Sino-American trade war that began during the Trump administration. Moreover, the fact that the Chinese government has inscribed fiber-optic networks into its overall BRI narrative and policy documents has further garnered international attention to these infrastructures. Aside from media debates around Huawei, the public in European countries such as Switzerland continues to be mostly oblivious to digital infrastructures in general, and the DSR in particular. It is mostly Chinese diplomats and Chinese companies that push the DSR narrative in Switzerland. Meanwhile, apart from some industry insiders like the Green Data Center head quoted earlier, few people in Switzerland would call themselves part of the BRI and its digital component, especially in public. While all these facets make the DSR difficult to grasp, it is precisely this ambiguity that "lies at the heart of the BRI" (Schatz and Silvey, introduction to this volume: 8).

This chapter has also highlighted the multidirectionality of the DSR. In Europe, the DSR is commonly perceived as moving from China to other countries. While Chinese ICT companies increasingly attract international media attention (e.g., Hope, 2023), China observers in Europe and elsewhere largely overlook the fact that Swiss cable makers play an important role in connecting infrastructure projects within China, and that European telecom operators such as Deutsche Telekom also run fiber-optic networks in China (even though they are not comparable in quantity). The British colonial expansion of telegraph lines is, in a way, a predecessor of the expansion of communication technology from Europe to Asia. Yet, paradoxically, the notion that the DSR is also a road from Europe or other places to China is precisely the image that Chinese telecom operators paint in the marketing material I collected. This is partly to try to attract European companies, based on a narrative of immense business opportunities in China, but also, in view of the ongoing Huawei debate as well as more general Western fears of Chinese neocolonialism, a Silk Road *to* (not just from) China may appear much less threatening to the rest of the world.

Finally, this chapter has shown that as BRI projects extend into Europe, and as the DSR speeds up the Internet in Switzerland in particular, China's role in all of this may be of little significance to the Swiss public. The Chinese Communist Party (CCP) is far from the only actor driving the BRI's expansion, and as such, the DSR may be better understood as a set of multinational investments than as an element of any coherent geopolitical strategy emanating from Beijing. Indeed, while Chinese companies are often owned by the state, aided by government policies, and publicly supported by CCP diplomats, they are also often competitors with one another, and they may even outcompete each other, as in the case of ZTE and Huawei in Switzerland. Nevertheless, when taken together, Chinese digital infrastructures certainly play an increasingly significant role in the digitalization of Switzerland, a fact that most people would not even have dared to imagine a few years ago.

8

Keeping Watch along the Digital Silk Road

CCTV Surveillance and Central Asians' Right to Privacy

Jasmin Dall'Agnola

Introduction

In the context of the COVID-19 pandemic, we witnessed a proliferation of smart city technologies to tackle the spread of infectious diseases. Even European governments, which previously condemned China's smart city equipment as restrictive of human rights, began to develop similar tools, including the unprecedented use of drone surveillance, data tracking, facial recognition, and other forms of biometrics for quarantine enforcement and contact tracing (Kitchin, 2020). Whereas face masks have disappeared, smart surveillance technologies, such as closed-circuit television (CCTV) cameras with integrated facial recognition software (FRS), have become part of everyday law enforcement and governmental practices everywhere. As such, the preliminary fear among surveillance scholars, such as French and Monahan (2020), that the global health crisis would be used by governments around the world—and authoritarian-leaning regimes in particular—to normalize mass surveillance and expand their control over the population has proven to be justified.

Thus far, we know little about how the pandemic shaped the use of smart city technologies by nondemocratic regimes to monitor their citizenry. Even less is known about whether the pandemic has helped Chinese technology companies, such as Huawei, Hikvision, and Dahua Technology, to position themselves as providers of affordable, high-quality surveillance cameras in authoritarian-leaning countries. Yet we do know that Chinese technology vendors are promoting and selling their high-resolution artificial intelligence (AI) surveillance cameras with FRS—under the banner of China's Digital Silk Road (DSR)—to Central Asia (Stryker, 2021; Yau, 2022b).

Apart from some studies describing the use of Chinese CCTV cameras to combat the COVID-19 virus in the Central Asian cities of Bishkek, Kyrgyzstan, and Almaty, Kazakhstan (Marat, 2020; Marat and Sutton, 2021), there is no significant public debate in Central Asia surrounding China's DSR. Similarly, we lack studies on the wider Central Asian public's attitude toward Chinese CCTV

Jasmin Dall'Agnola, *Keeping Watch along the Digital Silk Road* In: Seeing China's Belt and Road. Edited by: Edward Schatz and Rachel Silvey, Oxford University Press. © Oxford University Press 2025.
DOI: 10.1093/oso/9780197789261.003.0009

cameras' presence in public places. In this chapter, I argue that this is problematic because Chinese surveillance cameras not only are used by local elites to track people's whereabouts, but they also enable Chinese businesses and, by extension, Chinese authorities to collect and store big data on Central Asian citizens. As such, Chinese CCTV cameras can infringe upon Central Asians' privacy.

In investigating whether Central Asian people's privacy concerns over their government's unauthorized stockpiling of citizens' private information affects their approval of Chinese CCTV cameras in public spaces, this chapter seeks to illustrate what the normalization of mass state surveillance, intensified by China's DSR, has come to mean for individuals' data and privacy in Central Asia. Methodologically, this study uses an interpretative qualitative frame that features analysis of survey data from the World Value Survey (WVS) Wave 7 country data sets for Kazakhstan, Kyrgyzstan, and Tajikistan (Haerpfer et al., 2022),[1] along with some preliminary observations from my fieldwork on Chinese CCTV cameras conducted in the three Central Asian states in the summer of 2022.

The rest of this chapter is divided into four sections. The first provides an overview of the broader scholarly debate about the visibility of China's DSR in Central Asia and assesses China's growing influence through smart city technologies, especially CCTV cameras with FRS, in the region. Drawing on previous scholarship's findings and my visual documentation and assessment of Chinese CCTV cameras in the region in 2022, the first section demonstrates that Chinese technology firms such as Huawei, Dahua Technology, and Hikvision are indeed the dominant providers of surveillance cameras in Central Asia. The second section summarizes the existing scholarship on public perceptions of privacy and Chinese technologies in Central Asia, before I present the methodological approach employed. In the third section, I introduce the statistical analysis, which reveals that, despite a strong correlation between Central Asian citizens' privacy concerns and their support for the deployment of CCTV cameras in public areas, most Central Asians seem to approve of mass surveillance through outdoor video cameras. The study ends with a critical reflection on how Central Asians see Chinese surveillance cameras and, by extension, China's DSR in the region.

---

[1] Uzbekistan had to be excluded from this study because the Uzbek authorities are currently blocking the transfer of public opinion data that were collected by a local Uzbek polling center for the World Value Survey Secretariat in 2022 (Dall'Agnola, 2024). Turkmenistan had to be excluded, not only because it is the only Central Asian country where the implementation of the WVS wave has not been possible (Haerpfer and Kizilova, 2020), but also because it was impossible for the author to enter the country to conduct field research.

The Digital Silk Road and Chinese CCTV Cameras
in Central Asia

Since Xi Jinping visited Kazakhstan in September 2013 to unveil the "One Belt, One Road" strategy, since renamed the Belt and Road Initiative (BRI), China has pledged nearly $1 trillion in development assistance and infrastructure projects in more than 120 countries, including the Central Asian states of Kazakhstan, Kyrgyzstan, and Tajikistan (Vila Seoane, 2020) Recent scholarship on the BRI in Central Asia has predominantly focused on the scale of its economic infrastructure projects, from ports and roads to railways and gas pipelines.

Less attention has been paid to the BRI's digital element, the DSR. This is surprising given the growing popularity of Chinese digital, health, and smart city technologies during the pandemic (Chen, 2023). The reluctance of previous scholarship to investigate the DSR can be explained as follows: although some estimate that DSR-related investments in digital infrastructure projects outside China already surpass $79 billion, comprehensive data on the scale of DSR projects and investment are difficult to locate (Ghiasy and Krishnamurthy, 2021). Moreover, little is known about how Chinese firms engage in these developments and operate within the DSR (Vila Seoane, 2020). Whether a given information technology (IT) project is related to the DSR often remains unclear, as there is no official definition of a DSR project (Cheng and Zeng, 2023). Similar to the BRI more generally, "ambiguity lies at [its] heart" (Schatz and Silvey, introduction, this volume: 8). Given this ambiguity, it is impossible to separate DSR projects from China's foreign relations more generally. Also, while most infrastructure projects, such as new railroads and ports, are visible, the scale and impact of DSR projects and investments are less visible and are therefore harder to analyze (Oreglia, Ren, and Liao, 2021).[2]

Since its launch in 2015, the DSR not only acts as a door opener for Chinese technology giants such as Alibaba, Huawei, and Tencent but also helps them to promote their technological solutions in Central Asian countries (Kassenova and Duprey, 2021). On the one hand, the DSR is about the development and promotion of critical digital infrastructure such as transcontinental submarine data cables, cellular networks, and global satellite navigation systems (Shen, 2018; Vila Seoane, 2020). On the other hand, the DSR seeks to increase the connectivity between businesses and consumers through the promotion of Chinese smart city technologies (AI cameras, drones, facial recognition robots, and tracking apps), education technology platforms, apps, routers, smartphones,

---

[2] As Kaufmann (Chapter 7, p. 147 of this volume) argues, "This is not surprising, as most digital infrastructures are buried underground, in the ocean, or hidden from the public in remote and inaccessible data centers."

and computers (Kassenova and Duprey, 2021; Oreglia et al., 2021). Today, "Chinese surveillance technology is used in more than eighty countries" (Hillman, 2021: 11). Thanks to ethnographic fieldwork in various Central Asian cities in 2022, I can confirm previous scholars' speculation that the fight against COVID-19 indeed accelerated the spread of Chinese CCTV cameras in the region (Marat and Sutton, 2021; Stryker, 2021). My interlocutors in the field were unanimous in contending that Chinese technology firms, most notably Huawei, Dahua Technology, and Hikvision, had become the dominant suppliers of surveillance technologies in Central Asia.

In Kazakhstan, local authorities continued to rely on Chinese technology firms' supply of and knowledge about surveillance technology, but at the same time they invested in locally made surveillance tools that allowed the storage of data on local servers (Marat, 2020). The Astana-based tech firm Sergek Group,[3] in close collaboration with the Chinese technology company Dahua Technology, was building Kazakhstan's video surveillance capacity as part of the Kazakhstani government's "National Video Monitoring System" (Gussarova, 2020; Gussarova and Jaksylykov, 2021). According to Marat (2020), in Astana alone 14,000 Sergek video cameras were monitoring the movement of people. Despite previously raised concerns by the local human rights activist Serikzhan Bilash about Sergek cameras facilitating Chinese spying on local Uyghur communities in Almaty (Altynbayev, 2019), the system was rolled out in various cities, including Almaty, Atyrau, Shymkent, Semey, Taraz, Ust-Kamenogorsk, and Turkestan (Shesternyova, 2023). The cameras were originally installed to help decrease traffic accidents and criminal activities but were then used to monitor people violating quarantine regulations during the COVID-19 pandemic (Gussarova, 2020). In addition to Dahua Technology, Hikvision, another Chinese manufacturer of surveillance cameras under US sanctions,[4] also supplied CCTV cameras with FRS in major urban centers across Kazakhstan, including Almaty and Shymkent (Mukhitkyzy, 2019).

Moreover, during the summer of 2021, Kazakhstani officials rolled out the country's first Huawei-backed 5G installations in the capital Astana to facilitate a fully Chinese surveillance program (Yau, 2022b). Having documented and visually assessed the surveillance infrastructure in both Almaty and Astana in 2022, I can confirm that the number of Chinese CCTV cameras in Kazakhstan was substantially higher than official government reports suggested. From

---

[3] For information about Sergek Group and its AI-powered approach to traffic and mobility for smart cities, see https://sergek.tech/.

[4] In November 2022, the United States banned the integration of Chinese technology companies, such as the video surveillance companies Dahua Technology and Hikvision, into its critical infrastructure due to security concerns. For more details see the Federal Communication Commission's communiqué: https://www.fcc.gov/document/fcc-bans-authorizations-devices-pose-national-security-threat.

Figure 8.1 Photo of Hikvision camera in a university classroom in Almaty.
Source: Author.

the public entrance hall of their residency to their favorite gym or hairdresser, Chinese CCTV cameras were omnipresent in Kazakhstanis' lives in 2020. Even in universities funded by Western donors, Chinese video cameras were used by the administration to register students' and faculty's attendance in classrooms, as Figure 8.1 shows.

The omnipresence of Chinese surveillance cameras in Kazakhstanis' lives was problematic for two reasons. First, Kazakhstan's data protection law[5] provided the Kazakh government with unlimited access to citizens' personal information for any reason under the amorphously defined umbrella of "national security" (Gussarova and Jaksylykov, 2020, 2021). Second, the same law asked IT companies to store the collected data on a local server, but it did not clearly prohibit the storing of duplicate versions of the data outside the country, for example in China.[6] Chinese technology companies therefore could be expected to enjoy greater access to citizens' personal data than previously assumed.

---

[5] See https://online.zakon.kz/document/?doc_id = 31396226#pos = 3;-157.

[6] The danger of surveillance footage being exfiltrated by Chinese surveillance cameras to China was real. In 2020, the African Union (AU) discovered that Chinese CCTV equipment

Similarly, in Kyrgyzstan, most surveillance camera projects were implemented using foreign manufacturers of CCTV technology in direct cooperation with the Kyrgyz government. In 2018, Kyrgyzstan turned down Huawei's $60 million "safe city" project and instead signed a $33 million contract with the Russian technology company Vega to install 28 traffic-monitoring cameras in Bishkek and a total of 90 cameras across the whole country by September 2018 (Marat and Sutton, 2021). While the camera software was developed by a local Kyrgyz company, Vega oversaw the collection of data from its headquarters in Moscow (Marat, 2020). It also took a cut from all recorded traffic fines. In March 2019, the Kyrgyz government entered a similar agreement with China National Electronics Import and Export Corporation to install 60 Chinese-made CCTV cameras with FRS around Bishkek (Kudryavtseva, 2019; Mills and Wang, 2019). As part of this $5 million deal, the local authorities enjoyed access to FRS, but the intellectual property rights associated with the collected data remained with the Chinese company (Marat and Sutton, 2021: 257).

Despite a public outcry by some human rights campaigners over the potential for abuse of people's data and privacy rights by Chinese and local authorities (Mills and Wang, 2019), the Kyrgyz government has agreed to numerous other deals with Chinese technology firms since 2019. For example, as part of the second phase of Bishkek's "safe city" project, the local authorities opted for surveillance cameras with FRS that were installed by the Chinese company Shenzhen Sunwin Intelligent Co. Ltd. in 2022 (Kudryavtseva, 2021). The second stage of the "safe city" project covered all regions of the republic, two so-called republican cities, 15 so-called cities of regional significance, and 73 settlements. As a result, by October 2022, almost all Russian Vega cameras were replaced by Chinese CCTV cameras such as Hikvision and Dahua Technology in Bishkek city (fieldwork observation). Similar to Kazakhstan, the Kyrgyz government could access its citizens' personal data on the pretext of justice, national security, and the fight against terrorism or corruption.[7] Since 2017, state officials have sold citizens' private data to financial organizations and Chinese IT companies and some of them, as in the case of the presidential candidate Sooronbay Jeenbekov, even misused personal information to manipulate elections (Stryker, 2021).

Tajikistan's relationship with Chinese technology companies dates to 2013, when the government signed a $22 million deal for Huawei to install hundreds of CCTV and traffic cameras around Dushanbe (Yau, 2019). Quickly, over 870 Huawei CCTV cameras sprang up around the city, monitoring traffic and public

---

secretly transmitted surveillance footage from the AU headquarters in Ethiopia to servers in China (Hillman, 2021).

[7] See http://cbd.minjust.gov.kg/act/view/ru-ru/202269.

spaces, and sending the live footage to a panopticon-like TV-filled headquarters. By 2023, the number of cameras had doubled (Sputnik 2022). The loan was reportedly repayable within 20 years through fines that were collected from traffic offenders caught on camera. By 2019, the "Safe City" project begun in 2013 in Dushanbe had led to the issuance of fines in the amount of more than 132 million somoni ($13 million) per year (Rukhullo, 2019). Since those cameras lacked FRS, the Tajik government decided to modernize its CCTV infrastructure and to replace it with new Huawei cameras in 2019, not only in the center of the capital, but also at Dushanbe's airport, the railway station, and in every major shopping center (Rukhullo, 2019). Similar to Kyrgyzstan, the intellectual property rights associated with the data collected through Chinese CCTV cameras belonged to the Chinese company and therefore were often stored in data centers outside of Tajikistan. In October 2023, Tajikistan's authorities signed another deal that allowed Huawei ($25 million) to install Chinese surveillance cameras in Khujand starting in Spring 2024 (Mustafaeva, 2023). Having visited Dushanbe in the summer of 2022, I can attest that Chinese IT companies such as Huawei, Dahua Technology, and Hikvision dominated Tajikistan's video camera hardware market. Indeed, there were hundreds of Huawei cameras in Dushanbe's center. In the Rudaki park alone, there were several dozens of Chinese Huawei cameras watching pedestrians (Figure 8.2).

Tajikistan's personal data protection law, similar to Kazakhstan's and Kyrgyzstan's, stipulated that the Tajik government had the right to store information about anyone living in the country without citizens' consent if it was necessary for state authorities to carry out their functions or for the sake of national security (Narodnaya Gazeta, 2018).

Overall, Chinese CCTV cameras with FRS and AI were rolled out across Central Asia without public consultation or the necessary transparency, making it unclear if the government was failing to mitigate the potential impact of Chinese technology on citizens' privacy or was inherently in favor of undermining privacy due to its own desire for surveillance. This was problematic for two reasons. Advanced FRS in CCTV cameras in public spaces not only enabled the local elites to track and monitor people's habits and movements, but, due to loopholes in the Central Asian states' data regulations, Chinese CCTV cameras also enabled Chinese firms (and by proxy the Chinese government) to access and store sensitive information and data about Central Asian citizens. As part of the DSR, Central Asian states with more modest surveillance budgets, such as Kyrgyzstan and Tajikistan, in providing Chinese IT firms with unlimited access to people's data, were trading their citizens' privacy rights for new technology. This was a victory for local authorities, who were able to monitor their citizens while gaining access to cutting-edge technology that enabled them to do so. In all three Central Asian countries, state officials were willing to

Figure 8.2 Huawei camera in Dushanbe's Rudaki Park. Source: Author.

sacrifice the protection of their citizens' privacy in pursuit of rapid technological modernization.

Mass surveillance enabled by DSR infrastructure projects does not necessarily benefit the local population or local governments in Central Asia. Arguably, it may benefit the latter at the expense of the former. However, unless their partnership with Chinese companies is carefully regulated, regional authorities suffer under what some researchers call "data colonialism" (Couldry and Mejias, 2019: 337), a process that is also at play in other countries due to monopolization of the market by US-based technology firms (Zuboff, 2019). I therefore argue in this chapter that the increasing state-led use of Chinese surveillance cameras threatens Central Asian citizens' privacy rights.

Public Attitudes toward Privacy and Chinese Technologies in Central Asia

Thus far, we know little about how the public views local authorities' increased surveillance, which is enabled by Chinese technology, or about any corrosive impact this might have on Central Asian citizens' privacy rights. Several factors, including Central Asians' understanding of privacy and their attitudes toward Chinese technologies and their government, all affect the degree to which Central Asians approve their authorities' use of Chinese CCTV cameras in public spaces.

In this context, it seems important to emphasize that Central Asians' understanding of privacy is strongly influenced by communist ideology, which viewed citizens' privacy as secondary to social harmony. Until Khrushchev's mass housing project in the 1960s, which promoted the idea that every family should have its own apartment, there was no space for privacy in the dense communal flats (*kommunalki*) in Soviet Central Asia (Toqmadi and Zakharchenko, 2021). Claims to one's own private information had no place in this context where collective (state) ownership of individuals' information was the norm. The presumed ownership of citizens' data by the state has been inherited from this colonial past and continues to influence state policy agendas and discourses on CCTV cameras in public spaces (Marat and Sutton, 2021). Central Asian elites tend to subordinate concerns with privacy to their interest in protecting the country and its citizens from external and internal threats. Their emphasis on security shifts the focus away from possible accusations of state-led privacy infringements (Toqmadi and Zakharchenko, 2021). Surveillance cameras are often advertised by Central Asian authorities as an effective way to protect the public from harm by reducing crime (Marat and Sutton, 2021).

The culture of collectivism and the legacy of colonial history have contributed to the neglect of privacy both by the state and citizens in Central Asia. Privacy is often described by Central Asians as a foreign concept that originates in the West (Toqmadi and Zakharchenko, 2021; author's fieldnotes). While being alarmed by the immense penetration of the state into citizens' personal space, Central Asians entrust a vast majority of their information and data to their governments (Toqmadi and Zakharchenko, 2021; author's fieldnotes). In fact, in their study on data protection laws in Kazakhstan, Gussarova and Jaksylykov (2020) found that Kazakhstanis are more afraid of IT companies harvesting personal data without peoples' informed consent than of state-led mass surveillance. In their follow-up study on how Kazakhstanis' perceptions of data protection and privacy changed during the COVID-19 pandemic, Gussarova and Jaksylykov (2021) found their previous observation on Kazakhstanis' approval of mass surveillance to be reaffirmed: almost two-thirds of their respondents approved the state's use of Sergek video cameras, manufactured by Sergek Group with the help of Dahua Technology, to collect citizens' personal data for the purpose of improving national security. The Central Asia Barometer Survey Wave 11 (2022) for Kazakhstan, Kyrgyzstan, and Tajikistan confirms the trends identified by Gussarova and Jaksylykov (2021) in that it finds that Central Asians support the use of video surveillance systems in public places designed to reduce crime.

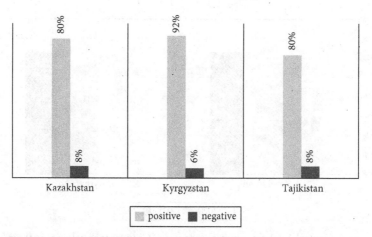

Figure 8.3 Central Asians' sentiments toward CCTV cameras in public spaces, designed to reduce crime. Source: Central Asia Barometer Wave 11 (2022).

According to the Central Asia Barometer Wave 11 (2022), as of 2022, almost 80 percent of respondents in Tajikistan and more than 90 percent of respondents in Kyrgyzstan and Kazakhstan felt very or somewhat positive about the use of CCTV cameras in public spaces for the purpose of reducing crime (Figure 8.3).

In this sense, Central Asian citizens typically are willing to give up a large share of their privacy rights in exchange for the greater public safety.

Moreover, since I am interested in observing how Central Asian citizens' privacy concerns influence their attitudes toward Chinese CCTV cameras, it seems sensible to analyze the available survey data on Central Asians' sentiments toward Chinese technologies, conducted by the Central Asia Barometer between 2020 and 2022.

Overall, the public opinion data collected by the Central Asia Barometer in Figure 8.4 suggest that Kazakhstanis and Kyrgyzstanis' support for Chinese technologies had increased since the outbreak of the COVID-19 pandemic in 2020. As of 2022, more than 60 percent of respondents in Kazakhstan and more than 70 percent of respondents in Kyrgyzstan approved of the use of Chinese technologies in their country. Unfortunately, the Central Asia Barometer did not survey people's attitudes toward Chinese technologies in Tajikistan. However, previous research found that Tajikistanis display more favorable attitudes toward China in general because Tajikistan has fewer economic partners to rely on than its neighbors (Laruelle and Royce, 2020). The country therefore appreciates Chinese investments and technological equipment more than its neighbors. Moreover, public discussions of a Chinese demographic threat are less prominent in Tajikistan than they are in Kazakhstan and Kyrgyzstan

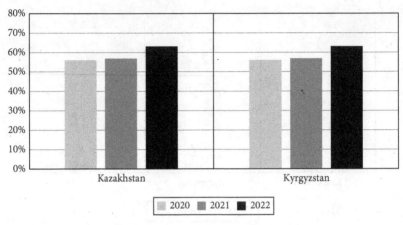

Figure 8.4 Central Asians' support for the use of Chinese technologies in their country. Source: Central Asia Barometer (2020–2022).

(author's fieldnotes). The survey data from the Central Asia Barometer Wave 11 (2022) seems to support my fieldwork notes inasmuch as they find that more than 60 percent of respondents described China as very friendly or somewhat friendly toward Tajikistan in late 2022. As such, it seems safe to assume that the wider public in Tajikistan welcomes the use of Chinese technologies in their country.

Drawing on previous studies on Central Asians' understanding of privacy and attitudes toward Chinese technologies, I therefore hypothesize that *Central Asian citizens approve of Chinese video cameras in public areas, despite the possible infringement to their right to privacy.*

Central Asian citizens' willingness to share personal information with the state through outdoor Chinese CCTV cameras has causes other than their understanding of privacy and opinion of China. Another possible explanation was put forward by Gussarova and Jaksylykov (2021), whose second public opinion poll recorded a certain sense of despair among the public regarding the Kazakhstani government's surveillance practices. Sixty-six percent of respondents believed that people in Kazakhstan have no choice other than to accept their government's invasive collection of personal information, because authorities will do what they want regardless of public opinion (Gussarova and Jaksylykov, 2021). Similar observations were reported by Toqmadi and Zakharchenko (2021) in a study on citizens' perception of privacy in Kyrgyzstan and Kazakhstan. Focus group participants frequently linked the widespread corruption of government structures with the state's possible misuse of people's personal data to falsify criminal records. Since anti-Chinese protests are often antigovernment in nature due to the popular assumption of an inherent link be-tween the two in Central Asia (Karibayeva, 2020), citizens who are in favor of their government can be assumed to display more welcoming attitudes toward China and therefore Chinese CCTV cameras. This leads to a second hypoth-esis: *the public's confidence in government predicts support for Chinese CCTV sur-veillance deployed by that government.*

Data and Methodology

To evaluate what the normalization of mass surveillance promoted by the DSR has come to mean for individuals' data and privacy, I turn to the WVS Wave 7 (Haerpfer et al., 2022) country data on Kazakhstan, Kyrgyzstan, and Tajikistan. The three surveys featured 3,600 respondents in total, but I narrowed this down to focus on those who answered the necessary questions (a total of 3,253 respondents). Participants were aged 18 and older. The interviewee selection procedure for the WVS surveys was designed to capture a representative sample of each country's adult population. The data were collected using a multistage stratified sampling method. The stratification was based on territorial admin-istrative units and rural and urban populations. Households were selected ran-domly within each stratum. In Tajikistan, the survey was conducted in Tajik or Russian, according to interviewee's choice of language, and carried out by the Research Center SHARQ/Oriens in Dushanbe. The interviews took place in January and February 2020 and covered all four provinces of Tajikistan: Gorno-Badakhshan, Sughd, Khatlon, and the Regions of Republican Subordination, as well as the capital city of Dushanbe. In Kazakhstan, the survey was also conducted in participants' language preference (Kazakh or Russian) by the Astana-based Public Opinion Research Institute in October and November 2018. It incorporated all five regions of Kazakhstan: North, Central, West, South, and East Kazakhstan, as well as the three cities with republican status: Astana (capital), Almaty, and Shymkent. In Kyrgyzstan, the survey was administered in respondents' language of choice (Kyrgyz or Russian) by the local staff of the nonprofit Central Asia Barometer Institute. The survey took place in December 2019 and January 2020 and featured participants from all seven regions of Kyrgyzstan: Batken, Chuy, Jalal-Abad, Naryn, Osh, Talas, and Issy-Kul, as well as the two cities with regional status: Bishkek (capital) and Osh.

The questionnaire item to capture people's approval of CCTV cameras in public spaces (my dependent variable) reads as follows: *Do you think this country's government should or should not have the right to do the following: keep people under video surveillance in public areas?* Respondents' answer to this question was initially recorded in four categories (1 = *Definitely should have the right*, 2 = *Probably should have the right*, 3 = *Probably should not have the right*, 4 = *Definitely should not have the right*). In order to change this ordinal four-point Likert scale into a binary variable, respondents who said that their government should either *definitely* or *probably* have the right to use surveillance cameras with FRS and AI in public areas were merged into the general category *should have*, and the remaining responses were merged into the general category *should not have*.

The statistical models in this study included a variety of controls, reflecting the findings in the previous literature regarding factors that influence people's attitudes toward CCTV cameras in their neighborhoods (Bradford et al., 2020; Gurinskaya, 2020; Gussarova and Jaksylykov, 2020, 2021; Marat and Sutton, 2021). Control variables consistently found by previous studies to be associated with citizens' concerns about surveillance cameras are age,[8] gender,[9] urban/rural residency,[10] and social class.[11] These control variables were included in the statistical models for this chapter.

In this study, the critical independent variable is respondents' privacy concerns about invasive harvesting of citizens' private data by their governments. Mass surveillance conducted by the state threatens citizens' right to privacy. In asking participants *if they think that their government should or should not have the right to collect information about anyone living in their country without their knowledge*, the WVS questionnaire captured Central Asians' attitudes toward possible privacy infringement due to state-led unauthorized mass collection of citizens' private information. Again, respondents' answers to this question were changed into binary variables, with *should definitely* or *should probably have the right to collect information* combined into the category *should* and the remaining ones into *should not*.

Since there may be other factors affecting Central Asian citizens' attitudes toward video surveillance cameras in public spaces in addition to their

---

[8] Younger people were found to display more welcoming attitudes toward the use of CCTV cameras in policing, because they are more frequently exposed to crime (Bradford et al., 2020; Gussarova and Jaksylykov, 2021).

[9] The gender of people can also influence their attitudes toward CCTV cameras. In her study on Russian youth's support for surveillance cameras in St. Petersburg, Gurinskaya (2020) found that women held more positive views of CCTV cameras with FRS and AI because they were more afraid of becoming the victim of a crime in public spaces than their male peers. We could thus expect Central Asian women to be more approving of CCTV surveillance because women seem to be more concerned about their safety in public spaces than men.

[10] Urbanites were found to display a less welcoming attitude toward the use of CCTV cameras in public spaces than their counterparts living in the countryside, mainly because they are more aware of privacy infringements thanks to their frequent exposure to the Internet and other technologies (Gussarova and Jaksylykov, 2021; Marat and Sutton, 2021).

[11] Working class people were found to be less likely to support their government's use of CCTV cameras than their middle- and upper-class counterparts, because people belonging to the working class often include internal migrants and populations engaged in the shadow economy that are the main target of the increased state surveillance (Marat and Sutton, 2021).

privacy concerns and demographic characteristics discussed earlier, one alternative explanation for respondents' acceptance of CCTV cameras was considered: whether a participant had a *great deal, quite a lot, not very much confidence,* or *none at all* in their government. This additional variable was measured by the WVS 7 with the following question: *Now I am going to name a number of organizations. For each one, could you tell me how much confidence you have in them: is it a great deal of confidence, quite a lot of confidence, not very much confidence or none at all? [the government (in your nation's capital)].* To include this additional independent variable was crucial because previous scholarship found citizens' trust in their government to be an important predictor of their acceptance or rejection of CCTV cameras in public spaces (Gurinskaya, 2020; Gussarova and Jaksylykov, 2020). I therefore merged *great deal* and *quite a lot of confidence* into the category of *trust* (1) and the remainder into the category of *no trust* (0).

While the WVS's questionnaire only captured Central Asian citizens' approval of the state's use of CCTV cameras more broadly and not specifically for Chinese providers of surveillance cameras, as previously discussed, it is reasonable to assume that Chinese firms such as Huawei, Dahua Technology, and Hikvision are by far the most dominant suppliers of surveillance cameras in Central Asia. Thus, the majority of surveillance cameras with FRS and AI in public areas are of Chinese origin, either directly (in the case of Kyrgyzstan and Tajikistan) or indirectly (in the case of Kazakhstan). Moreover, in contrast to previous scholars' assumptions (Marat and Sutton, 2021), I have good reason to believe that Central Asians know that Chinese firms are overwhelmingly involved in this space. Most Central Asians I met and interviewed during my fieldwork in 2022, when asked about the main manufacturer of CCTV cameras in their country, were aware that the majority of CCTV cameras in public spaces are produced by Chinese companies such as Huawei, Dahua Technology, and Hikvision. This statistical analysis is therefore valuable not only because it allows us to identify trends that can be investigated later in qualitative studies, but also because it is the first study to explore the wider Central Asian public's support for surveillance cameras beyond Kazakhstan and Kyrgyzstan.

Central Asian Citizens' Attitudes toward CCTV Cameras

Prior to presenting the regression analysis, it is worth providing a descriptive overview of how the support for CCTV cameras in the different Central Asian states varies across genders, generations, classes, and urban and rural residences. Table 8.1 illustrates citizens' support for CCTV cameras in Kazakhstan, Kyrgyzstan, and Tajikistan. Overall, Central Asians accept being kept under

Table 8.1 Descriptive statistics of Central Asians' support for CCTV cameras.

	Kazakhstan	Kyrgyzstan	Tajikistan
Gender[a]			
Women	62.3%	82.1%	82.6%
Men	59.6%	76.3%	78.1%
Generation[a]			
18–29 years old	67.4%	77.4%	73.7%
30–49 years old	58.8%	78.9%	80.5%
50+ years old	59.7%	83.2%	86.2%
Social class[a]			
Middle class	67.3%	83.8%	78.5%
Lower middle class	66.2%	73.3%	81.6%
Working class	48.8%	78.6%	81.2%
Area[a]			
Urban	57.5%	77.2%	76.7%
Rural	65.5%	81.6%	81.8%
Privacy concern[a]			
Concern	51.4%	72.7%	61.1%
No concern	87.7%	94.6%	92.7%
Government[a]			
Trust	66.2%	84.0%	81.0%
No Trust	48.1%	75.1%	74.1%

Source: Haerpfer et al. (2022).

[a] The government should *definitely* and *probably* have the right to keep people under video surveillance in public areas.

observation in public spaces without much opposition. More than 55 percent of respondents, irrespective of their country of residence, age, gender, or social class answered that the government should have the right to keep people under video surveillance in public areas. Apart from working class citizens in Kazakhstan (48.8 percent), Central Asian citizens, regardless of their social class, were in favor of electronic surveillance cameras.

In line with previous research on Russia (Gurinskaya, 2020), Central Asian women displayed a slightly more positive (3–6 percent) view of CCTV cameras than male citizens. Also, in line with previous studies' forecast on Kazakhstan and Kyrgyzstan (Gussarova and Jaksylykov, 2021; Marat and Sutton, 2021), Central Asians living in the countryside were slightly more supportive (4–7 percent) of surveillance cameras than their urban counterparts. Moreover, respondents who have more confidence in government were more approving (7–18 percent) of the introduction of video surveillance in their districts than those who had less trust in those institutions. For example, 66.3 percent of Kazakhstani respondents who trusted their government approved the state-led use of CCTV cameras in public spaces, whereas out of the respondents who did not trust their government, only 48.1 percent displayed favorable attitudes toward CCTV surveillance. Finally, the evidence presented in Table 8.1 supports previous studies' observations (Gussarova and Jaksylykov, 2021; Marat and Sutton, 2021) that Central Asian citizens are willing to trade their privacy rights for enhanced security brought to them by surveillance cameras. Even respondents who voiced general concerns about the state-led invasive collection of private information tended to approve of their government's use of video surveillance in public places. Kazakhstanis expressed the highest level of concern (48.6 percent) about mass surveillance via outdoor CCTV cameras in public areas. In Kyrgyzstan and Tajikistan only 27.3 percent and 38.9 percent of respondents, respectively, did so.

If we present the same information in graphical form (see Figure 8.5), the differences between the three states are even more pronounced. Overall, Tajikistanis were both more likely to approve video surveillance (more than 80 percent) and the state's collection of citizens' private information (more than 60 percent) than citizens in Kyrgyzstan. Kazakhstanis, by contrast, were more in favor of state-led mass data surveillance (73 percent) and expressed the highest level of concern about surveillance cameras (41 percent).

Similar to citizens in Tajikistan, the majority of respondents in Kyrgyzstan supported their government's use of CCTV cameras (79 percent).[12] Finally, given the Kyrgyzstani government's past misuse of citizens' private data (Stryker, 2021), it comes as no surprise that Kyrgyzstanis expressed the highest level of disapproval of their state's unauthorized collection of citizens' private information (68 percent). Overall, the descriptive results support the hypothesis that Central Asian citizens generally accept CCTV cameras, irrespective of their demographic characteristics or privacy concerns. Furthermore, the findings suggest that citizens in Tajikistan display a more welcoming attitude toward surveillance

---

[12] While the percentage of people who are favorable toward CCTV surveillance in Kyrgyzstan and Tajikistan resembles public support in the United Kingdom, where 86 percent backed the state's use of CCTV cameras in 2014 (Synectics White Paper, 2014), Kazakhstanis display a slightly lower, but still significant, level of support for video cameras.

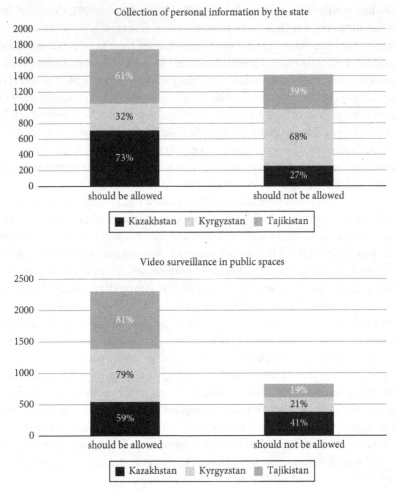

Figure 8.5 Central Asian citizens' approval of video surveillance and collection of private information by their government. Source: Haerpfer et al. (2022).

cameras, whether the cameras are Chinese or not, than their counterparts in Kazakhstan and Kyrgyzstan.

Table 8.2 presents models that test this chapter's first hypothesis, namely, that Central Asian people support video surveillance cameras in public places, which were manufactured by a Chinese technology firm, despite possible infringements on their privacy rights. Model 1 provides a baseline featuring the demographic control variables of *gender, age, social class, urban/rural,* and the critical independent variable of *privacy concerns.* In line with previous studies' findings on the Russian public's support for surveillance cameras (Gurinskaya, 2020), *female gender* is positively associated with citizens' support for CCTV cameras in public places. Central Asian women are more supportive of video surveillance than male citizens (significant at the $p < 0.01$ level). One way to interpret this is to argue that women are more in favor of surveillance cameras because they are more afraid of becoming victims of crimes than their male counterparts. Considering

Table 8.2 Regression analysis for Central Asians' support of CCTV in relation to their privacy concerns.

	Model 1	Model 2
Intercept	2.052 ***	2.120 ***
	(0.293)	(0.295)
Gender (f)	0.283 **	0.299 ***
	(0.087)	(0.087)
Age: 30–49	0.036	0.044
	(0.106)	(0.106)
Age: 50–91	0.229 *	0.233 *
	(0.118)	(0.118)
Lower middle class	−0.212*	−0.224 *
	(0.107)	(0.107)
Working class	−0.340 **	−0.324 **
	(0.108)	(0.105)
Urban	−0.304 ***	−0.275 ***
	(0.088)	(0.089)
Privacy concerns	−1.952 ***	−1.922 ***
	(0.113)	(0.114)
Confidence in government		−0.252 **
		(0.094)
AIC	3258.941	3253.742
BIC	3313.727	3314.616
Log Likelihood	−1620.470	−1616.871
Deviance	3240.941	3233.742
Respondents	3253	3253

*** $p < 0.001$, ** $p < 0.01$, * $p < 0.05$.

the rising numbers of bride kidnappings in Kyrgyzstan (Sultanalieva, 2021), as well as the growing incidence of "femicides" and gender-based violence against women and girls in Tajikistan and Kazakhstan (Human Rights Watch, 2019; Kabylova, 2021), this explanation is persuasive. Indeed, especially young un-married Central Asian women whom I met during my fieldwork in the region in 2022 argued that they felt safer and more secure thanks to the growing number of Chinese CCTV cameras in public spaces and public transport.

In addition to this, the findings in Table 8.2 partially confirm the observations from work on post-Soviet cities (Marat and Sutton, 2021) that the demo-graphic variables of *lower middle class* and *working class* are negatively related to respondents' acceptance of CCTV cameras in public spaces. Marat and Sutton (2021) suggest that the lower middle and working classes are less likely to sup-port surveillance cameras because they benefit less from increased surveillance than the middle class. The results in Table 8.2 also confirm Marat and Sutton's (2021) observations that urban people in Ukraine, Kazakhstan, and Kyrgyzstan tend to be less supportive of video cameras in public spaces, mainly because they are more sensitized to privacy issues than their counterparts living in the countryside (significant at the $p < 0.001$ level). Consistent with previous studies' findings on public attitudes toward CCTV cameras in Russia and Kazakhstan (Gurinskaya, 2020; Gussarova and Jaksylykov, 2021), respondents in their fifties and older display more positive feelings toward the presence of surveillance cameras than the youngest age cohort (significant at the $p < 0.05$ level). One pos-sible explanation is that young people are more targeted by cameras and there-fore display more negative feelings toward them.

Yet the findings reported in Table 8.2 demonstrate that it is not solely individuals' *demographics* that affect their views about surveillance cameras. As Model 2 in Table 8.2 shows, respondents' trust in their government correlates significantly and negatively with their support for surveillance cameras (signif-icant at the $p < 0.01$ level). Central Asians who distrust their government there-fore are less likely to accept its use of cameras to monitor citizens in public areas.

Moreover, despite citizens' widespread support for video surveillance cameras (see Figure 8.5) in all three Central Asian states, the results presented in Table 8.2 confirm previous scholarships' assumptions (Bradford et al., 2020; Gurinskaya, 2020) that people's privacy concerns influence their attitudes toward CCTV cameras. Central Asian citizens who strongly disagree with the state's invasive harvesting of personal data and information tend to be less likely to approve the government's utilization of video surveillance cameras in public spaces (signifi-cant at the $p < 0.001$ level). The evidence presented in Table 8.2 suggests that this trend will be even more pronounced for those people who distrust their gov-ernment. The evidence presented in this chapter therefore provides support for both hypotheses, in suggesting that only a minority of the population, namely, those Central Asians who distrust their government and/or disapprove of their state's unauthorized harvesting of citizens' private data, is less supportive of Chinese CCTV cameras in public spaces.

Conclusion

What has the normalization of mass surveillance, promoted and enabled by China's DSR, come to mean for individuals' data and privacy in Central Asia? Overall, the findings presented in this chapter show that most Central Asians approve of their government's use of Chinese CCTV cameras in public areas. Only a minority of Central Asians, namely, those individuals who distrust their government and disapprove of their state's unauthorized use of citizens' private data, tend to express opposition to the use of CCTV cameras in public spaces.

There are two somewhat interlinked explanations for Central Asians' wide acceptance of video surveillance cameras. One is that, due to the Soviet colonial legacy, Central Asians tend to underprioritize the right to privacy, which was not considered of essential value during Communist times, compared with other principles, such as public safety. Indeed, most Central Asians that I met during my research in the region in 2022 displayed a "nothing to hide" rhetoric and were convinced that Chinese CCTV cameras help to reduce the number of car accidents, street violence, as well as public lewdness in their city. For example, one taxi driver in Almaty explained to me because people (and taxi drivers in particular) are watched by Chinese cameras these days, they tend to urinate less in public.

The Soviet colonial legacy also explains why women are more receptive to CCTV cameras. Women are not more ignorant than their male counterparts, but they see the trade-off as worthwhile given their greater risk of suffering violent crime. Many of the Central Asian women I interviewed in 2022 expressed their support for their government's use of Chinese surveillance cameras because cameras increase the likelihood of video footage recording scenes of abduction or rape that could be used as evidence in criminal proceedings. In short, local authorities' branding strategy that CCTV cameras help to improve public safety seems to resonate well among the wider Central Asian public. Thus far, there are no representative and reliable studies that support my interviewees' and local authorities' claim that CCTV cameras reduce the crime rates in Central Asian cities and villages. Even less is known regarding whether and how video footage of scenes of abduction or rape are used in Central Asian courts. These are just some of the possible questions that future research could explore.

Another possible explanation for Central Asians' positive views about Chinese CCTV cameras is the authoritarian nature of governance in the region.

Given the sensitive political nature of the state's surveillance system, some WVS respondents may have felt pressured to self-censor and answer the question in line with their government's stance on CCTV cameras in public spaces. Such concerns are not abstract. According to Kasiet Ysmanova (2024), the director of the local opinion polling center Central Asia Barometer, Central Asian people have little trust in survey providers, and most believe that the opinion polling center is conducting research on behalf of the local government. This can lead to high rates of systematic nonresponses and/or biased answers, resulting in poor data (Ysmanova, 2024). Likewise, only a few Central Asians whom I met and interviewed in 2022 felt safe enough to share with me their distrust and disapproval of their government's use of Chinese CCTV cameras in public spaces. Although some of my interlocutors were concerned about the fact that these surveillance cameras served the government at the expense of the people, the same respondents anonymously agreed that nothing could be done about the government's invasive surveillance practices. As observed by previous scholars (Gussarova and Jaksylykov, 2021; Toqmadi and Zakharchenko, 2021), there seems to exist a certain sense of hopelessness among the Central Asian public regarding local authorities' surveillance practices.

As such, it seems wrong to assume that it is Central Asians' lack of awareness about their privacy rights that makes them more accepting of state surveillance, enhanced by China's DSR. It seems equally and perhaps more likely, based on the evidence presented here, that some Central Asians are aware of the broader implications of Chinese CCTV cameras but support their use anyway. Their support and understanding of CCTV surveillance and, by extension, their vision of China's DSR seems to be influenced by both historical legacies and the lack of democratic mechanisms.

9

Labor Migration Pathways under the BRI

A Case Study of Chinese Expatriates in Ethiopia

Ding Fei

Introduction

Since its first announcement by Chinese President Xi Jinping in 2013, the Belt and Road Initiative (BRI) has become a key strategy, narrative, and framework for the new era of China's globalization (Liu and Dunford, 2016). Between 2013 and 2018, the Chinese government committed an annual investment of $70 billion to fund BRI-related activities (Gonzalez-Vicente, 2019). In 2018 alone, 7,721 new contracts were executed in BRI countries, totaling at a value of $1.25 billion (Tang, 2020). In recent years, the BRI is further expanding from its initial focus on infrastructure connectivity, investment networks, and trade opportunities to diverse areas of cooperation such as the environment (i.e., the Green Silk Road), technology (i.e., the Digital Silk Road [DSR]), and health (i.e., the Health Silk Road).

While the BRI seemingly presents a unitary narrative of China's vision of international relations and development cooperation, emerging studies have revealed the contingency, complexity, and unevenness in how the BRI is framed and interpreted both within China and in the participating countries (Oliveira et al., 2020). Instead of being a highly coordinated and centralized state project, research shows that the BRI is an extremely loose and indeterminate assemblage, which necessitates a critical contextualization of its material entanglements to assess its downstream effects (Flint and Zhu, 2019; Jones and Zeng, 2019). Therefore, it is imperative to call into question some of the misconceptions about the BRI that Schatz and Silvey rightly identify in this volume's introduction.

In pursuit of the volume's overarching goal to "shed light on otherwise hard-to-see facets of the BRI and its varied impact" (Schatz and Silvey, introduction, this volume: 9), this chapter delves into the human dimension of the BRI. It aims to unveil the lived experiences of labor migration among Chinese expatriate managers and migrant workers in Africa. Studies have analyzed the growing Chinese migrant population in Africa with regard to their transnational livelihood strategies, identity formation, and intercultural encounters with local

Ding Fei, *Labor Migration Pathways under the BRI* In: Seeing China's Belt and Road. Edited by: Edward Schatz and Rachel Silvey, Oxford University Press. © Oxford University Press 2025. DOI: 10.1093/oso/9780197789261.003.0010

Africans (Giese, 2017; Hodzi, 2019; Sheridan, 2018). However, existing research primarily focuses on Chinese traders and entrepreneurs, often overlooking another significant group of migrants: expatriate Chinese managers and migrant laborers who are sent abroad by their employers (Yeh and Wharton, 2016). These individuals are often directly involved in implementing construction projects or carrying out investment activities under the BRI. Their transnational movement is typically short-term, work-based, and tied to their employment relations with globalized Chinese companies (Cranston, 2018).

Chinese laborers represent one of the most prominent and visible facets of the BRI (Hillman and Tippett, 2021; Kuo and Chen, 2021). However, their visibility is often subject to polarized portrayals. At one extreme is the Chinese official description of Chinese migrants as part of the "people-to-people" cooperation under the BRI who deliver physical infrastructure and skills training in host countries. At the other extreme is the perception of Chinese workers as extensions of the Chinese state or Chinese capital who impose harsh managerial practices upon African recruits or displace jobs within local communities (Baah and Jauch, 2009; Gadzala, 2010). In between the polarized portrayals, limited knowledge exists regarding migrants' heterogenous composition, varied migration experiences, and the impacts of overseas work on their lives.

This chapter addresses this oversight by examining the lives of Chinese expatriates within the context of the BRI. Here, the term "expatriates" is used to encompass a broad spectrum of Chinese individuals, ranging from managers to specialists to manual workers, whose transnational mobility is orchestrated by globalized Chinese companies. While their various job positions may imply class-based distinctions among Chinese migrants, in reality, these divisions are complex and often defy clear-cut categorization, as the empirical case examined in this chapter will demonstrate. The term "expatriates" therefore intends to capture the collective experiences of this distinct group of Chinese migrants who are recruited and managed by Chinese employers. Nonetheless, it is crucial to acknowledge that the term emphasizes not uniformity but, rather, the heterogeneity of individual migrant experiences, which often hinge on their unique social and economic characteristics (Fei, 2023).

The empirical focus of this chapter is on Chinese expatriates in Ethiopia, an East African country that actively participates in the BRI. In 2017, Ethiopia was one of only two African countries that sent a high-level delegation to attend China's first Belt and Road Forum for International Cooperation. Ethiopian leaders also consider the BRI to be a natural progression of growing ties between the two countries, boasting plans to continue leveraging the BRI to boost Ethiopia's infrastructural development and industrialization (Xinhua News Agency, 2019). Under this close interstate connection, Chinese companies and expatriates have become active players in multiple economic sectors in Ethiopia, providing a useful case study for examining the interregional movement of capital and labor.

This chapter begins with a review of the recent literature on the BRI, emphasizing the necessity for scholarly attention to the burgeoning cross-regional migration flows associated with the initiative. Subsequently, it delves into Chinese expatriates in the Global South, followed by a specific focus on Chinese expatriates in Africa. I then present a case study, drawing upon interviews and surveys with 66 Chinese expatriate managers, specialists, and migrant workers in Ethiopia. The empirical data were gathered during the author's research spanning from 2013 to 2020, while researching Chinese companies in construction, telecommunicatioins, and manufacturing sectors. The chapter concludes with a reflection on the downstream effects of the BRI on China's expatriated workers.

Grounding the BRI

Since its inception, the BRI has become an all-encompassing framework for capturing China's increasingly intensive and extensive global activities. Geopolitical interpretations take the BRI as a strategy for strengthening China's diplomatic relations and political influence in Asia and beyond, so as to contain and confront Western power in the region (Cheng, 2016; Lin, Sidaway, and Woon, 2019). The vagueness in the official delineation of the BRI by Beijing is seen as a calculated strategy to create "useful fuzziness" that allows for multiple interpretations, diverse forms of participation, and flexible adjustments by China and participating countries (Jones and Zeng, 2019; Narins and Agnew, 2020; Sidaway et al., 2020).[1] In addition to these geopolitical analyses, scholars also highlight the BRI's important geoeconomic agenda in terms of generating a multivector spatial fix to domestic overaccumulation, rising labor costs, and necessary industrial upgrades in China (Carmody, Taylor, and Zajontz, 2022). Hence, the BRI allows China to maintain and deepen its domestic economic reform by connecting the country's less developed inland regions to the outside world (Fei, 2017; Yeh and Wharton, 2016). Moreover, geocultural discussions draw attention to the pursuit of the Chinese dream of national rejuvenation as stated by President Xi Jinping (Winter, 2021). The BRI, in this sense, demonstrates a geopolitical culture that positions China in the center of an international community of shared destiny (Lin, Sidaway, and Woon, 2019; Zhao, 2020).

While geopolitical, geoeconomic, and geocultural analyses tend to approach the BRI as a coherent entity, a growing number of studies have

---

[1]   See also Kaneti, Chapter 4, this volume.

uncovered its variegated and contingent nature (Mohan, 2021). On the one hand, research reveals the unevenness of Chinese subnational politics and the development agenda that shape the profiles and impacts of the BRI (Summers, 2016; Ye, 2019). For example, Chen et al. (2020) examined the discrepancies, disjointed actions, and gaps among Chinese central, provincial, and local governments in implementing BRI projects. Similarly, Jones and Zeng (2019) showed how competing interests and struggles for power and resources in China influence the progress and development of the BRI. On the other hand, research also highlights the local specificities of particular BRI projects in participating countries to underline the local messiness, confusion, and contradictions that result from the vagueness of the BRI's official narrative and the absence of cartographic representation (Ang, 2019; Flint and Zhu, 2019; Oliveira et al., 2020).[2] The ambiguity of the BRI necessitates careful disaggregation that shows how its various projects are visualized and appropriated by a diverse range of actors from China and participating countries (Klinger and Muldavin, 2019; Sidaway et al., 2020).

So far, much has been discussed about the physical infrastructure projects of the BRI, such as railways, airports, dams, telecommunications, and economic zones (Bataineh, Bennon, and Fukuyama, 2019; Fei, 2017; Han and Webber, 2020; Lin and Ai, 2020). This chapter, however, focuses on the *people* who implement the various projects falling under the broad umbrella of the BRI. Although transnational flows of Chinese capital and labor to BRI countries existed before the formal launch of the initiative, the BRI has undeniably ushered in new resources and opportunities. Frequent diplomatic exchanges and increased policy commitments have not only mobilized intergovernmental interactions at provincial and municipal levels but also encouraged Chinese companies to actively seek projects and investment opportunities in BRI countries. As the agents who materialize and substantiate not only the grand narrative and agenda of the BRI but also the experiments and improvisions at subnational levels, the lives and experiences of migrant workers merit sustained attention. This chapter endeavors to explore the new migration pathways that have emerged as a result of the BRI and their impact on Chinese workers. It seeks to unravel the factors influencing migrants' decisions to either become expatriates or return to their home country, while also shedding light on the governance of the expatriation process.

---

[2] See also Murton, Chapter 5, this volume.

Chinese Contract Migrant Workers in the Global South

Notwithstanding their diverse job positions, Chinese expatriates engaged in overseas work under the BRI can be broadly categorized as *contract migrant workers*, aligning with the definition provided by the Organisation for Economic Co-operation and Development (OECD). According to the OECD (2008: 102), contract migrant workers are "persons working in a country other than their own under contractual arrangements that set limits on the period of employment and on the specific job held by the migrant." Yet, the unique national domestic context of China has given rise to distinct conditions of transnational labor migration that warrants close examination. In official accounts, Chinese overseas contract migrant workers fall under the categories of dispatched labor or service labor, and their transnational mobility is facilitated through two respective channels, detailed below (Xiang, 2003).

For one, workers are hired by globalized Chinese companies as *project laborers* to execute overseas contract projects, financed through loans by Chinese banks, international financial institutions, or governments of the host country (National Bureau of Statistics of China, 2012). In cases where Chinese financing is involved, contractors often abide by the loan contract to procure materials from China and employ Chinese workers (Corkin, 2016). For another, workers can also be recruited and managed by professional labor service companies as *service laborers* to work for foreign or Chinese companies abroad. Acting as intermediaries, the labor service companies sign contracts with companies looking to hire Chinese workers, oversee recruitment and selection of Chinese nationals, arrange for their migration, and perform managerial duties (National Bureau of Statistics of China, 2012). In sum, while project laborers are considered employees of Chinese contractors or subcontractors who work on overseas construction projects, service laborers are commonly organized and dispatched by certified domestic labor service companies to work for foreign employers in diverse sectors.

Since 2000, the number of Chinese overseas contract migrant workers increased steadily (see Figure 9.1). Between 2000 and 2019, the average rate of annual increase in the overseas labor stock was 3 percent for service laborers and 11.7 percent for project laborers. In 2014, the year after China announced the BRI, the number of Chinese service laborers increased by 23.7 percent, and the number of Chinese project laborers increased by 10.5 percent. By the end of 2019, there were 624,100 Chinese working abroad under labor service and 368,100 under contract projects. Geographically, Asia and Africa were the major continental destinations, respectively, accounting for 70.1 and 20.2 percent of the total Chinese overseas contract workers in 2018. A significant share

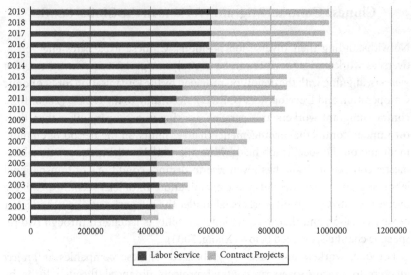

Figure 9.1 Year-end stock of Chinese overseas contract migrant workers (2000–2019). Source: China Africa Research Initiative, 2021.

(45.4 percent) of these workers was employed in the engineering and construction sector, followed by manufacturing (15.7 percent) and transportation (11.8 percent).

Provinces contributing to the greatest outward labor migration are Shandong, Guangdong, and Jiangsu, which took up 15.0, 11.1, and 10.5 percent of Chinese overseas contract workers in 2019, respectively (Ministry of Commerce, 2020). These three provinces are also at the frontline of winning engineering and construction projects in the BRI countries. In 2018, companies from Shandong province secured contracts at a value of $7.32 billion in the BRI countries, accounting for 60.2 percent of all overseas contracts that Shandong-based companies obtained in that year (Ministry of Commerce, 2020). The values were $9.43 billion (49.3 percent) for Guangdong and $3.28 billion (49.8 percent) for Jiangsu.

Overseas contract workers are often rural migrants or unemployed urban workers whose lives have been deeply influenced by domestic reforms since the late 1970s and the "Going Out" strategy starting in the early 2000s (Xiang, 2003). Under these reforms, state-owned enterprises (SOEs) underwent profound restructuring, and market-based rules were introduced to socialist labor systems, resulting in millions of Chinese being displaced from formal sectors. The "Going Out" strategy further mobilized domestic companies to venture abroad for markets, resources, and assets, primarily in developing countries. Labor service companies grew during this time, connecting workers searching for jobs with companies looking for a workforce. Many of these labor service companies, often under the name of "international economic and technological cooperation companies," were initially established as provincial SOEs but privatized during subsequent rounds of SOE reform (Xiang, 2012). In the late 1980s, fewer than 100 companies were certified to provide overseas labor service (Zhang, 2013). By 2017, over 2,000 companies operated in the sector (Ministry of Commerce, 2019). Therefore, it has been a common practice for globalized Chinese companies to either establish subsidiaries to handle labor services, or outsource the duties of labor recruitment and management to professional labor service companies in the market (Zhang, 2013; Zhao and Guo, 2015). As a result, globalized Chinese companies are able to shirk liability over overseas workers by delegating labor service to other domestic firms (Zhang, 2021).

As the number of overseas contract workers continues to grow, the Chinese government has intensified its measures to regulate labor dispatch and protect overseas contract workers. For example, the Ministry of Commerce put forward a mandate that specifies the legal responsibilities of overseas (sub)contractors and mechanisms for dispute resolution (Ministry of Commerce, 2006). The State Council also introduced regulations on overseas labor cooperation (State Council, 2012b). It set forth criteria to evaluate companies' qualifications to operate overseas labor services and provided detailed guidelines on the contents of labor contracts. In 2013, the National People's Congress issued the Amendment of Labor Contract Law that highlighted the "equal pay for equal work" principle entitled to dispatched workers (State Council, 2012a). According to the amendment, dispatched labor should receive the same compensation, including basic salary, bonuses, subsidies, and allowances, as formal employees in the same company. In 2017, the State Council passed the Amendment of Regulations on the Administration of Foreign Contracted Projects, which required Chinese overseas contractors to work with government-certified labor service companies for recruitment, and to sign formal labor contract with workers (State Council, 2017). Despite the various regulatory endeavors, overseas workers still face lingering issues such as absence of formal contracts, lack of benefits, and substandard working conditions (Franceschini, 2020; Halegua, 2020).

Chinese Expatriates in Africa

Between 2009 and 2019, Africa consistently ranked as the second-largest recipient region for Chinese contract migrant workers (see Figure 9.2). On average, the continent accounted for 23.24 percent of total overseas Chinese contract migrant workers in the period (Ministry of Commerce, 2020). However, it is important to note that official statistics likely underestimate the actual number of

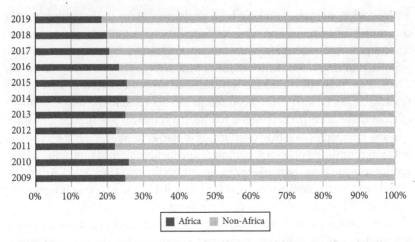

Figure 9.2 Year-end stock of Chinese contract migrant workers in Africa (2009–2019). Source: China Africa Research Initiative, 2021.

Chinese dispatched to work in Africa. Chinese expatriates in Africa comprise not only managerial personnel at mid- and low levels but also specialists such as accountants, engineers, and legal experts (Driessen, 2019; Fei, 2021b; Guccini and Zhang, 2021; Park, 2022). Although these individuals are often considered more skilled and better educated than contract migrant workers, the nature of their transnational movements is in many ways similar to that of other workers.

While the term "expatriates" is used in this chapter to describe Chinese workers in Africa regardless of their specific roles or skill levels, it is important to recognize that they do not fit the typical stereotype of privileged Western expatriates in developing countries (Cai and Su, 2021), or the emerging class of Chinese transnational elites in the Global North (Liu-Farrer, 2016). Unlike these groups, Chinese expatriates in Africa often lack the economic capacity, political resources, and social networks to gain prestige and privilege in the host society (Lin, 2012; Ong, 1999). Instead, they are in many ways vulnerable (but not completely agency-less) subjects to the prevailing social, political, and economic structures and forces at home and in host countries (Giese and Thiel, 2012; Driessen, 2021).

In addition, contemporary Chinese expatriates in Africa differ from the Chinese technicians dispatched by the socialist government between the 1950s and the 1970s to build railways and other public projects in Africa. Those expatriates were motivated by Maoist ideologies of a third-world alliance and a sense of communist heroism; their travels were also tightly controlled by the Chinese government (Monson, 2009). Moreover, they enjoyed the socialist cradle-to-grave employment protection system. In contrast, as will be discussed, contemporary expatriates under the market-based labor contract system are driven by diverse incentives and personal obligations; they also hold heterogenous values and worldviews.

Overseas Chinese companies are the major players in organizing expatriate sojourns to Africa. There are multiple reasons behind expatriation. First and foremost, expatriates can ensure managerial consistency and communicative efficiency between headquarters and subsidiaries (Gamble, 2000). This is especially the case for Chinese companies that engage in frequent communications with domestic headquarters, the Chinese government, and banks. Maintaining these lines of communication requires not just Chinese language proficiency but also someone who understands and abides by Chinese social and work norms (Fei, 2021b). Moreover, since many newly globalized Chinese companies lack overseas experience, using expatriates is also a way to ensure daily operational efficiency and productivity. Some scholars argue that expatriation is just a temporary strategy at the early stage of companies' internationalization (Tang, 2010). According to this argument, as business stabilizes over time, hiring Chinese expatriates will become less economically attractive. The reluctance of Chinese workers to stay for long periods in Africa may also push companies to turn to local workers to fulfill their labor needs (Corkin, 2007).

Other studies show that ownership types and companies' strategic agendas in Africa can influence expatriation/localization decisions. Private companies that have less home government support and weaker financial capacity are more likely to invest abroad in local workers to save on costs and build local linkages (Gu, 2009). Similarly, companies with long-term strategic plans in Africa tend to hire abroad in order to deepen their stake in local embeddedness and integration (Lee, 2014). Nonetheless, recent studies point to a shared perception among Chinese managers that African workers lack characteristics integral to an ideal industrial workforce, such as diligence, skillfulness, productivity, and willingness to work overtime, and this perception has sustained companies' reliance on expatriates (Fei, 2023).

While studies have examined considerations behind Chinese companies' decision to rely on expatriated labor, less is known about the perspectives and experiences of various Chinese people who are recruited to live and work in Africa. Most research has identified the monetary incentive behind migration: expatriates typically receive a major increase in salary in their overseas jobs, and their salaries are deposited directly into their bank accounts in China (Lee, 2014). In addition, their companies often provide overseas accommodations, resulting in additional savings for migrant workers (Fei, 2020).

Meanwhile, Chinese workers face mounting financial burdens back home, including rising costs of apartment mortgages, children's education, and elder care (Driessen, 2015, 2021). They thus experience growing pressure to migrate to earn sufficient income to meet these financial obligations. Yet these pressures affect different groups of Chinese expatriate workers in distinct ways. What sorts of financial pressures are different groups of overseas Chinese workers facing, and how do these pressures affect their motivation to migrate in the context of the BRI? What are other considerations that drive different groups of migrant workers to choose employment in Africa? How is the expatriation pathway arranged and regulated? The rest of this chapter explores these questions through a case study of Chinese expatriates in Ethiopia.

Case Study: Expatriation Pathways of Chinese in Ethiopia

Methods and Contexts

The primary data for this chapter were collected during the author's fieldwork in Ethiopia between 2013 and 2017. During this time, a total of 66 Chinese expatriates were surveyed to study their motivations to work abroad, the challenges they encountered, and potential reasons to return to China. A subset of 38 Chinese expatriates was interviewed after the survey to gain better understandings of their experiences before or during the process of expatriation and their plans to return. Between 2018 and 2020, the author had virtual conversations with 9 Chinese expatriates from the 38 interviewed Chinese expatriates to once again follow up on their work and receive life updates. While this sample may be small, it encompasses individuals with a diverse range of backgrounds in terms of age, place of origin within China, educational attainment, economic sector, and type of employer (see Figure 9.3). As a result, this sample provides a valuable opportunity to compare and analyze expatriation pathways across different groups, offering insights into the varied experiences of Chinese engaged in overseas work under the BRI.

Expatriates in this study were employed in three key sectors of Chinese investment in Ethiopia: construction, telecommunications, and manufacturing. Each sector possesses distinctive features that contribute to different expatriation regimes. In the construction sector, Chinese investment is primarily driven by SOEs. Between 2010 and 2019, the gross annual revenues of Chinese-contracted construction projects in Ethiopia averaged approximately $38.66 billion (China Africa Research Initiative, 2021). Notably, China Railway Engineering Corporation secured contracts worth $3.69 billion between 2011 and 2018, and China Communications Construction Company obtained contracts valued at $2.69 billion between 2009 and 2019 (American Enterprise Institute, 2021). Despite the dominance of SOEs in Ethiopia's construction sector, Chinese expatriates working in the sector do not necessarily hold positions as state

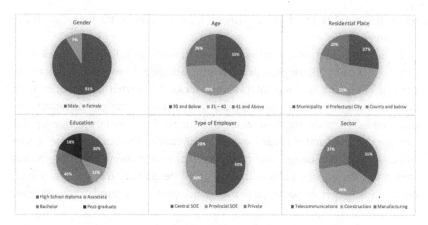

Figure 9.3 Summary of surveyed expatriates (N = 66).

employees. The expatriation regime in the sector is shaped by widespread informalization, primarily due to the utilization of outsourced labor and private subcontractors. As a result, the composition of expatriates in this sector is diverse, encompassing a mix of both formal and informal employees, as well as individuals employed by both state-owned and private entities (Fei, 2021c).

While construction is a labor-intensive sector attracting a less skilled workforce, telecommunications represent a knowledge- and technology-intensive sector that employs relatively well-educated groups of expatriates. For a long time, Ethiopia's telecommunications sector was dominated by one Chinese SOE that leveraged close interstate relations and Chinese state financing to succeed in the local market. In 2006, the SOE obtained $1.9 billion through vendor financing from the China Development Bank and the Export-Import Bank of China and became the exclusive contractor of national telecommunications projects in Ethiopia between the mid-2000s and early 2010s. The high profits of its Ethiopian subsidiary made the country a sought-after destination for expatriates within the SOE.

In contrast to the SOE domination in the construction and telecommunication sectors, Chinese involvement in Ethiopia's manufacturing sector is characterized by a large number of small, private investors. Between 2010 and 2016, a total of 510 manufacturing investors registered at the Ethiopian Investment Commission. These investors were engaged in diverse industries, with the major ones including plastic products (75 registered investors), textiles (71), food processing (39), and nonmetallic mineral products (38). Due to the relatively small-scale nature of their investments, these companies are highly sensitive to operational costs, including expenses related to expatriation. As a result, they tend to rely more heavily on local workforces for their day-to-day operations.

To analyze expatriation pathways, I addressed the following questions at three stages of an expatriate's process of transnational movement. Before the expatriates embark on their international travel, I ask what factors drive their decision to take up the new position and to what extent they can negotiate contract details. Then, during their tenure in Ethiopia, I explore how their everyday lives are regulated and managed, as well as the challenges they have experienced while working in a foreign country. Given that expatriation contracts typically span two to three years, I also examine what postexpatriation options they have, especially how they decide upon or experience contract renewal or repatriation.

Pre-expatriation

Although research often delineates migration along the lines of internal and international pathways, it is increasingly recognized that cross-border movement is a spatially extended form of mobility within China (Xiang, 2014). Among the 66 surveyed expatriates, 25 were cross-provincial migrants who had already established families in cities that were not their birthplaces before embarking on their overseas journeys. Unlike the pursuit of cosmopolitan lifestyles, higher education, or better social welfare commonly associated with the rising upper- and middle-class Chinese immigrants in developed countries, expatriates in Ethiopia reported more practical and mundane objectives driving their mobility. One primary driver was the salary offered by employers: managers and other specialists typically received a substantial raise, ranging between 200 and 300 percent, while contract workers experienced an increase of 30 to 50 percent. Regardless of the varying rates, all expatriates considered their salary increase as a major source of improvement for their families' lives in China. Young specialists, such as engineers, accountants, human resource officers, or legal experts who recently graduated and sought to establish themselves in large cities such as Shenzhen and Wuhan, found the salary particularly attractive, as it enabled them to purchase their first apartment, get married, or start a family. On the other hand, contract workers, with an average age of 41, acknowledged that they had become increasingly less competitive in the domestic job market and relied on overseas contracts to sustain their families' financial security.

In addition to salary, managers and specialists viewed their expatriation experience as a learning opportunity for personal growth and professional development, with the aim of leveraging these enhanced credentials to advance their careers. All surveyed expatriate managers had college or graduate degrees from prestigious Chinese universities. At an average age of 31, they recognized overseas work experiences as essential assets for their future development, especially as an increasing number of Chinese companies sought to establish themselves globally. Meanwhile, career advancement in domestic companies—especially SOEs—often hinged on intricate personal politics and years of relationship building. In contrast, expatriate managers in construction and telecommunications companies found that overseas service offered a relatively clear-cut career pathway. Many of these companies pledged promotion in job rank after a certain number of years of overseas service, instilling a sense of direction and purpose for expatriates' career mobility. Other motivations that expatriates mentioned during interviews included a desire to escape the hierarchical and bureaucratic work environment prevalent in Chinese SOEs, to pursue self-advancement by working in a foreign context, and to live in places with better climate and less air pollution compared with their home country.

Despite many shared motivations for working abroad, pre-expatriation experiences vary across groups and sectors in terms of recruitment processes and contract details. In the construction sector, the expatriate workforce typically comprised both formal employees and contract workers hired by contractors and subcontractors. For instance, in a stadium project in Ethiopia, the SOE contractor collaborated with at least five Chinese private subcontractors. Each party independently assembled its own workforce through domestic branches and labor intermediaries. In the period between 2016 and 2017, 80 percent of the total of 260 expatriates working for the project were employed by different subcontractors, even though all of them were recognized as employees of the main contractor on immigration documents.

Formal employees in the construction sector were typically offered two-year contracts with the benefit of annual vacation time to return to China. They enjoyed a certain level of employment security but had to follow job assignments from their domestic supervisors to "travel with projects" within Ethiopia and to other countries. For senior expatriate managers employed by the SOE contractor, there was an added incentive of a promised half-rank promotion upon their return to China. Outsourced workers in the sector were subject to more stringent contract terms: they were required to stay on throughout the project without any vacations, and there was no guarantee of continued employment after the completion of the current project.

During its peak operation, the Chinese SOE in the telecommunications sector employed a total of 200 Chinese expatriates, with the majority recruited from various domestic branches in China. Job openings were announced on the internal job board, allowing interested candidates to apply for positions. Given that the SOE operates in over 160 countries and regions, potential expatriates have some level of autonomy in choosing their preferred work locations. Yet, some admitted that working in developed countries is often considered a more desirable option and thus reserved for well-connected employees within the company. Others revealed that the rate of overseas compensation was determined based on a host country's level of economic development and political stability. Appointments in riskier or less developed regions often came with higher salaries as an incentive to attract and retain qualified expatriates. Therefore, those eager to maximize their earnings were often inclined to choose assignments in developing regions. The contract term in these cases was usually two to three years. Managers and specialists were promised a rank promotion after completing two consecutive terms of overseas service.

In the manufacturing sector, companies typically adopted a flat organizational structure that included only a few expatriates as managers, accountants, and senior technicians, while locals made up over 90 percent of the workforce. The hiring process was less formal, and there was no standardized process for recruiting expatriates. Some were employees of the company's domestic branches and dispatched to Ethiopia to set up a new factory. Some were hired from the Chinese labor market through labor service companies. Some were relatives of the owner and were recruited to help run family businesses abroad. Others had worked for the owner in China but had to relocate abroad after the domestic company went bankrupt. For many expatriates in the manufacturing sector, there was limited autonomy in choosing their work destinations, especially for those who had to relocate due to the closure of a domestic branch. Larger manufacturing companies offered formal contracts for a two- to three-year period, but for smaller companies, the employment contract was less formal. Given the small number of expatriates, negotiation of benefits usually unfolded on an individual, case-by-case basis; for example, some might request vacations when production in the factories was at a lull rather than specify terms of paid leave in their employment contracts.

All expatriates in the survey shared a common experience of not receiving formal training from their employers before departing for Ethiopia. Instead, their knowledge about the country was primarily derived from insights shared by colleagues or friends who had prior experience working there. They also gathered information by reading online posts about the lives of expatriates in Africa. As discussed further in the next subsection, many expatriates trusted their employers to handle the logistics for their overseas travel and accommodation, leading them to forgo making additional preparations on their own.

During Expatriation

While abroad, the mobility of Chinese workers was first controlled by the immigration policies of their host countries (Dobler, 2009). For most expatriates arriving in Ethiopia, their work visas were processed and obtained through their employers. However, the Ethiopian government gradually implemented stricter guidelines on visa issuance to foreign expatriates, with the goal of retaining jobs opportunities for the local population. As a result, visa applications took considerably longer to process. In addition, the Ethiopian government set minimum educational and skills requirements for applicants. While these requirements might be easily met by expatriates in the telecommunications sector, they posed significant challenges for construction and manufacturing companies. Many employees in these sectors possessed extensive work experience but lacked the necessary certification in higher education. To navigate these challenges, some companies opted to bring expatriates into the country on one-month tourist visas initially. Once in Ethiopia, these expatriates then worked to obtain residence cards, allowing them to stay and work legally in the country.

While Ethiopian immigration policies regulated the types of jobs and lengths of stay for expatriates, the everyday lives of Chinese expatriates in Ethiopia were primarily under the direct control of their Chinese employers. Surveyed companies in all three sectors provided live-in arrangements for expatriates, although the degree of managerial control and social-spatial confinement varied. The management regime in the construction sector was characterized by the use of gated compounds to house expatriates. All expatriates lived and socialized within the compound, but the specific arrangement—such as meal plans, the number of occupants per room, and the length of lunch breaks—might vary based on employers as well as workers' job titles. Expatriates, especially those not in managerial positions, were not permitted to leave the compound without supervisor approval. This practice was justified as a measure to protect employees and prevent potential conflicts between Chinese workers and locals. As a result, workers in construction companies experienced the strictest form of sociospatial confinement and immobility during their time in Ethiopia.

While collective management also prevailed in telecommunication companies, the living conditions for expatriates were much better than those in construction companies. Expatriates resided in multifamily houses leased by the company in affluent neighborhoods of the capital city. Each expatriate had their own room and could bring their spouse and children to live in Ethiopia. In some cases, spouses of higher-ranking employees or those who had completed a previous term abroad were eligible to receive family compensation. Company shuttles came to expatriates' residences every morning to transport them to the office. For those working late, evening shuttles ran every hour until midnight.

In addition to a canteen in the office building, the company operated a separate canteen near the expatriate houses to provide meals to families during the weekdays. The rented house thus became the primary place for expatriates to socialize. Expatriates of different ranks were often mixed in their residence, which contributed to congenial management-employee relations.

The accommodations for expatriates in the manufacturing sector showed similarities to the dormitory labor regimes observed in China's coastal special economic zones (SEZs) during the early years of economic reforms in the 1980s. In Ethiopia, Chinese investors established several industrial parks across the country to attract foreign investment, particularly in the manufacturing sector. One example is the Eastern Industrial Zone located at about 30 miles south of the capital city, where expatriates used to reside in rooms located on the upper levels of the factory sheds. Many factories in the zone set up kitchens inside the sheds to prepare meals for expatriates and, at times, local workers too. Over the past years, separate dormitories and canteens were developed within the zone to provide better accommodation for investors and expatriates. In the past, it was common for expatriates to venture out of the zone and explore nearby towns during weekends. However, due to political instability since 2016, most expatriates preferred to stay inside due to safety concerns. Thus, the industrial zone had evolved into enclosed and protected spaces for expatriates, increasingly disconnected from the surrounding Ethiopian communities (Giannecchini and Taylor, 2018).

The centralized management style of Chinese companies across sectors has effectively extended and enforced managerial control over expatriates' labor power, leading to limited everyday sociospatial mobility during their overseas tenure. However, this sociospatial immobility is compensated by their improved economic power and heightened social status in Ethiopia. Even contract workers were seen as holding positions of authority compared with local workers, with the ability to supervise groups of 20 to 50 local employees. Construction workers, despite being confined to their compounds, offered generous tips to local workers in exchange for bringing in outside goods like beer and cigarettes. Increased power and access to capital and resources enabled expatriates to enjoy a lifestyle that might be unattainable for them in China. Some expatriates pursued leisure activities such as hiring private coaches for tennis lessons on weekends. Others invested in their children's education, sending them to international schools in Ethiopia. In the telecommunications sector, some accompanying spouses seized economic opportunities by working as petty traders, importing clothes and accessories from China to sell in Ethiopia. Others found employment with other Chinese companies in the country, further augmenting their family's income. Those who went abroad to work alone highlighted the positive impact of remittances, which offered financial support to their families and relatives back in China.

Postexpatriation

Most expatriates working overseas under the BRI ultimately hoped to return to China. Their decision to take up an overseas assignment might be influenced by institutional, social, and economic pressures or driven by personal aspirations and concerns (Nyíri, 2021; Xiang, 2021). Nevertheless, their long-term plan was eventually to return China to build a better life or enhance their career prospects. However, my research revealed that the process of repatriation was not without its challenges. Most companies failed to develop a clear-cut and well-defined trajectory for expatriation and repatriation. Expatriates received little training or guidance on how to adjust to their foreign environment, nor were they provided with information about repatriation procedures. This lack of preparation and support contributed to a high turnover rate among expatriates.

During interviews, expatriates expressed various challenges that deterred them from completing their contracts or extending their overseas tenure. Communication emerged as the most challenging aspect of expatriate life, especially for contract workers who lacked English or local language proficiency but frequently interacted with locals for work purposes. Young specialists who recently graduated found the lack of social activities and subpar lodging conditions to be discouraging factors for making long-term plans in Ethiopia. Middle-aged specialists and managers primarily considered job satisfaction and family obligations in China when deciding to return.

In contrast, most workers in construction and manufacturing companies had adult, working-age children and were accustomed to living in challenging conditions and being separated from their families. As a result, factors such as lodging quality, social lives, or family duties were not significant reasons for their early return. Instead, poor health was cited as the primary cause for their premature departure, given the limited access to reliable and affordable healthcare services in Ethiopia. Moreover, these workers often felt disappointed by their take-home salaries, as they had to cover unexpected local expenses such as meals and medical costs. Unexplained salary cuts and default payments were also common for these workers, adding to their overall frustration and dissatisfaction with the expatriation experience.

For those who ended up staying longer in Ethiopia than originally planned, the notion of expatriation as a path to upward social mobility often did not materialize as hoped. The salary increases and elevated social status obtained through foreign work were temporary and limited to the duration of their overseas assignments. Once repatriated, most expatriates encountered salary deductions and rank demotions, as the benefits of their international experience were not fully recognized in the home country. Moreover, promises of promotion made before expatriation sometimes went unfulfilled, as domestic branches might not have suitable vacancies for returning employees. Meanwhile, the years spent living abroad often led to weakened relationships between expatriates and home branch supervisors, creating a significant disadvantage during the repatriation process. As one interviewee described,

> If someone spent some quality time at the headquarters or a domestic branch before coming abroad, and maintained good connections within the company, he [or she] has a higher chance of finding a position [after returning China]. Those who were sent abroad shortly after being recruited can hardly find any positions.[3]

The discrepancy between the initial expectations of career advancement and the realities of repatriation were disheartening for many expatriates. Faced with the dilemma of choosing between staying abroad or returning home, some expatriates opted to commit to another term in Ethiopia, hoping that additional years of service might enhance their prospects for future repatriation. Others accepted a lower salary and returned to China, only to venture abroad again shortly afterward. Among the 66 expatriates surveyed, 36 had previously worked in other countries before coming to Ethiopia. Despite expressing a desire to reunite with their families, they chose to remain abroad. Over the years, these workers had taken on various assignments across Asia, the Middle East, and Africa. In the years after my research concluded, several expatriates left Ethiopia to work in other countries. Particularly for those in the construction sector, "following the project" had become a norm. Companies moved workers around to implement projects in different locations. Workers, together with their managers, found themselves "floating" outside China and in between countries to make their living abroad.

The global ventures of Chinese companies under the BRI have led to increased transnational mobility for expatriates, but paradoxically, they have also reduced expatriates' mobility upon their attempted return to China. Only in rare cases does the transnational mobility of working abroad translate into expatriates' long-term upward social mobility in China. In the majority of cases, the decision to become expatriates, driven by the motivation to improve their economic, social, and professional situations in China, creates a form of involuntary dependency through which mobility becomes a new norm of life. As a result, what was

---

[3] Interview with an executive director, Nanjing, China, 2017.

initially intended as a short-term expatriate experience may evolve into indefinite and uncertain stays (Yan, Sautman, and Lu, 2019). Expatriates, therefore, find themselves caught between the challenges of adapting to life abroad and the setbacks and compromises associated with returning home.

Conclusion

This chapter ventures beyond the polarized discussions surrounding the BRI, which often revolve around either concerns over Chinese expansionism or celebration about win-win international development cooperation. Instead, it focuses on the real-life experiences of Chinese expatriates on the ground, shedding light on the downstream effects and overlooked aspects of the BRI. By doing so, it contributes to the volume's exploration of the politics of sight, providing a more nuanced perspective on the Chinese managers, specialists, and workers who are often sweepingly labeled as mere agents of the Chinese state or capital. Indeed, the grand narrative of the BRI often comes to life through the hard work and dedication of these expatriates.[4] Their experiences of expatriation are distinct from those of elite migrants in developed countries and from organized transnational labor migration during China's early posteconomic reform years. As this chapter delves deeper into the challenges faced by Chinese expatriates, it uncovers a reality different from what the grand narratives of the BRI may suggest.

This case study of Chinese expatriates in Ethiopia reveals that many individuals have been drawn to overseas positions in hopes of escaping their social immobility in China and pursuing upward mobility. However, their transnational mobility is shaped by their contractual relationships with Chinese employers, and for most, their socioeconomic challenges in China are mirrored during their sojourns in Africa. In particular, expatriates experience a temporary improvement in their incomes during the time they are abroad, but while they are in Ethiopia, their local spatial mobility remains tightly constrained. They are residentially and socially segregated from the local population, and the relative social insularity of their communities is reinforced by the collective nature of the residences, meals, and transportation provided to them by Chinese companies. They are further isolated by their perceived foreignness, limited local or English language ability, and the lack of predeparture cultural training. Worse still, upon repatriation, most expatriates face challenges of salary deduction and social reintegration, and some may be disappointed by the unmet expectations of career advancement.

---

[4] See also DiCarlo, Chapter 6, this volume.

The experiences of Chinese expatriates in Ethiopia shed light on some of the human costs of downstream BRI development. Intensified overseas ventures of Chinese companies in recent years have generated job opportunities for millions of Chinese workers seeking higher salaries or hoping to sustain or improve their socioeconomic status in China. However, this dramatic global job expansion has brought tremendous social costs in its wake. These circuits of transnational contract labor are reliant upon repeated international sojourns, involving long periods of social detachment from China that rarely translate into upward socioeconomic mobility. To pursue an imagined better future, expatriates often sacrifice the opportunity of building their lives in China or investing in social relationships beyond the sphere of their overseas coworkers.

The diverse individual motivations behind expatriation as well as people's narratives about their desires, challenges, and disappointments during the expatriation process are largely invisible under the grand narratives of the BRI. Instead of being driven by the official rhetoric of connectivity and people-to-people ties, seeing BRI through the lives of expatriates brings to light the very material and mundane interests that take people abroad. The deferred dreams and profound disillusionment expressed by expatriates further make visible the mismatch between the ambitions of the BRI and its downstream effects. As expatriates manage their unrealized aspirations by persistently displacing their hopes onto an imagined future that lies *elsewhere* and *elsewhen* (Bunnell, Gillen, and Ho, 2018; Xiang, 2021), many have shifted toward seeing their temporary overseas contract work as a norm. As people become increasingly locked in repeated travels in and out of their home country to pursue opportunities (Parreñas et al., 2019), they begin to question why they are actively contributing to BRI projects without receiving their fair share of the benefits. The disconnection between the promises of upward mobility and the reality of their life situations has left them grappling with a sense of unfulfilled potential and a yearning for better opportunities. These sentiments reflect the complexities and challenges faced by Chinese expatriates, shedding light on the need for a more nuanced understanding of the BRI's human impact.

Conclusion

Looking Downstream

Edward Schatz and Rachel Silvey

Introduction

In this concluding chapter, we elaborate a way to think about transnational, transformative power. Our claim is that the varied contributions to the volume all converge in that they are *looking downstream*. By elaborating on what we mean by *looking downstream*, we reflect here on what our chapter authors have revealed about the transformations associated with the Belt and Road Initiative (BRI) and consider their implications for how to understand large-scale changes in global power relations of the sort already unfolding in the 21st century.

Seeing Differently: The Politics of Sight

All our chapter authors—whatever their empirical coverage and theoretical priorities—have landed on a common concern with the politics of sight. They were initially invited to detail their research findings about the downstream effects of the BRI to shed light on some of the less well-reported tensions and contradictions at stake. As a whole, they have accomplished more than what each set out to do individually. Their attention to the politics of sight offers *ways of seeing* the BRI *differently* and more effectively than the approaches that predominate in most media and scholarly accounts.

Our contributors have shown that research that looks downstream allows for conceptual advances with respect to the politics of sight. This leads us to make an ontological claim and to propose an epistemological move. The ontological claim is that what people see is contingent on their lines of sight. For example, as Lemon and Jardine describe in Chapter 1, seeing the BRI from Central Asian states brings to the fore China's increasing military role beyond its borders and the conflicts that arise from it. Importantly, their perspective also enables them to demonstrate that the pathways that the BRI is carving—its meanings,

Edward Schatz and Rachel Silvey, *Conclusion* In: Seeing China's Belt and Road. Edited by: Edward Schatz and Rachel Silvey, Oxford University Press. © Oxford University Press 2025.
DOI: 10.1093/oso/9780197789261.003.0011

trajectories, and impacts—reflect not just China's actions and interests, but also those of the people and regions responding to China's military investments. As they show, even with processes as overtly power-laden as China-led securitization efforts, the rollout is neither smooth, nor linear, nor uniform. Rather, it is shaped and contested by the actors and institutions it confronts along the way. Ontologically, Lemon and Jardine do not assume a set of logics attached to the process but instead look downstream to investigate the BRI's security–development nexus as geographically specific, socially and politically mediated processes.

By positing an ontology based on lines of sight, we are naturally drawn to a series of related questions about the BRI: How have social actors been conditioned to see what they think constitutes the BRI? What is presented for them to see, and what is rather kept out of their sights? We have good reason to believe that this ontology is analytically productive for a wide range of phenomena, but we are certain that it makes sense for a multifaceted, multiscaled, ambiguous, and ambitious phenomenon like the BRI.

This leads to our epistemological move. While the conceit of normal science is that scholars and social analysts work at great analytic distance from the social processes that interest them, in fact scholars and analysts inhabit the world they study.[1] As an inevitable result, what they conclude is in significant part a function of what and how they see. The same questions apply: How have scholars and analysts been conditioned to see the BRI? What is presented for them to see, and what, rather, is kept out of their sights? With regard to scholars and other analysts, we add a further question: What steps have they taken, and what further steps might be taken to see differently and more effectively?

If one takes the politics of sight seriously, important implications follow. For instance, how might we address cause and effect, knowing that the social world is replete with multiple meanings and rife with multiple possibilities? At a bare minimum, any causal claim would have to be linked to the particular lines of sight that actors enjoy in specific times and places. Moreover, if an "outcome" reveals different facets when viewed from a different perspective, it becomes rather challenging to substantiate strong general claims about the context-independent effects of causes. Such a move may usefully complicate social analysis, improving its validity.[2]

To be clear, we have no interest in moving entirely away from making claims about cause and effect. We are not interested in an "anything goes" relativism, wherein all perspectives are equally valid or equally likely. One would

---

[1] See the discussion in Jackson (2008). Methodological and epistemological politics have long been central to feminist scholarship (for a recent review, see Liebman, Katz, and Marston, 2023).

[2] Sandra Harding's (1992) arguments about "strong objectivity" are relevant to this line of reasoning.

be hard-pressed, for example, to deny the material changes introduced by the BRI, even if what any given change comes to mean in concrete social contexts is underdetermined.[3] Introducing the politics of sight allows us—in fact, *requires* us—to recalibrate our causal claims without throwing up our hands up in collective frustration.

There is great value in posing large and hard-to-answer questions about the BRI, but we prefer phrasing them in ways that do not presuppose outcomes. So, instead of "Does the BRI cause debt-traps?" we ask, "How does the BRI relate to shifting global hierarchies of national indebtedness?" Instead of "Does the BRI's expansion lead to social resistance?" we pose, "How does the expansion of the BRI relate to resistance that emerges in its wake?" Rather than "Does the BRI enhance China's global standing?" we want to know the answer to "How does the BRI affect China's global power?" Even if these questions are impossible to answer with certainty or precision, they productively orient our inquiry. The most convincing answers will attend to variation, contingency, complexity, context, and indeterminacy.

Sediment and the Potential for Change

Given this complexity, how might we think effectively about transformations that are as potentially globally significant as those connected to the BRI? What framework or conceptual approach could provide insight into the BRI while acknowledging its continual motion?

Our approach to transnational, transformative power begins with the analogy offered by Schatz (2021), who studied how images of the United States filtered into Central Asian politics and society. Likening the process to a waterway carrying sediment over long distances, he showed that the United States and its hegemony, although physically remote and materially limited in its impact, nonetheless arrived in Central Asia as a potent symbol that local social and political actors used as they pursued their respective agendas. From Islamists to human rights activists to labor organizers, social actors "quarried" the symbolic "sediment" made available to them.

The analogy of sediment traveling in waterways is useful here, too, for it allows us to view social and political change differently. It emphasizes that novel influences indeed can move through physical space with relative ease; that the process of change may be gradual; and that what is socially consequential is how

---

[3] It is underdetermined in the sense that its outcomes are unpredictable. It is also *overdetermined* in the sense that Althusser (2005) used the term to think about the multiple, often opposed forces active simultaneously in any one situation.

actors in turn quarry the newly sedimented material. Whereas change is easiest to identify when it arrives quickly and when the triggers are proximate, consequential change can occur gradually and over long distances with triggers that are remote.

This is a productive starting point for thinking about the BRI. Like the United States, China's image increasingly looms large even over settings that are physically distant from Beijing. And even in the case of proximate neighbors, an imagination of China and its influence is not simply a function of its material influence. This point can reveal itself through fairly mundane interactions. During a visit to the University of Toronto by a Chinese delegation, one official from Beijing confidently proclaimed that anyone in Central Asia who was protesting the BRI was falling prey to "fake news." We take a different position. What do such protesters see, such that they feel motivated to object to some narratives presented to them? For us, what occurs downstream from BRI projects is socially very real, and the fact that it is socially constructed (or, in the view of our official visitor, "fake") does not make it any less so. Rather, the fact that information and disinformation are socially mediated is part of the puzzle. They are part of the sedimentary load, or sets of clues, to pursue analytically.

Yet, to capture the variety of downstream effects covered by our chapters, the analogy of sediment needs to be modified and extended. Of course, change is not guaranteed: sometimes sediment may fail to accumulate in sufficient quantities to be consequential. Moreover, while change can occur slowly—as the analogy suggests—it can also occur quickly (Nasritdinov, 2024; Yurchak, 2005). And change can be precipitated exogenously or emerge endogenously: it can be the product of external factors or internal dynamics. An approach that follows sediment as it travels over long distances and becomes bedrock in a new locale describes one important possibility, but by looking downstream, it becomes possible to see a wider range of potential processes at play.

Here, geographers have a great deal to offer our understanding of spatial socioeconomic and political change. Specifically, Doreen Massey's (1993) understanding of "power geometries" offers valuable additions to looking downstream. By power geometries, Massey (1993: 63) refers to the "highly complex social differentiation" in the geographies of political economic change, writing,

> The ways in which people are inserted into and placed within . . . [the flow of the BRI's expansion] . . . are highly complicated and extremely varied. It is necessary to think through with a bit more conceptual depth, a bit more analytical rigour, quite how these positions are differentiated.

Thinking carefully about how different positions (for example, relations within and between states, fieldwork angles, relations with BRI projects) affect ways of seeing the BRI can help us to sharpen our observations, identify our blind spots, and see elements of processes that may have been invisible yet prove to be consequential. Political geographies are not reducible to simple locations on maps. As Murton argues in Chapter 5, maps themselves represent ways of seeing, and they should be read as partial and positioned representations that can play a part in amplifying specific geopolitical narratives. This political effect is especially clear in those BRI maps that celebrate the increasingly global reach of the plans and projects.

The sense of politics at stake in our downstream research involves thinking about places as processes (rather than as objects), echoing the arguments about sedimentation processes. Approaching places as dynamic processes rather than containers allows observers to think beyond teleological spatial relations (Silvey and Lawson, 1999). Put another way, rather than assuming that the BRI serves as a geopolitical tool of China that will make "receiving states" weaker and more economically dependent (a teleology of "China's rise"), research can attend to the range of actors, institutions, and relationships within those "receiving states" and their varied capacities to accommodate or redirect the flow in line with their own interests and identities. Rather than superimposing assumptions about what the BRI means for how global power operates, this volume has favored empirical questions about how people see and respond to the political economic transformations that the BRI has set in motion.

Looking Downstream

Extending the analogy, we propose an approach to transnational transformations that we call *looking downstream*. On a basic level, this notion is intuitive. First, it invites analysts not simply to see whatever happens to appear in their field of vision or to follow some predetermined research protocol without reflexivity, but, rather, to act consciously in selecting where and how to train their gaze, in other words to *look relationally*. Second, we specifically invite a gaze *downstream*, which specifies a *relative* location of a thing X vis-à-vis another thing Y. This relative location raises the possibility that Y may be affected by X, though we emphasize that this is a possibility that requires confirmation. Third, by invoking a *flow*, we invite thinking about direction and power. As we discuss in the book's introduction, China and its BRI enjoy and project power that moves in particular directions. Such flows can affect what occurs downstream, even if they do not determine outcomes. Fourth, the notion invites thinking about space and time. A downstream thing Y is further along, both spatially and temporally, than an upstream thing X, prompting us to think about the longer term and not to be captivated by what happens this week, this month, or this year.

Finally, by enjoying a clear view of varied, contingent, complex, and indeterminate outcomes, we return our gaze upstream to the BRI, asking how attention to the politics of sight helps us better understand the BRI in light of the outcomes and processes that have been revealed.

If our approach seems familiar, this may be because it builds on historical institutionalism (HI), an epistemology that has gained traction in historical sociology and political science. While there are many strands of HI, in general it highlights the subtleties of endogenously produced social change, as well as the importance of critical junctures, which are circumstances when the chance for major change to occur rises significantly (Capoccia and Keleman, 2007; Pierson, 2000; Thelen, 1999). Like our approach, HI emphasizes not crisp outcomes, but process, and relies not on decontextualized correlational analysis to make causal claims, but, rather, on thick description and conjunctural causation.

However valuable, HI has limits that our collective research on the BRI makes clear. First, HI often succumbs to a methodological nationalism, wherein the outcomes, processes, and inputs being considered are assumed to be contained within the bounds of a national state (Hameiri, 2020). Such an approach cannot adequately contend with transnationally generated change, such as that which occurs with the BRI. Second, as HI's name suggests, it focuses on social and political *institutions*. While conceptually this should include both formal and informal institutions, in practice it tends to focus on formal institutions, which are more readily observed, than on informal ones, which require in-depth fieldwork to reveal. Moreover, while the emphasis on patterned and broadly predictable behavior that undergirds most thinking about institutions is understandable, *looking downstream* is equally interested in the agentic, contingent, and unpredictable factors that constitute stasis and change in human communities (see Schedler, 2007).

Looking downstream is thus a broad invitation to analysis that is open to surprise without losing focus, that appreciates contingencies without ignoring probabilities, and that builds in reflexivity without reducing research to navel-gazing. Can we move beyond the basic intuitions to push the analogy further? What specific aspects of hydrological science are useful for thinking about the downstream effects of the BRI? Basing our discussion on Sivakumar (2017), we highlight four: nonlinearity, threshold effects, sensitive dependence, and unpredictability.

In hydrologic systems, nonlinear relationships are normal. As Sivakumar (2017: 38) highlights, a change in rainfall does "not result in a proportional change in streamflow . . . since many other factors also influence the conversion of rainfall (input) to streamflow (output)." Note that the claim is *not* that there is *no* relationship between input and output, only that the relationship is complex, nonlinear, and context dependent. Returning to our simple upstream–downstream distinction, if I add 500 cubic meters per second of water to a river upstream, it will have one effect if the riverbed is dry and a very different one if the river is already on the verge of overflowing its banks. As a case in point, as Narins writes in Chapter 2, official lending from China for BRI projects took notably different forms before and after the COVID-19 pandemic, and these have varied over space in Laos, Sri Lanka, Pakistan, and Zambia. Similarly, as Paltiel and Yan describe in Chapter 3, Chinese-funded high-speed railway projects assume distinct forms in Malaysia and Indonesia. While both countries' railway projects are part of the BRI, they are mediated by pre-existing forces (and different political approaches to investments from China) in the places they land.

In hydrologic systems, threshold effects likewise are legion. When inputs cross a certain threshold, their effects jump significantly, but if they remain below the threshold, their effects are less significant or simply inconsequential. Not only are such threshold processes abundant, but they are in constant interaction with each other. As a result, seemingly small changes can cascade through a system to produce large-scale changes. The flip side, of course, is that processes that do not cross a threshold can be described as being at equilibrium. So, small changes need not produce large change, but they contain the ever-present potential to do so. This ambiguity is hinted at by Kaneti in Chapter 4, where she discusses the museum exhibit hosted by the Beijing National Museum, entitled "Sharing a Common Future." Despite obvious efforts to produce a "commonsense" narrative about China as the center of global historical processes, the exhibit also provided a platform to disrupt and coconstruct new visions.

Hydrologic systems are similarly characterized by what the literature describes as "sensitive dependence," in which the interdependence of factors means that a small initial change can set in motion ever-larger changes that ultimately result in enormous transformations.[4] In hydrologic systems, for example, the downstream effect of contaminants released upstream may "largely depend upon the time (e.g. rainy or dry season)" when they were released (Sivakumar, 2017: 48).

The analytic challenge implied here is enormous: what appear to be tiny moments of happenstance can either become enormously consequential or remain inconsequential and therefore go unnoticed. While in theory, one could identify the starting conditions to predict the outcome, in practice with respect to the BRI and its representations, most such initial starting conditions go unobserved. For example, perhaps one might anticipate that Indonesia's high-speed railway investment would be governed in a top-down manner, but as Paltiel and Yan demonstrate in Chapter 3, bilateralism is complex and unpredictable.

---

[4] As Sivakumar (2017: 48–49, referencing Lorenz [1969]) discusses, the notion was "popularized in the so-called 'butterfly effect;' i.e., a butterfly flapping its wings in one location ... could change the weather in a far-off location."

Further, we cannot know in advance and for certain that we are capturing all the relevant starting conditions necessary to offer a compelling explanation. In other words, we may not know where precisely upstream—that is, which actors and institutions are pushing for the BRI's expansion via the development of the high-speed railways or the coherence of the museum exhibition—to look in the first place.[5] In Chapter 8, Dall'Agnola comes closest to linking up to this crucial point. Whereas one might be tempted to tell the story of the expanding Digital Silk Road (DSR) through high-level bilateral negotiations, she shows that the relevant actors are in fact the general public in Central Asia. Instead of meeting the expansion of CCTV security technology with fear about privacy violations, the public has met it with relative sanguinity or acquiescence. There has been little public debate about the rapid and widespread adoption of CCTV technology, and the relative lack of opposition has smoothed the way for the expansion of the DSR in these countries.

At a minimum, the presence of so many confounding variables and unknowable conditions should induce humility about our ability to predict what happens downstream. While it is possible to assess the direction a stream is flowing and its general volume of water at any given time, these assessments will not tell you what tomorrow's direction or volume will be. The same can be said about the BRI. That is, we know that investment flows associated with the BRI have been massive, and it is clear that the global footprint of BRI projects has been expanding rapidly. However, its trajectory could shift quite suddenly, as the reverberations of the COVID-19 pandemic in the global economy made clear.

If we extend the analogy from hydrological dynamics to social ones, with self-conscious human actors exercising agency in ways that introduce even greater unpredictability, we must conclude that looking downstream is less an instruction sheet for how to reveal the dynamics of transformational processes than it is an invitation to a broad way of seeing politics and their geographies as they unfold.

In sum, as it applies to social dynamics, looking downstream has the following elements. It privileges the longer term over the shorter term. It has a view of the gradual and slow, even as it retains analytic space for seeing rapid change that overwhelms. It allows for unpredictability, even if the broad contours of social dynamics are largely and generally patterned. It has a clear view of recursivity, especially when human agency and place specificity are involved. Finally, it recognizes that even within systems that demonstrate stability, with the system absorbing and resisting change, that stability is always provisional, subject to forces that overwhelm and induce broad transformation.

---

[5] For further discussion, see Sivakumar (2017: 158–59).

Over the Horizon: Theorizing Possible Futures

There is always something unseen just over the horizon. As broad ranging as our coverage of the BRI and its effects has been, scholars have only begun to see some topics that deserve sustained attention. An honest accounting of this book's contribution should pause to consider these additional topics. Here we flag some questions that historians and critical development studies scholars would ask.

Critical development studies scholars underscore several questions—and indeed *hypotheses* about the ways that capitalist development unfolds—relevant to our discussion of the BRI. They turn our attention to what several generations of scholars have identified as patterns of capitalist expansion irrespective of national origin. Specifically, as David Harvey (2014), as well as many specialists of China,[6] would remind us, there are well-established patterns and logics that the history of capitalist expansion has prompted "downstream" in sites of investment. Some of these patterns, as Eric Wolf (1982), Immanuel Wallerstein (2011), Janet Abu-Lughod (1991), and Eric Hobsbawm (1989) have detailed, have global historical precedents. Here, we discuss a few.

First, world systems historians invite researchers to attend to the *longue durée* in the Braudelian sense. From the perspective of the past several centuries, many empires have risen and fallen. This longer history has several implications for how we understand the cases examined here. First, it serves as reminder that national economies and borders have always been contested terrain, and nation-states and their relations with one another are constituted by a much wider range of processes and variables than is generally acknowledged (Mitchell, 2002). The disruptions prompted by new forces with wide-ranging, unpredictable consequences, as well as sudden unanticipated ruptures in once-steady regimes, are not historically anomalous. Rather, disequilibrium, and not any imagined steady-state world order, is the historical norm. Second, attention to the *longue durée* attunes us to processes taking place at scales both broader and more finely grained than the nation-state, without sacrificing attention to the specific roles of particular nation-states in given moments. Analyzing the BRI through attention to its downstream effects allows observers to better distinguish processes that were in motion before the BRI from those that are prompted by BRI projects, and to better parse the consequences of specific contexts of the BRI.

Taking the long history of capitalist development as background, we might view the development of the BRI as the Chinese Communist Party's (CCP's) response to what David Harvey terms a crisis of overaccumulation. According to this perspective, which dates back to Lenin's theory of imperialism,[7] as excess

---

[6] For example, see Hung (2008) and Lee (2022).
[7] See Lenin (2010), originally published in 1917.

capital accumulates, it requires new outlets for investment in order to be profitable. The BRI's development of investment frontiers and new markets are "spatial fixes," or ways that China can find profitable outlets for the surplus funds it has accumulated in recent decades as a result of its rapid economic growth. By investing in connections of China's economy to other countries, the BRI is intended to stimulate economic activity and create demand for products made in China by opening up new territories for production and consumption. In this view, the BRI's expansion into new territory reflects a "natural tendency" of capital accumulation.

Yet as the chapters in this volume have shown, the processes of infrastructure investment assume a wide range of locally specific forms. Some BRI projects are more explicitly and evidently driven by the CCP, such as the export processing zones in Laos.[8] Others, such as the fiber optic cables enabling high-speed Internet in Switzerland, are simply owned by companies based in China.[9] In addition, all these different types of investments and relationships between state-owned and private investors within China are developing increasingly transnational ties through the BRI. This means that the variegated "downstream" effects of the BRI are influenced by sets of social forces and political processes that are themselves in motion as they articulate *across* national contexts. None of these logics or patterns implies predictable consequences in their specific local formations, but they do suggest likely logics at least of capital's trajectories, if not of the role of specific states. Capital does, as it turns out, tend to accumulate. Colonial extraction did (and does) rely on expropriation, exploitation, and expulsion alongside the development of railroads, ports, and factories. But the cultural politics and political geographies of particular people and places—as well as their respective politics of sight—affect the forms these patterns take downstream.

Looking Downstream at the BRI and "Global China"

As of 2023, a decade after the BRI was launched, its enormous scale was undeniable. Since 2013, cumulative global BRI engagement amounted to $962 billion: about $573 billion in construction contracts and $389 billion in nonfinancial investments (Wang, 2023). The large scale of these investments is evident in some form in all our chapters. However, as the collection has shown, the BRI as part of "global China" has manifested quite differently in Laos, Switzerland, Kyrgyzstan, and Ethiopia. The differences between these contexts of reception have been further complicated by the unexpectedly dramatic

---

[8] See DiCarlo, Chapter 6, this volume.
[9] See Kaufmann, Chapter 7, this volume.

economic contractions driven by the COVID-19 pandemic, as well as the unanticipated economic retrenchments within China.

It is impossible to predict what the next chapter of the BRI will bring. Yet, *looking downstream* as an epistemology suggests that additional effects will continue to reveal themselves as the years progress. We would do well to position ourselves with analytic questions to make sense of transformations—those that are anticipated and those that surprise—as they occur. Developed in that spirit, this volume is a modest step toward producing a framework both robust enough and flexible enough for the task.

Bibliography

Abu-Lughod, Janet L. *Before European Hegemony: The World System AD 1250–1350.* Oxford University Press, 1991.

Acharya, Amitav. "After Liberal Hegemony: The Advent of a Multiplex World Order." *Ethics & International Affairs*, 31, 3, 2017, pp. 271–85.

Acharya, Amitav. "From Heaven to Earth: 'Cultural Idealism' and 'Moral Realism' as Chinese Contributions to Global International Relations." *Chinese Journal of International Politics*, 12, 4, 2019, pp. 467–94.

Adeney, Katharine, and Filippo Boni. "How Pakistan and China Negotiate." Carnegie Endowment for International Peace. Accessed April 24, 2022, https://carnegieendowment. org/files/Adeney_Boni_Pakistan_and_China_final_1.pdf, 2021.

Adler-Nissen, Rebecca, Katrine Emilie Andersen, and Lene Hansen. "Images, Emotions, and International Politics: The Death of Alan Kurdi." *Review of International Studies*, 46, 2020, pp. 75–95.

Afrobarometer. "World Development Information Day: China's Growing Presence in Africa Wins Positive Popular Reviews (Afrobarometer Findings)." Accessed December 14, 2021, https://www.afrobarometer.org/articles/world-development-information-day-chinas-growing-presence-africa-wins-positive-popular-reviews/, 2016.

Alami, Ilias. "Money Power of Capital and Production of 'New State Spaces': A View from the Global South." *New Political Economy*, 23, 4, 2018, pp. 512–29.

Altynbayev, Kanat. "Chinese Hardware in Kazakh Cities Raises Spying Concerns." Caravanserai. Accessed January 9, 2024, https://central.asia-news.com/en_GB/articles/ cnmi_ca/features/2019/12/11/feature-01, 2019.

Ambrosio, Thomas. "The Legal Framework of the Shanghai Cooperation Organization: An Architecture of Authoritarianism." The Foreign Policy Centre. Accessed May 29, 2021, https://fpc.org.uk/sco-architecture-of-authoritarianism/. 2016.

American Enterprise Institute. "China Global Investment Tracker." American Enterprise Institute and Heritage Foundation. https://www.aei.org/china-global-investment-tracker/, 2021.

Amnesty International. "Return to Torture: Extradition, Forcible Returns and Removals to Central Asia." Accessed May 29, 2021, https://www.amnesty.org/en/documents/EUR04/ 001/2013/en/, 2013.

Anand, Nikhil, Akhil Gupta, and Hannah Appel, eds. *The Promise of Infrastructure.* Durham: Duke University Press, 2018.

Anderson, Benedict R. O. *Imagined Communities: Reflections on the Origin and Spread of Nationalism.* Rev. ed. London: Verso, 2006.

Andrews, John H. "Introduction: Meaning, Knowledge, and Power in the Map Philosophy of J.B. Harley." In Paul Laxton, ed., *J. B. Harley, The New Nature of Maps: Essays in the History of Cartography.* Baltimore: Johns Hopkins University Press, 2001, pp. 1–32.

Ang, Sylvia, Elaine Ho, and Brenda S.A.Yeoh. "Migration and New Racism beyond Colour and the "West": Co-ethnicity, Intersectionality and Postcoloniality." *Ethnic and Racial Studies*, 45, 4, 2022, pp. 585–94.

Ang, Yuen Yuen. "Demystifying Belt and Road: The Struggle to Define China's 'Project of the Century.'" *Foreign Affairs*. Accessed March 6, 2020, https://www.foreignaffairs.com/artic les/china/2019-05-22/demystifying-belt-and-road, 2019.

Apostolopoulou, Elia. "Tracing the Links between Infrastructure-Led Development, Urban Transformation, and Inequality in China's Belt and Road Initiative." *Antipode*, 53, 3, 2020, pp. 831–58.

Arase, David. "China's Rise, Deglobalization and the Future of Indo-Pacific Governance." *Asia Global Papers*, 2, 2020.

Areddy, James T. "Hidden Debt Plagues China's Belt and Road Infrastructure Plan, Studies Find." *Wall Street Journal*. Accessed February 2, 2024. https://www.wsj.com/articles/hidden-debt-plagues-chinas-belt-and-road-infrastructure-plan-studies-find-11632866461, 2021.

Army Recognition. "Chinese QW2 MANPADS Missile in Service with Turkmenistan Army." Accessed May 30, 2021. https://www.armyrecognition.com/january_2018_global_defense_security_army_news_industry/chinese_qw-2_manpads_missile_in_service_with_turkmenistan_army.html, 2018a.

Army Recognition. "Tajikistan: New Military Vehicles for GKNB Border Troops." Accessed May 29, 2021. https://www.armyrecognition.com/december_2018_global_defense_security_army_news_industry/tajikistan_new_military_vehicles_for_gknb_border_troops.html, 2018b.

Art China. "13 gè guó jiā，234 jiàn zuò pǐn，kàn sī chóu zhī lù shàng de 'shū fāng gòng xiǎng'" [13 Countries, 234 Works, See the "Community of Shared Future" on the Silk Road]. http://art.china.cn/zixun/2019-04/13/content_40718045.htm, 2019.

ASEAN–China Center. "Speech by Chinese President Xi Jinping to Indonesian Parliament." Accessed April 25, 2022, http://www.asean-china-center.org/english/2013-10/03/c_133062675.htm, 2013.

Baah, Anthony Yaw, and Herbert Jauch. "Chinese Investments in Africa: A Labour Perspective." In Anthony Yaw Baah and Herbert Jauch, eds., *Chinese Investments in Africa*. Accra: African Labour Researchers Network, 2009, p. 544.

Barder, Alexander. *Empire Within: International Hierarchy and Its Imperial Laboratories of Governance*. London: Routledge, 2015.

Bariyo, Nicholas. "Zambia's Opposition Wins Surprise Landslide as Defaulting Economy Reels." *Wall Street Journal*. Accessed February 2, 2024. https://www.wsj.com/articles/zambias-opposition-wins-surprise-landslide-as-defaulting-economy-reels-11629114113, 2021.

Barnett, Robert. "China Is Building Entire Villages in Another Country's Territory." *Foreign Policy*. Accessed June 22, 2024, https://foreignpolicy.com/2021/05/07/china-bhutan-border-villages-security-forces/, 2021.

Barney, Keith, and Kanya Souksakoun. "Credit Crunch: Chinese Infrastructure Lending and Lao Sovereign Debt." *Asia & the Pacific Policy Studies*, 8, 2021, pp. 94–113.

Barton, Benjamin. "Leveraging the 'String of Pearls' for Strategic Gains? An Assessment of the Maritime Silk Road Initiative's (MSRI) Economic/Security Nexus in the Indian Ocean Region (IOR)." *Asian Security*, 17, 2, 2020, pp. 216–35.

Bataineh, Bushra, Michael Bennon, and Francis Fukuyama. "How the Belt and Road Gained Steam: Causes and Implications of China's Rise in Global Infrastructure." King Center on Global Development, May, 2019. Working paper 1051.

BBC. "Kazakhstan's Land Reform Protests Explained." Accessed May 27, 2021, https://www.bbc.com/news/world-asia-36163103, 2016.

Bélanger, Danièle, and Rachel Silvey. "An Im/mobility Turn: Power Geometries of Care and Migration." *Journal of Ethnic and Migration Studies*, 46, 16, 2020, pp. 3423–40.

Belt and Road Forum for International Cooperation. "Joint Communique of the Leaders Roundtable of the Belt and Road Forum for International Cooperation." Accessed May 30, 2021, http://2017.beltandroadforum.org/english/n100/2017/0516/c22-423.html, 2017a.

Belt and Road Forum for International Cooperation. "Yang Jiechi Answers Questions from the Media on the Belt and Road Forum for International Cooperation." Accessed April 23, 2022, http://2017.beltandroadforum.org/n100/2017/0514/c24-332.html, 2017b.

Belt and Road Portal. "Joint Communique of the Leaders' Roundtable of the 2nd Belt and Road Forum for Regional Cooperation." Belt and Road Portal. Accessed September 30, 2021, https://eng.yidaiyilu.gov.cn/qwyw/rdxw/88230.htm, 2019.

Belt and Road Portal. "yǐ tóng zhōng guó qiān dìng gòng jiàn 'yī dài yī lù' hé zuò wén jiàn de guó jiā yī lǎn" [List of Countries That Have Signed Cooperation Documents with China to Jointly Build the "One Belt One Road"]. Accessed April 24, 2022, https://www.yidaiyilu.gov.cn/xwzx/roll/77298.htm, 2021.

Bennetts, Marc. "Dmitry Medvedev Threatens to Cut off the West's Internet." The Times. Accessed July 20, 2023, https://www.thetimes.co.uk/article/dmitry-medvedev-threatens-to-cut-off-the-wests-internet-pcsqsk2t3, 2023.

Berents, Helen, and Constance Duncombe. "Introduction: Violence, Visuality and World Politics." International Affairs, 96, 3, 2020, pp. 567–71.

Bērziņa-Čerenkova, Una Aleksandra. "BRI Instead of OBOR – China Edits the English Name of Its Most Ambitious International Project." Latvian Institute of International Affairs. Accessed April 20, 2022, https://web.archive.org/web/20170206061842/http://liia.lv/en/analysis/bri-instead-of-obor-china-edits-the-english-name-of-its-most-ambitious-international-project-532, 2016.

Bleiker, Roland. Aesthetics and World Politics. London: Palgrave Macmillan, 2009.

Bleiker, Roland, ed. Visual Global Politics. London: Taylor and Francis, 2018.

Bleiker, Roland. "Writing Visual Global Politics: In Defence of a Pluralist Approach—a Response to Gabi Schlag, 'Thinking and Writing Visual Global Politics.'" International Journal of Politics, Culture, and Society, 32, 1, 2019, pp. 115–23.

Boellstorff, Tom. "Culture of the Cloud." Journal for Virtual Worlds Research 2, 5, 2010, pp. 3–9.

Boni, Filippo, and Katharine Adeney. "The Impact of the China-Pakistan Economic Corridor on Pakistan's Federal System: The Politics of the CPEC." Asian Survey, 60, 3, 2020, pp. 441–65.

Bottici, Chiara. "Imaginal Politics." Thesis Eleven, 106, 2011, pp. 56–72.

Bowdler, Neil. "Kyrgyz Police Embrace Chinese Face-Recognition Technology." Radio Free Europe/Radio Liberty. Accessed May 30, 2021, https://www.rferl.org/a/kyrgyzstan-police-embrace-chinese-face-recognition-tech/30248431.html, 2019.

Bowker, Geoffrey, and Susan Leigh Star. Sorting Things Out: Classification and Its Consequences. Cambridge, MA: Massachusetts Institute of Technology Press, 1999.

Bradford, Ben, Julia Yesberg, Jonathan Jackson, and Paul Dawson. "Live Facial Recognition: Trust and Legitimacy as Predictors of Public Support for Police Use of New Technology." The British Journal of Criminology, 60, 6, 2020, pp. 1502–22.

Braga, Peter, and Kaneshko Sangar. "Strategy Amidst Ambiguity: The Belt and Road and China's Foreign Policy Approach to Eurasia." The Journal of Cross-Regional Dialogues, 2020.

Bräutigam, Deborah. "A Critical Look at Chinese 'Debt-trap Diplomacy': The Rise of a Meme." Area Development and Policy, 5, 1, 2020, pp. 1–14.

Bräutigam, Deborah. "How Zambia and China Co-Created a Debt 'Tragedy of the Commons.'" China Africa Research Initiative, Policy brief 61. https://static1.squarespace.com/static/5652847de4b033f56d2bdc29/t/6167389e16bd597c5abec114/1634154654419/V2+-+PB61+-+Zambia+Tragedy+of+the+Commons+-+October+2021.pdf, 2021.

Bräutigam, Deborah, and Meg Rithmire. "The Chinese 'Debt Trap' Is a Myth." The Atlantic. Accessed February 2, 2024, https://www.theatlantic.com/international/archive/2021/02/china-debt-trap-diplomacy/617953/, 2021.

Bräutigam, Deborah, and Yinxuan Wang. "Zambia's Chinese Debt in the Pandemic." China Africa Research Initiative. Policy brief 5. https://static1.squarespace.com/static/5652847de4b033f56d2bdc29/t/61578140e3542a5a82ef8e23/1633146947172/BP+5+%E2%80%93+Brautigam+Wang+%E2%80%93+Zambia+Chinese+Debt+Pandemic+Era.pdf, 2021.

Breuer, Peter, and Charles Cohen. "Time Is Ripe for Innovation in the World of Sovereign Debt Restructuring." International Monetary Fund. Accessed April 24, 2022, https://blogs.imf.

org/2020/11/19/time-is-ripe-for-innovation-in-the-world-of-sovereign-debt-restructur
ing/, 2020.

Büchenbacher, Katrin. "Ausländische Firmen haben kaum Chancen auf Beteiligung an Chinas neuer Seidenstrasse." *Neue Zürcher Zeitung.* Accessed October 8, 2021, https://www.nzz. ch/nzz-asien/neue-seidenstrasse-zwischenbilanz-fuer-die-schweiz-nzz-asien-ld.1554 970, 2020.

Bunnell, Tim, Jamie Gillen, and Elaine Lynn Ee Ho. "The Prospect of Elsewhere: Engaging the Future through Aspirations in Asia." *Annals of the American Association of Geographers,* 27, 108, 1, 2018, pp. 35–51.

Burg, Denis von, and Mischa Aebi. "5G: USA warnen nachdrücklich vor Huawei." *Tages-Anzeiger.* Accessed October 8, 2021, https://www.tagesanzeiger.ch/wirtschaft/unterneh men-und-konjunktur/5g-usa-warnen-nachdruecklich-vor-huawei/story/13645040, 2020.

Burkhanov, Aziz, and Yu-Wen Chen. "Kazakh Perspective on China, the Chinese, and Chinese Migration." *Ethnic and Racial Studies,* 39, 12, 2016, pp. 2129–48.

Brzezinski, Zbigniew. *Grand Chessboard: American Primacy and Its Geostrategic Imperatives.* New York: Basic Books, 1998.

Cai, Xiaomei, and Xiaobo Su. "Dwelling-in-Travelling: Western Expats and the Making of Temporary Home in Guangzhou, China." *Journal of Ethnic and Migration Studies,* 47, 12, 2021, pp. 2815–32.

CAICT. "White Paper on China International Optical Cable Interconnection (2018)." China Academy of Information and Communications Technology, 2018.

Callahan, William A. "Sino-Speak: Chinese Exceptionalism and the Politics of History." *The Journal of Asian Studies,* 71, 1, 2012, pp. 33–55.

Callahan, William A. *Sensible Politics: Visualizing International Relations.* New York: Oxford University Press, 2020.

Capoccia, Giovanni, and R. Daniel Kelemen. "The Study of Critical Junctures: Theory, Narrative, and Counterfactuals in Historical Institutionalism." *World Politics,* 59, 3, 2007, pp. 341–69.

Carmody, Pádraig, Ian Taylor, and Tim Zajontz. "China's Spatial Fix and 'Debt Diplomacy' in Africa: Constraining Belt or Road to Economic Transformation?" *Canadian Journal of African Studies,* 56, 1, 2022, pp. 57–77.

Carrai, Maria Adele. "Questioning the Debt-Trap Diplomacy Rhetoric Surrounding Hambantota Port." *Georgetown Journal of International Affairs.* 2021. https://gjia.georget own.edu/2021/06/05/questioning-the-debt-trap-diplomacy-rhetoric-surrounding-ham bantota-port/.

Carter, Paul. *The Road to Botany Bay.* Minneapolis: University of Minnesota Press, 2010.

Cavanna, Thomas. "Coercion Unbound? China's Belt and Road Initiative." In Daniel Drezner, Daniel, Henry Farrell, and Abraham Newman, eds., *The Uses and Abuses of Weaponized Interdependence.* Washington: Brookings Institution Press, 2021, 221–39.

Center for Strategic and International Studies. "Mapping Continental Ambitions." *Reconnecting Asia.* Accessed September 30, 2021. https://reconasia.csis.org/, 2021.

Central Asia Barometer Data. "Kazakhstan, Kyrgyzstan and Tajikistan." Wave 8–12, 2020–2022. Accessed January 5, 2024, http://www.ca-barometer.org.

Cerulus, Laurens, and Sarah Wheaton. "How Washington Chased Huawei out of Europe." *POLITICO.* Accessed July 28, 2023, https://www.politico.eu/article/us-china-huawei-eur ope-market/, 2022.

Chan, Alfred L. *Xi Jinping: Political Career, Governance, and Leadership, 1953–2018.* Oxford: Oxford University Press, 2022.

Chen, Jihong, Yijie Fei, Paul Tae-Woo Lee, and Xuezong Tao. "Overseas Port Investment Policy for China's Central and Local Governments in the Belt and Road Initiative." In Suisheng Zhao, ed., *China's New Global Strategy: The Belt and Road Initiative (BRI) and Asian Infrastructure Investment Bank (AIIB), Volume 1.* Routledge, 2020, pp. 120–39.

Chen, Shujie. "Duō guó lián hé bàn zhǎn de cháng shì yǔ sī kǎo —— yǐ 'shū fāng gòng xiǎng' zhǎn wéi lì" [Reflection on the Joint Multinational Exhibition: The Case of 'Sharing a Common Future' Exhibit]. *Journal of the National Museum of China*, 2019, pp. 145–54.

Chen, Wangjing K. "Sovereign Debt in the Making: Financial Entanglements and Labor Politics along the Belt and Road in Laos." *Economic Geography*, 96, 4, 2020, pp. 295–314.

Chen, Zhixin. "The Geopolitics of Public Health and China's Digital Silk Road in Asia." *Asiascape: Digital Asia*, 10, 1–2, 2023, pp. 121–36.

Cheng, Jing, and Jinghan Zeng. "'Digital Silk Road' as a Slogan Instead of a Grand Strategy." *Journal of Contemporary China*, 2023, pp. 1–16. https://doi.org/10.1080/10670 564.2023.2222269.

Cheng, Leonard K. "Three Questions on China's 'Belt and Road Initiative.'" *China Economic Review*, 40, 2016, pp. 309–13. https://doi.org/10.1163/22142312-bja10046.

Chettri, Mona, and Michael Eilenberg. *Development Zones in Asian Borderlands*. Amsterdam: Amsterdam University Press, 2021.

Chilkoti, Avantika, and Gabriele Steinhauser. "Covid's Next Economic Crisis: Developing-Nation Debt." *Wall Street Journal*. Accessed February 2, 2024, https://www.wsj.com/artic les/covid-coronavirus-developing-nation-africa-debt-crisis-11595455147, 2020.

Chin, Tamara. "The Invention of the Silk Road, 1877." *Critical Inquiry*, 40, 1, 2013, pp. 194–219.

China Africa Research Initiative. "Chinese Contracts in Africa." http://www.sais-cari.org/data-chinese-contracts-in-africa, 2021.

China Global Television Network. "Lao Deputy Prime Minister: Laos-China Railway Is a Successful Example of BRI Cooperation." Accessed June 5, 2023, https://news.cgtn.com/ news/2023-04-18/The-Laos-China-railway-is-a-successful-example-of-BRI-cooperation-1j6w10FXM9q/index.html, 2023.

China Internet Information Center. "Xi's Speech at 'Five Principles of Peaceful Coexistence.'" Accessed May 30, 2021, http://www.china.org.cn/world/2014-07/07/content_32876905. htm, 2014.

China Internet Information Center. "Chinese President Advocates New Type of Int'l Relations." Accessed May 19, 2021, http://www.china.org.cn/xivisitus2015/2015-09/29/ content_36708416.htm, 2015.

China Military Online. "In-Depth: How China Became the World's Third-Largest Supplier of Weapons Worldwide." Accessed May 29, 2021, http://english.chinamil.com.cn/view/2018-02/27/content_7953754.htm, 2018.

China Mobile International. "Global Resources." Accessed October 8, 2021, https://www.cmi. chinamobile.com/en/global-resources, 2020.

China Power. "How Is China Bolstering Its Military Diplomatic Relations?" Accessed May 29, 2021, https://chinapower.csis.org/china-military-diplomacy/, 2020.

China Telecom Europe. "CTE Solutions Overview: Digitally Transform Your Business with Cross Border Connectivity Solutions and Services." Accessed October 8, 2021, https://www. chinatelecomeurope.com/wp-content/uploads/2020/08/CTE-Company-brochure_27J uly2020.pdf, 2020.

China Telecom Americas. "Global Data Center Map." Accessed October 8, 2021, https://www. ctamericas.com/global-data-center-map/, 2021.

China Telecom Americas. "China Telecom Global Infrastructure Map." Accessed January 24, 2024, https://www.ctamericas.com/wp-content/uploads/2023/02/China-Telecom-Global-Infrastructure-Map.pdf, 2023.

China Telecom Europe. "About China Telecom (Europe)." Accessed October 8, 2021, https:// www.chinatelecomeurope.com/our-story/aboutcte/, 2021.

China Unicom. "China Unicom Global Map." Accessed October 8, 2021, https://network. chinaunicomglobal.com/, 2021.

Christopoulos, Dimitris. "The Governance of Networks: Heuristic or Formal Analysis? A Reply to Rachel Parker." *Political Studies*, 56, 2020, pp. 475–81.

CIPUC. "Tǎ jí kè sī tǎn guó ān wěi fǎn kǒng péi xùn bān zài wǒ yuàn kāi bān" [Tajikistan State Security Commission Counter-Terrorism Training Class Held in Our College]. Accessed May 30, 2021, http://news.cipuc.edu.cn/info/1030/11255.htm, 2014.

Clark, Ian. *The Hierarchy of States: Reform and Resistance in the International Order*. Cambridge: Cambridge University Press, 1989.

Clark, Ian. *Hegemony in International Society*. Oxford: Oxford University Press, 2011.

Clark, Ian. "International Society and China: The Power of Norms and the Norms of Power." *The Chinese Journal of International Politics*, 7, 3, 2014, pp. 315–40.

Clark, Ian. "Hierarchy, Hegemony, and the Norms of International Society." In Tim Dunne and Christian Reus-Smit, eds., *The Globalization of International Society*. Oxford: Oxford University Press, 2017, pp. 249–96.

Clark, James. "Jakarta-Bandung High-Speed Railway." Accessed September 20, 2021, https://futuresoutheastasia.com/java-high-speed-railway/, 2021.

Clarke, Michael. "The Belt and Road Initiative: China's New Grand Strategy?" *Asia Policy*, 24, 2017, pp. 71–79.

CNN. "Chinese Diplomat Killed in Kyrgyzstan." Accessed January 23, 2024, https://www.cnn.com/2002/WORLD/asiapcf/central/06/30/kyrgyzstan.diplomat/index.html, 2002.

Coduri, Michele, Hans Keller, and Eleonore Baumberger. "China." In HLS, a Company of the Swiss Academy of Humanities and Social Sciences, ed., *Historisches Lexikon der Schweiz*. Basel: Schwabe. Accessed October 8, 2021, http://www.hls-dhs-dss.ch/textes/d/D3405.php, 2009.

Colton, J. H., & Co. "Map Showing the Telegraph Lines in Operation, under Contract, and Contemplated, to Complete the Circuit of the Globe / Entered According to Act of Congress in the Year 1855." New York: G.W. & C.B. Colton & Co. Accessed through Library of Congress, October 8, 2021, https://lccn.loc.gov/86692708, 2020.

Commercial Register Office of the Canton of Zurich. "China Unicom (Europe) Operations Limited, London, Zweigniederlassung Zürich." *Handelsregisteramt des Kantons Zürich*. Accessed October 8, 2021, https://zh.chregister.ch/cr-portal/auszug/auszug.xhtml?uid=CHE-379.367.413, 2016.

Commercial Register Office of the Canton of Zurich. "China Telecom (Europe) Limited, London, Zweigniederlassung Zürich." *Handelsregisteramt des Kantons Zürich*. Accessed October 8, 2021, https://zh.chregister.ch/cr-portal/auszug/auszug.xhtml?uid=CHE-385.895.229, 2018.

Congressional Research Service. "Huawei and U.S. Law." Accessed January 23, 2024, https://sgp.fas.org/crs/misc/R46693.pdf, 2021.

Cons, Jason. *Sensitive Space: Fragmented Territory at the India-Bangladesh Border*. Seattle: University of Washington Press, 2019.

Consulate General of the People's Republic of China in Milan. Accessed July 15, 2023, http://milano.china-consulate.org/eng/xwdt/t1254263.htm, 2013.

Contessi, Nicola. "Foreign and Security Policy Diversification in Eurasia: Issue Splitting, Co-Alignment, and Relational Power." *Problems of Post-Communism*, 62, 5, 2015, pp. 299–311.

Cooley, Alexander. *Logics of Hierarchy: The Organization of Empires, States, and Military Occupations*. Ithaca: Cornell University Press, 2005.

Cooley, Alexander. *Base Politics: Democratic Change and the U.S. Military Overseas*. Ithaca: Cornell University Press, 2008.

Cooley, Alexander. *Great Games, Local Rules: The New Great Power Contest in Central Asia*. Oxford: Oxford University Press, 2012.

Corbet, Sylvie. "Debt-Plagued Zambia Reaches Deal with China, Other Nations to Rework $6.3B in Loans, French Say." *Associated Press*. https://apnews.com/article/zambia-debt-restructuring-deal-china-a0d14e7af986e2f873555685cedb86b3, 2023.

Corkin, Lucy. "The Strategic Entry of China's Emerging Multinationals into Africa." *China Report*, 43, 3, 2007, pp. 309–22.

Corkin, Lucy. *Uncovering African Agency: Angola's Management of China's Credit Lines.* London and New York: Routledge, 2016.

Cortada, James W. *The Digital Flood: The Diffusion of Information Technology across the U.S, Europe and Asia.* Oxford: Oxford University Press, 2012.

Costa Buranelli, Filippo. "Spheres of Influence as Negotiated Hegemony—The Case of Central Asia." *Geopolitics*, 23, 2, 2017, pp. 378–403.

Couldry, Nick, and Ulises A. Mejias. "Data Colonialism: Rethinking Big Data's Relation to the Contemporary Subject." *Television & New Media*, 20, 4, 2019, pp. 336–49.

Craib, Raymond. *Cartographic Mexico: A History of State Fixations and Fugitive Landscapes.* Durham: Duke University Press, 2004.

Crampton, Jeremy. *Mapping: A Critical Introduction to Cartography and GIS.* Malden: John Wiley and Sons, 2010.

Cranston, Sophie. "Calculating the Migration Industries: Knowing the Successful Expatriate in the Global Mobility Industry." *Journal of Ethnic and Migration Studies*, 44, 4, 2018, pp. 626–43.

Dadabaev, Timur. "Uzbekistan as Central Asian Game Changer? Uzbekistan's Foreign Policy Construction in the Post-Karimov Era." *Asian Journal of Comparative Politics*, 4, 2, 2019, pp. 162–75.

Dall'Agnola, Jasmin. "Smartphones and Public Support for LGBTQ+ in Central Asia." *Central Asian Survey*, 43, 1, 2024, pp. 123–42.

Dätwyler IT Infra. "Reference Projects & Case Studies." Accessed October 8, 2021, https://www.itinfra.datwyler.com/en/reference-projects.html, 2021.

Davis, Mike. *Planet of Slums.* New York: Verso, 2006.

Dehghan, Saeed K. "More than 100 Countries Face Spending Cuts as Covid Worsens Debt Crisis, Report Warns." *The Guardian*. Accessed February 2, 2024, https://www.theguardian.com/global-development/2021/sep/23/more-than-100-countries-face-spending-cuts-as-covid-worsens-debt-crisis-report-warns, 2021.

Deibert, Ronald. *RESET: Reclaiming the Internet for Civil Society.* Toronto: House of Anansi Press, 2020.

Demirgüç-Kunt, Asli, Micahel M. Lokshin, and Iván Torre. "Opening-Up for a Strong Economic Recovery: Lessons from the First Wave of Covid-19." World Bank. Accessed April 24, 2022, https://blogs.worldbank.org/developmenttalk/opening-strong-economic-recovery-lessons-first-wave-covid-19, 2020.

Denton, Kirk A. *Exhibiting the Past: Historical Memory and the Politics of Museums in Postsocialist China.* Honolulu: University of Hawai'i Press, 2014.

Department of Defense. *Military and Security Developments Involving the People's Republic of China.* Accessed May 29, 2021, https://media.defense.gov/2020/Sep/01/2002488689/-1/-1/1/2020-DOD-CHINA-MILITARY-POWER-REPORT-FINAL.PDF;https://media.defense.gov/2020/Sep/01/2002488689/-1/-1/1/2020-DOD-CHINA-MILITARY-POWER-REPORT-FINAL.PDF, 2020.

Deutsche Telekom. "Deutsche Telekom in China." Accessed October 8, 2021, https://www.telekom.com/en/company/worldwide/profile/deutsche-telekom-in-china-355812, 2021.

DiCarlo, Jessica. *Grounding Global China in Northern Laos: The Making of the Infrastructure Frontier.* Doctoral dissertation. Boulder: University of Colorado Boulder, 2021.

DiCarlo, Jessica. "Boten: Project Spotlight." *Global China Pulse*, 1, 1, 2022, pp. 141–59.

DiCarlo, Jessica. "Speed, Suspension, and Stasis: Life in the Shadow of Infrastructure." In Jean-Paul Addie, Michael Glass, and Jen Nelles, eds. *Infrastructural Times: Temporality and the Making of Global Urban Worlds.* Bristol: Bristol University Press, 2024, pp. 207–26.

Dobler, Gregor. "Chinese Shops and the Formation of a Chinese Expatriate Community in Namibia." *The China Quarterly*, 199, 2009, pp. 707–27.

Dommann, Monika, Hannes Rickli, and Max Stadler, eds. *Data Centers: Edges of a Digital Nation.* Zurich: Lars Müller Publishers, 2020.

Donnelly, Jack. "Sovereign Inequalities and Hierarchy in Anarchy: American Power and International Society." *European Journal of International Relations*, 12, 2, 2006, pp. 139–70.

Dreher, Axel, Andreas Fuchs, Bradley Parks, Austin Strange, and Michael J. Tierney. *Banking on Beijing: The Aims and Impacts of China's Overseas Development Program.* New York: Cambridge University Press, 2022.

Drew, FitzGerald, and Newley Purnell. "Facebook Drops Plan to Run Fiber Cable to Hong Kong Amid U.S. Pressure." *Wall Street Journal.* Accessed October 8, 2021, https://www.wsj.com/articles/facebook-drops-plan-to-run-fiber-cable-to-hong-kong-amid-u-s-pressure-11615400710, 2021.

Driessen, Miriam. "Migrating for the Bank: Housing and Chinese Labour Migration to Ethiopia." *The China Quarterly*, 221, 2015, pp. 143–60.

Drezner, Daniel, Farrell, Henry, and Newman, Abraham, eds. *The Uses and Abuses of Weaponized Interdependence.* Washington, DC: Brookings Institution Press, 2021.

Driessen, Miriam. *Tales of Hope, Tastes of Bitterness: Chinese Road Builders in Ethiopia.* Hong Kong: Hong Kong University Press, 2019.

Driessen, Miriam. "Chinese Workers in Ethiopia Caught between Remaining and Returning." *Pacific Affairs*, 94, 2, 2021, pp. 329–46.

Du, Shangze, Wei Ding, and Wendi Huang. "Promoting People to People Friendship: Jointly Develop the 'Silk Road Economic Belt.'" Accessed September 10, 2021, http://politics.people.com.cn/n/2013/0908/c1024-22842900.html, 2013.

Dwyer, Michael, and Thoumthone Vongvisouk. "The Long Land Grab: Market-Assisted Enclosure on the China-Lao Rubber Frontier." *Territory, Politics, Governance*, 7, 1, 2019, pp. 96–114.

Easterling, Keller. *Extrastatecraft: The Power of Infrastructure Space.* London: Verso, 2016.

Economist Intelligence Unit. "Global Outlook: Should Emerging Countries Worry about Their Rising Debt Pile-Ups?" Video. Accessed April 24, 2022, https://www.youtube.com/watch?v=BlY_4fwX1E4, 2021.

Edney, Matthew. *Mapping an Empire.* Chicago: University of Chicago Press, 1999.

Ekman, Alice, and Cristina de Esperanza Picardo. "Towards Urban Decoupling? China's Smart City Ambitions at the Time of COVID-19." European Union Institute for Security Studies. Accessed January 9, 2024, https://www.iss.europa.eu/content/towards-urban-decoupling-china%E2%80%99s-smart-city-ambitions-time-covid-19, 2020.

English, Jasmine, and Bernardo Zacka. "The Politics of Sight: Revisiting Timothy Pachirat's Every Twelve Seconds." *American Political Science Review*, 116, 3, 2022, pp. 1025–37.

Eom, Janet, Deborah Bräutigam, and Lina Benebdallah. "The Path Ahead: The 7th Forum on China-Africa Cooperation." *China Africa Research Initiative.* https://static1.squarespace.com/static/5652847de4b033f56d2bdc29/t/5c467754898583fc9a99131f/1548121941093/Briefing+Paper+1+-+August+2018+-+Final.pdf, 2018.

Esteban, Joan, Justin Yifu Lin, and Joseph E. Stiglitz, eds. *The Industrial Policy Revolution.* New York: Palgrave, 2013.

Eurasia Group. "The Digital Silk Road: Expanding China's Digital Footprint." Accessed October 8, 2021, https://www.eurasiagroup.net/files/upload/Digital-Silk-Road-Expanding-China-Digital-Footprint-1.pdf, 2020.

Eurasianet. "Tajikistan: Secret Chinese Base Becomes Slightly Less Secret." Accessed January 23, 2024, https://eurasianet.org/tajikistan-secret-chinese-base-becomes-slightly-less-secret, 2020.

European Bank for Reconstruction and Development. *Turkmenistan: Country Assessment.* Accessed February 11, 2024, https://www.ebrd.com/publications/transition-report-202122-turkmenistan, 2021.

Faul, Moira V. "Networks and Power: Why Networks Are Hierarchical Not Flat and What Can Be Done about It." *Global Policy*, 7, 2, 2015, pp. 185–97.

The Federal Council. "President Ueli Maurer Meets President Xi Jinping." Accessed October 8, 2021, https://www.admin.ch/gov/en/start/documentation/media-releases.msg-id-74817.html, 2019.

Federal Department of Foreign Affairs of the Swiss Confederation. "China Strategy 2021–24." https://www.eda.admin.ch/content/dam/eda/en/documents/publications/Schweizerisc heAussenpolitik/Strategie_China_210319_EN.pdf, 2021.

Fei, Ding. "Worlding Developmentalism: China's Economic Zones within and beyond Its Border." *Journal of International Development*, 29, 6, 2017, pp. 825–50.

Fei, Ding. "The Compound Labor Regime of Chinese Construction Projects in Ethiopia." *Geoforum*, 117, 2020, pp. 13–23.

Fei, Ding. "Chinese Telecommunications Companies in Ethiopia: The Influences of Host Government Intervention and Inter-Firm Competition." *The China Quarterly*, 245, 2021a, pp. 186–207.

Fei, Ding. "Employee Management Strategies of Chinese Telecommunications Companies in Ethiopia: Half-Way Localization and Internationalization." *Journal of Contemporary China*, 30, 130, 2021b, pp. 661–76.

Fei, Ding. "Networked Internationalization: Chinese Companies in Ethiopia's Infrastructure Construction Sector." *Professional Geographer*, 73, 2, 2021c, pp. 322–32.

Fei, Ding. "Chinese in Africa: Expatriation Regime and Lived Experience." *Journal of Ethnic and Migration Studies*, 49, 11, 2023, pp. 2720–41.

Fergana. "V Bishkeke ustanoviat 60 kamer s raspoznavaniem lits" [60 Cameras with Facial Recognition Will Be Installed in Bishkek]. Accessed May 30, 2021, https://fergana.agency/news/112048/, 2019.

Fernholz, Tim. "Eight Countries in Danger of Falling into China's 'Debt Trap.'" *Quartz*. Accessed February 2, 2024, https://qz.com/1223768/china-debt-trap-these-eight-countr ies-are-in-danger-of-debt-overloads-from-chinas-belt-and-road-plans/, 2018.

Financial Tribune. "China's BRI Initiative Hits Roadblock in 7 Countries." Accessed May 30, 2021, https://financialtribune.com/articles/world-economy/84692/china-s-bri-initiative-hits-roadblock-in-7-countries, 2018.

Fish, Adam. "The Place of the Internet in Anthropology." *Anthropology News*, 52, 3, 2011, p. 17.

Fleetwood, Lachlan. *Science on the Roof of the World: Empire and the Remaking of the Himalaya*. Cambridge: Cambridge University Press, 2022.

Flint, Colin, and Cuiping Zhu. "The Geopolitics of Connectivity, Cooperation, and Hegemonic Competition: The Belt and Road Initiative." *Geoforum*, 99, 2019, pp. 95–101.

Foot, Rosemary. "Remembering the Past to Secure the Present: Versailles Legacies in a Resurgent China." *International Affairs*, 95, 1, 2019, pp. 143–60.

Foot, Rosemary. "China's Rise and US Hegemony: Renegotiating Hegemonic Order in East Asia?" *International Politics*, 57, 2, 2020, pp. 150–65.

Franceschini, Ivan. "As Far Apart as Earth and Sky: A Survey of Chinese and Cambodian Construction Workers in Sihanoukville." *Critical Asian Studies*, 52, 4, 2020, pp. 512–29.

Frankopan, Peter. *The New Silk Roads: The New Asia and the Remaking of the World Order*. New York: Vintage Books, 2018.

French, Martin, and Torin Monahan. "Editorial: Disease Surveillance: How Might Surveillance Studies Address COVID-19?" *Surveillance & Society*, 18, 1, 2020, pp. 1–11.

Freymann, Eyck. *One Belt One Road: Chinese Power Meets the World*. Cambridge, MA: Harvard University Press, 2020.

Fu, Xiaolan. *China's Path to Innovation*. Cambridge: Cambridge University Press, 2015.

Fujimura, Kazuhiro. "The Increasing Presence of China in Laos Today: A Report on Fixed Point Observation of Local Newspapers from March 2007 to February 2009." Ritsumeikan Asia Pacific University. Accessed February 2, 2024, https://en.apu.ac.jp/rcaps/uploads/fckeditor/publications/journal/RJAPS_V27_Fujimura.pdf, 2010.

Fumagalli, Matteo. "Alignments and Realignments in Central Asia: The Rationale and Implications of Uzbekistan's Rapprochement with Russia." *International Political Science Review*, 28, 3, 2007, pp. 253–71.

Furlong, Kathryn. "Geographies of Infrastructure II: Concrete, Cloud and Layered (In)Visibilities." *Progress in Human Geography*, 45, 1, 2021, pp. 190–98.

Gadzala, Aleksandra W. "From Formal- to Informal-Sector Employment: Examining the Chinese Presence in Zambia." *Review of African Political Economy*, 37, 123, 2010, pp. 41–59.

Gallagher, Kevin, Amos Irwin, and Katherine Koleski. "The New Banks in Town: Chinese Finance in Latin America." Inter-American Dialogue. Accessed February 2, 2024, https://www.thedialo gue.org/analysis/the-new-banks-in-town-chinese-finance-in-latin-america/, 2012.

Gamble, Jos. "Localizing Management in Foreign-Invested Enterprises in China: Practical, Cultural, and Strategic Perspectives." *International Journal of Human Resource Management*, 11, 5, 2000, pp. 883–903.

Gardner, Kyle. *The Frontier Complex: Geopolitics and the Making of the India-China Border, 1846–1962*. Cambridge: Cambridge University Press, 2021.

Garlick, Jeremy. "Deconstructing the China-Pakistan Economic Corridor: Pipe Dreams versus Geopolitical Realities." *Journal of Contemporary China*, 27, 112, 2018, pp. 519–33.

Ge, Zhaoguang. *Here in "China" I Dwell: Reconstructing Historical Discourses of China for Our Time*. Leiden: Brill, 2017.

Ghiasy, Richard, and Rajeshwari Krishnamurthy. "China's Digital Silk Road and the Global Digital Order." *The Diplomat*. Accessed January 9, 2024, https://thediplomat.com/2021/04/chinas-digital-silk-road-and-the-global-digital-order/, 2021.

Giannecchini, Philip, and Ian Taylor. 2018. "The Eastern Industrial Zone in Ethiopia: Catalyst for Development?" *Geoforum*, 88, 2018, pp. 28–35.

Giese, Karsten. "Chinese Traders in Ghana: The Liminality Trap, and Challenges for Ethnic Formation and Integration." In Min Zhou, ed., *Contemporary Chinese Diasporas*. Singapore: Springer, 2017, pp. 53–77.

Giese, Karsten, and Alena Thiel. "The Vulnerable Other—Distorted Equity in Chinese–Ghanaian Employment Relations." *Ethnic and Racial Studies*, 37, 6, 2012, pp. 1101–20.

Gilpin, Robert. *The Political Economy of International Relations*. Princeton: Princeton University Press, 1987.

Global Times. "China-Laos Railway Roars in Full Swing, Brings Laos into Modern Transport Era amid BRI Endeavor." *Global Times*. Accessed April 24, 2022, https://www.globaltimes.cn/page/202112/1240592.shtml, 2021.

Goddard, Stacie. "Brokering Change: Networks and Entrepreneurs in International Politics." *International Theory*, 1, 2, 2009, pp. 249–81.

Goddard, Stacie. "Embedded Revisionism: Networks, Institutions, and Challenges to World Order." *International Organization*, 72, 4, 2018, pp. 763–97.

Gonzalez-Vicente, Ruben. "Make Development Great Again? Accumulation Regimes, Spaces of Sovereign Exception and the Elite Development Paradigm of China's Belt and Road Initiative." *Business and Politics*, 21, 4, 2019, pp. 487–513.

Gordon, David, and Meia Nouwens. *The Digital Silk Road China's Technological Rise and the Geopolitics of Cyberspace*. Abingdon: Routledge, 2022.

Gordon, David, Haoyu Tong, and Tabatha Anderson. "Beyond the Myths—Towards a Realistic Assessment of China's Belt and Road Initiative: The Development-Finance Dimension." The International Institute for Strategic Studies. https://www.iiss.org/globalassets/media-library---content—migration/files/research-papers/bri-report-one_beyond-the-myths_-development-finance---updated.pdf, 2020.

Graham, Stephen, and Simon Marvin. *Telecommunications and the City: Electronic Spaces, Urban Places*. London: Routledge, 2004.

Grayson, Kyle, and Jocelyn Mawdsley. "Scopic Regimes and the Visual Turn in International Relations: Seeing World Politics through the Drone." *European Journal of International Relations*, 25, 2, 2019, pp. 431–57.

Greater Zurich Area. "Huawei setzt mit 1'000 Forschungsstellen auf geballte Technologie-Kompetenz im stabilsten Umfeld Europas." Accessed October 8, 2021, https://www.greaterzuricharea.com/de/news/huawei-setzt-mit-1000-forschungsstellen-auf-geballte-technologie-kompetenz-im-stabilsten, 2019.

Greene, Paul, and Paul Triolo. "Will China Control the Global Internet via Its Digital Silk Road?" Carnegie Endowment for International Peace. Accessed October 8, 2021, https://carnegieendowment.org/2020/05/08/will-china-control-global-internet-via-its-digital-silk-road-pub-81857, 2020.

Grgić, Mladen. "Chinese Infrastructure Investments in the Balkans: Political Implications of the Highway Project in Montenegro." *Territory, Politics, Governance*, 7, 1, 2019, pp. 42–60.

Gu, Jing. "China's Private Enterprises in Africa and the Implications for African Development." *European Journal of Development Research*, 21, 4, 2009, pp. 570–87.

Guccini, Federica, and Mingyuan Zhang. "'Being Chinese' in Mauritius and Madagascar: Comparing Chinese Diasporic Communities in the Western Indian Ocean." *The Journal of Indian Ocean World Studies*, 4, 2, 2021, pp. 91–117.

Guifang, Xue, and Zheng Jie. "China's Building of Overseas Military Bases: Rationale and Challenges." *China Quarterly of International Strategic Studies*, 5, 4, 2019, pp. 493–510.

Guluzian, Christine R. "Making Inroads: China's New Silk Road Initiative." *Cato Journal*, 37, 1, 2017, pp. 135–47.

Gurinskaya, Anna. "Predicting Citizens' Support for Surveillance Cameras. Does Police Legitimacy Matter?" *International Journal of Comparative and Applied Criminal Justice*, 44, 1–2, 2020, pp. 63–83.

Gurung, Phurwa. "Challenging Infrastructural Orthodoxies: Political and Economic Geographies of a Himalayan Road." *Geoforum*, 120, 2021, pp. 103–12.

Gussarova, Anna. "Kazakhstan Experiments with Surveillance Technology to Battle Coronavirus Pandemic." The Jamestown Foundation. Accessed January 9, 2024, https://jamestown.org/program/kazakhstan-experiments-with-surveillance-technology-to-battle-coronavirus-pandemic/, 2020.

Gussarova, Anna, and Serik Jaksylykov. *Zashchita personal'nykh dannykh v Kazakhstane: Status, riski i vozmozhnosti.* Almata: Fond Soros-Kazakhstan, 2020.

Gussarova, Anna, and Serik Jaksylykov. *Zashchita personal'nykh dannykh v Kazakhstane 2.0: Zifrovoĭ Sled COVID-19.* Almata: Fond Soros-Kazakhstan, 2021.

Häberli, Stefan. "Ex-Chefbeamter gibt Huawei-freundliches Buch heraus." *Neue Zürcher Zeitung.* Accessed July 20, 2023, https://www.nzz.ch/wirtschaft/ex-chefbeamter-gibt-huawei-freundliches-buch-heraus-ld.1695157, 2022.

Haerpfer, Christian, Roland Inglehart, Alejandro Moreno, Christian Welzel, Kseniya Kizilov, Jaime Diez-Medrano, Marta Lagos, Pippa Norris, Eduard Ponarin, and Bi Puranen. *World Values Survey: Round Seven—Country-Pooled Datafile Version 3.0.* Madrid & Vienna: JD Systems Institute & WVSA Secretariat. https://doi.org/10.14281/18241.16, 2022.

Haerpfer, Christian, and Kseniya Kizilova. "Values and Transformation in Central Asia." In Anja Mihr, ed., *Transformation and Development.* Cham: Springer, 2020, pp. 7–28.

Hafner-Burton, Emilie, Miles Kahler, and Alexander Montgomery. "Network Analysis for International Relations." *International Organization*, 63, 3, 2009, pp. 559–92.

Haga, Kai Yin Allison. "The Asian Infrastructure Investment Bank: A Qualified Success for Beijing's Economic Statecraft." *Journal of Current Chinese Affairs*, 50, 3, 2021, pp. 391–421.

Hale, Thomas, Ryan McMorrow, and Andy Lin. "China Suffers Plunging Foreign DirectInvestment amid Geopolitical Tensions." *Financial Times*, https://www.ft.com/content/56294843-7eff-4b83-9fa2-c46fb4ac1278, 2023.

Halegua, Aaron. "Where Is the Belt and Road Initiative Taking International Labour Rights? An Examination of Worker Abuse by Chinese Firms in Saipan." In Jean-Christophe Defraigne, Maria Adele Carrai, and Jan Wouters, eds., *The Belt and Road Initiative and Global Governance.* Cheltenham: Edward Elgar Publishing, 2020, pp. 225–57.

Hameiri, Shahar. "Institutionalism beyond Methodological Nationalism? The New Interdependence Approach and the Limits of Historical Institutionalism." *Review of International Political Economy*, 27, 3, 2020, pp. 637–57.

Han, Xiao, and Michael Webber. "From Chinese Dam Building in Africa to the Belt and Road Initiative: Assembling Infrastructure Projects and Their Linkages." *Political Geography*, 77, 2020, 102102.

Hannon, Paul, and Saabira Chaudhuri. "Why the Economic Recovery Will Be More of a Swoosh than V-Shaped." *Wall Street Journal*. Accessed February 2, 2024, https://www.wsj.com/articles/why-the-economic-recovery-will-be-more-of-a-swoosh-than-v-shaped-1158 9203608, 2020.

Harding, Sandra. "Rethinking Standpoint Epistemology: What Is 'Strong Objectivity'?" In Linda Alcoff and Elizabeth Potter, eds., *Feminist Epistemologies*. New York: Routledge, 1992, pp. 49–82.

Hardy, Stephen. "U.S. Commerce Department Adds Fiberhome to Entity List." *Lightwave*. Accessed October 8, 2021,https://www.lightwaveonline.com/business/companies/article/14176645/us-commerce-department-adds-fiberhome-to-entity-list, 2020.

Harley, J. B. *The New Nature of Maps*. Baltimore: Johns Hopkins University Press, 2001.

Harris, Tina. *Geographical Diversions: Tibetan Trade, Global Transactions*. Athens: University of Georgia Press, 2013.

Hart, Gillian. "Relational Comparison Revisited: Marxist Postcolonial Geographies in Practice." *Progress in Human Geography*, 42, 3, 2018, pp. 371–94.

Harvey, David. *Seventeen Contradictions and the End of Capitalism*. Oxford: Oxford University Press, 2014.

Harvey, Penelope, Casper Jensen, and Atsuro Morita, eds. *Infrastructures and Social Complexity: A Companion*. 1st ed. London: Routledge, 2016. https://doi.org/10.4324/9781315622880.

Harvey, Penelope, Casper Bruun Jensen, and Atsuro Morita, eds. *Infrastructures and Social Complexity: A Routledge Companion*. London: Routledge, 2017.

Harvey, Penelope, and Hannah Knox. *Roads: An Anthropology of Infrastructure and Expertise*. Ithaca: Cornell University Press, 2015.

Hashimova, Umida. "Uzbekistan and Tajikistan Engage in Joint Military Exercises." *The Diplomat*. Accessed May 29, 2021, https://thediplomat.com/2020/03/uzbekistan-and-taj ikistan-engage-in-joint-military-exercises/, 2020.

Haynes, Naomi, and Jason Hickel. "Hierarchy, Value, and the Value of Hierarchy." *Social Analysis*, 60, 2016, pp. 1–20.

Hecht, Jeff. *City of Light: The Story of Fiber Optics*. New York: Oxford University Press, 1999.

Heeks, Richard, Angelica V. Ospina, Christopher Foster, Ping Gao, Nicholas Jepson, Seth Schindler, and Qingna Zhou. "China's Digital Expansion in the Global South: Systematic Literature Review and Future Research Agenda." Centre for Digital Development. https://hummedia.manchester.ac.uk/institutes/gdi/publications/workingpapers/di/dd_wp95.pdf, 2023.

Henry, Jacob. "Morality in Aversion?: Meditations on Slum Tourism and the Politics of Sight." *Hospitality & Society*, 10, 2, 2020, pp. 157–72.

Heslop, Luke, and Galen Murton, eds. *Highways and Hierarchies: Ethnographies of Mobility from the Himalaya to the Indian Ocean*. Amsterdam: Amsterdam University Press, 2021.

Hillman, Jennifer, and Alex Tippett. "Who Built That? Labor and the Belt and Road Initiative." *The Internationalist*. Accessed January 15, 2022, https://www.cfr.org/blog/who-built-labor-and-belt-and-road-initiative, 2021.

Hillman, Jonathan E. "The Hazards of China's Global Ambitions." *New Perspectives Quarterly*, 35, 2, 2018, pp. 17–20.

Hillman, Jonathan E. *The Emperor's New Road: China and the Project of the Century*. New Haven: Yale University Press, 2020.

Hillman, Jonathan E. *The Digital Silk Road: China's Quest to Wire the World and Win the Future*. New York: HarperCollins Publishers, 2021.

Ho, Elaine Lynn-Ee. *Citizens in Motion: Emigration, Immigration, and Re-migration across China's Borders*. Stanford: Stanford University Press, 2019.

Ho, Selina. "Infrastructure and Chinese Power." *International Affairs*, 96, 6, 2020, pp. 1461–85.

Hobsbawm, Eric J. *The Age of Empire, 1875–1914*. 1st ed. New York: Vintage Books, 1989.

Hobson, John. "The Twin Self-Delusions of IR: Why 'Hierarchy' and Not 'Anarchy' Is the Core Concept of IR." *Millennium*, 42, 3, 2014, pp. 557–75.

Hodzi, Obert. "Chinese in Africa: 'Chineseness' and the Complexities of Identities." *Asian Ethnicity*, 20, 1, 2019, pp. 1–7.

Hope, Arran. "This Is the State of Play at Huawei under Sanctions." The China Project. Accessed July 28, 2023, https://thechinaproject.com/2023/06/21/this-is-the-state-of-play-at-huawei-under-sanctions/, 2023.

Horn, Sebastian, Carmen M. Reinhart, and Christoph Trebesch. "China's Overseas Lending." National Bureau of Economic Research. Accessed February 2, 2024, https://www.nber.org/papers/w26050, 2019.

Horn, Sebastian, Carmen M. Reinhart, and Christoph Trebesch. "How Much Money Does the World Owe China?" *Harvard Business Review*. https://hbr.org/2020/02/how-much-money-does-the-world-owe-china, February 26, 2020.

Hu, Tung-Hui. *A Prehistory of the Cloud*. Cambridge, MA: The MIT Press, 2015.

Huawei. "Huawei Facts." Accessed October 8, 2021, https://www.huawei.com/en/facts, 2021.

Huawei. "Huawei in Switzerland." Accessed July 20, 2024, https://www.huawei.com/ch-en/corporate-information/local-states, 2024.

Hubei Government. "Zhōng guó guāng gǔ ， lí shì jiè guāng gǔ yǒu duō yuǎn ？" [How Far Is China's Optics Valley from the World's Optics Valley?] Accessed July 20, 2023, http://www.hubei.gov.cn/zhuanti/2020/2020zggg/index.shtml, 2023.

Human Rights Watch. "'Violence with Every Step': Weak State Response to Domestic Violence in Tajikistan." Human Rights Watch. Accessed January 9, 2024, https://www.hrw.org/report/2019/09/19/violence-every-step/weak-state-response-domestic-violence-tajikistan, 2019.

Hung, H. Fung. "Rise of China and the Global Overaccumulation Crisis." *Review of International Political Economy*, 15, 2, 2008, pp. 149–79.

IAMS (I. A. O. M. O. T. S. R.). "International Alliance of Museums of the Silk Road." Newsletter, Volume 3, 2019.

IGI Consulting. *China Telecom Volume 2: Fiber Optics Markets and Opportunities*. Boston: Information Gatekeepers Inc, 2001.

Ikenberry, G. John. "The Future of the Liberal World Order: Internationalism after America." *Foreign Affairs*, 90, 3, 2018, pp. 56–68.

Imamova, Navbahor. "Central Asians Balance Benefits, Risks of China's BRI." *Voice of America*. Accessed January 23, 2024, https://www.voanews.com/a/central-asians-balance-benefits-risks-of-china-s-bri/7308448.html, 2023.

International Household Survey Network. "Living Conditions Monitoring Survey VI 2010 Zambia, 2010." Central Statistical Office. Accessed April 24, 2022. https://catalog.ihsn.org/catalog/2597, 2010.

Ito, Asei. "China's Belt and Road Initiative and Japan's Response: From Non-Participation to Conditional Engagement." *East Asia*, 36, 2, 2019, pp. 115–28.

Izumikawa, Yazushiro. "Network Connections and the Emergence of the Hub-and-Spokes Alliance System in East Asia." *International Security*, 45, 2, 2020, pp. 7–50.

Jackson, Patrick Thaddeus. "Foregrounding Ontology: Dualism, Monism, and IR Theory." *Review of International Studies*, 34, 1, 2008, pp. 129–53.

Janes. 2019. "Uzbekistan Conducts First FD-2000 Air-Defense Test." Accessed May 30, 2021, www.janes.com/article/92799/uzbekistan-conducts-first-fd-2000-air-defence-test, 2019.

Jardine, Bradley. "China's Surveillance State Has Eyes on Central Asia." *Foreign Policy*. Accessed January 23, 2024, https://foreignpolicy.com/2019/11/15/huawei-xinjiang-kazakhstan-uzb ekistan-china-surveillance-state-eyes-central-asia/, 2019.

Jardine, Bradley, Edward Lemon, and Natalie Hall. "Globalizing Minority Persecution: China's Transnational Repression of the Uyghurs." *Globalizations*, 20, 4, 2023, pp. 564–80.

Jisi, Wang. "'Marching Westwards': The Rebalancing of China's Geostrategy." In Shao Binhong, ed., *The World in 2020 According to China: Chinese Foreign Policy Elites Discuss Emerging Trends in International Politics*. Amsterdam: Brill, 2014, 129–36.

Johnson, Alix. "Data Centers as Infrastructural In-Betweens: Expanding Connections and Enduring Marginalities in Iceland." *American Ethnologist*, 46, 1, 2019, pp. 75–88.

Johnston, Alastair Iain. "Socialization in International Institutions: The ASEAN Way and International Relations Theory." In G. J. Ikenberry and Michael Mastanduno, eds., *International Relations Theory and the Asia-Pacific*. New York: Columbia University Press, 2003, pp. 107–62.

Jones, Lee, and Shahar Hameiri. "Debunking the Myth of 'Debt-Trap Diplomacy': How Recipient Countries Shape China's Belt and Road Initiative." Chatham House. https://www. chathamhouse.org/2020/08/debunking-myth-debt-trap-diplomacy, 2020.

Jones, Lee, and Jinghan Zeng. "Understanding China's 'Belt and Road Initiative': Beyond 'Grand Strategy' to a State Transformation Analysis." *Third World Quarterly*, 40, 8, 2019, pp. 1415–39.

Jorgic, Drazen. "Fearing Debt Trap, Pakistan Rethinks Chinese 'Silk Road' Projects." *Reuters*. Accessed February 2, 2024, https://www.reuters.com/article/us-pakistan-silkroad-railway-insight/fearing-debt-trap-pakistan-rethinks-chinese-silk-road-projects-idUSKCN1MA 028, 2018.

Kabylova, Moldir. "Examining the Causes of Femicide in Kazakhstan." Central Asia Program. https://www.centralasiaprogram.org/wp-content/uploads/2021/04/CAP-Paper-256-by-Moldir-Kabylova-PDF.pdf, 2021.

Karavas, George. "How Images Frame China's Role in African Development." *International Affairs*, 96, 3, 2020, pp. 667–90.

Karibayeva, Akbota. "Public Attitudes toward China in Central Asia." Caspian Policy Center. Accessed January 9, 2024, https://api.caspianpolicy.org/media/uploads/2020/05/Public-Attitudes-Toward-China-in-Central-Asia.pdf, 2020.

Kassenova, Nargis, and Brendan Duprey, eds. *Digital Silk Road in Central Asia: Present and Future*. Cambridge: Davis Center for Russian and Eurasian Studies, 2021.

Kaufmann, Lena. "Altdorf–Shanghai–Shenzhen–Liebefeld: Swiss-Chinese Entanglements in Digital Infrastructures." In Monika Dommann, Hannes Rickli, and Max Stadler, eds., *Data Centers: Edges of a Digital Nation*. Zurich: Lars Müller Publishers, 2020, pp. 262–89.

Keohane, Robert, and Joseph Nye. "Power and Interdependence." *Survival*, 15, 4, 1973, pp. 158–65.

Keohane, Robert, and Joseph Nye. *Power and Interdependence: World Politics in Transition*. Boston: Little, Brown and Company, 1977.

Kerimkhanov, Abdul. "Tajikistan, Uzbekistan Intend to Establish Joint Production of Military Equipment." *AzerNews*. Accessed May 29, 2021, https://www.azernews.az/region/146868. html, 2019.

Khalili, Laleh. *Sinews of War and Trade. Shipping and Capitalism in the Arabian Peninsula*. London: Verso, 2020.

Khong, Yuen Foong. "Primacy or World Order? The United States and China's Rise—a Review Essay." *International Security*, 38, 3, 2013, pp. 153–75.

Kitchin, Rob. "Civil Liberties or Public Health, or Civil Liberties and Public Health? Using Surveillance Technologies to Tackle the Spread of COVID-19." *Space and Polity*, 24, 3, 2020, pp. 362–81.

Kliman, Daniel. "China's Power Play: The Role of Congress in Addressing the Belt and Road." Accessed July 15, 2023, https://www.cnas.org/publications/congressional-testimony/chinas-power-play-the-role-of-congress-in-addressing-the-belt-and-road, 2019.

Klinger, Julie Michelle, and Joshua S. S. Muldavin. "New Geographies of Development: Grounding China's Global Integration." *Territory, Politics, Governance*, 7, 1, 2019, pp. 1–21.

Knoke, David, and James Kuklinski. *Network Analysis*. London: Sage, 1982.

Knox, Hannah. "Traversing the Infrastructures of Digital Life." In Haidy Geismar and Hannah Knox, eds., *Digital Anthropology*. 2nd ed. Abingdon/New York: Routledge, 2021, pp. 178–96.

Kose, M. Ayhan, Franziska Ohnsorge, Peter Nagle, and Naotaka Sugawara. "Caught by the Cresting Debt Wave." *Finance & Development*, 57, 2, https://www.imf.org/Publications/fandd/issues/2020/06/COVID19-and-debt-in-developing-economies-kose, June 2020.

Kremlin. "Sovmestnoe zasedanie Rossiĭskoĭ Federatsii i Kitaĭskoĭ Narodnoĭ Respubliki ob uglublenii otnoshenii vseob"emliushchego partnerstva i vzaimodeĭstviia, vstupaiushchikh v novuiu obstanovku" [Joint Statement by the Russian Federation and the People's Republic of China on Deepening Comprehensive Partnership and Strategic Cooperation, Entering a New Era]. Accessed July 22, 2023, http://kremlin.ru/supplement/5920, 2022.

Krishna, Sankaran. "Cartographic Anxiety: Mapping the Body Politic in India." *Alternatives: Global, Local, Political*, 19, 4, 1994, pp. 507–21.

Kucera, Joshua. "Afghanistan, China, Pakistan, Tajikistan Deepen 'Anti-Terror' Ties." *Eurasianet*. Accessed May 29, 2021, https://eurasianet.org/afghanistan-china-pakistan-tajikistan-deepen-anti-terror-ties, 2016.

Kudryavtseva, Tatyana. "Aktivistyi trebuyut otmenit ustanovku kamer raspoznavaniya lits v Kyrgyzstane." *24.KG*. Accessed January 9, 2024, https://24.kg/obschestvo/134314_aktivistyi_trebuyut_otmenit_ustanovku_kamer_raspoznavaniya_lits_vkyirgyizstane/, 2019.

Kudryavtseva, Tatyana. "Safe City: Contract with Chinese Company Extended until March 10, 2022." *24.KG*. Accessed January 9, 2024, https://24.kg/english/199585_Safe_sity_Contract_with_Chinese_company_extended_until_March_10_2022/, 2021.

Kuik, Cheng-Chwee. "Laos's Enthusiastic Embrace of China's Belt and Road Initiative." *Asian Perspective*, 45, 4, 2021, pp. 735–59.

Kuik, Cheng-Chwee, and Zikri Rosli. "Laos-China Infrastructure Cooperation: Legitimation and the Limits of Host-Country Agency." *Journal of Contemporary East Asian Studies*, DOI: 10.1080/24761028.2023.2274236, 2023.

Kumoratih, Dewi, Gisela Anindita, Inda Ariesta, and Elghandiva Astrilia Tholkhah. "The Role of Visual Communication Design to Increase Public Literacy on the History of Spice Route in Supporting Indonesia's Proposal Toward UNESCO's World Cultural Heritage." *IOP Conference Series: Earth and Environmental Science*, 729, 2021.

Kuo, Lily, and Alicia Chen. "Chinese Workers Allege Forced Labor, Abuses in Xi's 'Belt and Road' Program." *The Washington Post*. Accessed January 15, 2022, https://www.washingtonpost.com/world/asia_pacific/china-labor-belt-road-covid/2021/04/30/f110e8de-9cd4-11eb-b2f5-7d2f0182750d_story.html, 2021.

Ladduwahetty, Ravi. "Hambantota Port Will Attract 36,000 Ships Annually—Ananda Kularatne." *Daily News*. Accessed February 2, 2024, http://archives.dailynews.lk/2002/06/18/bus04.html, 2002.

Lai, Karen P. Y., Shaun Lin, and James Sidaway. "Financing the Belt and Road Initiative (BRI): Research Agendas beyond the 'Debt-Trap' Discourse." *Eurasian Geography and Economics*, 61, 2, 2020, pp. 109–24.

Lake, David. *Hierarchy in International Relations*. Ithaca: Cornell University Press, 2009.

Lampton, David, Selina Ho, and Cheng-Chwee Kuik. *Rivers of Iron: Railroads and Chinese Power in Southeast Asia*. Oakland: University of California Press, 2020.

Larkin, Brian. "The Politics and Poetics of Infrastructure." *Annual Review of Anthropology*, 42, 1, 2013, pp. 327–43.

Larkin, Brian. *Signal and Noise: Media, Infrastructure, and Urban Culture in Nigeria.* Durham: Duke University Press, 2020.

Laruelle, Marlène, and Dylan Royce. "No Great Game: Central Asia's Public Opinions on Russia, China, and the U.S." *Kennan Cable,* 56, August 2020.

Lee, Ching Kwan. "The Spectre of Global China." *New Left Review,* 89, 2014, pp. 28–65.

Lee, Ching Kwan. *The Specter of Global China: Politics, Labor, and Foreign Investment in Africa.* Chicago: University of Chicago Press, 2017.

Lee, Ching Kwan. "Introduction. Global China at 20: Why, How and So What?" *The China Quarterly,* 250, pp. 313–31, 2022.

Lee, Clair. "Datafication, Dataveillance, and the Social Credit System as China's New Normal." *Online Information Review,* 43, 6, 2019, pp. 952–70.

Leiden Asia Centre. "The BRI and China's International Trade Map." Leiden Asia Centre. Accessed September 30, 2021, https://leidenasiacentre.nl/wp-content/uploads/2021/02/VERSIE-FINAL-30-DEC-PNG-1-1.png, 2021.

Lemon, Edward, and Bradley Jardine. "Avoiding Dependence? Central Asian Security in a Multipolar World." The Oxus Society for Central Asian Affairs. Accessed May 27, 2021, https://oxussociety.org/avoiding-dependence-central-asian-security-in-a-multipolar-world/, 2020a.

Lemon, Edward, and Bradley Jardine. "In Russia's Shadow: China's Rising Security Presence in Central Asia." *Kennan Cable,* 52. Accessed January 23, 2024, https://www.wilsoncenter.org/publication/kennan-cable-no-52-russias-shadow-chinas-rising-security-presence-central-asia, 2020b.

Lenin, Vladimir. *Imperialism, the Highest Stage of Capitalism.* London: Penguin Classics, 2010.

Li, Cheng. *Middle Class Shanghai: Reshaping US–China Engagement.* Washington, DC: Brookings Institution Press, 2021.

Lieberman, Evan S. "Nested Analysis as a Mixed-Method Strategy for Comparative Research," *American Political Science Review,* 99, 3, 2005, pp. 435–52.

Liebman, Alexander, Liana Katz, and Andrea Marston. "Aporias at the Intersection of Geography and Feminist Science and Technology Studies: Critical Engagements with Black Studies." *Progress in Human Geography,* 47, 2, 2023, pp. 238–58.

Lin, Shaun, James D. Sidaway, and Chih Yuan Woon. 2019. "Reordering China, Respacing the World: Belt and Road Initiative (一带一路) as an Emergent Geopolitical Culture." *Professional Geographer,* 71, 3, 2019, pp. 507–22.

Lin, Weiqiang. "Beyond Flexible Citizenship: Towards a Study of Many Chinese Transnationalisms." *Geoforum,* 43, 1, 2012, pp. 137–46.

Lin, Weiqiang, and Qi Ai. "'Aerial Silk Roads': Airport Infrastructures in China's Belt and Road Initiative." *Development and Change,* 51, 4, 2020, pp. 1123–45.

Lindtner, Silvia. *Prototype Nation: China and the Contested Promise of Innovation.* Princeton: Princeton University Press, 2020.

Liu, He. "Accelerating the Construction of a New Development Outlook Focused on the Domestic Big Cycle and the Mutual Promotion of the Domestic and International Economic Cycles." *Xinhua News Agency.* Accessed May 30, 2021, http://www.xinhuanet.com/politics/leaders/2020-11/25/c_1126785254.htm, 2020.

Liu, Jiahe. "Guó jì tōng xìn dà lù qiáo —— yà ōu lù dì guāng lǎn xì tǒng gōng chéng (TAE)" [Continental Bridge of International Communication: The Asia-Europe Terrestrial Optical Cable System Project (TAE)]. *Telecom Engineering Technics and Standardization,* 3, 1993, p. 2.

Liu, Weidong, and Michael Dunford. "Inclusive Globalization: Unpacking China's Belt and Road Initiative." *Area Development and Policy,* 1, 3, 2016, pp. 323–40.

Liu, Weidong, Yajing Zhang, and Wei Xiong. "Financing the Belt and Road Initiative." *Eurasian Geography and Economics,* 61, 2, 2020, pp. 137–45.

Liu-Farrer, Gracia. 2016. "Migration as Class-Based Consumption: The Emigration of the Rich in Contemporary China." *The China Quarterly,* 226, 2016, pp. 499–518.

Lookout. "Mobile APT Surveillance Campaigns Targeting Uyghurs." Accessed January 18, 2024, https://www.lookout.com/documents/threat-reports/us/lookout-uyghur-malware-tr-us.pdf, 2020.

Lu, Bin. "Zhōng é guāng lǎn jiàn shè wéi hù xié yì zài jīng qiān shǔ" [Chinese-Russian Fiber-Optic Cable Construction and Maintenance Agreement Signed in Beijing]. *People's Post and Telecommunications*, 2004.

Lu, Hui. "Full Text of Joint Communique of Leaders' Roundtable of 2nd BRF." *Xinhua News Agency*. Accessed February 11, 2024, http://www.xinhuanet.com/english/2019-04/27/c_13 8016073.htm, 2019.

Lu, Juliet. "Grounding Chinese Investment: Encounters between Chinese Capital and Local Land Politics in Laos." *Globalizations*, 18, 3, 2021, pp. 422–40.

Lu, Juliet, and Oliver Schönweger. "Great Expectations: Chinese Investment in Laos and the Myth of Empty Land." *Territory, Politics, Governance*, 7, 1, 2019, pp. 61–78.

Lugt, Sanne van der. "Exploring the Political, Economic, and Social Implications of the Digital Silk Road into East Africa: The Case of Ethiopia." In Florian Schneider, ed., *Global Perspectives on China's Belt and Road Initiative: Asserting Agency through Regional Connectivity*. Amsterdam: Amsterdam University Press, 2021, pp. 315–46.

Macikenaite, Vida. "China's Economic Statecraft: The Use of Economic Power in an Interdependent World." *Journal of Contemporary East Asia Studies*, 9, 2, 2020, pp. 108–26.

Macikenaite, Vida. "China's Economic Statecraft: The Use of Economic Power in an Interdependent World." *Journal of Contemporary East Asia*, 9, 2, 2020, pp. 108–26.

Mahmood, Shahid, Ghaffar Ali, Rashid Menhas, and Muazzam Sabir. "Belt and Road Initiative as a Catalyst of Infrastructure Development: Assessment of Resident's Perception and Attitude towards China-Pakistan Economic Corridor." *PloS One*, 17, 7, 2022, p. e0271243.

Malik, Ammar A., Bradley Parks, Brooke Russell, Joyce Jiahui Lin, Katherine Walsh, Kyra Solomon, Sheng Zhang, Thai-Binh Elston, and Seth Goodman. "Banking on the Belt and Road: Insights from a New Global Dataset of 13,427 Chinese Development Projects." AidData. Accessed February 2, 2024, https://www.aiddata.org/publications/banking-on-the-belt-and-road, 2021.

Marat, Erica. "Chinese Artificial Intelligence Projects Expand in Eurasian Cities." Program on New Approaches to Research and Security in Eurasia. Accessed January 9, 2024, https://www.ponarseurasia.org/chinese-artificial-intelligence-projects-expand-in-eurasian-cities/, 2018.

Marat, Erica. "Video Surveillance and COVID-19 in Eurasia." Program of New Approaches to Research and Security in Eurasia. Accessed January 9, 2024, https://www.ponarseurasia.org/video-surveillance-and-covid-19-in-eurasia/, 2020.

Marat, Erica, and Deborah Sutton. "Technological Solutions for Complex Problems: Emerging Electronic Surveillance Regimes in Eurasian Cities." *Europe-Asia Studies*, 73, 1, 2021, pp. 243–67.

Maoz, Zeev. "How Network Analysis Can Inform the Study of International Relations." *Conflict Management and Peace Science*, 29, 3, 2012, pp. 247–56.

Marandi, Rosemary. "China-Led AIIB to Spend $3.5bn with Focus on India." *Nikkei*. Accessed May 20, 2021, https://asia.nikkei.com/Economy/China-led-AIIB-to-spend-3.5bn-with-focus-on-India, 2018.

Markey, Daniel S. *China's Western Horizon: Beijing and the New Geopolitics of Eurasia*. New York: Oxford University Press, 2020.

Marti, Tobias. "Bern fürchtet den Zorn Amerikas: Chinas Entwicklungszentren in der Schweiz." *Blick*. Accessed October 8, 2021, https://www.blick.ch/news/politik/weil-china-entwicklungszentren-in-der-schweiz-plant-bern-fuerchtet-den-zorn-amerikas-id15293 817.html, 2019.

Massey, Doreen. "Power-Geometry and a Progressive Sense of Place." In Jon Bird, Barry Curtis, Tim Putnam, George Robertson, and Lisa Tickner, eds., *Mapping the Futures: Local Cultures, Global Change*. London: Routledge, 1993, pp. 60–69.

Mastro, Oriana Skylar. "The Stealth Superpower: How China Hid Its Global Ambitions." *Foreign Affairs.* Accessed July 22, 2024, https://www.foreignaffairs.com/articles/china/china-plan-rule-asia, 2019.

Mattern, Janice, and Ayşe Zarakol. "Hierarchies in World Politics." *International Organization,* 70, 3, 2016, pp. 623–54.

Mawdsley, Emma. "South-South Cooperation 3.0? Managing the Consequences of Success in the Decade Ahead." *Oxford Development Studies,* 47, 3, 2019, pp. 259–74.

Mayer, Maximilian. *China's Rise as Eurasian Power: The Revival of the Silk Road and Its Consequences.* Singapore: Springer, 2017.

Mayer, Maximilian. "China's Historical Statecraft and the Return of History." *International Affairs,* 94, 6, 2018a, pp. 1217–35.

Mayer, Maximilian. *Rethinking the Silk Road: China's Belt and Road Initiative and Emerging Eurasian Relations.* Singapore: Springer, 2018b.

McConaughey, Meghan, Paul Musgrave, and Dan Nexon. "Beyond Anarchy: Logics of Political Organization, Hierarchy, and International Structure." *International Theory,* 10, 2, 2018, pp. 181–218.

McCormack, David. *Great Powers and International Hierarchy.* New York: Palgrave Macmillan, 2018.

Mercator Institute for China Studies. "Mapping the Belt and Road Initiative: This Is Where We Stand." Mercator Institute for China Studies. Accessed September 30, 2021, https://merics.org/en/analysis/mapping-belt-and-road-initiative-where-we-stand, 2018.

Miksic, John N. *Singapore and the Silk Road of the Sea, 1300–1800.* Singapore: NUS Press, 2013.

Military News. "Zhōng guó guó chǎn yùn shū jī jī bài měi é chǎn pǐn ： chū kǒu zhōng yà ràng wài méi fàn suàn." [Chinese Domestic Transport Aircraft Beat US and Russian Products in Central Asia]. *Military News.* Accessed May 30, 2021, https://mil.news.sina.com.cn/jssd/2018-10-11/doc-ihmhafiq9908390.shtml, 2018.

Mills, Laura, and Maya Wang. "Facial Recognition Deal in Kyrgyzstan Poses Risks to Rights." Human Rights Watch. Accessed January 9, 2024, https://www.hrw.org/news/2019/11/15/facial-recognition-deal-kyrgyzstan-poses-risks-rights, 2019.

Minhas, Shahryar, Peter Hoff, and Michael Ward. "A New Approach to Analyzing Coevolving Longitudinal Networks in International Relations." *Journal of Peace Research,* 53, 3, 2016, pp. 491–505.

Ministry of Commerce. "Notice of the Ministry of Commerce on Issuing the Business Statistical System for the Contracting of Foreign Projects and the Business Statistical System for Foreign Labor Cooperation." http://www.mofcom.gov.cn/article/b/bf/200602/2006020 1553432.shtml, 2006.

Ministry of Commerce. *Annual Report on China International Labor Cooperation, 2017–2018.* Accessed on June 10, 2021, https://www.chinca.org/CICA/PublicationsList/TP/1712111 0551111, 2019.

Ministry of Commerce. *Annual Report on China International Project Contracting (2018–2019).* Accessed on June 10, 2021, https://www.chinca.org/cica/PublicationsList/TP/201 20409085711, 2020.

Ministry of Commerce. *Annual Report on China International Labor Cooperation, 2018–2019.* Accessed on June 10, 2021, https://www.chinca.org/CICA/PublicationsList/TP/2005110 9211311, 2021.

Ministry of Defense. "Cháng wàn quán yǔ hā sà kè sī tǎn guó fáng bù cháng jǔ xíng huì tán" [Chang Wanquan Holds Talks with Kazakhstan's Defense Minister]. Accessed May 30, 2021, http://www.mod.gov.cn/leaders/2016-06/07/content_4675251.htm, 2016.

Ministry of Finance and National Planning. *2020 Annual Economic Report.* Accessed April 24, 2022, https://www.mofnp.gov.zm/?wpdmpro=2020-annual-economic-report, 2020.

Ministry of Foreign Affairs. "Joint Communique of the Leaders' Roundtable on the 2nd Belt and Road Forum for International Cooperation." Accessed July 19, 2024, https://www.fmprc.gov.cn/eng/wjdt_665385/2649_665393/201904/t20190427_679562.html, 2019.

Ministry of Foreign Affairs. "Speech Chinese President Xi Jinping at Kazakhstan's Nazarbayev University." Accessed April 25, 2022, https://worldjpn.net/documents/texts/BR/20130907. O1E.html, 2013.

Ministry of Foreign Affairs. *List of Instruments Signed and Exchanged between Nepal and China.* Accessed September 30, 2021, https://mofa.gov.np/list-of-instruments-singed-and-exchanged- between-nepal-and-china/, 2019.

Ministry of Foreign Affairs. "America's Coercive Diplomacy and Its Harm." https://www.fmprc. gov.cn/eng/wjbxw/202305/t20230518_11079589.html, May 18, 2023.

Ministry of Foreign Affairs. Ministry of Foreign Affairs Speeches. China.

Mitchell, Timothy. "The Limits of the State: Beyond Statist Approaches and Their Critics." *The American Political Science Review*, 85, 1, 1991, pp. 77–96.

Mitchell, Timothy. *Rule of Experts: Egypt, Techno-politics, Modernity.* Berkeley: University of California Press, 2002.

Mitchell, William J. T. "Pictorial Turn." In Roland Bleiker, ed., *Visual Global Politics.* Abingdon: Routledge, 2018.

Mohan, Giles. "Below the Belt? Territory and Development in China's International Rise." *Development and Change*, 52, 1, 2021, pp. 54–75.

Mohseni-Cheraghlou, Amin, and Naomi Aladekoba. "The Global Infrastructure Financing Gap: Where Sovereign Wealth Funds and Pension Funds Can Play a Role." *Atlantic Council.* Accessed July 22, 2023, https://www.atlanticcouncil.org/blogs/econographics/the-global-infrastructure-financing-gap-where-sovereign-wealth-funds-swfs-and-pension-funds-can-come-in/, 2022.

Monson, Jamie. *Africa's Freedom Railway.* Bloomington: Indiana University Press, 2009.

Morgenthau, Hans. *Politics among Nations.* New York: McGraw-Hill, 1948.

Morrison, Amanda. "Patriotic Blockbusters Mean Big Box Office for Chinese Filmmakers." *Foreign Policy.* https://foreignpolicy.com/2021/02/22/china-communism-films-national ism-censorship/, 2021.

Mozur, Paul, and Ruth Perlroth. "China's Software Stalked Uighurs Earlier and More Widely." *New York Times.* Accessed May 29, 2021, https://www.nytimes.com/2020/07/01/technol ogy/china-uighurs-hackers-malware-hackers-smartphones.html, 2020.

Mukhitkyzy, Asemgul. "Raspoznaet dazhe liudei v maskakh. Nuzhny li Kazakhstanu kamery Hikvision." *Radio Asia.* Accessed January 9, 2024, https://rus.azattyq.org/a/kazakhstan-china-survellience-camera/30210035.html, 2019.

Mundy, Barbara. *The Mapping of New Spain.* Chicago: University of Chicago Press, 1996.

Murton, Galen. "Post-disaster Development Zones and Dry Ports as Geopolitical Infrastructures in Nepal." In Mona Chettri and Michael Eilenberg, eds., *Development Zones in Asian Borderlands.* Amsterdam: Amsterdam University Press, 2021, pp. 33–54.

Murton, Galen. "Beyond the BRI: The Volumetric Presence of China in Nepal." *Territory, Politics, Governance*, 12, 1, 2024, pp. 72–92.

Murton, Galen, and Austin Lord. "Trans-Himalayan Power Corridors: Infrastructural Politics and China's Belt and Road Initiative in Nepal." *Political Geography*, 77, 2020, p. 102100.

Murton, Galen, Austin Lord, and Robert Beazley. "'A Handshake across the Himalayas:' Chinese Investment, Hydropower Development, and State Formation in Nepal." *Eurasian Geography and Economics*, 57, 3, 2016, pp. 403–32.

Murton, Galen, and Nadine Plachta. "China in Nepal: On the Politics of Belt and Road Development in South Asia." In Joseph Chinyong Liow, Liu Hong, and Gong Xue, eds., *Research Handbook on the Belt and Road Initiative.* London: Edward Elgar Publishing, 2021, pp. 332–41.

Mustafaeva, Lenura. "V Khudshande v nachale 2024 goda planiruyut zapustit' sistemu 'Bezopasnii gorod.'" [In Khujand, They Plan to Launch the 'Safe City' System at the Beginning of 2024]. *Asia-Plus.* Accessed January 9, 2024, https://www.asiaplustj.info/ru/ news/tajikistan/security/20231027/v-hudzhande-v-nachale-2024-goda-planiruyut-zapus tit-sistemu-bezopasnii-gorod, 2023.

Narins, Tom, and John Agnew. "Missing from the Map: Chinese Exceptionalism, Sovereignty Regimes and the Belt Road Initiative." *Geopolitics*, 25, 4, 2020, pp. 809–37.

Narins, Tom, and John Agnew. "Veiled Futures? Debt Burdens, the Belt Road Initiative, and Official Chinese Lending after Coronavirus." *Human Geography*, 15, 2, 2021, pp. 190–205.

Narodnaya Gazeta. "Zakony Respubliki Tadzhikistan." Accessed January 9, 2024, http://www.narodnaya.tj/index.php?option=com_content&view=article&id=7232:2018-08-08-07-09-50&catid=69:zakoni&Itemid=171, 2018.

Nasritdinov, Emil. "On Edward Schatz's 'Slow Anti-Americanism.'" *Central Asian Affairs* 11, 1, 2024, pp. 85–87.

Nataraj, Geethanjali, and Richa Sekhani. "China's One Belt One Road: An Indian Perspective." *Economic and Political Weekly*, 50, 49, 2015, pp. 67–71.

National Bureau of Statistics of China. *China's Statistical Year Book*. Accessed August 23, 2015, https://www.stats.gov.cn/sj/ndsj/2012/indexeh.htm, 2012.

National Museum of China. *Sharing a Common Future Exhibition*, 2019.

NDRC. "Outline of the 13th Five Year Plan." National Development and Reform Commission. Accessed May 30, 2021, https://www.ndrc.gov.cn/fggz/fzzlgh/gjfzgh/201603/P020191104614882474091.pdf, 2016.

Newman, Abraham, and Henry Farrell. "Weaponized Interdependence: How Global Economic Networks Shape State Coercion," *International Security*, 44, 1, 2019, pp. 42–79.

NL Times. "Huawei Was Able to Eavesdrop on Dutch Mobile Network KPN: Report." *NL Times*. Accessed October 8, 2021, https://nltimes.nl/2021/04/17/huawei-able-eavesdrop-dutch-mobile-network-kpn-report, 2021.

Nourzhanov, Kirill. "Omnibalancing in Tajikistan's Foreign Policy: Security-Driven Discourses of Alignment with Iran." *Journal of Balkan and Near Eastern Studies*, 14, 3, 2012, pp. 363–81.

Nyíri, Pál. "Migration and the Globalisation of Chinese Capital." *Made in China Journal*, 5, 3, 2021, pp. 42–47.

Oakes, Tim. "The BRI as an Exercise in Infrastructural Thinking." *Transformations: Downstream Effects of the BRI*. Accessed January 30, 2024, https://munkschool.utoronto.ca/belt-road/research/bri-exercise-infrastructural-thinking, 2021.

OECD. *OECD Glossary of Statistical Terms*, https://doi.org/10.1787/9789264055087-en. Accessed July 24, 2024, Paris: OECD Publishing, 2008.

Ofstad, Arve, and Elling Tjønneland. "Zambia's Looming Debt Crisis—Is China to Blame? *Chr. Michelsen Institute*. Accessed February 2, 2024, https://www.cmi.no/publications/6866-zambias-looming-debt-crisis-is-china-to-blame, 2019.

Oliveira, Gustavo de L. T. "Boosters, Brokers, Bureaucrats and Businessmen: Assembling Chinese Capital with Brazilian Agribusiness." *Territory, Politics, Governance*, 7, 1, 2019, pp. 22–41.

Oliveira, Gustavo de L. T., Galen Murton, Alessandro Rippa, Tyler Harlan, and Yang Yang. "China's Belt and Road Initiative: Views from the Ground." *Political Geography*, 82, 102225, 2020.

Oliveira, Gustavo de L. T., and Margaret Myers. "The Tenuous Co-production of China's Belt and Road Initiative in Brazil and Latin America." *Journal of Contemporary China*, 30, 129, 2021, pp. 481–99.

Ong, Aihwa. *Flexible Citizenship: The Cultural Logics of Transnationality*. Durham: Duke University Press, 1999.

Oreglia, Elisa, Hongyi Ren, and Chia-Chi Liao. "The Puzzle of the Digital Silk Road." In Nargis Kassenova and Brendan Duprey, eds. *Digital Silk Road in Central Asia: Present and Future*. Cambridge: Davis Center for Russian and Eurasian Studies, 2021, pp. 1–7.

Organski, A. F. K. *World Politics*. New York: Alfred A. Knopf, 1958.

Organski, A. F. K., and Jacek Kugler. *The War Ledger*. Chicago: University of Chicago Press, 1980.

Osborne, Hilary, and Sam Cutler. "Chinese Border Guards Put Secret Surveillance App on Tourists' Phones." *The Guardian*. Accessed May 29, 2021, https://www.theguardian.com/world/2019/jul/02/chinese-border-guards-surveillance-app-tourists-phones, 2019.

Pachirat, Timothy. *Every Twelve Seconds: Industrialized Slaughter and the Politics of Sight*. New Haven: Yale University Press, 2011.

Page, Jeremy, Kate O'Keeffe, and Rob Taylor. "America's Undersea Battle with China for Control of the Global Internet Grid." *Wall Street Journal*. Accessed October 8, 2021, https://www.wsj.com/articles/u-s-takes-on-chinas-huawei-in-undersea-battle-over-the-global-internet-grid-11552407466, 2019.

Paltiel, Jeremy. "China's Regionalization Policies: Illiberal Internationalism or Neo-Mencian Benevolence?" In Emilian Kavalski, ed., *China and the Global Politics of Regionalization*. Farnham: Ashgate, 2009, pp. 47–62.

Pan, Jianxin, ed. *Shàng hǎi nián jià*n [Shanghai Yearbook]. Shanghai: Shanghai Bureau of Statistics, 1999.

Panamarov, Vladimir. "China & Central Asia: Present & Future Economic Cooperation." Conflict Studies Research Centre. Accessed January 23, 2024, https://www.files.ethz.ch/isn/92589/05_May.pdf, 2005.

Park, Yoon Jung. "Forever Foreign? Is There a Future for Chinese People in Africa?" *Journal of Ethnic and Migration Studies*, 48, 4, 2022, pp. 894–912.

Parreñas, Rhacel Salazar, Rachel Silvey, Maria Cecilia Hwang, and Carolyn Areum Choi. "Serial Labor Migration: Precarity and Itinerancy among Filipino and Indonesian Domestic Workers." *International Migration Review*, 53, 4, 2019, pp. 1230–58.

Patey, Luke. *How China Loses: The Pushback against Chinese Global Ambitions*. New York: Oxford University Press, 2020.

Paudel, Dinesh. "Himalayan BRI: An Infrastructural Conjuncture and Shifting Development in Nepal." *Area, Development, Policy*, 7, 1, 2021, pp. 1–21.

Paul, Boban Varghese, Arden Finn, Sarang Chaudhary, Renata Mayer Gukovas, and Ramya Sundaram. "COVID-19, Poverty, and Social Safety Net Response in Zambia." *World Bank Group*. Accessed February 2, 2024, https://openknowledge.worldbank.org/handle/10986/35249, 2021.

PEACE Cable. "PEACE Cable System." Accessed July 20, 2023, http://www.peacecable.net, 2023.

Pearson, Margaret M., Meg Rithmire, and Kellee S. Tsai. "China's Party-State Capitalism and International Backlash: From Interdependence to Insecurity." *International Security*, 47, 2, 2022, pp. 135–76.

People's Daily. "China Pledges 40 Bln USD for Silk Road Fund." *People's Daily*. Accessed May 19, 2021, http://en.people.cn/n/2014/1109/c90883-8806435.html, 2014.

People's Daily. "A Closer Look at the Jakarta-Bandung High-Speed Rail Project." *People's Daily*. Accessed September 20, 2021, http://pic.people.com.cn/n1/2020/1121/c1016-31939304.html, 2020.

Perlez, Jane. "China Surprises U.N. with $100 Million and Thousands of Troops for Peacekeeping." *New York Times*. Accessed May 30, 2021, https://www.nytimes.com/interactive/projects/cp/reporters-notebook/xi-jinping-visit/china-surprisesu-n-with-100-million-and-thousands-of-troops-for-peacekeeping, 2015.

Perragin, Charles. "Verkabelter Ozean." *Die Tageszeitung: taz*. Accessed January 24, 2024, https://taz.de/!5770921/, 2021.

Peyrouse, Sebastien. "Military Cooperation between China and Central Asia: Breakthroughs, Limits, and Prospects." Jamestown Foundation. Accessed May 30, 2021, https://jamestown.org/program/military-cooperation-between-china-and-central-asia-breakthrough-limits-and-prospects/, 2010.

Peyrouse, Sebastien. "Discussing China: Sinophilia and Sinophobia in Central Asia." *Journal of Eurasian Studies*, 7, 1, 2016, pp. 14–23.

Pierson, Paul. "Increasing Returns, Path Dependence, and the Study of Politics." *American Political Science Review*, 94, 2, 2000, pp. 251–67.

Pitkin, Hanna F. *Wittgenstein and Justice: On the Significance of Ludwig Wittgenstein for Social and Political Thought.* Berkeley: University of California Press, 1993.

Plachta, Nadine. "Post-disaster Development at the Margins: Development, Profit and Insecurities across Nepal's Northern Borderlands. In Mona Chettri and Michael Eilenberg, eds., *Development Zones in Asian Borderlands.* Amsterdam: Amsterdam University Press, 2021, pp. 187–210.

Putz, Catherine. "China in Central Asia: Building Border Posts in Tajikistan." *The Diplomat.* Accessed May 27, 2021, https://thediplomat.com/2016/09/china-in-central-asia-building-border-posts-in-tajikistan/, 2016.

Qin, Yaqing. "A Relational Theory of World Politics." *International Studies Review*, 18, 1, 2016, pp. 33–47.

Qin, Yaqing. *A Relational Theory of World Politics.* Cambridge: Cambridge University Press, 2018.

Qin, Yaqing, and Astrid H. M. Nordin. "Relationality and Rationality in Confucian and Western Traditions of Thought." *Cambridge Review of International Affairs*, 32, 5, 2019, pp. 601–14.

Ramaphosa, Cyril. "Global Response Is Needed to Prevent a Debt Crisis in Africa." *Financial Times.* Accessed February 2, 2024, https://www.ft.com/content/5f428a4d-bd29-44e6-a307-c97b3f325d7b, 2020.

Ramaswamy, Sumathi. *Terrestrial Lessons: The Conquest of the World as Globe.* Chicago: University of Chicago Press, 2017.

Ramzy, Austin, and Charles Buckley. "'Absolutely No Mercy': Leaked Files Expose How China Organized Mass Detentions of Muslims." *New York Times.* Accessed May 28, 2021, https://www.nytimes.com/interactive/2019/11/16/world/asia/china-xinjiang-documents.html, 2019.

Rancière, Jacques. *The Emancipated Spectator.* London, Verso, 2011.

Rancière, Jacques. *Dissensus: On Politics and Aesthetics.* London: Bloomsbury Publishing, 2013a.

Rancière, Jacques. *The Politics of Aesthetics.* London: Bloomsbury Publishing, 2013b.

Rankin, Katharine N., Pushpa Hamal, Elsie Lewison, Tulasi Sharan Sigdel. "Corruption as a Diagnostic of Power: Navigating the Blurred Boundaries of the Relational State." *South Asia: Journal of South Asian Studies*, 42, 5, 2019, pp. 920–36.

Rankin, Katharine N., Tulasi Sharan Sigdel, Lagan Rai, Shyam Kunwar, and Pushpa Hamal. "Political Economies and Political Rationalities of Road Building in Nepal." *Studies in Nepali History and Society*, 22, 1, 2017, pp. 43–84.

Rankin, Katharine N., and Edward Simpson. "Roads and the Politics of Thought: Climate in India, Democracy in Nepal." In Galen Murton and Luke Heslop, eds., *Highways and Hierarchies: Ethnographies of Mobility from the Himalaya to the Indian Ocean.* Amsterdam: Amsterdam University Press, 2021, pp. 197–220.

Rathie, Martin. "The History and Evolution of the Lao People's Revolutionary Party." In Vanina Boute and Vatthana Pholsena, eds., *Changing Lives in Laos: Society, Politics, and Culture in a Post-socialist State.* Singapore: National University of Singapore Press, 2017, pp. 19–55.

Ray, Himanshu Prabha. *The Archaeology of Seafaring in Ancient South Asia.* Cambridge: Cambridge University Pres, 2003.

Ray, Himanshu Prabha. "'Project Mausam.' India's Transnational Initiative: Revisiting UNESCO's World Heritage Convention." In Burkhard Schnepel and Tansen Sen, eds., *Travelling Pasts: The Politics of Cultural Heritage in the Indian Ocean World.* Leiden: Brill, 2019.

Ray, Himanshu Prabha. "Sailing Ships, Naval Expeditions and 'Project Mausam.'" *India Quarterly*, 76, 3, 2020, pp. 411–24.

Reed, Tristan, and Alexander Trubetskoy. "Assessing the Value of Market Access from Belt and Road Projects." The World Bank Group. Accessed September 30, 2021, http://documents1.

worldbank.org/curated/en/333001554988427234/pdf/Assessing-the-Value-of-Market-Acc
ess-from-Belt-and-Road-Projects.pdf, 2020.

Reilly, James. *Orchestration: China's Economic Statecraft across Asia and Europe.*
Oxford: Oxford University Press, 2021.

Reinhart, Carmen, and Vincent Reinhart. "The Pandemic Depression: The Global Economy
Will Never Be the Same." *Foreign Affairs.* Accessed February 2, 2024, https://www.for
eignaffairs.com/articles/united-states/2020-08-06/coronavirus-depression-global-econ
omy, 2020.

Research and Markets. "Global & Chinese Optical Fiber Preform Markets, Forecast to
2025: Supply & Demand, Regional Distribution, Price, Competitive Pattern, Development
Trends." *GlobeNewswire.* Accessed October 8, 2021, http://www.globenewswire.com/news-
release/2019/09/02/1909635/0/en/Global-Chinese-Optical-Fiber-Preform-Markets-Forec
ast-to-2025-Supply-Demand-Regional-Distribution-Price-Competitive-Pattern-Deve
lopment-Trends.html, 2019.

Reus-Smit, Chris. "Cultural Diversity and International Order." *International Organization,*
71, 4, 2017, 851–85.

Reuters. "Indonesian Companies Ask China to Up Stake in High-Speed Rail Project." *Reuters.*
Accessed September 15, 2021, https://www.reuters.com/article/indonesia-railway-idUSL4
N2M80V7, 2021a.

Reuters. "Lawyers Urge ICC to Probe Alleged Forced Deportations of Uyghurs from Tajikistan."
Reuters. Accessed January 23, 2024, https://www.reuters.com/world/asia-pacific/lawyers-
urge-icc-probe-alleged-forced-deportations-uyghurs-tajikistan-2021-06-10/, 2021b.

Reuters. "Zambia Owes Nearly $27 Billion in Foreign and Local Public Debt. *Reuters.* zambia-
owes-nearly-27-billion-in-foreign-and-local-public-debt-idUSKBN2HA2L5, 2021c.

Reuters. "Local Public Debt." *Reuters.* Accessed April 24, 2022. https://www.reuters.com/arti
cle/zambia-debt/.

RFE/RL. "Voennoe sotrudnichestvo mezhdu Kitaem i T͡Sentral'noĭ Azieĭ: proryv, predely
i perspektivy" [Military Cooperation between China and Central Asia: A Breakthrough,
Limits and Prospects]. Accessed May 30, 2021, https://rus.azattyq.org/a/central_asia_china
_millitary_help/1986304.html, 2010.

RFE/RL. "Kyrgyz Government Cancels $275 Million Chinese Project amid Protests." Accessed
May 30, 2021, https://www.rferl.org/a/kyrgyz-government-cancels-275-million-chinese-
project-amid-protests/30451825.html, 2020.

Rippa, Alessandro, Galen Murton, and Matthäus Rest. "Building Highland Asia in the 21st
Century." *Verge: Studies in Global Asias,* 6, 2, 2020, pp. 83–111.

Roberts, Sean. *The War on the Uyghurs.* Princeton: Princeton University Press, 2020.

Robertson, Holly. "The World's Emptiest Airport Is a Red Flag." *Next City.* Accessed February
2, 2024, https://nextcity.org/features/the-worlds-emptiest-airport-is-a-red-flag, 2018.

Rolland, Nadège. *China's Eurasian Century? Political and Strategic Implications of the Belt and
Road Initiative.* Washington: The National Bureau of Asian Research, 2017.

Rolland, Nadège. "China's Vision for a New World Order: Implications for the United States."
National Bureau of Asian Research. https://www.nbr.org/publication/chinas-vision-for-a-
new-world-order-implications-for-the-united-states/, October 2, 2020.

Rosenberger, Felix. "Fiche: China." State Secretariat for Economic Affairs. Accessed July 28,
2023, https://www.seco.admin.ch/seco/en/home/Aussenwirtschaftspolitik_Wirtschaftl
iche_Zusammenarbeit/Wirtschaftsbeziehungen/laenderinformationen/asien/ostasien/
china.html, 2022.

Rowedder, Simon. "Railroading Land-Linked Laos: China's Regional Profits, Laos' Domestic
Costs?" *Eurasian Geography and Economics,* 61, 2, 2020, pp. 152–61.

Rukhullo, Sarvinoz. "V Dushanbe ulichye kamery nachnut raspoznavat' litsa." [In Dushanbe,
Street Cameras Will Begin to Recognize Faces]. *Radio Ozod.* Accessed January 9, 2024,
https://rus.ozodi.org/a/30003322.html, 2019.

Schatz, Edward. *Slow Anti-Americanism: Social Movements and Symbolic Politics in Central Asia*. Stanford: Stanford University Press, 2021.

Schedler, Andreas. "Mapping Contingency." In Ian Shapiro and Sonu Bedi, eds., *Political Contingency: Studying the Unexpected, the Accidental, and the Unforeseen*. New York: New York University Press, 2007, pp. 54–78.

Schindler. "About Schindler: Company Facts." Accessed October 8, 2021, https://www.schindler.com/content/com/internet/en/about-schindler/_jcr_content/contentPar/downloadlist/downloadList/19_1461919093155.download.asset.19_1461919093155/schindler-company-facts.pdf, 2019.

Schlag, Gabi. "Thinking and Writing Visual Global Politics —a Review of R. Bleiker's Visual Global Politics." *International Journal of Politics, Culture, and Society*, 32, 1, 2019, pp. 105–14.

Schneider, Florian. Global Perspectives on China's Belt and Road Initiative. Amsterdam: Amsterdam University Press, 2021.

Schubert, Renate, and Ioana Marinica. "Wait, My Data Goes Where?" In Monika Dommann, Hannes Rickli, and Max Stadler, eds., *Data Centers: Edges of a Digital Nation*. Zurich: Lars Müller Publishers, 2020, pp. 310–39.

Schwenkel, Christina. "Spectacular Infrastructure and Its Breakdown in Socialist Vietnam." *American Ethnologist*, 42, 3, 2015, pp. 520–34.

Scott, James C. *Seeing Like a State: How Certain Schemes to Improve the Human Condition Have Failed*. London and New Haven: Yale University Press, 1998

Scott, John. *Social Network Analysis*. London: Sage, 2000.

SEA-ME-WE 5. "About the SEA-ME-WE 5 Submarine Cable." Accessed October 8, 2021, https://seamewe5.com/about/about-smw5/, 2015.

The Second Belt and Road Forum for International Cooperation. "Joint Communiqué of the Leaders' Roundtable of the 2nd Belt and Road Forum for International Cooperation." Accessed May 30, 2021, http://www.beltandroadforum.org/english/n100/2019/0427/c36-1311.html, 2019.

Security Assistance Monitor. "Uzbekistan Purchases Military Drones from China." Accessed May 29, 2021. https://securityassistance.org/content/uzbekistan-purchases-military-drones-china, 2014.

Segal, Adam. "Huawei, 5G, and Weaponized Interdependence." In Daniel Drezner, Henry Farrell, and Abraham Newman, eds., *The Uses and Abuses of Weaponized Interdependence*. Washington: Brookings Institute Press, 2021, 149–68.

Shakya, Tsering. "Interview: Beyond Development and Diversity." *Himal Southasian*. Accessed September 30, 2021, https://www.himalmag.com/beyond-development-and-diversity-historian-tsering-shakya-interview/, 2018.

Shambaugh, David. *China Goes Global: The Partial Power*. New York: Oxford University Press, 2013.

Shao, Dahai. "Zhōng guó lián tōng ruì shì fēn gōng sī zài sū lí shì chéng lì" [China Unicom Switzerland Branch Established in Zurich]. Swiss Broadcasting Corporation. Accessed October 8, 2021. https://www.swissinfo.ch/chi/business/中国电信企业进入瑞士_中国联通瑞士分公司在苏黎世成立/43563680, 2017.

Shen, Hong. "Building a Digital Silk Road? Situating the Internet in China's Belt and Road Initiative." *International Journal of Communication*, 12, 2018, pp. 2683–701.

Sheridan, Derek. "'If You Greet Them, They Ignore You': Chinese Migrants, (Refused) Greetings, and the Inter-Personal Ethics of Global Inequality in Tanzania." *Anthropological Quarterly*, 91, 1, 2018, pp. 237–65.

Shesternyova, Svetlana. "Kazakhstan's Surveillance Cameras Installed in Namangan." *Daryo*. Accessed January 9, 2024, https://daryo.uz/en/2023/03/03/kazakhstans-surveillance-cameras-installed-in-namangan, 2023.

Shih, Gary. "In Central Asia's Forbidding Highlands, a Quiet Newcomer: Chinese Troops." *Washington Post*. Accessed May 27, 2021, https://www.washingtonpost.com/world/

asia_pacific/in-central-asias-forbidding-highlands-a-quiet-newcomer-chinese-troops/2019/02/18/78d4a8d0-1e62-11e9-a759-2b8541bbbe20_story.html, 2019.

Shipton, Eric. *The Six Mountain Travel Books.* Seattle: The Mountaineers Books, 2010.

Sidaway, James, Simon Rowedder, Chih Yuan Woon, Weiqiang Lin, and Vatthana Pholsena. "Introduction: Research Agendas Raised by the Belt and Road Initiative." *Environment and Planning C: Politics and Space*, 38, 5, 2020, pp. 795–802.

Sidaway, James, and Chih Yuan Woon. "Chinese Narratives on 'One Belt, One Road' (一带一路) in Geopolitical and Imperial Contexts." *The Professional Geographer*, 69, 4, 2017, pp. 591–603.

Sidhu, Ravinder K., Ho Kong Chong, and Brenda S. A. Yeoh. *Student Mobilities and International Education in Asia: Emotional Geographies of Knowledge Spaces.* Cham: Palgrave Macmillan, 2020.

Silvey, Rachel, and Victoria Lawson. "Placing the Migrant." *Annals of the Association of American Geographers*, 89, 1, 1999, pp. 121–32.

Sims, Kearrin. "Laos Set Its Own Debt Trap." East Asia Forum. Accessed February 2, 2024, https://www.eastasiaforum.org/2020/10/31/laos-set-its-own-debt-trap/, 2020.

Sina Military. "Zhōng guó de wǔ qì huán bù bèi rèn kě? Yǒu xiē guó jiā yǐ jīng bèi liè rù hēi míng dān" [China's Weapons Have Not Yet Been Approved? Some Countries Have Been Blacklisted]. Accessed May 29, 2021, https://mil.sina.cn/sd/2019-01-21/detail-ihqfskcn9151073.d.html?cre=tianyi&mod=wpage&loc=15&r=32&rfunc=59&tj=none&tr=32, 2019.

Siu, Ricardo C. S. "China's Belt and Road Initiative: Reducing or Increasing the World Uncertainties?" *Journal of Economic Issues*, 53, 2, 2019, pp. 571–78.

Sivakumar, Bellie. *Chaos in Hydrology: Bridging Determinism and Stochasticity.* 1st ed. Dordrecht: Springer, 2017.

Small, Andrew. "Returning to the Shadows: China, Pakistan, and the Fate of CPEC." The German Marshall Fund of the United States. Accessed February 2, 2024, https://www.gmfus.org/news/returning-shadows-china-pakistan-and-fate-cpec, 2020.

Smith, Richard J. *Mapping China and Managing the World: Culture, Cartography and Cosmology in Late Imperial Times.* London: Routledge, 2013.

Smith, Stephen N. "China's 'Major Country Diplomacy': Legitimation and Foreign Policy Change." *Foreign Policy Analysis*, 17, 2, 2021, pp. 1–18.

Sohail, Safdar. "Debt Sustainability and the China Pakistan Economic Corridor." United Nations Conference on Trade and Development. Accessed July 26, 2023, https://unctad.org/system/files/information-document/BRI-Project_policy-brief-06_en.pdf, 2022.

Sputnik. "V Tashkente mogut vnedrit' sistemu raspoznavaniia lits" [Facial Recognition System May Be Introduced in Tashkent]. Accessed May 30, 2021, https://uz.sputniknews.ru/20190717/V-Tashkente-mogut-vnedrit-sistemu-raspoznavaniya-lits-12021304.html, 2019.

Sputnik. "Stalo izvestno, skolk'ko kamer nablyudayut za zhitelyami Dushanbe." [It became known how many cameras are watching the residents of Dushanbe]. *Sputniknews*. Accessed July 17, 2024. https://tj.sputniknews.ru/20221031/kameri-nabludenie-dushanbe-1052531026.html, 2022.

Stallings, Barbara. "A Dependency Perspective on the United States, China, and Latin America." In Aldo Madariaga and Stefano Palestini, eds., *Dependent Capitalisms in Contemporary Latin America and Europe.* Cham: Palgrave Macmillan, 2021, pp. 29–53.

Standish, Reid. "Tajikistan Approves Construction of New Chinese-Funded Base as Beijing's Security Presence in Central Asia Grows." *Radio Free Europe/Radio Liberty*. Accessed July 28, 2023, https://www.rferl.org/a/tajikistan-approves-chinese-base/31532078.html, 2021.

Star, Susan L. "The Ethnography of Infrastructure." *The American Behavioral Scientist*, 43, 3, 1999, pp. 377–91.

Starosielski, Nicole. *The Undersea Network.* Durham: Duke University Press, 2015.

State Council Gazette. "The State Council's Decision to Establish Leading Office of the Development of Western Regions." *Gazette of the State Council of the People's Republic of China*, 6, 6–7, 2000.

State Council Information Office. "What Are Six Economic Corridors under Belt and Road Initiative?" Accessed April 24, 2022. http://english.scio.gov.cn/beltandroad/2020-08/04/content_76345602.htm, 2020.

State Council of the People's Republic of China. "The Executive Office of the State Council Issues Notices from the Western Development Office's Implementation Measures on Policies Concerning the Western Development Project." Accessed May 16, 2021, http://www.gov.cn/gongbao/content/2001/content_61158.htm, 2001.

State Council of the People's Republic of China. "Labor Contract Law of the People's Republic of China (Amendment)." Accessed January 23, 2021, http://www.npc.gov.cn/zgrdw/english npc/Law/2009-02/20/content_1471106.htm, 2012a.

State Council of the People's Republic of China. "Regulation on the Administration of Foreign Labor Cooperation." Accessed January 23, 2021, http://www.gov.cn/zwgk/2012-06/11/cont ent_2157905.htm, 2012b.

State Council of the People's Republic of China. "China Unveils Action Plan on Belt and Road Initiative." Accessed July 17, 2023, http://english.www.gov.cn/news/top_news/2015/03/28/content_281475079055789.htm, 2015a.

State Council of the People's Republic of China. "Full Text: Action Plan on the Belt and Road Initiative." Accessed May 30, 2021, http://english.www.gov.cn/archive/publications/2015/03/30/content_281475080249035.htm, 2015b.

State Council of the People's Republic of China. "The SASAC Hosts Work Meeting on Promoting Central SOEs to Participate in the Development of the BRI and International Capacity and Manufacturing Equipment." Accessed May 30, 2021, http://www.gov.cn/guowuyuan/2015-06/23/content_2882766.htm, 2015c.

State Council of the People's Republic of China. "Regulations on the Administration of Foreign Contracted Projects (Amendment)." Accessed on January 23, 2021, https://www.lawinfoch ina.com/display.aspx?id=27432&lib=law&EncodingName=big5, 2017.

State Council of the People's Republic of China. "Full Text of Xi Jinping's Keynote Speech at China-Central Asia Summit." Accessed July 28, 2023, https://english.www.gov.cn/news/202 305/19/content_WS6467059dc6d03ffcca6ed305.html, 2023.

Steinhauser, Gabriel, and Joe Wallace. "Africa's First Pandemic Default Tests New Effort to Ease Debt from China." *Wall Street Journal*. Accessed February 2, 2024, https://www.wsj.com/articles/africas-first-pandemic-default-tests-new-effort-to-ease-debt-from-china-11605619 676, 2020.

Strangio, Sebastian. *In the Dragon's Shadow: Southeast Asia in the Chinese Century*. New Haven: Yale University Press, 2020.

Strategic Advisory Committee for Building a Manufacturing Superpower. "《Zhōng guó zhì zào 2025》zhòng diǎn lǐng yù jì shù lù xiàn tú" [Roadmap of Major Technical Domains for "Made in China 2025"]. Accessed January 24, 2024, http://www.cae.cn/cae/html/files/2015-10/29/20151029105822561730637.pdf, 2015.

Stryker, Cian. "Digital Silk Road and Surveillance Technology in Central Asia." In Nargis Kassenova and Brendan Duprey, eds. *Digital Silk Road in Central Asia: Present and Future*. Cambridge: Davis Center for Russian and Eurasian Studies, 2021, pp. 17–54.

Stuart-Fox, Martin. "Southeast Asia and China: The Role of History and Culture in Shaping Future Relations." *Contemporary Southeast Asia*, 26, 1, 2004, pp. 116–39.

Stuart-Haentjens, Remy. "China and the AIIB on the Belt and Road: Powers sans Control." *Global Risk Insights*. Accessed May 30, 2021, https://globalriskinsights.com/2017/07/china-aiib-belt-road-power-sans-control/, 2017.

Stuart-Haentjens, Remy. "Power sans Control on Belt and Road: China's Control over the AIIB Is Eroding." *Frontera*. Accessed April 22, 2022, https://frontera.net/news/asia/power-sans-control-on-belt-and-road-chinas-control-over-the-aiib-is-eroding/, 2017.

Stubbs, Jack. "China Hacked Asian Telecos to Spy on Uighur Travelers: Sources." *Reuters*. Accessed May 29, 2021, https://www.reuters.com/article/us-china-cyber-uighurs/china-hacked-asian-telcos-to-spy-on-uighur-travelers-sources-idUSKCN1VQ1A5, 2019.

Submarine Telecoms Forum. *Submarine Telecoms Industry Report 2012*. Accessed October 8, 2021, https://subtelforum.com/articles/wp-content/IndustryReport-2012.pdf, 2012.

Submarine Telecoms Forum. *Submarine Telecoms Industry Report 2022/2023*. Accessed January 24, 2024, https://subtelforum.com/industry-report/#, 2022.

Submarine Telecoms Forum. "Submarine Cable Almanac." Accessed January 24, 2024, https://subtelforum.com/almanac/, 2023.

Suhardiman, Diana, Jessica DiCarlo, Oulavanh Keovilignavong, Jonathan Rigg, and Alan Nicol. "(Re)constructing State Power and Livelihoods through the Laos-China Railway Project." *Geoforum*, 124, 2021, pp. 79–88.

Sultanalieva, Syinat. "Another Woman Killed in Scourge of Kyrgyzstan 'Bride Kidnappings.' Authorities Should Provide Justice, End to Deadly Crime against Women." Human Rights Watch. Accessed January 9, 2024, https://www.hrw.org/news/2021/04/09/another-woman-killed-scourge-kyrgyzstan-bride-kidnappings, 2021.

Summers, Tim. "China's 'New Silk Roads': Sub-National Regions and Networks of Global Political Economy." *Third World Quarterly*, 37, 9, 2016, pp. 1628–43.

Summers, Tim. "Negotiating the Boundaries of China's Belt and Road Initiative." *Environment and Planning C: Politics and Space*, 38, 5, 2020, pp. 809–13.

Sun, Yun. "Winning Projects and Hearts? Three Cases of Chinese Mega-Infrastructure Projects in Southeast Asia." *The Asan Forum*. https://theasanforum.org/winning-projects-and-hearts-three-cases-of-chinese-mega-infrastructure-projects-in-southeast-asia, 2017.

Swisscom. "Cyber Security Threat Radar 2020/2021." Accessed October 8, 2021, https://www.swisscom.ch/content/dam/swisscom/en/about/news/2021/04/16-woher-die-gefahr-droht/sc_sr_en_20210413final.pdf.res/sc_sr_en_20210413final.pdf, 2021.

Swiss Official Gazette of Commerce. "Deletion ZTE Switzerland AG in Liquidation, Bern." Accessed October 8, 2021, *Swiss Official Gazette of Commerce*. https://www.shab.ch/#!/search/publications/detail/542c0a4c-4e5b-4795-87c9-0690e999849a, 2021.

Synectics. "CCTV in the UK. What We Can Learn from Public Attitudes Towards Surveillance?" White paper. London: Synectic Systems Group Limited, 2014.

Szadziewski, Henryk, Mary Mostafanezhad, and Galen Murton. "Territorialization on Tour: The Tourist Gaze along the Silk Road Economic Belt in Kashgar, China." *Geoforum*, 128, 2022, pp. 135–47.

Tan, Danielle. "Chinese Enclaves in the Golden Triangle Borderlands: An Alternative Account of State Formation in Laos." In Pál Nyíri and Danielle Tan, eds., *Chinese Encounters in Southeast Asia: How People, Money, and Ideas from China Are Changing a Region*. Seattle: University of Washington Press, 2017, pp. 136–56.

Tang, Xiaoyang. "Bulldozer or Locomotive? The Impact of Chinese Enterprises on the Local Employment in Angola and the DRC." *Journal of Asian and African Studies*, 45, 3, 2010, pp. 350–68.

Tang, Xiaoyang. "Co-Evolutionary Pragmatism: Re-Examine 'China Model' and Its Impact on Developing Countries." *Journal of Contemporary China*, 29, 126, 2020, pp. 853–70.

TeleGeography. "Submarine Cable Map." Accessed October 8, 2021, https://www.submarinecablemap.com/, 2021.

TeleGeography. "Submarine Cable Frequently Asked Questions." Accessed January 24, 2024, https://www2.telegeography.com/submarine-cable-faqs-frequently-asked-questions, 2024.

Teles Fazendeiro, Bernardo. *Uzbekistan's Foreign Policy: The Struggle for Recognition and Self-Reliance under Karimov*. Abingdon: Routledge, 2018.

Tengri News. "Kitaĭ byl gotov predostavitʹ voennuiu pomoshchʹ - glava MID Kazakhstana" [China Was Ready to Provide Military Assistance - Kazakh Foreign Minister]. Accessed July 29, 2023, https://tengrinews.kz/kazakhstan_news/kitay-gotov-predostavit-voennuyu-pomosch-glava-mid-459624/, 2022.

Thanabouasy, Phayboune. "Buddhist Ceremony Held to Mark Laos-China Railway Inauguration." *Laotian Times*. Accessed February 2, 2024, https://laotiantimes.com/2021/12/03/buddhist-ceremony-held-to-mark-laos-china-railway-inauguration/, 2021.

Thelen, Kathleen. "Historical Institutionalism in Comparative Politics." *Annual Review of Political Science*, 2, 1, 1999, pp. 369–404.

Thorat, Dhanashree. "Colonial Topographies of Internet Infrastructure: The Sedimented and Linked Networks of the Telegraph." *South Asian Review*, 40, 3, 2019, pp. 252–67.

Tidy, Joanna, and Joe Turner. "The Intimate International Relations of Museums: A Method." *Millennium*, 48, 2, 2020, pp. 117–42.

Toqmadi, Malika, and Natalia Zakharchenko. "I Agree to the Terms and Conditions: Negotiating Privacy in Central Asia." *eJournal of eDemocracy and Open Government*, 13, 1, 2021, pp. 71–100.

Tskhay, Aliya, and Costa Buranelli, Filippo. "Accommodating Revisionism through Balancing Regionalism: The Case of Central Asia." *Europe-Asia Studies*, 72, 6, 2020, pp. 1033–52.

Tsunashima, Toru. "China Rises as World's Data Superpower as Internet Fractures." *Nikkei Asia*. Accessed October 8, 2021. https://asia.nikkei.com/Politics/International-relations/China-rises-as-world-s-data-superpower-as-internet-fractures, 2020.

Turtiainen, Hannu, Andrei Costin, Timo Hamalainen, and Tuomo Lahtinen. "Towards Large-Scale, Automated, Accurate Detection of CCTV Camera Objects Using Computer Vision Applications and Implications for Privacy, Anonymity, Surveillance, Safety, and Cybersecurity." arXiv. Accessed January 9, 2024, https://arxiv.org/abs/2006.03870, 2021.

Umarov, Temur. "China Looms Large in Central Asia." Carnegie Endowment for International Peace. Accessed February 18, 2024, https://carnegiemoscow.org/commentary/81402, 2020.

UNDP. "Covid-19 Pakistan Socio-economic Impact and Assessment & Response Plan." United Nations Development Programme. Accessed April 24, 2022, https://www.undp.org/sites/g/files/zskgke326/files/migration/asia_pacific_rbap/Pakistan---COVID-19-Socio-econo mic-Impact-Assessment-and-Response-Plan-1-May-2020.pdf, 2020.

UNICEF. "Tackling the COVID-19 Economic Crisis in Sri Lanka: Providing Universal, Lifecycle Social Protection Transfers to Protect Lives and Bolster Economic Recovery." United Nations Children's Fund. Accessed February 2, 2024, https://www.unicef.org/srila nka/media/1501/file/UNICEF_Brief_SocialProtectionResponseSL_Summary_2020Jul30. pdf, 2020.

U.S. Bureau of Industry and Security. "Supplement No. 4 to Part 744 - Entity List." Accessed October 8, 2021, https://www.bis.doc.gov/index.php/documents/regulations-docs/2326-supplement-no-4-to-part-744-entity-list-4/file, 2021.

U.S.-China Economic and Security Review Commission. *2022 Report to Congress of the U.S.-China Economic and Security Review Commission*. Accessed July 15, 2023, https://www.uscc.gov/sites/default/files/2022-11/2022_Annual_Report_to_Congress.pdf, 2022.

U.S. House of Representatives. *Adverse Report of the Committee on Armed Services, House of Representatives on H. Res. 640 Together with Dissenting Views*. Washington: US Government Printing Office, 2004.

Vaenkeo, Souksakhone. "Think Tank: Laos-China Railway Opens Doors for Establishment of SEZs." *Vientiane Times*. Accessed December 5, 2018, https://laos.opendevelopmentmek ong.net/news/think-tank-laos-china-railway-opens-doors-for-establishment-of-sezs/ , 2018.

Vanderhill, Rachel, Sandra Joireman, and Roza Tulepbayeva. 2020. "Between the Bear and the Dragon: Multivectorism in Kazakhstan as a Model Strategy for Secondary Powers." *International Affairs*, 96, 4, 2020, pp. 975–93.

Van Der Kley, Dirk. "China's Security Activities in Tajikistan and Afghanistan's Wakhan Corridor." In Nadege Rolland, ed., *Securing the Belt and Road Initiative*. Washington: National Bureau of Asian Research, 2019, pp. 71–90.

Varutti, Marzia. *Museums in China: The Politics of Representation after Mao*. Suffolk: Boydell & Brewer, 2014.

Vila Seoane, Maximiliano Facundo. "Alibaba's Discourse for the Digital Silk Road: The Electronic World Trade Platform and 'Inclusive Globalization.'" *Chinese Journal of Communication*, 13, 1, 2020, pp. 68–83.

Vonderau, Asta. "Scaling the Cloud: Making State and Infrastructure in Sweden." *Ethnos*, 84, 4, 2019, pp. 698–718.

Vuori, Juha, and Rune Saugmann Andersen, eds. *Visual Security Studies: Sights and Spectacles of Insecurity and War*. Abingdon: Routledge, 2018.

Wallerstein, Immanuel. *The Modern World-System I: Capitalist Agriculture and the Origins of the European World-Economy in the Sixteenth Century*. 1st ed. Berkeley: University of California Press, 2011.

Waltz, Kenneth. *Theory of International Politics*. Long Grove: Waveland Press, 1979.

Wang, Christoph Nedopil. *China Belt and Road Initiative (BRI) Investment Report 2022*. Green Finance and Development Center. Accessed November 3, 2023. https://greenfdc.org/china-belt-and-road-initiative-bri-investment-report-2022/, 2023.

Wang, Chunfa. "Shū fāng gòng xiǎng" [Sharing a Common Future]. National Museum of China. Accessed April 25, 2022, http://www.chnmuseum.cn/portals/0/web/zt/20190411s fgx/, 2019.

Wang, Hongyan. "Zhōng guó lián tōng guó jì gōng sī ruì shì fēn gōng sī zhèng shì guà pái chéng lì" [China Unicom International Corporation Switzerland Branch Was Officially Established]. CCTIME. Accessed October 8, 2021, http://www.cctime.com/html/2017-9-28/1324605.htm, 2017.

Wang, Lin. "How SOEs Can Become the 'Main Corps' and the 'Pathfinding Goat' in the BRI?" *China Youth Daily*, August 2, 2015, p. 3.

Wang, Wen, Jinjing Jia, Xiaochen Chen, Yuwei Hu, Junyong Xiang, Zhen Li, and Yang Cheng. "The 'BRI' Will Establish a New Structure of Opening to the Outside during the 13th Five Year Plan." *Xinhua News Agency*. Accessed May 30, 2021, http://www.xinhuanet.com/polit ics/2015-10/27/c_128363076.htm, 2015.

Wedeen, Lisa. *Ambiguities of Domination: Politics, Rhetoric, and Symbols in Contemporary Syria*. Chicago: University of Chicago Press, 1999.

Wedeen, Lisa. "Reflections on Ethnographic Work in Political Science." *Annual Review of Political Science*, 13, 2010, pp. 255–72.

Wei, Changhao. "A Guide to 2018 State Council Institutional Reforms." *NPC Observer*. Accessed September 20, 2021, https://npcobserver.com/2018/03/14/a-guide-to-2018-state-council-institutional-reforms/, 2018.

Wen, Yun. *The Huawei Model: The Rise of China's Technology Giant*. Urbana/Chicago/Springfield: University of Illinois Press, 2020.

Weng, Lingfei, Lan Xue, Jeffrey Sayer, Rebecca Anne Riggs, James Douglas Langston, and Agni Klintuni Boedhihartono. "Challenges Faced by Chinese Firms Implementing the 'Belt and Road Initiative': Evidence from Three Railway Projects." *Research in Globalization*, 3, 100074, 2021.

Werner, Cynthia. "Bride Abduction in Post-Soviet Central Asia: Marking a Shift Towards Patriarchy through Local Discourses of Shame and Tradition." *Journal of the Royal Anthropological Institute*, 15, 2, 2009, pp. 314–31.

White, Edward. "'Hidden Debt' on China's Belt and Road Tops $385 billion, Says New Study." *Financial Times*. Accessed February 2, 2024, https://www.ft.com/content/297beae8-7243-4d93-9fac-09e515e82972, 2021.

Wignaraja, Ganeshan, Dinusha Panditaratne, Pabasara Kannangara, and Divya Hundlani. "Chinese Investment and the BRI in Sri Lanka." Chatham House. https://www.chath amhouse.org/2020/03/chinese-investment-and-bri-sri-lanka-0/2-labour-and-environm ent, 2020.

Williams, Michael C. "International Relations in the Age of the Image." *International Studies Quarterly*, 62, 4, 2018, pp. 880–91.

Williams, Ollie. "Zambia's Default Fuels Fears of African 'Debt Tsunami' as Covid Impact Bites." *The Guardian*. https://www.theguardian.com/global-development/2020/nov/25/zambias-default-fuels-fears-of-african-debt-tsunami-as-covid-impact-bites, 2020.

Winter, Tim. *Geocultural Power: China's Quest to Revive the Silk Roads for the Twenty-First Century*. Chicago: The University of Chicago Press, 2019.

Winter, Tim. "Silk Road Diplomacy: Geopolitics and Histories of Connectivity." *International Journal of Cultural Policy: CP*, 26, 7, 2020, pp. 898–912.

Winter, Tim. "Geocultural Power: China's Belt and Road Initiative." *Geopolitics*, 26, 5, 2021, pp. 1376–99.

Winter, Tim. *The Silk Road: Connecting Histories and Futures*. New York: Oxford University Press, 2022.

Wolf, Diane. *Factory Daughters: Gender, Household Dynamics, and Rural Industrialization in Java*. Berkeley and Los Angeles: University of California Press, 1992.

Wolf, Eric R. *Europe and the People without History*. 2nd ed. Berkeley: University of California Press, 1982.

Wong, Audrye. "More than Peripheral: How Provinces Influence China's Foreign Policy." *China Quarterly*, 235, 2018, pp. 735–57.

Wood, Denis. *Rethinking the Power of Maps*. New York: Guilford Press, 2010.

Woods, Kevin. "Rubber out of the Ashes: Locating Chinese Agribusiness Investments in 'Armed Sovereignties' in the Myanmar–China Borderlands." *Territory, Politics, Governance*, 7, 1, 2019, pp. 79–95.

Woodworth, Max, and Agnieszka Joniak-Lüthi. "Exploring China's Borderlands in an Era of BRI-induced Change. *Eurasian Geography and Economics*, 61, 1, 2020, pp. 1–12.

World Bank. *From Landlocked to Land-Linked: Unlocking the Potential of Lao-China Rail Connectivity*, Accessed February 2, 2024, https://documents1.worldbank.org/curated/en/648271591174002567/pdf/Main-Report.pdf, 2020a.

World Bank. "Global Economic Prospects." Accessed April 24, 2022, https://openknowledge.worldbank.org/entities/publication/d29e6c95-4753-58e8-b368-d03c78cacab5, 2020b.

Wu, Gang, and Shuang Yan. "Xi Jinping Pledges Great Renewal of Chinese Nation." *Global Times*. Accessed February 18, 2024, https://www.globaltimes.cn/content/747443.shtml, 2012.

Xi, Jinping. "Work Together for a Bright Future of China-Iran Relations." *Xinhua News Agency*, 2016.

Xi, Jinping. "Work Together to Build the Silk Road Economic Belt and the 21st Century Maritime Silk Road. Opening Ceremony of the First Belt Road Forum." *Xinhua News Agency*, http://www.xinhuanet.com/english/2017-05/14/c_136282982.htm, 2017.

Xi, Jinping. "Working Together to Deliver a Brighter Future for Belt and Road Cooperation." Ministry of Foreign Affairs. Accessed May 30, 2021, https://www.fmprc.gov.cn/mfa_eng/wjdt_665385/zyjh_665391/201904/t20190426_678729.html, 2019.

Xiang, Biao. "Emigration from China: A Sending Country Perspective." *International Migration*, 41, 3, 2003, pp. 21–48.

Xiang, Biao. "Predatory Princes and Princely Peddlers: The State and International Labour Migration Intermediaries in China." *Pacific Affairs*, 85, 1, 2012, pp. 47–68.

Xiang, Biao. "The Would-Be Migrant: Post-socialist Primitive Accumulation, Potential Transnational Mobility, and the Displacement of the Present in Northeast China." *TRaNS: Trans-Regional and -National Studies of Southeast Asia*, 2, 2, 2014, pp. 183–99.

Xiang, Biao. "Introduction: Suspension: Seeking Agency for Change in the Hypermobile World." *Pacific Affairs*, 94, 2, 2021, pp. 233–50.

Xinhua News Agency. "The Central Committee of the Chinese Communist Party Publishes 'Plans Concerning Deepening the Reforms of Party and State Administrations.'" Accessed September 18, 2021, http://www.xinhuanet.com/politics/2018-03/21/c_1122570517.htm, 2018.

Xinhua News Agency. "China's National Defence in the New Era." *Xinhua News Agency.* https://english.www.gov.cn/archive/whitepaper/201907/24/content_WS5d3941ddc6d08 408f502283d.html, 2019a.

Xinhua News Agency. "Interview: BRI to Further Boost Comprehensive Ethiopia-China Ties." Xinhua News Agency. http://www.xinhuanet.com/english/2019-04/22/c_137999185. htm, 2019b.

Xinhua News Agency. "Indonesia's 1st 'Bullet Train Home': Jakarta-Bandung Railway's Complex Building Topped Out." *Xinhua News Agency.* Accessed September 15, 2021, http:// www.xinhuanet.com/english/2021-04/05/c_139858980.htm, 2021.

Xinhua News Agency. "China-Central Asia Cooperation in Numbers." *Xinhua News Agency.* Accessed January 23, 2024, https://english.news.cn/20230516/1f486fbe7274411581702 21544fc8211/c.html, 2023.

Xu, Wang. "BRI Offers New Platform for Japan." *China Daily.* https://www.chinadaily.com.cn/ a/201907/03/WS5d1c0b79a3105895c2e7b5f3.html, 2019.

Yan, Hairong, Barry Sautman, and Yao Lu. "Chinese and 'Self-Segregation' in Africa." *Asian Ethnicity,* 20, 1, 2019, pp. 40–66.

Yan, Karl. "The Railroad Economic Belt: Grand Strategy, Economic Statecraft, and a New Type of International Relations." *British Journal of Politics and International Relations,* 23, 2, 2021, pp. 262–79.

Yan, Karl. "Navigating between China and Japan: Indonesia and Economic Hedging." *Pacific Review,* 36, 4, 2023, pp. 755–83.

Yau, Niva. "China Business Briefing: Not Happy with Kyrgyzstan." *Eurasianet.* Accessed May 30, 2021, https://eurasianet.org/china-business-briefing-not-happy-with-kyrgyzstan, 2020.

Yau, Niva. "China's Security Management towards Central Asia." Foreign Policy Research Initiative. Accessed February 18, 2024, https://www.fpri.org/article/2022/04/chinas-secur ity-management-towards-central-asia/, 2022a.

Yau, Niva. "Chinese Governance Export in Central Asia." *Security and Human Rights,* 32, 2022b, pp. 28–40.

Yau, Niva, and Dirk van der Kley. "The Growth, Adaptation and Limitations of Chinese Private Security Companies in Central Asia." National Bureau of Asian Research, 2020.

Yau, Tsz Yan. "Smart Cities or Surveillance? Huawei in Central Asia." *The Diplomat.* Accessed January 9, 2024, https://thediplomat.com/2019/08/smart-cities-or-surveillance-huawei-in-central-asia/, 2019.

Ye, Min. "Fragmentation and Mobilization: Domestic Politics of the Belt and Road in China." *Journal of Contemporary China,* 28, 119, 2019, pp. 696–711.

Ye, Min. *The Belt Road and Beyond: State-Mobilized Globalization in China: 1998–2018.* Cambridge: Cambridge University Press, 2020.

Ye, Min. "Adapting or Atrophying? China's Belt and Road after the Covid-19 Pandemic." *Asian Policy,* 16, 1, 2021, pp. 65–95.

Yeh, Emily T. "Introduction: The Geoeconomics and Geopolitics of Chinese Development and Investment in Asia." *Eurasian Geography and Economics,* 57, 3, 2016, pp. 275–85. https:// muse.jhu.edu/article/781803.

Yeh, Emily T. "'The Land Belonged to Nepal but the People Belonged to Tibet': Overlapping Sovereignties and Mobility in the Limi Valley Borderland." *Geopolitics,* 26, 3, 2021, pp. 919–45.

Yeh, Emily T., and Elizabeth Wharton. "Going West and Going Out: Discourses, Migrants, and Models in Chinese Development." *Eurasian Geography and Economics,* 57, 3, 2016, pp. 286–315.

Yergaliyeva, Aidana. "Aqkol Becomes First Smart City in Kazakhstan." *Astana Times.* Accessed May 30, 2021, https://astanatimes.com/2019/01/aqkol-becomes-first-smart-city-in-kaz akhstan/, 2019.

Yu, Hong. "Motivation behind China's 'One Belt, One Road' Initiatives and Establishment of the Asian Infrastructure Investment Bank." *Journal of Contemporary China*, 26, 105, 2017, pp. 353–68.

Ysmanova, Kasiet. "Pitfalls and Promise for Public Opinion Research in Central Asia." In Jasmin Dall'Agnola and Aijan Sharshenova, eds., *Researching Central Asia: Navigating Positionality in the Field*. Cham: Springer, 2024, pp. 19–26.

Yurchak, Alexei. *Everything Was Forever, until It Was No More: The Last Soviet Generation*. Princeton: Princeton University Press, 2005.

Zakaria, Rafia. "The Pandemic Depression." *Dawn*. https://www.dawn.com/news/1573991, August 12, 2020.

Zeng, Jinghan. *Slogan Politics: Understanding Chinese Foreign Policy Concepts*. Singapore: Springer, 2020.

Zhang, Falin. "Rising Illusion and Illusion of Rising: Mapping Global Financial Governance and Relocating China." *International Studies Review*, 23, 1, 2020, pp. 1–29.

Zhang, Jing. "Wǒ guó láo wù pài qiǎn de xiàn zhuàng wèn tí jí jiě jué duì cè" [Status, Challenges, and Coping Strategies for Overseas Labor Service Industry]. *Academic Exchange*, 232, 7, 2013, pp. 73–77.

Zhang, Ketian. "Cautious Bully: Reputation, Resolve, and Beijing's Use of Coercion in the South China Sea." *International Security*, 44, 1, 2019, pp. 117–59.

Zhang, Lu. 2021. "Contextualizing Precarious Work: Labor Dispatch, Boundary-Drawing, and the Politics of Labor Regulation in Post-socialist China." *Labor History*, 62, 5–6, pp. 556–74.

Zhang, Xue. "A Jesuit Atlas of Asia in Eighteenth-Century China." Asian and African Studies. Accessed April 25, 2022, https://blogs.bl.uk/asian-and-african/2019/04/a-jesuit-atlas-of-asia-in-eighteenth-century-china.html, 2019.

Zhao, Jinjing, and Jongchul Lee. "The Belt and Road Initiative, Asian Infrastructure Investment Bank, and the Role of Enterprise Heterogeneity in China's Outward Foreign Direct Investment." *Post-Communist Economies*, 33, 4, 2021, pp. 379–401.

Zhao, Suisheng. "China's Belt-Road Initiative as the Signature of President Xi Jinping Diplomacy: Easier Said than Done." *Journal of Contemporary China*, 29, 123, 2020, pp. 319–35.

Zhao, Yingjie, and Lu Guo. "Lùn wǒ guó láo wù pài qiǎn fǎ lǜ zhì dù de wán shàn" [Instituional Development for Overseas Labor Dispatching]. *Academic Exchange*, 251, 2, 2015, pp. 64–69.

Zhu, Jiejin. "Is the AIIB a China-Controlled Bank? China's Evolving Multilateralism in Three Dimensions (3D)." Global Policy, 10, 4, 2019, pp. 653–59.

Zhu, Zhenming. "China's Economic Aid to CLMV and Its Economic Cooperation with Them." Economic Research Institute for ASEAN and East Asia. Accessed April 24, 2022, https://www.ide.go.jp/library/English/Publish/Reports/Brc/pdf/01_chinaseconomic.pdf, 2015.

Zuboff, Shoshana. *The Age of Surveillance Capitalism: The Fight for a Human Future at the New Frontier of Power*. New York: PublicAffairs, 2019.

Index